Tombstone Inscriptions of Alexandria Virginia

Volume 1

Wesley E. Pippenger

HERITAGE BOOKS
2008

HERITAGE BOOKS
AN IMPRINT OF HERITAGE BOOKS, INC.

Books, CDs, and more—Worldwide

For our listing of thousands of titles see our website at
www.HeritageBooks.com

Published 2008 by
HERITAGE BOOKS, INC.
100 Railroad Ave. #104
Westminster, Maryland 21157

Copyright © 1992, 1994 (Revised) Wesley E. Pippenger

All rights reserved. No part of this book may be reproduced or transmitted in any form or by any means, electronic or mechanical, including photocopying, recording or by any information storage and retrieval system without written permission from the author, except for the inclusion of brief quotations in a review.

International Standard Book Number: 978-1-58549-210-7

TABLE OF CONTENTS

INTRODUCTION 1
    Area Plan by Author 3

First Presbyterian Church Cemetery (1809) 5
    Plans 89

First Presbyterian Church Graveyard (1773) 97
    Burials After the c.1809 Stoppage 111
    Plan by Author 114

Trinity United Methodist Church Cemetery (1808) 115
    Plan by Author 147

Home of Peace Cemetery (1860) 149
    Plan by Author 159
    Plan by Author 160

Agudas Achim Cemetery (1933) 161
    Plan by Author 166

Penny Hill Cemetery (c.1796) 167
    Plan by Author 169

INDEX 171

INTRODUCTION

Some of the most valuable information available for genealogical and biographical research is that which is found inscribed on tombstones. It is often intriguing to speculate any reasons for the choice of epitaph, cited scripture, or craft of monument - some of them being quite ingenious or ornate. Perhaps rising costs have caused the considerable decline in expression on monuments, either in the form of scripture, epitaphs, or configuration. Few twentieth-century monuments bear inscriptions beyond a name, and birth and death dates.

Permanent as the original intent may have been, many of the monuments are extremely vulnerable to the destructive forces of the weather and vandals. Many have not survived these forces, and the message they once displayed may be lost forever.

Because of this critical element of timeliness, this project is initiated to preserve what visibly remains in the cemeteries of Alexandria, Virginia. Unless the data is readily available, no extra effort will be made to: (1) abstract the history behind the land parcels which the cemeteries occupy; (2) document evolution of the religious organizations that are or have been associated with them; or (3) extensively study or make speculation into the sometimes numerous unmarked graves. Therefore, the purpose of this project is to preserve the inscriptions on the tombstones and monuments in these cemeteries. Though much enthusiasm has been received toward this project, it has been initiated and in most part performed directly by the author. Hence, the project will continue as time permits. Initially this work will concentrate on twelve cemeteries which surround the western bounds of Wilkes Street at Hamilton Lane. These cemeteries generally were first established as extensions of those within the city limits which were ordered closed to further burials sometime after about 1809. Vestry records of Christ Episcopal Church reflect an entry on April 20, 1809, that further burials in the churchyard would cease after the "first day of May, next.[1]" Despite the stoppage order, some burials are known to have occurred within the city limits after this time.

The Alexandria City Council declared no additional burial lots would be sold within the corporation limits after March 27, 1804[2]. This concern was voiced along with other issues of health and sanitation. The policy stated that:

> No burying ground shall be opened, or allotted for the interment of human bodies within the limits of the corporation. Any person who shall dig a grave, or cause it to be done with a view of burying a human body therein in any ground within the corporation, not opened or allotted before the twenty-seventh day of March, eighteen hundred and four to that purpose, shall forfeit and pay twenty dollars for each offence, and moreover be compelled to remove the corpse, if discovered within three days after interment, under the penalty of twenty dollars for neglect.

---

[1] Alexexandria Library, Lloyd House, microfilm reel #295.
[2] Alexandria City Council, The Charter and Laws, of the City of Alexandria, Va., and An Historical Sketch of Its Government (Alexandria: Gazette Book and Job Office, 1874), p. 66.

Most monuments are headstones; upright and inscribed slabs of stone placed in the ground at the head of the deceased. Exceptions to this are generally noted, and include: tablets (flat stones which cover the entire grave and are often level to the ground or slightly raised); table stones (tablet stones which are elevated above ground by a number of columns, usually six, and open underneath); boxtombs (like table stones but all sides are enclosed); and obelisks.

Every effort has been made to preserve the tombstone inscriptions exactly as they appear, including capitalization of words, spelling, punctuation, and word count per line. In this work, all personal names are capitalized as a finding aid. If inscriptions were done in all capital letters, lower case has been used here to save space. A slash ("/") indicates a new line, and that new line may be on a different face of the stone in cases where inscriptions appear on multiple faces.

Rather than an account by name, this work is organized by tombstone. With this in mind it is pointed out that oftentimes a tombstone marks the burial for many of a family, and as such may contain more than one surname inscription. All names included in this work also may be found in the index.

Obituary notices of the Alexandria Gazette, which also may be found in Obituary Notices From the Alexandria Gazette, 1784-1915 (Bowie: Heritage Books, Inc., 1978), were consulted in cases where the tombstone could not be clearly read. Because in some instances the date of death given in this publication and that found on a tombstone are not the same, it is suggested that users of this work resolve conflicts by consulting any available alternate sources, the newspaper, and by visiting the cemetery. If additional information was learned from the newspaper, a citing follows each entry and gives the date and page of the newspaper, i.e. "AG:22/9/83:3." It is noted that many tombstones may be found for which there is no death record evident in the available newspapers. Keep in mind that the actual title of the Alexandria Gazette has changed multiple times since its beginning in 1784.

My greatest appreciation goes to the late Mrs. Carrie White Avery whose untiring efforts led to her own preparation of a manuscript made during the early 1920's which contained a good number of early tombstone transcriptions. Without this manuscript now housed in the Manuscript Division of the Library of Congress in Washington, D.C., many of the tombstones which are now in varying stages of decay would be illegible and the information forever lost. For those who would like to pursue this source, see Genealogical Records (Gathered from Graveyards, Public Monuments and Family Papers, in Virginia, Maryland and the District of Columbia), 1922, 4 volumes, file #2522.

I am grateful to Yvonne Carignan and Sandy O'Keefe of the Alexandria Library, Lloyd House for making records housed there available for review and use in this work. Additional thanks are in order for the generosity of William R. Sengel of Alexandria who provided original surveys and burial records of the First Presbyterian Church cemetery, and Ruth Sinberg Baker who provided initial data for the Jewish cemeteries Home of Peace and Agudas Achim.

Wesley E. Pippenger
Alexandria, Virginia

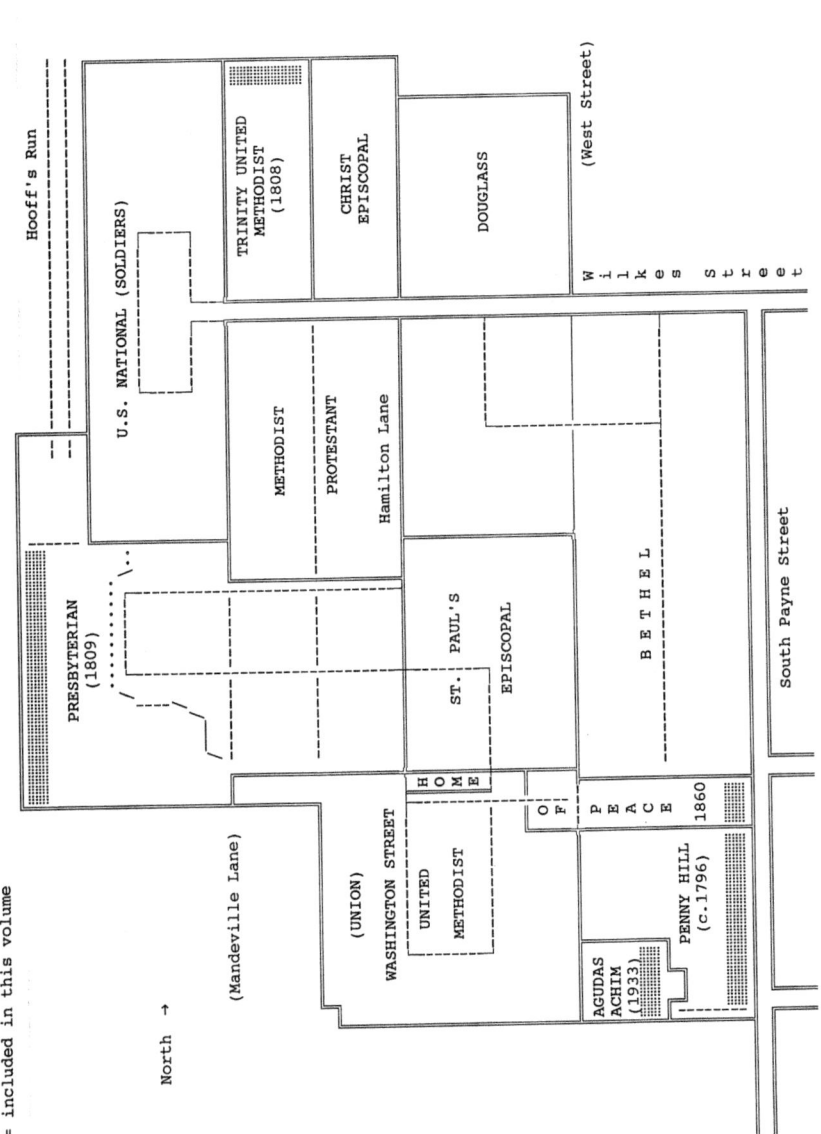

Area Plan by Author

First Presbyterian Church Cemetery (1809)
Hamilton Lane, off Wilkes Street

The cemetery for what was initially known as the First Presbyterian Church of Alexandria was set aside in 1809. Though the original Fairfax County property conveyance record has been lost[1], a subsequent deed of February 6, 1813, helps reconstruct record that on June 22, 1809, members Thomas Vowell, James Irwin, Joseph Riddle, Richard Veitch, Hugh Smith, Joseph Deane, Andrew Jamieson, Alexander McKenzie and Joseph Harper (since deceased), of the Committee of the Presbyterian Congregation of the Town of Alexandria, made an agreement to lease from Philip G. Marsteller and his wife Christiana D. Marsteller, a "square of ground" in the vicinity of the town of Alexandria, situate on the south side of Gibbon Street, north side of Franklin Street, west side of Hamilton Lane, and the east side of Mandeville Lane, for an annual rent of $45.00. With executing the 1813 deed, the trustees paid consideration of $450 to confirm ownership of the parcel[2]. The cemetery is active.

Originally established as the First Presbyterian Church of Alexandria, the church building was occupied in the twentieth century by a different congregation and is now known as the Old Presbyterian Meeting House.

For each tombstone that is currently visible, the section and lot numbers are included in parenthesis at the end of each entry. The entries which begin with a "B," i.e. (B:194), indicate the grave is located within the identified border area which surrounds the oldest part of the cemetery. For the entries which do not include location information, the tombstone was not found at the time this information was compiled, and the information for it may have been taken from Mrs. Carrie White Avery's genealogical notes as described in the Introduction of this volume. Most monuments are headstones, but a few which are table stones, boxtombs or tablets are so noted.

A cemetery survey done in July 1890 by Howell & Greenough of Washington, D.C. which was updated October 24, 1939 by A.B. Garrett of Alexandria, Virginia was provided by Rev. William R. Sengel of Alexandria. Rev. Sengel was also instrumental in obtaining from Everly-Wheatley Funeral Home a loan to the compiler of a record of burials in the cemetery after January 1, 1936. Drawings of lot locations were provided by the Alexandria Library, Lloyd House, as supplied by Rev. Sengel. Initial data collection was completed October 14, 1991. Walk through and verification was assisted by Edmund M. Bedsworth and Tod J. Johnston, and completed November 17, 1991.

Some information was gleaned from a record of funerals kept by Rev. Dr. Muir, entitled:

---

[1] Fairfax County Deeds, Bk. K No. 2, p. 14.
[2] Fairfax County Deeds, Bk. M No. 2, pp. 311-315.

First Presbyterian Church Cemetery (1809)

Register of Baptisms, Marriages, and Funerals During the Ministry of the Revd Doctr James Muir in the Presbyterian Church of Alexandria, D.C., as well as a subsequent yet largely incomplete church record which covers the period 1818 to 1861. References from these sources are prefaced with abbreviations "MR" and "FR," respectively, and are followed by a page number from which the information was taken, i.e. "MR:funeral held 9 NOV:6." See notes on page 97 for additional information on the first of these sources.

An additional note regarding burial is indicated with "BR," for burials beginning January 1, 1936, and is followed by the burial date and an abbreviation for the hosting funeral home or location, i.e. "BR:14 DEC:W."

Names of the following funeral homes have been extracted from the burial record, and are abbreviated as below. These are given as stated in the record, and as the actual funeral home name may have changed, no attempt has been made to follow chronology of business ownership.

> A=Arnold Funeral Home; Ar=Arlington Funeral Home (est. 1956); B=J.F. Birch, Washington DC; Ba=Baker Funeral Home (est. 1946); C=Cunningham Funeral Home; Ch=W.W. Chambers (est. 1914); Co=Covington-Martin; Col=Colonial Funeral Home (est. 1963); Dl=W.W. Deal; D=Demaine Funeral Home (est. 1841); E=Everly or Everly-Wheatley (est. 1849); G=Joseph Gawler & Sons (est. 1850); Gr=W.F. Gross Funeral Home; H=S.H. Hines (est. c.1873); Hy=Hardesty Funeral Home; H&I=Hill and Irving; I=Ives (Ives-Pearson) Funeral Home (est. 1910); M=Murphy; Ma=Mattingly Funeral Home; Mc=McGuire; Mu=Mullens Funeral Home; P=O.C. Pearson; Pu=R.A. Pumphrey (est. 1854); R=James T. Ryan; T=Taylor Funeral Home; W=Wheatley Funeral Home; and Wh=Welch

Wesley E. Pippenger
Alexandria, Virginia

First Presbyterian Church Cemetery (1809)

Surname Unknown

____, [Catey?]. ____ / born Dec. 5, 1852 / died / Sept. 19, 1903. (25:11)
____, Isabella. ____ also of their daughter / ISABELLA / who died Decr. 12th 1841 / in the 3d year of her age. (41:1)
____, John. To / the memory of / JOHN ____ / who departed this life / December 6th 183[6] / in the 25th year / of his age. (44:132)
____, Sonny. No surname, no dates. (18:18)

A

ABBOTT, Sallie Monroe. SALLIE MONROE ABBOTT / 1900-1900. (B:183)
ACTON, Eliza Virginia. ELIZA VIRGINIA / beloved wife of / THEODORE M. ACTON / born May 1842 / died Feb. 1900. (B:173, footstone "E.V.A.")
ACTON, James Herman. JAMES HERMAN ACTON / 1870-1895.
ACTON, John S. [BR:28 JUL 1943:D]. (B:173, stone below soil, footstone "J.S.A.")
ACTON, Mathew. [BR:14 JUL 1941]. (B:173, no stone; BR entry indicates body may have been removed to St. Mary's Co. Md.)
ACTON, R. Carlton. R. CARLTON ACTON / 1879-1919. (B:173)
ACTON, Theodore M. THEODORE M. ACTON / born Feb. 1840 / died June 1912. (B:173, footstone "T.M.A.")
ADAM. In memoriam / within these sacred / precints lie the / departed members of / the ADAM family / ELIZA CAMPBELL ADAM / beloved daughter of / JOHN and MARY / DUNLAP ADAM / born Sept. 12, 1819 / died May 29, 1909 / JANE DADE / daughter of ROBERT / and ANNA ADAM / died Jan. 23, 1873 / aged 89 years / widow of CHARLES / STUART DADE who was / lost at sea July 1811 / CHARLES IRVIN / son of / JOHN and MARY ADAM / died Jan. 1823 / aged 5 years / THOMAS IRWIN / son of / JOHN and MARY ADAM / died Jan. 19, 1879 / JOHN ADAM / eldest son of / ROBERT ADAM / First Wor. Master of / the Alexandria / Washington Lodge / of Masons / Grandson of the / Rev. JOHN and JANET / CAMPBELL ADAM / of Kilbride, Scotland / died Sept. 30, 1843 / aged 62 years / MARY DUNLAP / widow of JOHN ADAM / died Jan. 29, 1873 / JAMES IRWIN / of Belfast, Ireland / The faithful / guardian of JOHN ADAM / died Sept. 5, 1822 [AG:24/1/73:2; 31/12/09:1]. (41:14)
ADAM, John. Departed this life / Augt. 4th, 1848 / JOHN ADAM / aged 73 years / *It may truly be said he was / the noblest work of God, an / honest man.* (41:13; Alexandria Wills, Bk. 5, p. 79, men. wife Mary, and daughter Mary Ann who is wife of John S. Mills)
ADAM, John G. JOHN G. ADAM / son of / JOHN and MARY ADAM / was born 6th March, 1811 / died 21st August, 1848 / in the 38th year of his age. (41:13)
ADAM, Mary D. MARY / wife of / JOHN ADAM / born Nov. 4th, 1780 / died Jan. 25, 1857. (41:13; Alexandria Wills, Bk. 7, p. 197)

First Presbyterian Church Cemetery (1809)

ADAM, Robert F. Sacred / to the memory of / ROBERT F. ADAM / son of / JOHN and MARY ADAM who was born / on the 8th day of June 1801 / and departed this life / on the 8th of June 1840, aged 38 years. (41:13)

ADAMS, Leonard. In memory of / LEONARD ADAMS / born at Sandisfield, Berkshire County, Massachusetts / April 19th 1773 / died in Washington, D.C. / March 3d 1856 / in the 83d year of his age. (41:17)

ADAMS, Sally. Sacred / to the memory of / SALLY / wife of / LEONARD ADAMS / who died Nov. 7, 1811 / in the 39 year of her / age. [MR:funeral on 9 NOV]. (41:17)

ADDISON, John Daingerfield. JOHN DAINGERFIELD ADDISON / son of THOMAS DULANY and / MARY B.S. ADDISON / Jan. 19 / 1888 / Mar. 26 / 1966 [BR:28 MAR:D]. (25:4)

ADDISON, Mary Brockenbrough Smith. MARY BROCKENBROUGH ADDISON / daughter of / Dr. JOHN PHILIP & SALLY B.N. SMITH / May 24 / 1859 / Dec. 12 / 1938. (25:5; BR:14 DEC:W)

ADDISON, Thomas Dulany. THOMAS DULANY ADDISON / son of / Dr. EDWARD C. & ELIZA B. ADDISON / Oct. 1 / 1846 / Feb. 23 / 1925. (25:4)

ADLER, Berwin. An owner of section 1, site 38. (no stone)

ADLER, Edna O. [BR:18 OCT 1963:D]. (1:38, no stone)

AGNEW, Anne Rebecca. In memory of / ANNE REBECCA / beloved daughter of / JOHN PARK and MATILDA / ELIZABETH AGNEW / 1851-1934 / *I shall see him face to face.* (44:149)

AGNEW, Augustus Harrison. In memory of / AUGUSTUS HARRISON / beloved son of / JOHN PARK and MATILDA / ELIZABETH AGNEW / 1861-1946 / and his wife / MABEL AGNEW / 1876-1949. (44:149)

AGNEW, David Smith. Sacred / to the memory of / DAVID SMITH / son of / JOHN P. & MATILDA E. AGNEW / died March 26, 1874 / in the 17th year of his age [AG:27/3/74:2]. (44:149)

AGNEW, Elizabeth H. ELIZABETH H. AGNEW / 1898-1950. (15:6)

AGNEW, John Park. In memory of / JOHN PARK AGNEW / born in Ebensburg, Pa. / December 25, 1819 / died in Alexandria, Va. / June 7, 1892 / *He shall dwell before God / forever.* (44:149)

AGNEW, John Park. JOHN PARK AGNEW / 1887-1961. (15:6)

AGNEW, Laura Bell. LAURA BELL / wife of / PARK AGNEW / 1850-1916. (15:6)

AGNEW, Laura Thomas. LAURA THOMAS / daughter of / PARK & LAURA E. / AGNEW / born June 7, 1875 / died May 10, 1881. (44:149)

AGNEW, Margaretta Linton. In memory of / MARGARETTA LINTON / beloved daughter of / JOHN PARK and MATILDA / ELIZABETH AGNEW / 1866-1941 / *In thy presence is fullness of joy.* (44:149)

AGNEW, Mary Virginia. In memory of / MARY VIRGINIA / beloved daughter of / JOHN PARK and MATILDA / ELIZABETH AGNEW / 1853-1932 / *Life forevermore.* (44:149)

AGNEW, Matilda Elizabeth. In memory of / MATILDA ELIZABETH / beloved wife of / JOHN PARK AGNEW / 1823-1917 / *Blessed are the pure in heart / for they shall see God.* (44:149)

AGNEW, Minniehaha. MINNIEHAHA / daughter of / J.P. and M.E. AGNEW / born / Oct. 15, 1863 / died Aug. 12, 1867 [AG:12/8/67:3]. (44:149)

First Presbyterian Church Cemetery (1809)

AGNEW, Park. PARK AGNEW / 1847-1910 [AG:31/12/10:1, gives death 14 JUL 1910]. (15:6)

AITCHESON, Alan Carlyle. ALAN CARLYLE / son of / JOHN & CAROLINE / AITCHESON / Nov. 21, 1887 / Oct. 7, 1888. (B:184)

AITCHESON, Benjamin M. BENJAMIN M. AITCHESON / beloved husband / of / S. MAUDE DOWNHAM / 1870-1920 / S. MAUDE DOWNHAM / beloved wife / of / BENJAMIN M. AITCHESON / 1877-1964. (25:22)

AITCHESON, Benjamin M. [BR:28 APR 1977:E]. (25:22, no stone)

AITCHESON, John. JOHN AITCHESON / March 25, 1851 - Jan. 17, 1939 [BR:20 JAN:W] / CAROLINE AITCHESON / Oct. 13, 1857 - Feb. 20, 1940 [BR:22 FEB:W] / DAVID W. AITCHESON / Aug. 22, 1883 - Aug. 9, 1943 / NANNIE A. AITCHESON / Sept. 28, 1889 - Dec. 31, 1949 / JESSIE O. AITCHESON / Sept. 19, 1885 - Feb. 19, 1970 [BR:21 FEB:E]. (B:184)

AITCHESON, Mary C. MARY C. AITCHESON / June 10, 1892 / April 12, 1989 [BR:cremation:C]. (B:184)

AITCHESON, Sarah M.D. [BR:20 JUN 1964:E]. (25:22, no stone)

ALEXANDER, Amos. Owner of west half of section 41, lot 7. (no headstone, only one footstone visible)

ALLEN, Ada Alice. Sacred / to the memory of / ADA ALICE / infant daughter of / WILLIAM W. & MARY / DRUCILLA ALLEN / born Oct. 28, 1851 / died July 21, 1852 / aged 8 months & 26 days. (13:3)

ALLEN, Ernest Linwood. ERNEST LINWOOD ALLEN / 1856-1939 [BR:19 JUN:C] / A member of / Alexandria Washington Lodge / No. 22, A.F. and A.M. (13:3)

ALLEN, Mary Drusilla Skidmore. In memory of / M. DRUSILLA SKIDMORE ALLEN / 1831-1914. (13:3)

ALLEN, William Lewis. WILLIAM LEWIS ALLEN / August 15, 1853 / April 8, 1938 [BR:11 APR] / P.M. Andrew Jackson Lodge No. 120, A.F. and A.M. (13:3)

ALLISON, Robert, Jr. In memory / of / ROBERT ALLISON, JR. / who fell / in battle on the 5th Septr. 1814 / at the white house / in gallantly defending his country / aged 27 years / Our lives belong to God, & our country / He was a dutiful son / an affectionate Brother / conciliating in manners / beloved by all / erected by his kinsman / JAMES M. STEWART. [MR:funeral 6 SEP]. (42:74)

ANDERSON, John. Erected to the memory / of / JOHN ANDERSON / a native of Ireland / who departed this life / October 6th, 1811 / aged 36 years. South and next to this Tomb / lies JANE, the widow of / THOMAS CHURCH / who departed this life Jan. 20, 1814 / aged 94 years / Justly respected by all who knew her.

ANDERSON, Robert. In memory of / ROBERT ANDERSON / a native of Stirling in Scotland / who departed this life / on the 1st day of July 1833 / in the 64th year / of his age. / As an honest man and useful citizen, he / was ___ reputation that during ... [AG:6/7/33]. (41:25, tablet; Alexandria Wills, Bk. 4, p. 60, men. sister Margaret Anderson, wife of Robert Conway)

ANSLEY, Harriet Fuller. HARRIET FULLER / wife of / HARRIE CRAIG ANSLEY / May 23, 1853 / Dec. 31, 1906 / And they shall be mine saith / the Lord of host in that day / when I make up my jewels. / URQUHART ANSLEY / January 25, 1898 / September 12, 1960 [BR:29 SEP:Cape May NJ] / HARRIE CRAIG ANSLEY / April 28, 1850 / March 28, 1924 / He giveth his beloved sleep. / LEWIS M. ANSLEY / August 29, 1888

First Presbyterian Church Cemetery (1809)

/ August 25, 1946 / ANNE W. ANSLEY / January 12, 1883 / May 29, 1952 / HARRIE CRAIG / eldest son of / H.C. and H.F. ANSLEY / Aug. 1, 1881 / Dec. 29, 1901 / *But thanks be to God which / giveth us the victory through / our Lord Jesus Christ* [AG:31/12/07:1; 31/12/01:1]. (14:14, obelisk)

APPICH, Barbara Ann. In memory of / BARBARA ANN / wife of / DAVID APPICH / who departed this life / September 9th, 1852 / in the 43rd year of her / age. (43:99)

APPICH, Caroline C. Sacred / to the memory of / CAROLINE C. / wife of DAVID APPICH / died January 16th, 1865 / in the 32nd year of / her age [AG:16/1/65:2]. (43:99)

APPICH, Christina. CHRISTINA APPICH / 1836-1920. (44:156)

APPICH, David. In memory of / our father / DAVID APPICH / born in / Wurtemberg / Germany / Oct. 12, 1801 / died April 13, 1887 [AG:13/4/87:3]. (43:99)

APPICH, George David. In memory of / GEORGE DAVID / only son of GOTLIEB and BARBARA APPICH / born December 28th, 1833 / was killed while discharging his duty as a Fireman / November 17th, 1855 / *Dearest David thou hast left us / here thy loss we deeply feel / But tis God who has bereft us / He can all our sorrows heal.* (43:99)

APPICH, Gertrude Barbara. In memory of / GERTRUDE BARBARA / wife of GOTTLIEB APPICH / born in Wirtemberg, Germany / 1801 / died in Alexandria, Va. / August 31, 1874 / *Sleep mother dear and take your rest / God called you home / He thought it best.* (43:99)

APPICH, Gottlieb. In memory of / GOTTLIEB APPICH / born in Wirtemberg, Germany / October 10, 1802 / died in Alexandria, Va. / October 12, 1866 / *He is not dead, but sleepeth.* (43:99; Alexandria Wills, Bk. 8, p. 443)

APPICH, Jacob D. JACOB D. APPICH / born June 19, 1837 / died Jan. 1, 1870 / *The Lord gave, and the Lord / hath taken away, blessed be the / house of the Lord.* [AG:1/1/70:2]. (44:156, footstone "J.D.A.")

APPICH, John A. Gottlieb. Sacred / to the memory of / JOHN A. GOTTLIEB / son of DAVID APPICH / died February 4th, 1861 / in the 39th year of / his age. (43:99)

ARCHIE, Harry W. HARRY W. ARCHIE / Pvt. U.S. Marine Corps / World War II / Feb. 18, 1927 - Mar. 13, 1985. (44:146E:8)

ARMSTRONG. ANTHONY W. ARMSTRONG / died Dec. 24, 1901 / WAYNE E. ARMSTRONG / died July 11, 1884 / JESSIE R. ARMSTRONG / died Aug. 21, 1909 / LOUISE R. ARMSTRONG / died Feb. 22, 1919 / ANTHONY G. ARMSTRONG / died Jan. 23, / 1921 / JOHN T. ARMSTRONG / died Oct. 18, 1879 / LUCY LYNCH ARMSTRONG / died Nov. 20, 1897 / MARION E. VICKROY ARMSTRONG / died Nov. 26, 1897 / GEORGE L. ARMSTRONG / died June 12, 1869 / ALICE DeK. SHATTUCK / died March 20, 1907 / LUCIOUS H.[OLMAN] SHATTUCK / died June 12, 1887 [AG:29/6/77:3]. (43:109)

[ARMSTRONG?], Catherine. Sacred / to the memory of / CATHERINE / daughter of / J. & E. [ARMSTRONG?] / who departed this life / March 22, 183[3] / aged 2 yrs. / _____. (43:108)

ARNOLD, Annie Laurie. ANNIE LAURIE / beloved wife of / HOWARD L. ARNOLD / 1899-1921 / *Blessed are the pure in / heart for they shall / see God.* (42:59)

ARNOLD, James Brooke. JAMES BROOKE ARNOLD / 1855-1916 / *At rest.* / AMANDA V. ARNOLD / 1858-1942. (42:59)

ARNOLD, J. Raymond. J. RAYMOND / ARNOLD / Aug. 20, 1896 / July 1, 1973 [BR:5 JUL:E] / LUCILLE W. / Oct 4, 1899 - [blank]. (42:59)

First Presbyterian Church Cemetery (1809)

ARNOTT, Henry. Sacred / to the memory of / HENRY ARNOTT / who died in this city / on the 16th day of November / A.D. 1835 / aged 64 years / *A native of Fifeshire / in Scotland, and upwards of / Thirty Years, a Merchant of / the Island of Barbadoes / From his upright / and Honorable conduct / his Humane and charitible / actions, and his urbane / and Hospitible disposition / He acquired universal respect / and esteem. He will long be / deeply and sincerely / Lamented by his relatives / and numerous / Friends.* (43:125)

ARRINGTON, Emma C. EMMA C. / wife of / CHAS. H. ARRINGTON / born June 19, 1874 / died April 15, 1927 / D. of A. / *She gave all for others.* (17:10)

ASHBY, F. Westwood. F. WESTWOOD ASHBY / born / May 25, 1819 / died / July 17, 1870. (44:142)

ASHBY, Margaret Douglas. MARGARET DOUGLAS / wife of / F. WESTWOOD ASHBY / born April 27, 1831 / died Feb. 24, 1892. (44:141)

ASHER, George Gordon. In loving memory / of / GEORGE GORDON ASHER / 1872-1915 / son of / JOHN and MILDRED MOORE / MABEN ASHER / and seventh in descent from / Sir ALEXANDER SPOTSWOOD / Colonial Governor of Virginia. (16:8)

ATKINSON, David Wayne. DAVID WAYNE / beloved son of / JANET and ROSCOE / ATKINSON / December 28, 1959 / August 26, 1966 [BR:30 AUG:E] / *Jesus loves me.* (19:4:7)

AUMAN, William Richard. WILLIAM RICHARD / [blank]. [BR:14 SEP 1991:E] / EDITH FAIRFIELD / 1892-1974 [BR:1 JUL 1974:E] / EVELYN FAIRFIELD / [blank]. (18:22W)

AUSTIN, Mariana. Sacred / to the memory of / MARIANA / the wife of / JOHN AUSTIN / who departed this life / Oct. 12th, 1820, in the ___ th year of her age. / *Released from all her cares and woes / She rests in calm and sweet repose.* (41:15)

AVERY, Hattie E. In memory / of / HATTIE E. / wife of / R.W. AVERY / born July 30, 1844 / died March 7, 1897. (43:92)

AVERY, Richard W. RICHARD W. AVERY / born Nov. 22, 1839 / died May 24, 1899 [AG:30/12/99:1]. (43:92)

AVERY, Wesley. Father & Mother / WESLEY AVERY / born Sep. 29, 1813 / died Jan. 10, 1886 / MARY, his wife / born May 15, 1816 / died Feb. 10, 1886. (43:92)

B

BAADER, Caroline. Mother / CAROLINE BAADER / died Sept. 19, 1928 / aged 78 years. (B:182)

BAADER, Carrie. In memory / of / CARRIE / beloved daughter of / CAROLINE & HENRY / BAADER / born Feb. 18, 1884 / died Jan. 5, 1887. (B:182)

BAADER, Charlie. In memory / of / CHARLIE / beloved son of / CAROLINE & HENRY / BAADER / born Oct. 23, 1871 / died April 4, 1885. (B:182)

BAADER, Emma. In memory / of / EMMA / beloved daughter of / CAROLINE & HENRY BAADER / born March 3, 1886 / died Nov. 22, 1886. (B:182)

BAADER, Henry. Father / HENRY BAADER / died Nov. 16, 1911 / aged 65 years. (B:182)

BAADER, Lizzie. In memory / of / LIZZIE / beloved daughter of / CAROLINE & HENRY / BAADER / born March 16, 1880 / died March 31, 1896. (B:182)

BAADER, Mamie. In memory / of / MAMIE / beloved daughter of / CAROLINE & HENRY

First Presbyterian Church Cemetery (1809)

/ BAADER / born March 3, 1882 / died Feb. 10, 1885 / CAROLINE ALICE ARCHER / aged 9 months. (B:182)

BAADER, Rosa Lee. ROSA LEE BAADER / April 26, 1874 / June 15, 1938 [BR:18 JUN:D]. (B:182)

BAGGETT, Mary Ann Appich. Our / Mother / MARY ANN / consort of / A.W. BAGGETT / and eldest daughter of / DAVID APPICH / born May 10, 1829 / died May 3, 1871 [AG:4/5/71:3]. (44:156, footstone "M.A.B.")

BAGOT, Julia A.E.B. Our Mother / JULIA ANN ELIZA BERNICE / wife of / JOHN C. BAGOT / born Jan. 15, 1821 / died Jan. 12, 1902 / *He giveth his beloved sleep.* (B:215)

BAIN, William E. WILLIAM E. BAIN / 1857-1920 / his wife / FANNIE C. MASON / 1885-1931. (16:10)

BAKER, Clara Edith Graves / June 14, 1902 / Oct. 16, 1980. (19:1)

BAKER, Selden Stewart. BAKER / SELDEN STEWART / March 11, 1908 / June 6, 1970 / EVELYN PICKETT / Feb. 4, 1911 / June 20, 1977 [BR:23 JUN:E]. (3:16:1 & 2)

BARKER, Mary E. Moore. MARY E. MOORE / wife of / ROGER F. BARKER / born Sept. 19, 1874 / died / Jan. 24, 1903 / *At rest.* (15:1)

BARLEY, J.R. McKim. J.R. McK. BARLEY / born Sept. 14, 1850 / died June 1, 1877 / *Trusting in Jesus.* [AG:2/6/77:3]. (44:152)

BARNES, Thelma Clark. Daughter / THELMA C. BARNES / Jan. 30, 1904 / Nov. 10, 1959 [BR:12 NOV:C]. (13:13)

BARTLE, Samuel. [Multiple stones] SAMUEL BARTLE'S / FAMILY / burial ground 1854. [another stone] JOHN SELLERS and his wife SUSAN C., natives of / Germantown, Pennsylvania. / *For a long time resident of this place, their age not recollected / Erected by S. Bartle.* / [white place stone] J.S. & S.C.S. / [white stone] THOMAS, PHEBE ANN, JAMES & ANDREW / Children of SAMUEL & SUSAN BARTLE. / [white place stone] T., P.A., J., A. (43:88)

BARTLEMAN, Ann Edwards. Sacred / To the memory of / ANN EDWARDS / the daughter of / WILLIAM & MARGARET / BARTLEMAN / who died Oct. 30, 1859 / aged 29 years / *She was lovely in life / and peaceful in death / now she is blessed.* (41:31)

BARTLEMAN, Isabella Paterson. Sacred / to the memory of / ISABELLA PATERSON / the daughter of / WILLIAM & MARGARET / BARTLEMAN / who died Oct. 3d, 1837 / aged 34 years / *She was lovely in life / And peaceful in death / Now she is blessed.* (41:31)

BARTLEMAN, Margaret Douglas. MARGARET / wife of / WILLIAM BARTLEMAN / and daughter of / REV. JAMES & MARGT. DOUGLAS / born in Ireland / January 11, 1776 / died at Alexandria / April 4, 1861 [AG:5/4/61:2]. (41:31; Alexandria Wills, Bk. 8, p. 81)

BARTLEMAN, Rebecca Jane. REBECCA JANE / daughter of / WILLIAM and MARG'T / BARTLEMAN / born Sept. 20, 1807 / died July 15, 1880 / *Be thou Faithful unto / death and I will give / thee a crown of life.* (41:31)

BARTLEMAN, William. WILLIAM BARTLEMAN / Dec. 21, 1842 / In memory of / WILLIAM BARTLEMAN / long a respectable merchant / in Alexandria, born in the island of Lewis / Ross Shire / Scotland / died here Dec. 21, 1842 / in the 75 year of his age. (41:31; Alexandria Wills, Bk. 4, p. 312)

BASCELL, Louis A. [BR:7 MAR 1942:D]. (15:16, no stone)

First Presbyterian Church Cemetery (1809)

BASHFORD, Maude. [BR:D]. (4:7, no stone)
BAUMANN, David Marshall / June 16, 1907 / Feb. 21, 1947 [BR:24 FEB:W]. (19:6)
BAYLISS, Burt L. Owner of section 1, site 37. (no stone)
BAYLISS, Tillie Mae. TILLIE M. / Jan. 12, 1888 / Sept. 12, 1963 [BR:16 SEP:D] / STUART I. / July 31, 1888 / April 26, 1965 [BR:26 APR:D]. (1:30 and 31)
BEACHUM, Thomas W. To the memory / of / THOMAS WILLIAM BEACHUM / who departed this life / ____ 1803 / ____ years. (41:16)
BEALL, Eugene L. EUGENE L. / Jan. 12, 1886 / Dec. 15, 1971 [BR:E] / FLORENCE M. / Nov. 3, 1899 / Dec. 26, 1982. (1:17)
BEALL, James Barry. JAMES BARRY BEALL / PFC US Army / Korea / Jul. 20, 1933 / Dec. 14, 1979. (1:17)
BELKOSKY, John P. BELKOSKY / JOHN P. / May 3, 1896 / March 22, 1976 [BR:E] / MARGARET J. / June 10, 1897 / April 13, 1984 [BR:16 APR:E]. (17:12:3 & 8)
BELL, James Entwistle. / ____ / ____ / JAMES ENTWISTLE / and MARGARET ANN / infant son & daughter of / ROBERT and MARY BELL / who departed this life / the 27th Nov. 1841 [Margaret Ann] / the other on the 26th [James Entwistle] / aged 7 weeks / They were lovely and pleasant / in their lives, and on their / death they were not divided. (43:122)
BELL, Lewis Verdun. LEWIS VERDUN BELL / May 22, 1906 / March 16, 1964 [BR:18 MAR:E]. (15:10)
BELL, Lizzie Tinsley. LIZZIE TINSLEY / wife of / ROBERT BELL, JR. / Fell asleep in Jesus / August 24, 1874 / aged 36 years. (44:152)
BELL, Maggie Calhoun. MAGGIE CALHOUN BELL / Fell asleep / June 7, 1881 / aged 8 years. (44:152)
BELL, Margaret Ann. In / memory of / MARGARET ANN / daughter of / ROBERT and MARY BELL / who died / Mar. 20, 1834 / aged 13 months. (43:122)
BELL, Mary Sidney. MARY SIDNEY / infant of / ROBERT, JR. and / L.T. BELL / died July 9, 1870 / aged 4 mos. & 12 days [AG:8/7/70:3]. (44:152)
BELL, Robert. ROBERT BELL / born in the / Isle of Ely, England / 1809-1885 / *Called and chosen / and faithful* / MARY GREENHALGH / wife of ROBERT BELL / born in Lancashire / 1816-1891 / ELIZABETH BLINKHORN / BELL / aged 90 years [AG:31/12/85:2, gives death 16 JUL 1885; AG:31/12/91:1, gives death 15 APR 1891]. (43:122)
BERKLEY, Harold P. HAROLD P. BERKLEY / born / Nov. 15, 1854 / died / Jan. 12, 1924. (18:18)
BERKLEY, William Norris, Jr. [BR:26 OCT 1959]. (18:18, no stone)
BERKLEY, William Norris, Sr. WILLIAM N. BERKLEY / Sept. 19, 1898 / Jan. 6, 1969 [BR:6 JAN:I]. (18:18:3)
BERRY, Blanche D. BERRY / BLANCHE D. / 1893-1965 [BR:2 DEC:G]. (16:25)
BERRY, Charles Adams. BERRY / CHARLES ADAMS / 1875-1961. (16:25)
BERRY, Elizabeth. Our Mother / ELIZABETH / wife of THOS. BERRY / born March 5, 1809 / died March 24, 1893 [AG:30/12/93:2]. (B:181)
BERRY, E. Louise Payne. BERRY / E. LOUISE PAYNE / 1879-1940 [BR:10 JUN]. (16:25)
BERRY, John Harper. JOHN HARPER BERRY / born July 14, 1848 / died April 20, 1910. (42:43)
BERRY, Margaret Fox. BERRY / MARGARET FOX / 1912-1981 [BR:G]. (16:25:1)

First Presbyterian Church Cemetery (1809)

BERRY, Thomas. [BR:19 SEP 1991:G]. (16:25:3, no stone)

BERRY, Winifred M. Smith. BERRY / WINIFRED M. SMITH / 1902-1967 [BR:6 OCT:G]. (16:25:4)

BERRYMAN, Charlotte Louise Cazenove. CHARLOTTE LOUISE / widow of / JOHN BERRYMAN, M.D. / daughter of / LOUIS A. & FRANCES A. / CAZENOVE / born Nov. 12, 1841 / died April 13, 1914; (second stone) CHARLOTTE CAZENOVE / widow of / JOHN BERRYMAN, M.D. / 1841-1914 / daughter of / LOUIS A. & FRANCES A. / CAZENOVE / *Grant O Lord Eternal Rest* / born Nov. 12, 1841 / died April 13, 1914. (43:93)

BEST, Martha Elizabeth Hannon. MARTHA ELIZABETH HANNON / wife of / Dr. JOSIAH JANNEY BEST / May 6, 1860 / May 24, 1941 [BR:26 MAY:W] / *They that dwell in the hearts / of the living are not dead.* (25:16)

BIERS, Sarah. SARAH BIERS / born ___ 29, 1800 / died Feb. 5, 1882. (43:103)

BIERS, William R. Sacred / to the memory of / WILLIAM R. BIERS / born Sept. 19, 1798 / died May 24, 1872. (43:103)

BITZER, Ellen Turner. ELLEN TURNER BITZER / September 28, 1924 / JAMES HERVEY BITZER / March 11, 1947. (25:28)

BLACK, David. In memory of / DAVID BLACK / & ELIZA / his wife. Sacred to the memory / of / ORLAND KING SHAY / aged 9 mos. and VIRGINIA aged 22 / mos. who died the same hour, Augt. / 21, 1834. They sleep on the remains of their grandfather / DAVID BLACK / and lie by the side of their sister / MARY JANE who died Aug. 29th, / 1839 aged 11 years, 8 mo. and their / brothers ORLANDO EUGENIUS / who died Sept. 11th, 1840, aged 5 years / 2 mos. 23 days, and HENRY JAMES / who died May 23, 1842, aged 9 mos. 22 days. / / Children of SAMUEL & JANE ELIZA KING / SHAY. [stone very worn, can be seen in midday sun]. (41:11)

BLACK, David. D.M.B. / born 1799 / died 1827 [AG:15/2/27:3]. (41:11)

BLACK, Capt. David. D.B. / born 1762 / died 1831 [AG:5/1/31:3]. (41:11)

BLACK, Eliza. E.B. / born 1777 / died 1850 [AG:20/2/50:2]. (41:11; Alexandria Wills, Bk. 5, p. 224)

BLACK, Helen Ann. H.A.B. / born 1812 / died 1845 [AG:3/10/45:3]. (41:11)

BLACKLOCK, Nicholas Frederick. In memory of / NICHOLAS F. BLACKLOCK / who died / Aug. 25th, 1818, / aged 28 years / ELIZA J. / his wife / died Jan. 18th, 1849 / aged 58 years. (42:72; Alexandria Wills, Bk. 2, p. 256)

BLACKLOCK, Robert S. In memory of / ROBERT S. BLACKLOCK, / who died / Nov. 10th, 1832 / aged 37 years / ANN M. / his wife / died April 30th 1837 / aged 41 years / also their daughter / ELIZABETH VIRGINIA / and her infant / wife of / WM. A. DUNCAN / who died February 17th / 1854. (42:72)

BLACKLOCK, William Ramsay. In memory of / WILLIAM RAMSAY / BLACKLOCK / son of / ROBERT S. & ANN M. BLACKLOCK / who departed this life / Nov. 14th, 1822 / aged 5 years & 9 months. / *E'vn sin could blight or sorrow fade / death came with friendly care / the opening bid to heaven coming / and bade a blessing there.* (42:72)

BLACKWELL, Mary S. In memory of / MARY S. BLACKWELL / wife of / JOSEPH H. BLACKWELL / and daughter of / DR. A. H. and ELLEN MOORE / SAUNDERS / born September 25, 1852 / died February 23, 1923 / *Numbered with Thy saints/ in glory everlasting.* (44:167)

BLAKE, William J., Sr. WILLIAM J. / Feb. 28, 1866 / July 19, 1953 [BR:29 JUL:C] /

First Presbyterian Church Cemetery (1809)

EMMA L. / Dec. 24, 1870 / July 26, 1967 [BR:29 JUL:C]. (24:10)
BLUNT, Sarah. Owner of section 41, lot 39. (no stone)
BLYTHE, Washington. In memory of / WASHINGTON BLYTHE / Surveyor / Civil Engineer and draughtsman / born May 27, 1810 / near Fairfield & Gettsburg / Adams County, Pennsylvania / died March 2nd 1882 / in Alexandria, Va. (44:154)
BOLAND, Edward J. EDWARD J. / Oct. 23, 1919 / Aug. 10, 1964 [BR:12 AUG:D] / DAVID S[cott]. BOLAND / Feb. 6, 1965 - May 3, 1969. (1:1A)
BOLTON, Walter A. / 1883-1937 / HELEN P. LEEF BOLTON / 1885-1933. (15:26)
BOSWELL, Lillie W. / 1856-1924. (17:22)
BOUSH, Mary A. May. In loving memory / of / MARY MAY / wife of / SAMUEL COLEMAN BOUSH / March 16, 1940 [BR:16 MAR:W]. (16:8)
BOUSH, Samuel Coleman. In memory / of / SAMUEL COLEMAN BOUSH / born in Alexandria / Virginia / 1842-1918 / member of the Washington / Artillery of New Orleans / C.S.A. (16:8)
BOWLES, William Elmer. WM. ELMER / June 22, 1896 / Aug. 21, 1977 [BR:24 AUG:C] / ELSIE F. / March 8, 1897 / June 17, 1979 [BR:C] / *At Rest*. (3:9:3 & 4)
BOYD, Charles W. CHARLES W. / born / Jan. 24, 1867 / died / June 13, 1871 / WILLIAM R. BOYD / born / May 22, 186[9] / died / Aug. 20, 1879 / MINNIE W. / born May 13, 1871 / died / April 19, 1877. (41:4)
BOYD, Harry P. HARRY P. BOYD / born June 10, 1886 / died Sept. 4, 1886. (41:4)
BOYD, John T. JOHN T. BOYD / born / Jan. 4, 1839 / died / Aug. 4, 1909 / MARTHA A. BOYD / born / July 28, 1844 / died / Feb. 14, 1929. (41:4)
BOYD, John Thomas. JOHN THOMAS / son of / JOHN T. & MARTHA A. BOYD / born Jan. 16, 1884 / died June 29, 1904 / *Rest sweet rest*. (41:4)
BOYD, Lillie Mildred. LILLIE MILDRED / daughter of / JOHN T. & MARTHA A. BOYD / born Nov. 14, 1874 / died Dec. 18, 1896 / *Blessed are they which are / called unto the marriage / supper of the Lamb*. (41:4)
BOYD, Mary R. MARY R. BOYD / born Oct. 26, 1881 / died Sept. 20, 1887. (41:4)
BOYD, Richard Theodore. RICHARD THEODORE / January 29, 1908 / September 9, 1972 [BR:13 SEP:Mc] / MARIE THOMAS / [blank]. (42:81)
BRADLEY, C. James. C. JAMES, SR. / Feb. 21, 1907 / July 22, 1971 [BR:E] / HELEN M. / Aug. 31, 1910 / [blank]. (18:9)
BRADLEY, Florence E. FLORENCE E. / BRADLEY / September 3, 1923 / April 7, 1989 / *A true companion*. (18:9)
BRENNER, Charles Francis. [BR:26 DEC 1957:D]. (13:10, no stone)
BRENNER, John E. JOHN E. BRENNER / born Feb. 10, 1873 / died April 2, 1938 [BR:5 APR:C] / ADDIE CRUMP / wife of / JOHN E. BRENNER / born Dec. 20, 1875 / died Nov. 27, 1928. (15:13)
BRENNER, Mary E. [BR:3 AUG 1937:D]. (13:10, no stone)
BRENNER, Nellie A. Fones. NELLIE FONES / Dec. 4, 1899 / Feb. 21, 1968 [BR:24 FEB:C] / GEORGE E. / OCT. 11, 1900 / June 28, 1971 [BR:C]. (15:13)
BRENNER, Sarah Elizabeth. SARAH ELIZABETH / wife of / ANTHONY BRENNER / 1849-1912 / ANTHONY BRENNER / 1843-1923 / daughter / JULIA C. BRENNER / 1873-1962 [BR:6 FEB:C]. (17:3)
BROCKET, Annabela. Remember Death / In memory of ANNABELA, the affectionate wife / of ROBERT BROCKET / and the sincere lover of her Famely, who / departed this life

First Presbyterian Church Cemetery (1809)

/ October 20th, 1808 / aged 54 years, and whose irreparable / loss is justly lamented / *O Sister, dust unfold thy Charms / Shortly fall into thy Arms* / 1st grave north and next to this Tomb / lies the body of WALTER the oldest son of / ANNABELLA & ROBERT BROCKET / who departed this life May 23d 1816 / aged 35 years / 2d ANDREW, son of / ELIZABETH & ROBERT BROCKET, JR. / who departed this life July 15th 1819 / aged 10 months. (41:9, boxtomb; FR:3, Andrew died of teething)

BROCKETT, Albert Doyle. ALBERT DOYLE BROCKETT / July 15, 1863 / May 17, 1922. (41:9, tablet)

BROCKETT, Caroline Elizabeth / 1831-1893 [AG:30/12/93:2, gives death 23 JUL 1893]. (44:148)

BROCKETT, Edgar Longden / 1825-1837. (44:148)

BROCKETT, Elizabeth Longden / 1795-1882. (44:148)

BROCKETT, Franklin Longden / 1822-1891 [AG:31/12/91:1, gives death 20 MAY 1891]. (44:148)

BROCKETT, Georgeanna Seymour / 1828-1898. (44:148)

BROCKETT, Hattie Nourse. HATTIE NOURSE BROCKETT / February 22, 1866 / January 21, 1941 [BR:23 JAN:W]. (41:9, tablet)

BROCKETT, Laura Virginia / 1833-1908 [AG:31/12/08:1, gives death 20 FEB 1908]. (44:148)

BROCKETT, Robert / 1792-1867 [AG:24/6/67:3]. (44:148)

BROCKETT, Robert. Beneath this tomb / is deposited the mortal remains of / ROBERT BROCKETT / a native of / Lanark Shire, Scotland / who departed this life March 29th, 1829 / aged 78 / *During a residence of 45 years in Alexandria he maintained the character of a worthy citizen & honest man*. (41:9, boxtomb)

BROCKETT, Virginia Eveleth / 1834-1927. (44:148)

BROCKETT, Walter Burnett / 1828-1889 [AG:31/12/89:2; gives death 5 JUL 1889]. (44:148)

BRODBECK, Annie Elizabeth. ANNIE ELIZABETH / died Jan. 1848 / aged 19 mo. & 8 dys. / ELIZA MAGRUDER / died Jan. 23, 1853 / aged 16 mo. 4 dys. / daughters of JACOB & MARY A. BRODBECK. (stone not found)

BROOKS, John Turpin. JOHN TURPIN BROOKS / Member of the Baptist Church / in Alexandria / Was called from time into Eternity / January 26, 1821 / aged 66 years / *At midnight the cry came / Behold the Bride groom cometh; go / Ye out to meet him / Blessed is that Servant who when his / Lord cometh shall be found watching*. (42:71, tablet; Alexandria Wills, Bk. 2, p. 410)

BROWN. Father and Mother / ARTHUR R. / born July 9, 1851 / died May 12, 1932 / ELLA H. / born Jan. 22, 1857 / died Nov. 11, 1931. (26:8)

BROWN, George Rush. GEORGE RUSH BROWN / Dec. 15, 1886 / May 22, 1970 / EDNA H. BROWN / wife of / JAMES H. WHITE / Aug. 28, 1890 / Dec. 31, 1931. (26:8)

BROWN, Georgianna. In memory / of / GEORGIANNA / wife of / LEONARD BROWN / died Feb. 15, 1901 / aged 64 years [AG:31/12/01:1]. (26:8)

BROWN, Leonard. In memory / of / LEONARD BROWN / died / Jan. 11, 1908 / aged 78 years [AG:31/12/08:1]. (26:8)

BROWN, Mary Emily. MARY [EMILY] BROWN / died / September 1, 189<u>8</u>. (stone not found)

BROWN, Mary Ramsay. MARY RAMSAY BROWN / wife of / Rt. REV. WILLIAM A. BROWN / June 21, 1877 / May 9, 1935. (B:212)

BRUSH, Mary P.S. MARY P.S. BRUSH / born Sept. 22, 1891 / died Dec. 21, 1907 / *Under*

First Presbyterian Church Cemetery (1809)

the sod and the dew / awaiting the judgment day. (15:16)
BRYANT, Arthur D. / 1881-1916. (16:21)
BURGESS, Albert C. ALBERT C. / 1884-1938 [BR:8 AUG:W] / MARY LINUS / 1891- [blank]. (14:23)
BURGESS, Benjamin F. To my husband / BENJ. F. BURGESS / born / March 26, 1845 / died / Dec. 14, 1894 / *At Rest*. / LILLIAN L. BURGESS / born / May 10, 1853 / died / June 19, 1932. (B:196, obelisk)
BURGESS, Bennie. BENNIE / son of EUGENE S. & AMELIA B. / BURGESS / 1901-1907 / *Asleep in Jesus*. (B:196)
BURGESS, Enock N. ENOCK N. BURGESS / husband of / LILLIAN L. BURGESS / 1847-1916 / *At Rest*. (B:196)
BURGESS, Lillian Eliza. LILLIAN ELIZA / daughter of / B.F. & LILLIAN L. BURGESS / born Sept. 4, 1891 / died June 26, 1892. (B:196)
BURROUGHS, Ida May / July 8, 1926 / Dec. 24, 1987 / *Loved and missed / by all who knew her*. [BR:29 DEC:E]. (16:21:7)
BUTLER, Catherine. Mother / CATHERINE BUTLER / 1855-1928 / *At rest*. (42:74)
BUTLER, Walter A. Died March 28, 1936. [BR:31 MAR]. (42:74, no stone)

C

CAGLE, Caroline. [BR:1 NOV 1972:I]. (16:12:3, no stone)
CALDWELL, Anthony / Aug. 31, 1957 / Dec. 22, 1976. (4:8)
CALDWELL, Charles. [BR:1976:E]. (4:21, no stone)
CALDWELL, Hannah Lyles. HANNAH LYLES CALDWELL / 1862-1935 / MARY E. DORSEY / 1882-1958 [BR:20 MAY:Ar] / LAURA M. DORSEY / 1879-1968 [BR:16 MAR:Ar]. (43:123)
CAMPBELL, Joseph F. JOSEPH F. CAMPBELL / Dec. 13, 1918 / July 10, 1967 [BR:14 JUL:Ch]. (B:175SW)
CAMPBELL, William. WM. CAMPBELL / Jan. 1, 1863 - Feb. 9, 1958 [BR:11 SEP:W]. (25:31N)
CARLIN, John Frank. JOHN FRANK / Aug. 26, 1861 / Aug. 17, 1917 / SARAH V. RUDD / Nov. 26, 1862 / Dec. 21, 1945. (14:23)
CARPENTER, Ralph L. / Pennsylvania / Sgt. Co. B 34 / Sig. Const. Bn. / World War II / Sept. 14, 1912 - Oct. 28, 1964 [second marker]. (16:16)
CARPENTER, Ralph Lester. RALPH LESTER / Sept. 14, 1912 - Oct. 28, 1964 / and his wife / ANNIE LAWS ASHTON / Nov. 22, 1901 - July 3, 1987 / <u>ASHTON</u> / LEETTA ERVIN WILKINS / wife of HENRY ASHTON / May 28, 1865 - Nov. 22, 1948 / OUIDA WATTLES BRESTER / Sept. 21, 1902 - Sept. 8, 1979 / <u>WATTLES</u> / NANNIE GORDON WATTLES / nee WILKINS / July 11, 1862 - April 5, 1914 / WILLIAM HERBERT / Sept. 16, 1882 - Sept. 2, 1928 / ALVIN MORTON / Oct. 20, 1872 - Nov. 10, 1911 / sons of A.J. & M.E. WATTLES. (16:16)
CARTER, Claude. <u>CARTER</u> / CLAUDE / 1872-1904. (25:23)
CARTER, Elisabeth Janney / October 23, 1869 / October 15, 1933. (15:25)
CARTER, Elizabeth. <u>CARTER</u> / ELIZABETH / 1866-1936. (25:23)
CARTER, Margaret Lisle. MARGARET LISLE / wife of J. NEWTON CARTER / and daughter of S. & A.S. MARK / died February 3, 1872.

First Presbyterian Church Cemetery (1809)

CARTER, Richard C. CARTER / RICHARD C. / 1855-1947. (25:23)
CARTER, Thomas T. THOMAS T. CARTER / Sept. 5, 1818 / Oct. 6, 1901 / his wife / SARAH TALIAFERRO / 1830-1916. (25:23)
CARTER, Thomas L. THOMAS L. CARTER / April 5, 1868 / May 2, 1938 [BR:4 MAY:C] / He left no nobler / heart behind. / J. BROOKE CARTER / Feb. 29, 1863 / March 11, 1943. (25:23)
CARTWRIGHT, Eliza. Erected / to the memory of / MRS. ELIZA CARTWRIGHT / wife of / MR. JOHNATHAN CARTWRIGHT / of Alexandria, D.C. / born in the year 1789 / died January 8th, 1840 / aged 41 years [AG:10/1/40:3]. (44:134)
CARTWRIGHT, Johnathan. To the memory of / JOHNATHAN CARTWRIGHT / who departed this life / the 13th of November 1848 / aged 52 years. (44:134; Alexandria Wills, Bk. 5, p. 105)
CATTS, Fannie Dulany. FANNIE DULANY / eldest daughter of / ROSIER D. & FANNIE A. / CATTS / born March 10, 1867 / died March 22, 1883 / What I do Thou knowest / not now but Thou shalt / know hereafter. / J.H. CATTS / Dec. 27, 1864 / Sept. 16, 1907 / SAMUEL R. CATTS, M.D. / Sept. 19, 1877 / Aug. 29, 1913 / LILLIAN L. COAKLEY / 1871-1944 / ROSIER D. CATTS / May 10, 1840 / Oct. 24, 1922 / his wife / FANNIE A. / Jan. 24, 1837 / July 24, 1909. (B:206)
CAZENOVE (also see DECAZENOVE).
CAZENOVE, Anne Hogan. In memory of / ANNE CAZENOVE / consort of / ANTONY CHARLES CAZENOVE / who departed this life / on Sunday the / 9th of July 1843 / in the 68th year of her age. (43:107, obelisk)
CAZENOVE, Anne. Asleep in Jesus. / ANNE / daughter of W.G. & / MARY E. CAZENOVE / born Augt. 23, 1854 / died Jany. 25, 1866 / She was a child of rare / promise, and of the / lovliest character. / Affectionate, docile, obedient, and pious / she was greatly beloved / and lamented. (43:107)
CAZENOVE, Antony Charles. In memory of / ANTY. CHAS. / CAZENOVE / a native of Geneva / Switzerland / but for nearly 60 years / an esteemed citizen / of Alexandria / where he departed / this life / on Saturday the / 16th day of Octr. 1852 / in the 78th year / of his age / universally / respected and beloved / born in Geneva / Switzerland / April 5th, 1775 / lived for nearly 60 / years in Alex. Va. / The spirit shall return / unto God who gave it. (43:107, obelisk; Alexandria Wills, Bk. 6, p. 157)
CAZENOVE, Antony Charles. In memoriam / ANTONY CHARLES / son of / WILLIAM GARDNER CAZENOVE / and MARY STANARD, his wife / born Alexandria, Va. / October 29, 1848 / died Baltimore, Md. / May 4, 1897. (43:107, statue)
CAZENOVE, Frances Eliza. Beneath this stone repose / the mortal remains of / FRANCES ELIZA / wife of LOUIS A. CAZENOVE / who died Apl. 2d 1847 / aged 27 yrs. & 17 days / and of / their youngest daughter / ELEUTHERA DUPONT / who died May 16, 1847 / aged 3 yrs. & 14 days. (43:104)
CAZENOVE, James O'Hara. 888 / JAMES O'HARA CAZENOVE / son of / LOUIS A. CAZENOVE, M.D. / and / MARY O'HARA CAZENOVE / March 25, 1880 - November 5, 1971 / Because I live you shall live also. (B:189)
CAZENOVE, Louis A. Sacred / to the memory of / LOUIS A. CAZENOVE / born Nov. 29th, 1807 / departed this life March 7th, 1852. (43:104, boxtomb)
CAZENOVE, Louis A. LOUIS A. CAZENOVE, M.D. / son of / LOUIS A. and HARRIOT E. / CAZENOVE / 1851-1925. (B:189)

First Presbyterian Church Cemetery (1809)

CAZENOVE, Mary O'Hara. In / loving memory of / MARY O'HARA / wife of / LOUIS A. CAZENOVE, M.D. / Sept. 10, 1853 / Nov. 30, 1890 / *Being justified freely by his / grace through the redemption / that is in Christ Jesus / Faithful in the discharge of / Every duty a most devoted / Selfsacrificing wife & mother / a steadfast friend. / Her children arise up and call / her blessed, her husband also / and he praiseth her.* (B:190, obelisk)

CAZENOVE, Mary Elizabeth Stanard. Sacred / to the memory of / MARY ELIZABETH STANDARD / wife of / WM. G. CAZENOVE / born / January 5, 1822 / died / November 14, 1892 / *Blessed are the pure in heart / for they shall see God / Thanks be to God who giveth / Us the victory through our / Lord Jesus Christ / He trusted in Jesus Christ / Loved truth, practiced virtue / and left to his children the / priceless inheritance of a / pure and stainless name / then are they glad because / they are at rest and so he / bringeth them into the house / where they would be.* (43:107)

CAZENOVE, Mary Stanard. In memory of / MARY STANARD / only daughter of / WM. G. and MARY E. CAZENOVE / born June 5th 1851 / died April 28th 1853. / *Blessed is the kingdom of Heaven.* (43:107)

CAZENOVE, Octavus Antony. Sacred / to the memory of / OCTAVIUS ANTY. CAZENOVE / who departed this life / 23 April 1841 / aged 27 yrs. 3 [m]ons. & 27 ds. / *Thou are gone to the...* (43:104, table; Alexandria Wills, Bk. 4, p. 299)

CAZENOVE, William Gardner. Sacred / to the memory of / WM. GARDNER CAZENOVE / born / October 27, 1819 / died August 8, 1877 / *Believe in the Lord / Jesus Christ and thee shall be saved.* (43:107, obelisk)

CHAMBERLAIN, Jacob. Here lies the remains / of / JACOB CHAMBERLAIN / who departed this life / June 15th 1831 / in the 20th year of his age / *In bright hope of eternal life / his last hours were employed for warning / his survivors to prepareth ____ / Let me die the death of the righteous / and let my last end be like his.* (41:2, tablet; Alexandria Wills, Bk. 4, p. 21, men. mother Jane L. Chamberlain)

CHAMBERLAIN, Luther. Here lies the remains of / LUTHER CHAMBERLAIN / who departed this life December 4th 1828 / in the 29th year of his age / *He desired to live that he might glorify his / Redeemer; but was willing to die in the hour / of eternal life. / He employed his last hours in warning his / survivors to prepare to meet their God. / He was soon followed by an infant son, a loved / child of the same name, aged 9 months / deposited in the same place.* [AG:8/12/28:3]. (41:13, tablet; Alexandria Wills, Bk. 3, p. 320, men. wife Jane Lelina Chamberlain)

CHAPMAN, John Seabury. JOHN SEABURY CHAPMAN / 1835-1880 / his wife / JULIA GREGORY / 1842-1912 / MARY LONG CHAPMAN / 1876-1878 / C.S.A. [AG:11/9/80:2, gives death 10 SEP 1880; AG:31/12/12:1, gives death 26 DEC 1912; AG:24/9/78:2, gives death 23 SEP 1878]. (44:142)

CHAPMAN, William Gregory. WILLIAM GREGORY CHAPMAN / 1872-1948 [BR:21 JUL:C]. (44:142)

CARPENTER, Ralph. [BR:31 OCT 1964:E]. (16:16, no stone)

CHATHAM, Fanny. FANNY / wife of / HENRY CHATHAM / died / Decr. 9th, 1830 / aged 40 years / *Not lost but gone before.* (41:36, obelisk)

CHATHAM, Henry. Our father / HENRY CHATHAM / died / December 30th, 1865 / aged 85 years. (41:36; Alexandria Wills, Bk. 8, p. 299, men. daughter Mary who is wife of John Graham, daughter Jane Chatham who is wife of Nathaniel Boush, and daughter

First Presbyterian Church Cemetery (1809)

Fanny who is wife of John A. Dixon)
CHAUNCEY, Frank. [BR:21 JUL 1936:W]. (44:147, no stone)
CHAUNCEY, John F. JOHN F. CHAUNCEY / 1830-1908 / his wife / MARY CATHARINE / 1832-1867 [AG:31/12/08:1, gives death 4 MAR 1908; AG:26/4/67:2, gives death 26 APR 1867]. (44:157)
CHESHIRE, Andrew H. CHESHIRE / ANDREW H. / April 14, 1921 / Feb. 16, 1972 [BR:19 FEB:D] / VICTORIA R. / Oct. 3, 1918 / June 10, 1979 [BR:15 JUN:E]. (17:12:1 & 2)
CHINAULT, Louis Avery / Dec. 26, 1903 - Dec. 29, 1972. (18:6)
CHURCH, Gilbert. In memory of / GILBERT CHURCH / who departed this / life March 4th 1813 / aged 40 years. (41:13)
CLARK, Clifton Power. CLARK / CLIFTON POWER / 1875-1949 / ALTA KELLY / 1879-1978. (44:144)
CLARK, Elizabeth Wood. [BR:11 JUN 1964:E]. (44:159, no stone)
CLARK, Robert E. [BR:20 APR 1966:E]. (44:159, no stone)
CLARVOE, Annie Gertrude. Gertie's Grave / Sacred / to the memory of / ANNIE GERTRUDE / beloved wife of / NAPOLEON B. CLARVOE / born Oct. 27, 1863 / died July 11, 1891. (43:110)
CLARVOE, Mary. MARY CLARVOE / born / Nov. 18, 1853 / died / Sept. 23, 1931 / *Out of suffering / came to rest.* (43:110)
CLARVOE, Napoleon B. In memory of / NAPOLEON B. CLARVOE / born / June 27, 1840 / died / Dec. 28, 1904. (43:110)
CLIFT, Percy E. PERCY E. CLIFT / 1864-1938 [BR:20 NOV:C] / his wife / FLORENCE HENDERSON / 1874-1932 / HENDERSON / INDIANA BALL HENDERSON / 1843-1913 / JOHN ALBERT HENDERSON / 1868-1918 / WILLIAM AVERY HENDERSON / 1866-1921 / ANNIE BALL PIERPOINT / 1839-1931. (15:20)
CLYBURN, Clifford L. [BR:25 MAR 1937:C]. (44:157, no stone)
COAKLEY, Lillian Lee. [BR:1 MAY 1944:D]. (B:206, no stone)
COE, Theodore Irving. THEODORE IRVING COE / August 18, 1872 / November 12, 1960 [BR:17 NOV:H, cremation] / MARTHA BROCKETT COE / April 6, 1865 / January 1, 1962 [BR:3 JAN:H, cremation]. (41:9, moved to 44:148)
COGAN, Charles A. In memory of / CHARLES A. COGAN / 1867-1892 / *Jehovah God is love.* / COGAN / In memory of / ELLA I. ROBERTSON / beloved wife of / CHARLES A. COGAN / 1868-1922 / *Simply trusting.* (B:211)
COGAN, Charles A. [BR:24 SEP 1942:Ch]. (B:211, no stone)
COGAN, Edward. [BR:10 JUL 1938:D]. (B:211, no stone)
COGAN, Ida M. Campbell. IDA M. CAMPBELL / wife of / JOHN A. COGAN / 1857-1924 / *A faithful wife.* (B:217)
COGAN, John A. / 1856-1926 / *At Rest.* (B:217)
COGAN, John P. JOHN P. / COGAN / 1822-1903 [AG:31/12/03:1, gives date 4 MAR 1903]. (B:211)
COGAN, Katherine. In memoriam / KATHERINE / beloved wife of / JOHN COGAN / born in Cranard / Co. Longford, Ireland / died in Alexandria, Va. / July 3, 1898 / aged 59 years / *May her soul rest in peace. / Blessed are the dead / who died in the Lord.* (B:211)
COGAN, Richard B. RICHARD B. COGAN / born / Jan. 16, 1863 / died / April 25, 1913.

First Presbyterian Church Cemetery (1809)

[another stone] RICHARD B. COGAN / 1863-1913 / his wife / MARY V. FOX / 1865-1935. (B:211)

COGAN, Virginia Barton. VIRGINIA BARTON / wife of / WILLIAM COGAN / born / Aug. 28, 1836 / died / Dec. 21, 1912 / *Well done good and faithful servant; / Enter thou into the joy of thy Lord.* (B:211)

COGAN, William. In memory of / my husband / WILLIAM COGAN / died / July 8, 1888 / aged / 60 years / native of London / England. (B:211)

COGAN, William W. WILLIAM W. COGAN / 1859-1916 / ALBERT C. COGAN / 1865-1918. (B:211)

CONWAY, Robert. Sacred / to the memory of / ROBERT and MARGARET / CONWAY / who departed this life / the former on the 1st of January 1837 / the latter on the 22nd Septr. 1832. (44:131, tablet)

COOK, Henry. HENRY COOK / Born / at St. Ives Hunts. / England / Sept. 16, 1806 / Died / Dec. 10, 1868. / *There remaineth therefore a rest to the people of God.* (43:115)

COOK, Hortense H. [BR:22 AUG 1967:D]. (43:115, no stone)

COOK, Hortensia H. Mark. HORTENSIA H. / Relict of / HENRY COOK / And Daughter of / SAMUEL & ANN S. MARK / Born in Alex. D.C. / March 24, 1818 / Died Nov. 14, 1880. / *Great peace have they which love thy [name].* (43:115)

COOK, Llewellyn M. LLEWELLYN M. COOK / born Aug. 28, 1854 / died / May 26, 1920. (43:115)

COOK, Lucy Ashby. LUCY ASHBY / wife of / LLEWELLYN M. COOK / died May 15, 1899. (43:115)

COOK, Mary Seymour. MARY SEYMOUR COOK / born in Alexandria / March 15th 1848 / died in Baltimore / Decr. 13th 1863 / *Even so them also which sleep in / Jesus will God bring with Him.* (43:115, tablet)

COOPER, Samuel. SAMUEL COOPER / departed this life / April 3, 1811 / in the 39 year / of his age. [MR:funeral held 4 APR]. (41:26)

COPE, C. Duane. C. DUANE COPE / Mar. 2, 1927 / Nov. 30, 1982. (25:32)

COPE, Oliver Wilson. OLIVER WILSON / Oct. 13, 1894 / June 3, 1978 [BR:E] / FAY GRIER / Sept. 29, 1894 / Oct. 28, 1978. (25:32)

CORNELL, Claudia Maynard. [BR:2_ FEB 1937:W]. (15:3, no stone)

CORSA, Ralph W. CORSA / RALPH W. / Aug. 6, 1904 / May 28, 1967 [BR:1 JUN:C] / MARY F. FONES / March 25, 1905 / [blank]. (3:8)

COX, Charles N. CHARLES N. COX / Dec. 23, 1882 / Dec. 15, 1970 / married Sept. 21, 1910 / REBECCA B. COX / March 25, 1879 / Aug. 31, 1969 [BR:3 SEP:D]. (1:26 & 25)

COX, Gilbert Jefferson. GILBERT JEFFERSON COX / 1862-1938 [BR:19 FEB:W] / ELLA LAWRENCE COX / 1864-1917. (36:10, Celtic cross)

COX, Gilbert Jefferson, Jr. GILBERT JEFFERSON / COX, JR. / February 8, 1895 / August 12, 1973 [BR:15 AUG:E]. (36:11:2)

COX, Meade E. MEADE EVERARD / FIELD COX / October 11, 1902 / March 23, 1988 [BR:26 MAR:E]. (36:11:1)

COX, Sarah Bowie. SARAH BOWIE / COX / June 16, 1899 / February 24, 1977 [BR:28 FEB:E]. (36:11:1)

COX, Thomas Wallace / July 23, 1869 / Sept. 29, 1940 [BR:1 OCT:H]. (16:3)

CRADLIN, George Nelson. GEORGE N. CRADLIN / Oct. 3, 1869 / May 31, 1953 [BR:31

First Presbyterian Church Cemetery (1809)

MAY:I]. (19:14)
CRADLIN, Lillie M. LILLIE M. / daughter of / G.N. & R.I. CRADLIN / 1902-1924 / *Rest sweet rest.* (19:14)
CRADLIN, Rose I. Boyd. ROSE I. BOYD / beloved wife of / GEORGE N. CRADLIN / Oct. 11, 1864 / Jan. 10, 1940 [BR:13 JAN:I]. (19:14)
CRAGG, Mabel Isbelle Hunter / 1885-1953 [BR:24 MAR]. (16:23E)
CRAGG, Mary Virginia / 1912-1939 [BR:27 JUL:C]. (16:23E)
CRAGG, Thomas Mark / 1882-1952 [BR:24 JAN:C]. (16:23E)
CRAMLEY, Helen Sue. [BR:11 AUG 1967:D]. (1:1J, no stone)
CRANE, John Aubrey. JOHN AUBREY / Dec. 20, 1905 / Jan. 28, 1975 [BR:31 JAN:C] / ELSIE VIRGINIA / Aug. 13, 1910 / Aug. 10, 1989. (3:15)
CRANE, Richard Allen. Son / RICHARD ALLEN CRANE / Jan. 6, 1902 / Jan. 25, 1918. (13:13)
CRANE, Richard Edward. Father / RICHARD EDWARD CRANE / Sept. 25, 1873 / Aug. 21, 1927. (13:13)
CRANE, Sarah Ann. Mother / SARAH ANN CRANE / Nov. 23, 1877 / Sept. 30, 1956 [BR:3 OCT:C]. (13:13)
CRANSTON, Annie E. Bagot. ANNIE E. BAGOT / wife of / JOHN D. CRANSTON / died Feb. 19, 1923 / JOHN D. CRANSTON / 1855-1934. (B:215)
CRUMBAUGH, Edward L. [BR:28 DEC 1978:C, no location given].
CRUMBAUGH, Etta Lee. [BR:30 OCT 1948:C, no location given].
CUMPSTON, Anna Ramsey. [BR:2 FEB 1968, cremation]. (41:31, no stone)
CUMPSTON, Wilhelmina Bartleman. WILHELIMINA B. / daughter of E.H. / & Anna B. CUMPSTON / born Dec. 12, 1875 / died June 9, 1878 / *Them also which sleep in / Jesus will God bring / with him* [AG:11/6/78:3]. (41:31)
CURTIN, Benjamin F. / Sept. 14, 1896 / April 23, 1923 / *Veteran of Foreign Wars.* (13:12)
CURTIN, Christopher. CHRISTOPHER CURTIN / March 8, 1854 / July 30, 1931 / *Rest in peace.* (13:9)
CURTIN, Christopher. CHRISTOPHER CURTIN / 1900-1912. (13:9)
CURTIN, Christopher. CHR. CURTIN, JR. No dates. (13:10)
CURTIN, Elizabeth Jane. ELIZABETH JANE CURTIN / wife of / CHRISTOPHER CURTIN / April 3, 1858 / Sept. 17, 1932 / *Rest in peace.* (13:9)
CURTIN, George R. Mc. GEORGE R. Mc. CURTIN / 1875-1906. (13:9)
CURTIN, James E. / 1866-1918. (13:13)
CURTIN, James E. JAMES EDW. / Nov. 24, 1891 / July 19, 1969 [BR:21 JUL:D] / MARGARET H. / April 8, 1893 / Feb. 6, 1965 [BR:8 FEB:D]. (13:13)
CURTIN, James E., Jr. JAMES E., Jr. / Nov. 6, 1915 / July 9, 1991 / WILLIE LOUISE / July 19, 1917 / [blank] / father / married Aug. 29, 1936 / mother. (2)
CURTIN, John T. My beloved husband / JOHN T. CURTIN / July 12, 1889 / Jan. 21, 1923. (13:12)
CURTIN, Willie. [BR:28 JAN 1972:C]. (13:13, no stone)

D

DAINGERFIELD, Edward. EDWARD DAINGERFIELD / born in Alexa. Va., April 1, 1805 / died May 12, 1861. (42:44, obelisk)

First Presbyterian Church Cemetery (1809)

DAINGERFIELD, Edward Lonsdale. EDWARD LONSDALE / infant son of / EDWARD L. and / S.V. DAINGERFIELD / born May 1, 1887 / died July 1, 1888 / *Spotless and pure / He lives in Paradise*. (25:20)

DAINGERFIELD, Edward Lonsdale. EDWARD LONSDALE DAINGERFIELD / son of / JOHN B. & REBECCA DAINGERFIELD / Nov. 5 / 1847 / Oct. 14 / 1925. (25:20)

DAINGERFIELD, Edward Lonsdale. In blessed memory / EDWARD LONSDALE DAINGERFIELD / Nov. 5, 1847 - Oct. 14, 1925 / his wife / SARAH VOWELL SMITH DAINGERFIELD / March 23, 1853 - May 16, 1906 / their son / FRANCIS LEE DAINGERFIELD / July 16, 1883 - Aug. 8, 1927. (25:7, statue and cross)

DAINGERFIELD, Francis Lee. FRANCIS LEE DAINGERFIELD / son of / EDWARD L. & SARAH S. DAINGERFIELD / July 16 / 1883 / Aug. 8 / 1927. (25:20)

DAINGERFIELD, John Bathurst. JOHN BATHURST / infant son of / EDWARD L. and / S.V. DAINGERFIELD / born Aug. 31, 1878 / died Aug. 7, 1879 / *Safe from the world / of temptations*. (25:20)

DAINGERFIELD, Margaret Boyd. In loving memory of / MARGARET BOYD DAINGERFIELD / wife of EDWARD DAINGERFIELD / and daughter of JOHN C. and / MARY VOWELL of Alexandria, Va. / born Oct. 13th 1811 / died Oct. 10th 1887 [AG:11/10/87:2]. (42:44)

DAINGERFIELD, Mary H. MARY H. DAINGERFIELD / daughter of / EDWARD L. and SARAH S. / DAINGERFIELD / July 2, 1880 - June 6, 1965. (25:7)

DAINGERFIELD, Rosalie Taylor. In memory of / ROSALIE DAINGERFIELD / wife of HENRY DAINGERFIELD / of Alexandria / and Daughter of / ROBT. I. TAYLOR / born January 8th 1817 / died June 22nd 1841 / aged 24 years 5 months. (41:22, obelisk)

DAINGERFIELD, Sarah Vowell Smith. SARAH VOWELL SMITH / wife of / EDWARD LONSDALE DAINGERFIELD / March 23 / 1853 / May 16 / 1906. (25:20)

DALE, A. Caldwell. A. CALDWELL DALE / his wife / JANE R. DALE / their sons and daughter / ROBERT and JAMES / ROSANNA. (43:95)

DALE, Mary Jane. MARY JANE / daughter of / GEORGE & ELIZA / DALE / departed 9th May 1827 / aged two years & 1 five months. (43:95)

DARST, Florence Wise. FLORENCE WISE / beloved wife of / Rev. THOS. C. DARST. 1876-1914 / *She served the Lord / with gladness*. [AG:31/12/14:1, gives death 12 JAN 1914]. (13:1)

DAVIDSON, Alberta Maria English. In memory of / ALBERTA MARIA ENGLISH / wife of / FRANCIS JAMES DAVIDSON / 1843-1935. (44:145)

DAVIDSON, Ann Elizabeth. In memory of / ANN ELIZABETH / daughter of / FRANCIS K. & JANE W. / DAVIDSON / died Oct. 20, 1925. (44:145)

DAVIDSON, Eva T. EVA T. DAVIDSON / [blank] / JOHN S. / June 26, 1893 / Dec. 28, 1975 [BR:31 DEC:E]. (3:14)

DAVIDSON, Faith Henderson. In memory of / FAITH HENDERSON DAVIDSON / wife of / FRANCIS JAMES DAVIDSON, JR. / born / April 7, 1892 / died / April 29, 1972. (44:145)

DAVIDSON, Francis James. In memory of / FRANCIS JAMES DAVIDSON / 1838-1921. (44:145)

DAVIDSON, Francis James, Jr. In memory of / FRANCIS JAMES DAVIDSON, Jr. / born / March 17, 1879 / died / April 27, 1959. (44:145)

DAVIDSON, Francis James, III. In memory of / FRANCIS JAMES DAVIDSON, III / born

First Presbyterian Church Cemetery (1809)

/ December 19, 1912 / died / May 21, 1985 [BR:24 MAY:G]. (44:145)
DAVIDSON, Francis K. In memory of / FRANCIS K. DAVIDSON / 1810-1888 / *Them also which sleep in / Jesus will God bring with him.* [AG:31/12/88:1, gives death 29 JUL 1888]. (44:145)
DAVIDSON, Jane Welborne. In memory of / JANE WELBORNE / wife of / FRANCIS K. DAVIDSON / 1812-1888. (44:145)
DAVIDSON, William K. In memory of / WILLIAM K. / son of / FRANCIS K. & JANE W. / DAVIDSON / died Aug. 17, 1914. (44:145)
DAVIS, Albert. In / memory of / ALBERT & EDWIN / sons of / GEO. & SARAH E. DAVIS / who died Sept. 9th & 11th, 1832 / aged 9 years & 5 years. (43:102)
DAVIS, Charles E. CHARLES E. DAVIS / Nov. 25, 1850 / July 7, 1903. (43:85)
DAVIS, Charlie. CHARLIE / son of / C.E. & E.M. DAVIS / 1877-1878. (43:85)
DAVIS, Charlotte Vowell. CHARLOTTE VOWELL DAVIS / 1820-1897 / ELIZA KNOX DAVIS / 1822-1901 [AG:31/12/97:1, gives death 4 MAR 1897; AG:31/12/01:1, gives death 18 MAR 1901]. (44:141)
DAVIS, Constance Gardner. CONSTANCE GARDNER / wife of / HENRY WINTER DAVIS / born July 17, 1820 / married Oct. 30, 1845 / died May 12, 1849. / *Thy faith hath saved thee, / Go in peace. / CONSTANCE / And hope and love and beauty's bloom / are blossoms gathered for the lamb. / There's nothing true but Heaven.* (43:104)
DAVIS, C. Randolph. C. RANDOLPH / DAVIS / 1868-1913 [AG:31/12/13:1, gives date 21 MAY 1913]. (25:9)
DAVIS, Eleanor W. [BR:3 MAR 1981:E]. (18:21:4, no stone)
DAVIS, Eliza Ann. In / memory of ELIZA ANN & ANN ELIZA daughters of GEO. & SARAH E. DAVIS / who died Augt. 5th 1825 / July 18, 1829, aged 3 years & 9 months & 5 months. (43:102)
DAVIS, Ella L.F. ELLA LEE FAIRFAX / DAVIS / 1872-1943 [BR:20 DEC:W]. (25:8)
DAVIS, Emma M. EMMA M. / wife of / CHAS. E. DAVIS / Dec. 11, 1848 / June 18, 1922.
DAVIS, George Oscar. In / Memory of / GEORGE OSCAR & GEORGIANA / children of / GEO. & SARAH E. DAVIS / who died Decr. 25, 1832 / aged 13 years & 7 years / *Rest gentle spirit.* (43:102)
DAVIS, James H. [BR:5 JAN 1982:E]. (18:21:1, no stone)
DAVIS, John Randolph Fairfax. JOHN RANDOLPH FAIRFAX DAVIS / Aug. 26, 1909 - Oct. 22, 1978 [BR:23 OCT:C] / his wife / LILLIAN BERTHA FRENCH DAVIS / May 16, 1912 - Dec. 4, 1984 [BR:7 DEC:C]. (24:16:3 & 4)
DAVIS, Josiah H. JOSIAH H. DAVIS / born Dec. 31, 1783 / died April 30, 1862 / SALLY M. DAVIS / his wife / died June 25, 1844 / in her 58 year / THOMAS V[owell]. / son of J.H. & S.M. DAVIS / born Feb. 22, 1824 / died Jan. 10, 1868 / JOHN H. DAVIS / son of J.H. & S.M. DAVIS / born Feb. 3, 1826 / died April 3, 1852 / J. HEWES DAVIS / born Sept. 2, 1816 / died June 17, 1871 / SARAH W[ells]. / wife of J.H. DAVIS / born March 12, 1795 / died Feb. 11, 1861 / HANNAH ANN / daughter of / J.H. & S.M. DAVIS / born Feb. 20, 1815 / died Feb. 12, 1845. (43:114)
DAVIS, Mildred Bradley / May 8, 1917 / January 24, 1979 / *A Gallant Lady.* (18:10)
DAVIS, Ray Osborne / 1893-1945. (25:8)
DAWSON, Christine N. [BR:FEB 1936:D]. (25:11, no stone)
DEAKINS, Jane Milburn. MRS. JANE DEAKINS / born at Newcastle Upon / Tyne, England / Oct. 3rd A.D. 1788 / died at Washington City, D.C. / Aug. 2nd A.D. 1863. (42:62,

First Presbyterian Church Cemetery (1809)

obelisk)
DEAKINS, Joseph Milburn. JOSEPH M. DEAKINS / grandson of / JOSEPH & MARGARET MILBURN / died 26th November 1832 / aged 28 years. (42:62)
DEAN, Charles Agustus. [BR:13 MAR 1954:C]. (16:9, no stone)
DEAN, Elizabeth Wyer. ELIZABETH WYER / and JAMES FOSTER / children of / WILLIAM & MARY A. DEAN / *Rest sweet babes you're safe at H[eaven?]*. (42:75)
DEAN, Elwood. [BR:2 AUG 1962:C]. (16:9, no stone)
DEAN, Joseph. JOSEPH DEAN / died April 21, 1818 / aged 55 years / HANNAH DEAN / died Feb. 6, 1843 / aged 76 years / JANE DEAN / died April 11, 1846 / aged 47 years / ELIZABETH W. DEAN / died / April 15, 1844 / aged 6 years & 9 months / JAMES F. DEAN / died June 7, 1844 / aged 4 months / WM. H[enry]. DEAN / died April 14, 1851 / aged 5 years & 10 months / MARY A. DEAN / wife of WM. DEAN / died August 1, 1854 / aged 41 years / MARY J. DEAN / died January 7, 1863 / aged 20 years / & 5 months. (42:75)
DEAN, Mary Isabel. [BR:31 MAR 1941:C]. (16:9, no stone)
DEANE, James. In memory of / JAMES DEANE / 1838-1918 / MARGARET / wife of / JAMES DEANE / 1828-1903 / *Rest.* / ANNIE M. DEANE / 1860-1926 / JAMES B. DEANE / 1868-1930 / MARGARET DEANE / 1865-1934 / JAMES DEANE DAVIS / 1900-1920 / MARY ESTHER DAVIS / 1896-1921 / ESTHER DAVIS / GRILLBORTZER / 1896-1927 / SANDRA JEAN / STRAUB / 1949-1950 / FRANCES DEANE DAVIS / 1862-1901 / Husband / ARTHUR G. DAVIS / 1870-1947 / ARCHIE L. STRAUB / 1891-1965 / His wife / ANNA DAVIS STRAUB / 1897-1965 [AG:31/12/01:1, gives death for Fannie D. Davis on 15 SEP 1901]. (B:214)
[DEANE?], J.B. Place stone for J.B.D. only. (14:25)
[DEANE?], M. Place stone for M.D. only. (14:25)
DEARBORN, Harriet. Sacred / to the memory of / HARRIET / the amiable consort of / SIMON DEARBORN / who departed this life Oct. 30, 1821 / Aged 37 years / *Heaven [broken] pledge of felicity to ___ / Rest th__!, rest in the sweet balm of / heaven.* (43:87, tablet)
DEBOGANDE, Ada Henderson Thomas / February 3, 1845 - February 23, 1917 / *She was tired and fell asleep.* (43:90, statue and cross)
DECAZENOVE, Infant. Infant son of / LOUIS A. & ELIZABETH A. / DECAZENOVE / born July 3, 1908 / died July 5, 1908. (B:189)
DECAZENOVE. 1888 - HELGA THORGJERD GRONVOLD - 1945 / wife of / 1878 - LOUIS A. DECAZENOVE - 1952. (B:189)
DECAZENOVE, Louis A. LOUIS A. / son of / LOUIS A. & ELIZABETH A. / DECAZENOVE / born March 31, 1911 / died April 5, 1911. (B:189)
DECAZENOVE, Louis A. [BR:24 JAN 1952:W]. (B:189, no stone)
DEEBLE, Joseph H. In memory of / JOS. H. DEEBLE / who departed this / life Ocr. 8th, 1813 / aged 25 years [AG:12/10/13:3]. (41:21)
DEIKE, Frederick / 1880-1920. (24:14)
DEIKE, Mary / 1847-1919. (24:14)
DELANEY, Baby. [BR:29 AUG 1938:D]. (42:57, no stone)
DELANEY, Child of Dr. Martin. [BR:2 JAN 1941:D]. (42:57)
DELANEY, Catharine O'Donoghue. CATHARINE O'DONOGHUE / (BABA) / Beloved wife of / DR. MARTIN D. DELANEY, SR. / July 11 [no year] / August 22, 1971. (42:47)

First Presbyterian Church Cemetery (1809)

DELANEY, Dorothy Devine / Mary 7, 1919 / July 30, 1970 [BR:3 AUG:D]. (42:57)
DELANEY, Martin Donohue. MARTIN DONOHUE / DELANEY / April 27, 1876 / February 10, 1933 / *He excelled in the art and / science of healing the / sick and the afflicted.* (42:57)
DELANEY, Dr. Martin, Jr. / June 5, 1907 / March 10, 1986. (42:57)
DELANEY, Paul Lyne / April 6, 1909 / March 29, 1990 / SARAH CARTER DELANEY / his wife / September 25, 1915 / [blank]. (B:201)
DEMAINE, Alice K. ALICE K. DEMAINE / 1866-1942 [BR:21 JAN:B]. (16:14W)
DEMAINE, Charles W.D. CHARLES W. DEMAINE / 1895-1936 [BR:died 4 APR 1936:B]. (16:14)
DEMAINE, Janie W. / 1889-1956 [BR:16 APR]. (16:14)
DEMAREST, Alma Ethel. DEMAREST / ALMA E. / 1869-1941 [BR:11 JAN:P] / DAVID T. / 1839-1923 / MARGARET C. / 1842-1924. (14:24)
DEMAREST, Dorothy / 1915-1918. (15:5)
DEMAREST, Henry Everett. HENRY E. DEMAREST / 1878-1960 [BR:19 MAR:A]. (15:5)
DEMAREST, Margaretta Agnew. MARGARETTA A. DEMAREST / 1878-1958 [BR:27 OCT:Ar]. (15:5)
DEMOLL, Bessie Scrivener / November 5, 1898 / July 27, 1927. (17:8)
DEMPSEY, James. JAMES DEMPSEY / 1809-1865 / ESTHER W. SANFORD / his wife / 1811-1899 / ANNA MILLER / their daughter / 1842-1913 / JAMES DEMPSEY / 1874-1878 / ANNA DEMPSEY / 1876-1878 / Children of / A.H. & S.D. THOMSON / ALFRED THOMSON / 1872-1944 / SUE ELLEN SMOOT / wife of / ALFRED THOMSON / 1868-1941 [BR:11 DEC:W] / ALFRED H. / 1841-1915 / SARAH McK. DEMPSEY / wife of / A.H. THOMSON / 1847-1911 / their daughter / MARY THOMSON / 1881-1941 [BR:20 DEC:W; AG:27/10/65:3, gives date 26 OCT 1865; AG:31/12/13:1, gives date 24 OCT 1913]. (44:136, obelisk)
DETTERER, Lewis A. LEWIS A. DETTERER / beloved husband of / MARGUERITE E. DETTERER / April 14, 1892 - July 9, 1957 [BR:12 JUL:G]. (17:24)
DETTERER, Lewis A., Jr. DETTERER / LEWIS A., JR. / Jan. 21, 1913 / Feb. 9, 1989 [BR:13 FEB:I] / GLADYS K. / Mar. 30, 1902 / July 3, 1990. (17:24)
DETTERER, Marguerite E. MARGUERITE E. DETTERER / Our beloved mother / May 27, 1889 - Jan. 15, 1963 [BR:19 JAN:G]. (17:24)
DETWILER, Richard Walter / May 30, 1958 / November 22, 1977 [BR:26 NOV:D, cremation]. (18:24)
DEVINE, Charles E. DEVINE / CHARLES E. / 1865-1924. (19:4)
DEVINE, Charles Joseph. [BR:30 AUG 1957:W]. (19:4, no stone)
DEVINE, Homer Leroy. DEVINE / HOMER L. / 1908-1959 [BR:6 JUN:W]. (19:4)
DEVINE, Julia A. JULIA A. / 1872-1965 [BR:15 JAN:E]. (19:4)
DEVINE, Robert E. DEVINE / ROBERT E. / 1893-1935. (19:4)
DIBBLE, Dorothy S. / February 12, 1912 / March 2, 1990 [BR:7 MAR:Col]. (25:1:1)
DICK, David. In / memory of / DAVID DICK / a native of Ireland / and 34 years a resident / of / Alexandria / who died 20th March 1833 / in the 67th year / of his age. (42:70)
DIEDEL, Adolph. In memory of / ADOLPH DIEDEL / born in Treysa / Kurhessen, Germany / Mar. 2, 1829 / died Mar. 26, 1888 / his wife / CAROLINA MAGDELENE / Jan. 16, 1834 / Feb. 15, 1918. (43:91)
DIEDEL, Caroline L. CAROLINE L. / infant daughter of / ADOLPH & CAROLINE M. /

First Presbyterian Church Cemetery (1809)

DIEDEL / born Mar. 29, 1875 / died July 7, 1875. (43:91, obelisk)
DIEDEL, Charles. CHARLES DIEDEL, D.D.S. / Nov. 13, 1865 - Apr. 30, 1937 [BR:3 MAY:G] / his wife / FANNIE ELIZABETH KING / June 13, 1870 - Oct. 6, 1927 / VIRGINIA DIEDEL / 1901-1979. (17:23)
DIXON, Mary J. Paton. MARY J. / daughter of / JOHN B. PATON / and wife of / TURNER DIXON / died / Dec. 11, 1870 / WILLIAM PATON DIXON / died / May 31, 1847 / TURNER DIXON / died / July 1864 / MARY / infant daughter. (42:77)
DODSON, Emmitt Otis. [BR:21 JUN 1960:C; disinterred and removed to Mt. Comfort cem. in 1969]. (was 14:9)
DOGAN, Leonard. In memory of our dear / Father / LEONARD DOGAN / who / departed this life / April 25, 1891 / in his 62nd year. (41:north border)
DOGAN, Mary M. In memory of our dear / Mother / MARY M. DOGAN / who / departed this life / February 14, 1904 / in her 62nd year. (41:north border)
DOLPHIN, Dolly. DOLLY DOLIPHAN / *Beloved adopted sister* / Sept. 2, 1886 - Jan. 29, 1962 [BR:1 FEB:B]. (14:10)
DOUGLAS, Eliza Kincaid. ELIZA KINCAID / wife of JAMES DOUGLAS / a native of Malone / Ireland / died / March 13th, 1876 / aged 85 years. (41:24)
DOUGLAS, Harriet Frances Whittington. HARRIET FRANCES / wife of / JAMES S. DOUGLAS / and daughter of / THOMAS & MARGARET C. / WHITTINGTON / born June 10, 1836 / died Feby. 21, 1889. (41:24)
DOUGLAS, James. JAMES DOUGLAS / a native of the County / Derry, Ireland / died November 2d, 1847 / aged 62 years. (41:24)
DOUGLAS, James S. JAMES S. DOUGLAS / born Jan. 11th, 1826 / died / June 25th, 1907. (41:24)
DOUGLAS, James S., Jr. / 1886-1968 [BR:16 SEP:E] / Captain, Inf. U.S.A. / 1917-1928. (14:20:4)
DOUGLAS, James Sidney. J. SIDNEY DOUGLAS / 1856-1949 [BR:1 MAR:W]. (14:21)
DOUGLAS, John G. / March 20, 1913 / May 7, 1981 [BR:11 MAY:E]. (4:22)
DOUGLAS, Sallie Wooden / 1860-1952 [BR:19 FEB:W]. (14:20)
DOUGLAS, Stuart. STUART DOUGLAS / son of / R.S. & V.T. DOUGLAS / born Jan. 29, 1860 / died Oct. 14, 1894 / *Blessed are the pure in heart / for they shall see God.* (41:24)
DOUGLASS, Catharine. CATHARINE / daughter of / JAMES & MARGARET / DOUGLASS / died Dec. 10, 1901 / *The eternal God is thy / refuge and underneath / are the everlasting arms.* (41:34)
DOUGLASS, Eliza C.K. Sacred / to the memory of / ELIZA CONTEE KEITH / daughter of JOHN C. VOWELL / wife of JOHN DOUGLASS / born Jan. 24th, 1801 / fell asleep in Jesus / Dec. 7th, 1865. (44:135)
DOUGLASS, Helen D. James. HELEN D. JAMES / daughter of / JOHN & ELIZA C.K. / DOUGLASS / born Sept. 15, 1836 / died Feb. 3, 1919. (44:135)
DOUGLASS, J. Edwards. J. EDWARDS DOUGLASS / born May 25, 1828 / died Nov. 11, 1875 / *God sent not his son unto the / world to condemn the world / but that the world through / him might be saved.* (41:34)
DOUGLASS, Margaret. Sacred / To the memory of / MRS. MARGARET DOUGLASS / who departed this life / on the 26th August, 1852 / in the 52nd year of her age / *I am the resurrection and the life, he / that believeth in me though he were / dead yet shall he live*

First Presbyterian Church Cemetery (1809)

and whosoever liveth / and believeth in me shall never die. (41:34)

DOUGLASS, R. Stuart. C.S.A. / R. STUART DOUGLASS / Quartermasters Dept. / died Sept. 1, 1894. (41:24)

DOUGLASS, Sarah. SARAH / daughter of / JAMES & MARGARET / DOUGLASS / Entered into rest / April 16, 1892 / *He giveth his beloved sleep.* [AG:31/12/92:2].

DOUGLASS, Thomas Vowell. In / memory of / THOMAS VOWELL / son of / JOHN & ELIZA C.K. DOUGLASS / born Dec. 13, 1833 / died July 27, 1865. (44:135)

DOWNHAM, E.E. E.E. DOWNHAM / beloved husband of / SARAH M. DOWNHAM / 1839-1921 / P.M. of A.J. Lodge No. 120, A.F. & A.M. / P.G.C. of Grand Commandery, Va. / Rep. of Acca Temple 23 years / Emeritus member of the / Imperial Council of A.A.O.N.M.S. / of North America / SARAH M[iranda]. DOWNHAM / beloved wife of / E.E. DOWNHAM / 1845-1937 [BR:12 NOV:W]. (25:22)

DOWNHAM, E. Francis. Father / E. FRANCIS / 1869-1950 / Mother / ESTHER M. / 1874-1940 [BR:10 JUL:W] / infant / ESTHER M. / died 1900 / EVERLINA / UNDERWOOD / 1886-1931. (B:213)

DOWNHAM, Harry A. HARRY A. DOWNHAM / beloved husband / of / GRACE E. DOWNHAM / 1867-1918 / *He hath answered / his / makers call.* / GRACE E. [Acton] DOWNHAM / 1867-1948 [BR:4 SEP:W]. (25:21)

DOWNHAM, Horace E. HORACE E. DOWNHAM / 1871-1872 / HORACE E. DOWNHAM / 1874-1902 / *At Rest. / Leave him to God's watching eye / Trust him to the hand that made him / Mortal love weeps idly by / God alone has power to aid him.* / BELLE H. TAYLOR / 1852-1938 / *Faithful to the end.* (25:21)

DRISCOLL, Theodore G. THEODORE G. / 1892-1963 [BR:28 OCT:D] / HARRIETTE C. / 1900-1988 [BR:21 OCT:D]. (16:26E)

DROWNS, Harvey Carroll. HARVEY C. DROWNS / Dec. 16, 1884 - April 18, 1957 / *At rest.* [BR:20 APR 1957:C]. (42:76W)

DROWNS, Ida V. IDA V. / wife of JOHN T. DROWNS / 1866-1939 [BR:25 MAY] / *At rest.* (42:76)

DROWNS, John T. / 1846-1904 / *At rest.* (42:76)

DROWNS, Marion L. / Dec. 17, 1888 - Oct. 1, 1972 / *At rest.* (42:76)

DUDLEY, Edward Lee. [BR:25 OCT 1965:C]. (2:9, no stone)

DUFFEY, Constance S. [BR:17 AUG 1967:D]. (1:32)

DUFFEY, Cora. CORA DUFFEY / died November 16, 1957 / ELLA LOUISE DUFFEY PALMER / Oct. 5, 1866 - March 31, 1923 / CHARLES WILLS DUFFEY / Feb. 28, 1854 - May 5, 1932 / JOSEPHINE DRAMOND HOUGH DUFFEY / June 14, 1861 - Sept. 23, 1948 [BR:24 SEP:W] / EDWARD LOUIS FOX / Oct. 23, 1886 - June 14, 1925 / REBECCA HEISHLEY FOX / Jan. 19, 1879 - June 14, 1938 [BR:15 JUN:W]. D.A.R. marker included. (18:17)

DUNCAN, George M. GEORGE M. / Feb. 23, 1892 / June 26, 1984 [BR:29 JUN:E] / *There is rest in heaven.* (14:26)

DUNCAN, James Arthur. JAMES A. DUNCAN / March 2, 1889 / March 1, 1951 [BR:5 MAR:C]. (14:13)

DUNCAN, James E. / April 5, 1930 / Nov. 8, 1982 [BR:12 NOV:E]. (14:26:6)

DUNCAN, Martha M. MARTHA M. / Dec. 22, 1899 / Dec. 18, 1983 / CLARENCE E. / Sept. 12, 1897 / [blank]. (14:26)

DUNCAN, Virginia. Sacred / to the memory of / VIRGINIA / the devoted and / beloved wife

First Presbyterian Church Cemetery (1809)

of / WILLIAM A. DUNCAN / her lovely babe / reposes with her / they died / February 17, 1854. (42:72)

DUNCAN, William. WILLIAM DUNCAN / 1858-1910 / his wife / AMELIA HAAG / 1860-1928. (14:13)

DUNCAN, William Harvey. WILLIAM H. DUNCAN / 1887-1970 [BR:17 MAR:C]. (14:13)

DUNDAS, Agnes Hepburn. Owner of section 42, lot 69 [AG:24/5/20:2, gives death for Agnes Dundas on 23 MAY 1820]. (A four-sided obelisk sits in this lot, but all inscriptions have been eroded by weather. The north side appears to contain the name Agnes Dundas: Sacred / to the memory of / AGNES DUNDAS / wife of JOHN DUNDAS / who departed this life / May 23, 1820]. (42:69, obelisk; Alexandria Wills, Bk. 2, p. 365; Bk. 1, p. 239)

DUNDAS, John. Died of dropsy, 29 AUG 1813 [AG:1/9/13:4, age 54y; MR:funeral held 1 SEP 1813; Alexandria Wills, Bk. 1, p. 239, men. daughter Nancy Moore Keene, daughter Sophia Matilda Peyton and father-in-law William Hepburn].

DUNLAP, Ann. To the memory of / ANN, the affectionate wife / of WM. DUNLAP / who departed this life / on the 11th of March, 1811, in the / 37th year of her age / *Her tender anxiety and Persevering exertions / for her family & welfare, will ever be cherished / in fond remembrance by her Husband, whom with / five surviving children she hath left to lament / their irreparable loss.* [MR:funeral held 13 MAR]. (41:23, tablet)

DUNLAP, James, no dates. (41:23)

DUNLAP, William, no dates. (41:23)

DuPIGNAC, Sarah Poythress Smith. SARAH POYTHRESS SMITH / DuPIGNAC / daughter of MARY CAMPBELL & LAROUCHE JAQUELIN SMITH / 1874-1962 [BR:13 JUN:Mt. Risco NY]. (43:86)

DYER, Ann Maria. ANN MARIA / wife of / JAS. W. DYER / born 1840 / died March 26, 1902 / ANN M. / wife of J.W. DYER / aged 61 years. (41:28)

DYER, Cordelia H. CORDELIA H. DYER / daughter of / FRANCIS and / MARGARET MORRIS DYER / born / Jan. 31, 1820 / died July 2, 1892. (42:50)

DYER, Henrietta Dent. In / memory of / HENRIETTA DENT, DYER / Daughter of / FRANCIS & MARGARET M. DYER / who departed this life / Nov. 5, 1822 / aged 1 year & 10 days / *Suffer little children and / forbid them not to come unto / me: for of such is the kingdom / of Heaven.* (42:50)

DYER, John Francis. JOHN FRANCIS DYER / born in / Alexandria, Va. / Feb. 5, 1817 / died / July 27, 1890. (B:195)

DYER, Lucy. LUCY DYER / daughter of / JOHN FRANCIS & / ROSALIE H. DYER / born in / Alexandria, Va. / Oct. 9, 1851 / died May 20, 1923. (B:195)

DYER, Margaret. MARGARET DYER / daughter of / JOHN FRANCIS & / ROSALIE H. DYER / born in / Alexandria, Va. / July 31, 1845 / died Oct. 21, 1920. (B:195)

DYER, Rosalie H. ROSALIE H. DYER / born Sept. 21, 1847 / died April 4, 1918. (B:195)

DYER, Rosalie H. ROSALIE H. wife of / JOHN FRANCIS DYER / born / May 16, 1818 / died / April 23, 1891. (B:195)

DYER, Virginia. VIRGINIA DYER / daughter of JOHN FRANCIS & / ROSALIE H. DYER / born Sept. 21, 1847 / died April 4, 1918. (B:195)

First Presbyterian Church Cemetery (1809)

E

EDELEN, Eva Dawkins. EVA DAWKINS EDELEN / of Maryland / wife of J. STEED EDELEN / and daughter of / YOUNG P. and ALETHEA P. / DAWKINS / born May 27, 1864 / died March 2, 1917. (26:13, Celtic cross)

EDELEN, James Steed. JAMES STEED EDELEN / of Maryland / son of PHILIP R. EDELEN / and FRANCES R. EDELEN / born August 15, 1865 / died February 24, 1919. (26:13, Celtic cross)

EDMONDS, Edmund. Sacred / to the memory of / EDMUND EDMONDS / late of Alexa. D.C. who sweetly passed from Time into Eternity / April 20th, 1824 / aged 68 years [AG:22/4/24]. (42:71, tablet)

EGGBORN, Infant. Infant EGGBORN / J.A. & A.R. EGGBORN. (26:16)

EGGBORN, J. Armistead. J. ARMISTEAD EGGBORN / 1872-1930 / ANITA ROBBINS EGGBORN / 1873-1965 [BR:1 MAR:E] / MARGARET EGGBORN / 1911-1976 [BR:24 DEC:E]. (26:16)

ELDRIDGE, Edward E. In memory of / my beloved husband / EDWARD E. ELDRIDGE / born / July 4, 1859 / died / October 13, 1893. (44:166, footstone "E.E.E.")

ELDRIDGE, Elizabeth M. In memory of / our beloved mother / ELIZABETH M. / wife of / E.E. ELDRIDGE / born / Dec. 19, 1862 / died Dec. 30, 1932. (44:166)

ELDRIDGE, Georgie H. GEORGIE H. / darling son of / MANCHESTER & SYBIL / H. ELDRIDGE / died June 15, 1859 / aged 5 years. (44:166, footstone "G.H.E.")

ELDRIDGE, Joseph Everett. JOSEPH EVERETT / Nov. 26, 1890 / April 1, 1951 / LUCINDA ALLEN / Dec. 31, 1892 / Dec. 29, 1984 [BR:13 JAN 1985]. (17:24)

ELDRIDGE, Manchester. Father / MANCHESTER ELDRIDGE / died / June 13, 1899. (44:166, footstone "M.E.")

ELDRIDGE, Sybil H. Mother / SYBIL H. ELDRIDGE / died / August 30, 1899. (44:166, footstone "S.H.E.")

ELKINS, Lucy Douglas / 1884-1929. (14:20)

ELLIS, Beverley C. In memory / of / BEVERLEY C. ELLIS / born Sept. 22, 1855 / died July 18, 1879. (44:163)

ELLIS, William Foster. My husband / WM. FOSTER ELLIS / born / Oct. 17, 1862 / died / Aug. 15, 1903 / *At rest*. / LULA B. ELLIS / JENNINGS / born / Nov. 26, 1867 / died / June 9, 1946 [BR:9 SEP 1946:Dl] / *At rest*. (44:164)

EMERSON, Ellen. Sacred / to the memory of / ELLEN EMERSON / relict of WM. D. EMERSON / departed this life Feby. 27th, 1855 / aged 57 years. (44:134)

EMERSON, William D. In / memory of / WILLIAM D. EMERSON / who departed this life / on the 17th day of Sep. 1838 / in the 37 year of his age / after an illness of four days / also ERASLUS and ELLEN ELIZA / infant children / of WILLIAM D. & ELLEN EMERSON. (44:134)

EMM, Martha Carol / Jan. 3, 1952 / Dec. 10, 1973 [BR:14 DEC:E]. (18:11:5)

ENGLISH, Emily Howe. In memory of / EMILY HOWE / daughter of JAMES A. & / MARIA S. ENGLISH / born Dec. 21, 1839 / died Aug. 12, 1917 [AG:14/8/17:1]. [two stones] (44:151, obelisk)

ENGLISH, Edwin. In memory of / EDWIN / son of JAMES A. & MARIA S. / ENGLISH / died October 13, 1873 / aged 21 years, 1 month / & 14 days. [two stones] (44:151, footstone "E.E.")

ENGLISH, Francis Clifton. FRANCIS CLIFTON / son of JOHN A. & / HENRIETTA E.

First Presbyterian Church Cemetery (1809)

ENGLISH / departed this life / 27th April 1854 / aged 10 months & 22 days. (44:150)
ENGLISH, Horace Lycurgus. In memory of / HORACE LYCURGUS / son of JAMES A. & / MARIA S. ENGLISH / born July 11, 1848 / died Dec. 30, 1928. (44:151)
ENGLISH, James Albert / born October 8, 1816 / died July 26, 1868 / aged 51 years, 10 months & / 18 days. (44:151, footstone "J.A.E.")
ENGLISH, Maria Seabury. [two stones] In memory of / JAMES A. ENGLISH / died / July 26, 1868 / aged 51 years / MARIA SEABURY / wife of / JAMES A. ENGLISH / died December 13, 1853 / aged 37 years. Our child / WILLIAM / son of JAMES A. / and MARIA S. ENGLISH / died June 16, 1852 / aged 11 mos. & 16 days. [second stone with lengthy epitaph] (44:151, obelisk)
ERBECK, Evelyn V. / September 23, 1921 / April 30, 1991 [BR, cremation] / *Mom, we love you.* (13:11)
ESPOSITO, Nance C. [BR:2 MAY 1963:D]. (1:29, no stone)
EVANS, Catherine / 1839-1928. (14:20)
EVANS, James Douglas / 1910-1911. (14:20)
EVANS, Percy / 1874-1916. (14:20)
EVANS, Victoria L. [BR:21 FEB 1966:D]. (1:1H, no stone)
EVELETH, Harriot MacKenzie. HARRIOT MacKENZIE / wife of / JAMES EVELETH / of Washington, D.C. / Entered into rest / July 18, 1891 / *She hath done what / she could.* (44:153)
EVELETH, James / 1841-1915 [AG:31/12/15:2, gives death 29 MAR 1915]. (15:8)
EVELETH, Kate P. / [1]844-1920. (15:8)
EVELETH, Sally S. / 1836-1918. (15:8)
EVERHARDT, John D., Jr. / January 1898 / December 1970 [BR:1 JAN 1971]. (4:6)

F

FADELEY, Milton McN. MILTON McN. FADELEY / born Sept. 17, 1842 / died Jan. 14, 1923 / ANNA M. FADELEY / born Nov. 11, 1848 / died July 1, 1906. (15:14)
FAIRFAX, Susanna. SUSANNA / wife of / THOMAS M. [FAIRFAX] / 1851-1917. (25:8)
FAIRFAX, Thomas M. / 1840-1912 [AG:31/12/12:1, gives death 26 MAY 1912]. (25:8)
FARRAR, Rupert G. RUPERT G. / Jan. 28, 1869 / May 28, 1903 / DOLLY HEISLEY / Jan. 15, 1873 / June 23, 1958. (14:18)
FEAGAN, Stella H. Schreiner / Aug. 13, 1869 - April 2, 1953. (14:2)
FENDALL, Elizabeth. ELIZABETH FENDALL / 1847-1903. (42:53)
FENDALL, Florence F. / 1841-1926. (42:53)
FENDALL, Mary Lee. MARY LEE FENDALL / born Jan. 20, 1828 / died March 29, 1911. (42:53)
FENDALL, Philip Richard. PHILIP RICHARD FENDALL / born 18 December 1794 / died / 16 Feb. 1868 [AG:17/2/68:2] / ELIZABETH MARY FENDALL / wife of PHILIP R. FENDALL / born 7 October 1804 / [died] 7 October 1859 / ROBERT YOUNG FENDALL / second child of / PHILIP R. and / ELIZABETH M. FENDALL / born 8 August 1829 / died 13 June 1832. (42:53, obelisk)
FENDALL, Philip R. PHILIP R. FENDALL / Maj. U.S. Marine Corps / born / in Washington, D.C. / Feb. 23, 1832 / died / in Portsmouth, N.H. / March 21, 1879. (42:53)

First Presbyterian Church Cemetery (1809)

FERNANDEZ, Ricardo J. / March 5, 1930 / March 31, 1977. (4:8)

FIELD, Alice H. ALICE H. / wife of / R. LEE FIELD / Dec. 31, 1871 / May 6, 1920. (17:20)

FIELD, R. Lee / March 10, 1862 / March 31, 1932. (17:20)

FIELD, Ruth Swain. RUTH SWAIN FIELD / 1864-1936. (B:172)

FIELD, Saidee Markell. SAIDEE M. FIELD / Feb. 5, 1884 / July 18, 1940 [BR:19 JUL:C]. (17:20)

FINKS, Robert Earl. Baby / ROBERT EARL / infant son of / PAUL & VIRGINIA / FINKS / Jan. 24, 1933 / March 17, 1933. (26:14)

FINKS, Thomas L. THOMAS L. FINKS / 1868-1916 / LUCY LEEF FINKS / died Dec. 5, 1946. (26:14)

FISHER, Elizabeth Leftwich. ELIZABETH LEFTWICH / wife of / THOMAS A. FISHER / 1866-1936 [BR:25 DEC:C]. (B:188)

FISHER, Isaiah / 1828-1892 [AG:31/12/92:2, gives date 23 MAR 1892]. (B:188)

FISHER, John Henry / 1862-1937 [BR:1 DEC:C]. (B:188)

FISHER, Sallie Ann / 1842-1911 [AG:30/12/11:4, gives date 29 APR 1911]. (B:188)

FISHER, Samuel P. / 1876-1916. (B:188)

FISHER, Thomas A. / 1870-1947 [BR:25 SEP:C]. (B:188)

FITZGERALD, John F. / Aug. 20, 1923 / Oct. 1, 1978 [BR:5 OCT:E]. (19:7E:4)

FITZGERALD, John Francis / MM3 US Coast Guard / World War II / 1923-1978 [second marker]. (19:7)

FITZPATRICK, Bernard W. BERNARD W. / Nov. 17, 1880 / Apr. 23, 1924 / RUTH L. / July 9, 1883 / July 31, 1972 [BR:2 AUG]. (24:12:3)

FLEMING, Andrew. In / memory of / ANDREW FLEMING / who died / July 6th, 1820 / aged 61 years / and of / JAMES / his son / who died / August 1st, 1828 / aged 31 years. (41:34)

FLEMING, Andrew J. ANDREW J. FLEMING / born / Aug. 24, 1810 / died / April 3, 1889 / I heard a voice from heaven / saying unto me, write / Blessed are the dead which die / in the Lord. [AG:31/12/89:2].

FLEMING, Ann Paton. no dates. (B:198)

FLEMING, Catharine. In / memory of / CATHARINE FLEMING / who died / March 26th, 1846 / aged 73 years [AG:27/3/46:3]. (41:34)

FLEMING, Edgar S. EDGAR S. FLEMING / MARIA A. FLEMING / ROBERTA FLEMING McCOY / MAMIE LAMAR FLEMING [BR:17 JAN:H]. No dates [AG:31/12/04:1, gives death for Edgar S. Fleming on 12 NOV 1908; AG:31/12/07:1, gives death for Maria A. Fleming on 2 AUG 1907]. (15:14)

FLEMING, Eliza. ELIZA / daughter of / ANDREW & CATHARINE / FLEMING / died May 10, 1885 / He giveth his beloved sleep. [AG:31/12/85:2]. (41:34)

FLEMING, Grace Irwin. GRACE / daughter of / WILLIAM H. and ANN PATON IRWIN / wife of / THOMAS FLEMING / died Jan. 3, 1917. (B:198)

FLEMING, James Paton / 1889-1922. (B:199)

FLEMING, Mary. In memory of / MARY FLEMING / who died / July 30, 1863 [AG:31/7/63:3]. (41:34)

FLEMING, Mary Lee / 1892-1922. (B:199)

FLEMING, Robert Fleming / 1885-1973 / IDA vonLENGERKE FLEMING / 1891-1976. (B:198)

First Presbyterian Church Cemetery (1809)

FLEMING, Thomas / 1851-1922. (B:198)
FLETCHER, George E. GEORGE E. / 1862-1925 / LEILA DABNEY / 1859-1933 / infant son / 1895-THOMAS WHITE-1896 / OWENS / MARIAN FLETCHER / 1899-1959. (B:197)
FOGLEMAN, Lyman M., Jr. / March 15, 1918 / May 20, 1971 [BR:24 MAY:E]. (20:3:1)
FONES, Linwood B. LINWOOD B. FONES / May 10, 1902 - Oct. 16, 1968 [BR:18 OCT:C] / CLARICE T. FONES / June 2, 1902 / [blank]. (4:6:1)
FONES, Mary E. Penn. MARY E. PENN / wife of / THOMAS R. FONES / 1875-1930 / *At rest.* / THOMAS R. FONES / April 18, 1872 / Nov. 28, 1953 [BR:31 NOV:C] / *At rest.* (15:13)
FONES, Melvin M. MELVIN M. / Oct. 17, 1895 / Aug. 17, 1980 / S. CATHERINE / Dec. 24, 1896 / Feb. 9, 1991 / *Faithful unto death.* (3:9)
FONES, Virginia H. VIRGINIA H. / beloved wife of / ALBERT R. FONES / born April 26, 1879 / died July 14, 1933. (B:174, footstone "V.H.F.")
FOOTE, Catharine Ramsay. In / memory of / CATHARINE R. FOOTE / consort of / F. FOOTE of Virginia and daughter of / the late JOHN RAMSAY of Alexandria / who departed this life / on the 11th January 1837 / in the 38th year of her age. / *In the various duties of Daughter, Wife, / Mother and Friend she was preeminent / and as she lived she died / regretted by all who knew her.* / In the same grave is deposited her infant / son born 11th January 1837 / and who died on the 15th of the same month. (41:8, tablet)
FORREST, Dora / 1851-1934. (14:16)
FORREST, James Pitt. J. PITT FORREST / born / Dec. 20, 1843 / died May 20, 1903. (14:16)
FORTENEY, Catherine. In memory of / CATHERINE FORTENEY / wife of / JACOB FORTENEY, Snr. / who departed this life / May 25, 1814 / aged 67 years. (42:67)
FORTENEY, Elizabeth. In memory of / ELIZABETH FORTENEY / daughter of JACOB and / CATHERINE FORTENEY / who departed this life / June 17th, 1814, aged / 36 years [AG:21/6/14:3]. (42:67, tablet)
FORTENEY, Jacob. In memory of / JACOB FORTENEY / Senior / who departed this life December 16th, 1816 / aged 72 years. (42:67, broken)
FOWLE, Anne Eliza. ANNE ELIZA / daughter of the late / LT. COL. JOHN FOWLE, U.S. Army / & PAULINA C. FOWLE / departed this life April 10th, 1843 / aged 8 years & 3 months. (43:104)
FOWLE, John Charles. In / memory of / JOHN CHARLES / son of the late / LT. COL. JOHN FOWLE / of the United States Army / & PAULINE C. FOWLE / He departed this life on the / 2nd of January 1845 / aged 3 years, 3 months / & 11 days. (43:104)
FOWLE, Col. John Charles. JOHN CHARLES FOWLE / born October 10, 1836 / died January 22, 1840 / ANNE ELIZA FOWLE / born January 13, 1835 / died April 10, 1843 / PAULINA CAZENOVE / born April 13, 1806 / married JOHN FOWLE / May 26, 1831 / died / April 21, 1891 / LIEUT. COLONEL JOHN FOWLE, U.S.A. / born Nov. 3, 1789 / at Watertown, Mass. / *Killed by the explosion / of the steamboat Moselle / at Cincinnatti* / April 23, 1838. (43:107; Alexandria Wills, Bk. 4, p. 165)
FREEMAN, Ethel Hoof. ETHEL HOOF FREEMAN / 1896 - [blank]. (44:144)
FRENCH, George E. GEO. E. FRENCH / died Aug. 17, 1890 / aged 67 years / *A good man, Gods noblest work* / also his wife / VIRGINIA C. FRENCH / died Aug. 13, 1894 /

First Presbyterian Church Cemetery (1809)

WILLIE P. FRENCH / died March 13, 1889, aged 29 years / MARY H. WHITE / died Jan. 1, 1876 / aged 50 years / EDGAR D. WHITE / died June 10, 1860 / aged 27 years / ROBT. L. WHITE / died March 2, 1845 / aged 50 years. (43:117, obelisk)

FRINKS, Alvin W. ALVIN WARREN / Sept. 15, 1912 / [blank] / MARGUERITE J. / Dec. 6, 1912 / [blank]. (19:3)

FULLMORE, Elizabeth C. In memory of / Our Mother / ELIZABETH C. FULLMORE / her children erected this stone / She died January 1st, 1866 / in the 67th year of her age. (43:98)

G

GARDNER, Catherine Cocke. CATHERINE COCKE GARDNER / 1892-1985 / WM. CAZENOVE / 1875-1934 [Loving Funeral Home marker for Catherine]. (43:105)

GARDNER, C. Cazenove. C. CAZENOVE GARDNER / died 30th May 1844 / aged 27. / *Blessed are the pure in heart for they shall see God.* (43:107, boxtomb)

GARDNER, Charles Cazenove. CHARLES CAZENOVE GARDNER / son of / DORSEY GARDNER / born Oct. 21, 1868 / died June 26, 1911. (43:119)

GARDNER, Dorsey. DORSEY GARDNER / August 1, 1842 / November 30, 1894. (43:105)

GARDNER, Eliza Cazenove / 1871-1925. (43:105)

GARDNER, Eliza Frances. In memory of / MRS. ELIZA FRANCES GARDNER / widow of the late / WILLIAM C. GARDNER / who died February 2d, 1857 / in the 59th year of her age. (43:104, boxtomb; Alexandria Wills, Bk. 7, p. 184, men. daughter Ann Eliza as the wife of Cassius F. Lee)

GARDNER, Harriet C. HARRIET C. GARDNER / wife of WILLIAM F. GARDNER / 1841-1911 / *Love is the fulfilling of the law.* (43:105)

GARDNER, Mary. Mary / daughter of WILLIAM & ELIZA GARDNER / departed the 5th April 1825 / aged 2 years, 9 months. (43:104, footstone)

GARDNER, Paul. PAUL / infant son of / WILLIAM F. & HURRIET [sic] C. GARDNER / April 24, 1879. (43:105)

GARDNER, William C. Departed this life / on the 20th of Novr. 1844 / WM. C. GARDNER / a native of Newport, Rhode Island / aged 55. / *For many years a resident of Alexandria, D.C. / when he died universally esteemed and lamented. / The Lord shall be thine everlasting light / and the days in thy mourning shall be ended.* (43:104, boxtomb; Alexandria Wills, Bk. 4, p. 390)

GARDNER, William C. WILLIAM C. / son of WM. C. & ELISA F. GARDNER / 1840-1907 / *My hope is thee.* (43:105)

GARDNER, William Cazenove. WM. CAZENOVE / 1875-1934. (43:105)

GARDNER, William F. WILLIAM F. GARDNER / son of WM. C. & ELIZA F. GARDNER / 1840-1907. (43:105)

GARNER, James A. / PHM / U.S. Navy / Sep. 15, 1917 - Jan. 22, 1974 [BR:26 JAN:E]. (14:2:8)

GARNER, William. In / memory of / WILLIAM GARNER / A native of ENGLAND / who departed this life / Nov. 15th, 1819 / aged 38 years / *His soul we hope is with his God / an angel's bliss to find / He bravely bore the human rod / this world with ease resigned.* (42:84)

GARNETT, Frank M. FRANK / son of / R.P.W. and SALLIE B. GARNETT / born Sept. 9,

First Presbyterian Church Cemetery (1809)

1860 / died Mar. 6, 1879 [AG:6/3/79:2]. (44:147)
GARNETT, Muscoe. MUSCOE / son of / R.P.W. and SALLIE B. GARNETT / born Dec. 4, 1856 / died Mar. 12, 1872. (44:147)
GARST, Paul E. PAUL E. / June 20, 1902 / Sept. 23, 1965 [BR:25 SEP:D] / ERMA E. / Jan. 28, 1910 / Oct. 8, 1868 [BR:10 OCT:D]. (1:45 & 44)
GAUSE, Harriet Douglas / 1888-1958. (14:21)
GEDNEY, Emma Elizabeth. EMMA E. / 1849-1854 / SUSAN A. / 1854-1855 / children of SAMUEL / and SUSAN GEDNEY. (44:140)
GERBER, Charles F. CHARLES F. / March 14, 1910 / Aug. 11, 1980 / JULIA B[enton]. / April 22, 1906 / Aug. 22, 1981 [BR:25 AUG:E]. (20:4)
GIBBS, Edward C. [BR:28 MAR 1963:E]. (14:5, no stone)
GIBBS, J. Norman / 1855-1933. (B:203, no stone)
GIBBS, Louise Paff. [BR:1 JUN 1961:E]. (14:5, no stone)
GIBBS, Margaret Harrison / 1862-1922. (B:203)
GIRD, John Henry. JOHN HENRY GIRD / died November 4, 1844 / aged 25 years / *To memory dear.* [AG:5/11/44:3]. (41:38)
GIRD, Sarah Kennedy. In memory of / SARAH / wife of JOHN GIRD / and daughter of / JAMES KENNEDY / who died / November 25, 1834 / aged 52 years.
GLANVILL, Joseph. JOSEPH GLANVILL / departed this life / July 12th, 1818 / aged 40 years / *How blest is ____ brother bereft / of all that ____ of burden his mind / How easy ____ soul that has left / his weari__ body behind.* (41:21)
GODFREY, Courtney N. COURTNEY N. GODFREY / born July 29, 1903 / died September 18, 1990 / ELEANOR BARNES NUGENT / born August 7, 1897 / died February 11, 1991. (17:15)
GOLAS, Janet Lee. In loving memory / JANET LEE GOLAS. No dates [BR:8 MAY 1989:D]. (4:21)
GOODMAN, Nellie L. / Sept. 6, 1915 / May 24, 1967 [BR:27 MAY:D]. (1:48)
GORHAM, Michael J.V. [BR:4 FEB 1977:D, cremation]. (1:22, no stone)
GOWAN, Margaret M. [BR:9 DEC 1965:D]. (1:46, no stone)
GRAHAM, Alice Montrose / 1890-1913. (16:17)
GRAHAM, Edythe Marie. EDYTHE / MARIE / GRAHAM / 1897-1897. (16:17)
GRAHAM, Robert M. ROBERT M. GRAHAM, 1865-1937 / his wife / ALICE H. GRAHAM, 1871-1929. (16:17)
GRAVES, Herbert Cornelius. HERBERT CORNELIUS GRAVES / born Alex. Va. / Aug. 17, 1869 / died Winsford, Eng. / July 26, 1919 / CLARA E. WALTER GRAVES / born Georgetown, D.C. / Dec. 14, 1873 / died Washington, D.C. / Jan. 17, 1966. (19:1)
GRAVES, Lucy Mariah / 1871-1946 [BR:29 JUN:W] / *The righteous shall be / in everlasting remembrance.* (19:2)
GRAVES, Myrtilla Melvina / 1868-1939 [BR:7 DEC:W] / *Blessed are the pure in heart: / for they shall see God.* (19:2)
GRAVES, Willard Purdy. In loving memory / of / WILLARD PURDY / GRAVES, JR. / 1878-1913 / *Greater love hath no man / than this, that a man lay down / his life for his friends.* [AG:31/12/13:1, gives death for W.P. Graves, Jr. on 20 JUN 1913]. (19:2)
GRAVES, Willard Purdy. WILLARD PURDY GRAVES, JR. / 1878-1913 [second engraving] / WILLARD PURDY GRAVES / 1838-1922 / LUCY M. LIBBY / beloved wife of / WILLARD P. GRAVES / 1838-1912 / *The gift of God is eternal / life through Jesus*

35

First Presbyterian Church Cemetery (1809)

Christ / our Lord. (19:2)

GRAY, Harrison B. HARRISON B. / June 24, 1883 / Sept. 25, 1958 [BR:26 SEP:C] / EVA V. KETLAND / March 19, 1891 / May 12, 1962 [BR:15 MAY:C]. (1:4 & 5)

GRECHANIK, Walter. WALTER / Captain, SC, USN / December 27, 1924 / [blank] / CYNTHIA / RHODES / July 4, 1928 / April 21, 1971 [BR:24 APR:W]. (3:19:2)

GREEN, Henry. HENRY GREEN / 1839-1897 / his wife / S. VIRGINIA GREEN / 1853-1932 [AG:31/12/97:1, gives date 1 MAY 1897]. (B:204)

GREEN, Judith Bradley / July 3, 1921 / October 24, 1976 [BR:26 OCT:E]. (18:10:5)

GREEN, Linda Mae. [BR:11 FEB 1963:D]. (1:37, no stone)

GREENAWAY, Coralie. CORALIE GREENAWAY / 1893-1962. (18:16)

GREENAWAY, Irene C. [BR:28 APR 1962:E]. (18:16, no stone)

GREENAWAY, Irene Wooddy / 1869-1902. (18:16)

GREENAWAY, Mary C.D. / 1858-1940 [BR:31 MAY]. (18:16)

GREENAWAY, Nevell Summerfield. No dates. D.A.R. marker. (18:16)

GREENAWAY, Nevell Summerfield. NEVELL SUMMERFIELD GREENAWAY / 1860-1922 / *A christian gentleman / a devoted husband / an affectionate father / a true friend / a zealous mason.* (18:16)

GREGORY, Boyd. BOYD / son of WM. & MARY D. / GREGORY / died / July 2d, 1852 / aged 7 years / & 6 months. (44:142)

GREGORY, Charles N. [BR:26 JUL 1948:P]. (15:4, no stone)

GREGORY, Douglas S. DOUGLAS S. GREGORY / born / October 27, 1824 / died / July 22, 1872 / *For so he giveth his beloved sleep.* (44:142)

GREGORY, Margaret Douglas Bartleman. Sacred to the memory / of / MARGARET DOUGLAS / the affectionate wife of / WILLIAM GREGORY / and daughter of / WILLIAM & MARGARET BARTLEMAN / She died at Bridgetown / in the island of Barbados / on the 19th day of June 1833 / in the 33d year / of her age / and her earthly remains / were deposited here on the 9th day / of July following / *Say what the daughter, mother, wife and friend should be / In this imperfect state and th__ she / Think what the humble Christian's dying prize / That need she now possesses in the skies / Her full reward - eternally alone / To kindred, sainted spirits can make known / Reader aspire make not this earth thy home / Live here by faith and hope for heaven to come.* (41:31, tablet)

GREGORY, Mary Donaldson. MARY DONALDSON GREGORY / born / January 31, 1809 / died / November 6, 1896 / WILLIAM GREGORY / born in / Kilmarnock, Scotland / March 3, 1789 / died / July 13, 1875 / WILLIAM B. GREGORY, M.D. / born March 13, 1829 / died May 18, 1887 / C.S.A. (44:141, obelisk)

GREGORY, Mary S. Mark. MARY S. MARK / wife of / DOUGLAS S. GREGORY / born June 5, 1829 / died October 28, 1881 / *Calm as the evening sky / was her pure mind / And lighted up with hopes / of heaven / She sweetly sank to rest.* (44:142)

GREGORY, Peter Mallard. In memory of / PETER MALLARD GREGORY / a native of Kilmarnock / in Scotland, who / departed this life on / the 17 day of March / 1817 / after a very short illness / in the 20th year of his / age. (41:25)

GRILLBORTZER, Eve C. GRILLBORTZER / Mother / EVE C. APPICH / wife of / JOHN A. GRILLBORTZER / 1804-1845. (43:99)

GRIMES, Hunter Fuller. HUNTER F. GRIMES / beloved husband of / MARY A. GRIMES / died Dec. 20, 1938 [BR:22 DEC:H] / MARY A. GRIMES / died Feb. 9, 1940 [BR:12

First Presbyterian Church Cemetery (1809)

FEB:H] / *He giveth his beloved sleep.* (43:103)
GRIMES, Joseph S. JOSEPH S. GRIMES / died Dec. 21, 1916 / his wife / CAROLINE HAMMILL / died Dec. 21, 1916. (15:22)
GRISAMORE, Jesse W. / 1886-1960. (3:24)
GRISAMORE, Oscar L. / 1894-1958. (3:24)
GRONAU, Robert Edward. ROBERT EDWARD GRONAU / born / December 10, 1859 / died / November 11, 1918 / his wife / ALICE PRICE / born / January 20, 1854 / died / July 21, 1941 [BR:23 JUL:C] / ALICE VIRGINIA FIELD / wife of / GORDON M. DENNIS / born / March 14, 1933 / died / June 2, 1964 [BR:5 JUN:E] / M. ALICE GRONAU / born / Feb. 25, 1891 / died Aug. 1, 1969 / STEPHEN HENRY FIELD / Sept. 18, 1893 / Mar. 6, 1944 / his wife / JANET VIRGINIA / Sept. 5, 1893 / May 11, 1967 [BR:15 MAY:E]. (17:9, obelisk)
GROSS, Ida B. Windsor / wife of W.B. GROSS / 1863-1937 [BR:6 AUG:D]. (18:14)
GROTTO, Wilhelmina Newton. WILHELMINA N. GROTTO / Nov. 7, 1919 / Dec. 24, 1986 [BR:27 DEC:E]. (26:18)
GROVES, Mary E. My darling / MARY E. / wife of / THOMAS A. GROVES / born April 1, 1844 / died August 22, 1885 / *Asleep in Jesus.* / THOS. A. GROVES / born April 23, 1843 / died Sept. 8, 1915 / LILLIAN E. GROVES / born Sept. 17, 1891 / died June 14, 1918. (15:7)
GUTHRIE, N. Rawlins. N. RAWLINS GUTHRIE / Dec. 26, 1871 / June 14, 1958 / his wife / LOUISE D. GUTHRIE / Sept. 16, 1876 / Dec. 16, 1954. (43:91)

H

HAAG, Clara Gertrude. CLARA G. HAAG / July 12, 1864 / June 22, 1955. (14:26)
HALL, B.F. / 1863-1919. (13:9)
HALL, George W. GEORGE W. HALL / 1838-1921 / MARTHA ANN / wife of / GEORGE W. HALL / 1839-1918. (13:9)
HALL, R. Clifford / Oct. 30, 1885 / Oct. 15, 1977. (3:5)
HALLEY, Esther. In / memory of / ESTHER HALLEY / relict of / WILLIAM HALLEY / who died 19th Sept. 1831 / aged 75 years [AG:30/9/31:3; Alexandria Wills, Bk. 4, p. 27]. (42:71)
HAMERSLEY, Florence. [BR:11 APR 1989:M]. (18:9, no stone)
HAMERSLEY, Florence A. Mother / FLORENCE A. / HAMERSLEY / Dec. 22, 1888 / Aug. 21, 1976. (18:9:8)
HAMMILL, C. Perry / 1895-1932 / HELEN E. HAMMILL / 1889-1929. (15:22)
HAMMILL, Daisy V. [BR:18 OCT 1965:I]. (16:12, no stone)
HAMMILL, Lucy Ashby. LUCY ASHBY / wife of / EDWARD HAMMILL / died Feb. 3, 1917 / EDWARD HAMMILL / died Dec. 7, 1923. (15:22)
HAMMILL, Paul E. [BR:21 FEB 1955:G]. (16:12, no stone)
HAMMILL, Reuben C. / 1874-1927. (15:22)
HAMMILL, Rita D. / 1902-1973 / HUNTER A. HAMMILL / 1897-1977. (15:22)
HAMMILL, Rose. ROSE HAMMILL / 1872-1936. [BR:17 FEB 1936:W]. (15:22)
HAMMILL, Sophia Hunter / wife of / J.H. HAMMILL / 1834-1923. (16:6)
HAMMILL, William R. [BR:10 OCT 1978:I]. (16:12, no stone)
HAMMOND. Children of J.W. & S.V. HAMMOND. (25:12)

First Presbyterian Church Cemetery (1809)

HAMMOND, James W. / 1843-1917. (25:12)
HAMMOND, J.T. To the memory of / my beloved husband / my darling / NAN. / 1881-1897 / from God you are / and when He calls his / own He gives you back to Him. / J.T. HAMMOND / born / August 30th, 1853 / died / August 11th, 1881 / You knew Him but to / love him / None mourned him but / To praise. / My angel mother / MARY HAMMOND / HOLMES / 1854-1908. (B:207)
HAMMOND, Mary / 1848-1931. (25:12)
HAMMOND, Sarah V. / 1843-1921. (25:12)
HANNOE, Julia Lucas. JULIA LUCAS HANNOE / born Mar. 2, 1844 / died Apr. 11, 1933 / JOHN LUCAS / / JOSEPH HANNOE / died Mar. 2, 1928. (41:north)
HARDIN, Randolph Tupper. RANDOLPH TUPPER / July 23, 1876 - July 10, 1947 / ANNIE ETHEL / April 23, 1881 - Jan. 23, 1985. (19:15)
HARDING, Claudia M. [BR:15 JAN 1968:H]. (17:4, no stone)
HARDING, Helen Louise. [BR:9 JUL 1938:Dl]. (17:4, no stone)
HARDING, William A., Jr. [BR:14 SEP 1959:H]. (17:4, no stone)
HARDING, William Alpheus, Sr. HARDING / WILLIAM ALPHEUS / Nov. 12, 1867 / Jan. 19, 1939 [BR:20 JAN:D] / CLAUDIA UNDERWOOD / Nov. 23, 1871 / Aug. 15, 1951. (17:4)
HARMAN, Richard A. / 1892-1948 [BR:5 MAR 1948:D]. (1:14)
[HARMON?], Anne. ANNE / Jan. 31, 1848 / ___ [19, 1868?]. (42:80)
HARMON, Allen C. / Aug. 4, 1819 / Feb. 2, 1892. (42:80)
HARMON, Charles P. C.S.A. / CHAS. P. HARMON / Co. A / 17th Va. Regt. / died / Dec. 1, 1875.
HARMON, Elizabeth. [BR:20 MAR 1963, cremation]. (43:106, no stone)
HARMON, Mary Honour. In / Remembrance of / MARY HONOUR HARMON / Daughter of AARON D. & MARY / HARMON / who died Dec. 17th, 1824 / aged 4-1/2 months / This lovely babe so young & fair / call'd home by early doom / Just come to shew [sic] how sweet a flo*wer* / in Paradise will bloom. (43:106)
HARMON, Philippa Ann. In memory of / PHILIPPA ANN / who died July 14, 1832 / aged 14 months / and WM. W. ALTON / who died Feb. 20, 1837 / aged 2 years & 8 months / children of A.D. & MARY HARMON. (43:106)
HARMON, Thomas D. THOMAS D. HARMON / May 15, 1850 / Oct. 18, 1884. (42:80)
HARPER, Catharine Fleming. CATHARINE FLEMING / daughter of / WILLIAM W. & ISABELLA / HARPER / died June 20, 1883 / We know that when he shall / appear, we shall be like him. (44:147)
HARPER, Ellen A. In memory of / ELLEN A. / daughter of / JOHN & SALLY HARPER / born Nov. 7, 18[15?] / died Dec. 22, 1881 [AG:24/12/81:2]. (42:43)
HARPER, Emma Danforth. EMMA DANFORTH HARPER / born June 30, 1857 / died Sept. 20th, 1866. (44:147)
HARPER, F.S. / 1852-1910 [AG:31/12/10:1, gives date 23 JUN 1910]. (44:147)
HARPER, Hannah A.D. To / the memory of / H.A.D. HARPER / daughter of / JOHN & SARAH HARPER / who departed this life / June 2d 1845 / in the 24th year of her age [AG:4/6/45:3]. (42:43)
HARPER, Isabella Fleming. ISABELLA FLEMING / wife of / WILLIAM W. HARPER / 1816-1907 / I am the resurrection and the life / he that believeth in me, though he / were dead, yet shall he live; / and whosoever liveth and believeth / in me shall never die.

First Presbyterian Church Cemetery (1809)

(44:147)
HARPER, Jane Eliza. JANE ELIZA / daughter of / DR. WM. & MARY T. HARPER / born Dec. 26, 1816 / died April 3, 1891. (43:111)
HARPER, [Capt.?] John. In / memory of / JOHN HARPER... [remainder illegible; AG:20 MAR 1838:3, *Capt. John Harper died Monday Morning 19th inst. in the 56th year of his age.*] (42:43)
HARPER, Margaret Douglass. MARGARET DOUGLASS / daughter of / WILLIAM WELLS & CATHARINE / ISABELLA FLEMING HARPER / died Feb. 15, 1934. (44:147)
HARPER, Mary A. Sacred to the memory of / MARY A. HARPER / wife of ROBERT HARPER / who departed this life March / 13th 1840, Aged 60 years / *Many are the affliction of the / righteous but the Lord delive / reth [him] out of them all.* (43:114)
HARPER, Mary T. Newton. MARY T. HARPER / wife of WM. HARPER / daughter of JOHN and MARY T. NEWTON / of Little Falls plantation, Stafford Co. / born Aug. 16, 1789 / died May 10, 1841 / aged 51 years / *To do good was her / delight and her / end was peace.* (43:111)
HARPER, M.M. / 1857-1919. (44:147)
HARPER, Capt. Samuel B. In / memory of SAMUEL B. HARPER / who died / September 11, 1838 / aged 26 years [AG:12/9/38:3]. (42:43)
HARPER, Samuel D. SAMUEL D. HARPER / born / December 22, 1828 / died / November 26, 1875 [AG:27/11/75:3]. (42:43)
HARPER, Sarah. In / memory of / SARAH HARPER / beloved wife of / Capt. JOHN HARPER / born March 1786 / died February 22, 18[63]. (42:43)
HARPER, Wells Andrew. Sacred to the memory of / WELLS ANDREW HARPER / eldest son of DR. WM and / MARY T. HARPER / born in Alexandria, Va. / Sept. 2, 1818 / died Dec. 7, 1876 / Sacred to the memory of all / the children of DR. WM. and MARY T. HARPER / MARTHA A., MARGARET A. / WELLS A., MARIA ANN / MARY LOUISE / JANE ELIZA / THOS. POWELL / WILLIAM WALTON HARPER, born July 1829 / died Dec. 25, 1911 / *Because I live he shall / live also.* (43:111, obelisk)
HARPER, Capt. William. WM. HARPER / departed this life / April 18, 1829 / aged 69 / *Blessed are the dead who / die in the Lord* [AG:22/4/29:3; Alexandria Wills, Bk. 3, p. 340]. (42:43)
HARPER, Dr. William. Sacred to the memory of / DR. WILLIAM HARPER / born in Alexandria, Va. / April 23, 1787 / died OCT 7, 1852 / A ruling elder of the 2nd Presbyterian Church of / that city / MARY T. HARPER / his wife / daughter of John and / MARY T. NEWTON / of Little Falls Plantation / Stafford Co. Va. was / born Aug. 16, 1789 / died May 10, 1841. (43:111)
HARPER, William W. WILLIAM W. HARPER / born Dec. 6, 1808 / died Oct. 12, 1886. (44:147)
HARPER, Willie. WILLIE / son of W. WALTON / HARPER / born Oct. 16, 1856 / died July 28, 1864 / *Suffer little children / to come unto me and / forbid them not for of / such is the Kingdom of / Heaven.* (43:111)
HARRELL, Emma Topping. EMMA TOPPING / wife of / Dr. ROY B. HARRELL / 1896-1919. (15:21)
HARRINGTON, Charles G. In memory of / CHARLES G. / HARRINGTON / 1843-1928. (B:215)
HARRINGTON, Edward B. EDWARD B. / son of J.H. & E.L. / HARRINGTON / born Dec.

First Presbyterian Church Cemetery (1809)

15, 1901 / died April 21, 1903. (B:215)

HARRINGTON, Elizabeth Lawrence. In memory of / ELIZ. L. HARRINGTON / Nov. 23, 1877 / Feb. 18, 1960 / *Rest in Peace.* (B:215)

HARRINGTON, John H. In memory of / JOHN H. / HARRINGTON / April 21, 1876 / March 24, 1949 [BR:28 MAR:W] / *Rest in Peace.* (B:215)

HARRINGTON, Margaret. In memory of / MARGARET HARRINGTON / 1861-1933. (B:215)

HARRIS, Gordon William. [BR:23 APR 1942:W]. (16:7, no stone)

HARRIS, Irene Cornelia / born Aug. 5, 1884 / Warrenton, Va. / died March 17, 1967 [BR:21 MAR:E] / Knoxville, Tenn. (16:7)

HARRIS, John Wade. JOHN WADE / son of / SAMUEL & LAURA HARRIS / who departed this life / August 10th 1838 / aged 9 months & 23 days. (42:54)

HARRIS, Jordan William / 1850-1942. (16:7)

HARRIS, Joseph. Stone is generally not legible except for a few words and date at the very bottom, "July 21, 1854" which may relate to a wife or child. The <u>Alexandria Gazette</u>, of 25 APR 1848, p. 3, announces the death of Joseph Harris who was owner of this lot. (42:54)

HARRIS, Laura Wadsworth. Sacred / to the memory of / LAURA WADSWORTH / wife of / SAMUEL HARRIS / who departed this life / the 6th day of November 1843 [AG:7/11/43:2]. (42:54)

HARRIS, Lute Miller / 1857-1930. (16:7)

HARRIS, Nick / Dec. 18, 1899 / June 16, 1980 / *At Rest.* (4:22)

HARRISON, Albert R. / 1869-1946. (B:203)

HARRISON, Albert W. ALBERT W. HARRISON / Jan. 21st 1834 / Mar. 2nd 1911. (B:203)

HARRISON, Alice R. [BR:9 SEP 1951:H]. (17:4, no stone)

HARRISON, Angeline Crane. ANGELINE CRANE / wife of / ALBERT W. HARRISON / September 24, 1896. (B:219)

HARRISON, Clara B. / 1859-1919. (B:203)

HARRISON, Rev. Elias. ELIAS HARRISON, D.D. / born in Orange Co., New York [January 22, 1790[1]] / and for 41 years Pastor of the First Presbyterian Church, Alexandria / departed this life Feb. 13th, 1863, aged 73 years. / *He was a good man and full of the Holy Ghost / and of faith; and much people was added unto the Lord.* / *Acts 11th Chap. 24th Ver.* (43:93; Alexandria Wills, Bk. 8, p. 144)

HARRISON, Elizabeth Veitch. Sacred to the memory of / ELIZABETH the beloved wife of the / Revd. ELIAS HARRISON / who departed this life, May the 6th / A.D. 1824, in the 26th year of her age. / *Perfect she was not, else she had not been / mortal yet what she was and whence she / would hardly be disposed to memory. / A winning openness of manner / a sincerity without smile a disposition / amiable and affectionate a piety modest / and _____ her a / grateful measurable and th__ _____ / the _____ sweet. / The heart of her husband could solely / trust in her for looking well in the way / of her household and has long...* (43:93, tablet)

---

[1] <u>Sengel</u>, p. 51; the son of Thomas Harrison and Mary Osburn.

First Presbyterian Church Cemetery (1809)

HARRISON, Mary C. / 1864-1929. (B:203)
HARRISON, Mary Newton. Sacred / to the memory of / MARY NEWTON / daughter of / Rev. ELIAS HARRISON / died Oct. 18, 1887 / in the 67th year / of her age / *Blessed are the pure in heart.* (42:45, footstone "M.N.")
HART, Elizabeth Brockett / 1866-1877. (44:148)
HART, John T. 1st Sgt. / JOHN T. HART / Co. I / 17th Regt. / Va. Inf. / C.S.A. / 1838-1862. (43:98)
HART, Nancy Craig / 1832-1896 [AG:31/12/96:1, gives death of Nannie C. Hart on 1 JAN 1896]. (44:148)
HART, William Andrew / 1826-1902. (44:148)
HARVEY, Alva L. / 1900-[blank] / LILLIAN E. / 1903-1978 [BR:15 JUL:E]. (3:21:1)
HEINAMAN, Jacob. JACOB HEINAMAN / and his wife / MARY A. No. dates. (43:85; AG:1/4/30:3, announces death of Mary Ann Heineman; FR:6, indicates Jacob died from a wound in his back, funeral 6 JUN 1821)
HEISLEY, [Phoebe]. 1845 / Mother / 1906 / wife of / FERDINAND F. HEISLEY [AG:31/12/06:1, gives death of Phoebe Heisley on 19 JAN 1906]. (14:2)
HEISLEY, Ferdinand F. My husband / FERDINAND F. HEISLEY / born / Sept. 30, 1842 / died / May 24, 1900 / *A kind and affectionate Husband / A loving Father and a / dear friend.* (14:2)
HEISLEY, George Edgar. GEORGE EDGAR / Oct. 5, 1886 / Jan. 31, 1952 [BR:4 FEB:H] / MARIE FOOTE / Sept. 2, 1888 / May 26, 1972 / *Faithful and true.* (14:18)
HEISLEY, George W. My husband / GEORGE W. HEISLEY / 1850-1904 [AG:31/12/04:1, gives death 1 FEB 1904] / *At rest.* / EMELINE HEISLEY / 1851-1936 [BR:4 APR:D]. (14:18)
HEISLEY, Katherine H. / 1872-1910 [AG:31/12/10:1, gives death of Kate Heisley on 19 NOV 1910]. (14:2)
HENDERSON, Alice Virginia. Sister / ALICE VIRGINIA / 4th daughter / of the late JOHN E. / & EMILY HENDERSON / born Jan. 22, 1855 / died Dec. 19, 1904. (43:90)
HENDERSON, Annie S. ANNIE S. HENDERSON / daughter of / JOHN E. and EMILY / HENDERSON / 1839-1923. (43:90)
HENDERSON, Archibald Murray. In memory of / ARCHIBALD MURRAY / infant son of / Gen. ARCHIBALD and / ANNE M. HENDERSON / born July 1, 1845 / died August 29th, 1846. (43:104)
HENDERSON, James Edward. JAMES EDWARD / 3rd son / of the late JOHN E. / & EMILY HENDERSON / died Oct. 13, 1893 / aged 43 years. (43:90)
HENDERSON, John E. / died / May 6, 1863 / aged 53 years / EMILY C. / died / Feby. 12, 1864 / aged 46 years / WM. F. / died Aug. 1, 1874 / aged 33 years / JULIAN F. / died / Feby. 16, 1884 / aged 31 years / JOHN J. THOMAS / U.S.N. / born Nov. 15, 1852 / died / June 23, 1884. (43:90, obelisk; Alexandria Wills, Bk. 8, p. 153)
HENDERSON, Lois Hall. [BR:7 APR 1974:E]. (4:17:7, no stone)
HENDERSON, Paulina Cazenove. PAULINA / daughter of / ARCHIBALD and ANN M. / HENDERSON / died 29th July 1833 / in her fourth year / *God took thee in his mercy*

First Presbyterian Church Cemetery (1809)

/ A lamb, unmastred / untried / he fought the fight for thee / He won the victory / And thou art sanctioned. [AG:1/8/33:3] (43:104)

HENDLEY, John R. JOHN R. HENDLEY / died Dec. 1, 1923 / his wife / MARY ROSALIE BAGOT / died March 2, 1929. (B:215)

HENKEL, James S. JAMES S. / April 29, 1866 / Oct. 25, 1948 / NANCY W. / May 20, 1870 / Dec. 11, 1960. (14:8)

HENKEL, Oscar. [BR:11 SEP 1986:E]. (14:8, no stone)

HEPBURN, George E. In memory of / my beloved husband / GEORGE E. HEPBURN / died Oct. 6, 1918 / NELLIE E. BAGOT / wife of GEORGE E. HEPBURN / died Aug. 17, 1924. (B:215)

HERBERT, Ethel M. / May 13, 1908 / May 30, 1970 / *She is Just asleep.* (3:26)

HERBERT, Linwood A. / July 18, 1903 / Dec. 24, 1973 [BR:30 DEC:C] / *Rest in peace.* (3:26:1)

HERBERT, Linwood A., Jr. / July 12, 1929 / April 27, 1977 [BR:2 MAY:C] / *Peace be His.* (3:25S)

HERRICK, Doreen. DOREEN HERRICK / Oct. 13, 1928 / Nov. 6, 1964 [BR:9 NOV:E] / *Your memory will always / be with me.* "*Russ*" (17:18:6)

HERRICK, Edna Mae Clark. Mother / EDNA MAE CLARK / wife of / JAMES B. HERRICK, SR. / April 13, 1889 - Jan. 15, 1951. (17:18)

HERRICK, James B., Sr. Father / JAMES B. HERRICK, SR. / husband of / EDNA MAE CLARK / Jan. 2, 1889 - March 16, 1956. (17:18)

HERRICK, James B., Jr. Beloved Brother / JAMES B. HERRICK, JR. / Oct. 25, 1912 / July 22, 1968 / *Rest in Peace.* (17:18)

HERRING, Margaretta Iden. MARGARETTA IDEN / HERRING / June 3, 1869 / Oct. 14, 1949 [BR:17 OCT:D]. (B:185)

HICKS, Gerald V. HICKS / GERALD V. / June 22, 1905 / Aug. 7, 1977 [BR:10 AUG:D] / VELLA H. / Dec. 21, 1907 / [blank]. (18:12E)

HIGGINBOTHAM, James A. / August 13, 1889 / April 5, 1963 [BR:8 APR:D]. (1:21)

HILDEBRAND, Anna Loucile / April 14, 1891 / August 9, 1971. (15:25)

HILDEBRAND, Edith Janney. Mother / EDITH JANNEY HILDEBRAND / Nov. 24, 1870 - Mar. 3, 1936 [BR:3 MAR:W] / *Blessed are the pure / in heart, for they / shall see God.* (15:25)

HILDEBRAND, Simpson V. REV. SIMPSON V. / HILDEBRAND / April 12, 1862 / April 6, 1943 [BR:8 APR:I]. (15:25)

HILLS, Mercy A. Sacred / to the memory of / MERCY A. HILLS / who died on the / 9th August 1862 / in the / 49th year of her age. (44:137)

HILLS, Samuel Bartlett. SAMUEL BARTLETT / Obt. Dec. 6th, 1844 / AE 5 yrs. / FRANCIS JAMES / Obt. Jany. 10th, 1845 / AE 5 mos. / children of J.B. & MERCY ANN HILLS. (44:137)

HIMES, Walter Lester. WALTER L. HIMES / 1887-1961 [BR:8 JUN:D]. (1:18)

HINN, William B. WILLIAM B. / HINN / Capt. / Army Air Forces / World War II / May 16, 1916 / Dec. 20, 1974. (18:12W:1)

HIPKINS, Jennie E. [BR:6 MAR 1937:I]. (42:67, no stone)

HIPKINS, Lewis. In memory of / LEWIS HIPKINS / died / March 18, 1888 / in the 70th year of / his age [AG:19/3/88:3]. (42:67)

HOEFT, Baby Girl / July 28, 1945. (B:191)

First Presbyterian Church Cemetery (1809)

HOEFT, John Farrell / Jan. 6, 1916 / Oct. 24, 1989 [BR:27 OCT:T]. (B:191)
HOFFMAN, Mabel S. [BR:25 APR 1974:E]. (16:24:2, no stone)
HOLBERT, Infant Son. [BR:4 OCT 1965:C]. (2:6, no stone).
HOLLOWAY, Charles Percy Evans / 1916-1961 [BR:7 NOV:E, cremation]. (14:20)
HOLMES, E.C. Sacred / to the memory of / my husband / E.C. HOLMES / 1850-1888 [AG:31/12/88:1, gives death 11 MAY 1888]. (B:207)
HOOFF, Philip Henry. PHILIP HENRY HOOFF 3rd / 1869-1952 [BR:20 MAY:I] / LAURA WILSON / 1873-1958 [BR:28 JUN:I]. (44:144)
HOOFF, Wilson Lee / 1906 - [blank] / LAURA CLARK / 1908 - [blank]. (44:144)
HOOKES, Mary Ann. Sacred / to the memory of / MARY ANN / wife of / JACOB HOOKES / who departed this life / Nov. 20, 1828 / in the 64th year [AG:28/11/28:3]. (42:64, broken tablet)
HOOKS, Jacob. In memory of / JACOB HOOKS / who departed this life / August 20th, 1821 / in the 53rd year / of his age. (42:64)
HOPKINS, Benedict Marion. BENEDICT MARION / Sept. 11, 1890 / July 26, 1951 [BR:28 JUL:W] / ALETHA TAYLOR / Dec. 19, 1893 / April 2, 1975 [BR:4 APR:D]. (24:15)
HOPKINS, Frank E. FRANK E. HOPKINS / son of / L.A. and H.T. HOPKINS / May 2, 1911 - Sept. 12, 1924. (18:7)
HOPKINS, Lawrence A. LAWRENCE A. HOPKINS / July 15, 1886 - April 3, 1960 [BR:5 APR:E] / and his wife / HILDRED T. HOPKINS / April 24, 1888 - September 6, 1977 [BR:8 SEP:E]. (18:7)
HOWARD, Elizabeth. In / memory of / ELIZABETH / wife of / BEAL HOWARD / who departed this life / Octr. 6th, 1821 / aged 20 years. (44:127)
HOWDERSHELL, Clarence E. CLARENCE E. HOWDERSHELL / 1883-1935 / BERTHA M. HOWDERSHELL / 1893 - [blank]. (B:217)
HOWDERSHELL, James E. JAMES ERASTUS / June 10, 1846 - Mar. 18, 1928 / his wife / AMANDA S. NALLS / Jan. 29, 1854 - Oct. 20, 1933 / *Until the day break and / the shadows flee away.* (B:217)
HOWDERSHELL, Julian R. HOWDERSHELL / JULIAN RYLAND / Aug. 10, 1873 - Nov. 25, 1943 [BR:29 NOV:H] / his wife / VIRGINIA M. COGAN / July 15, 1883 - July 22, 1961 [BR:28 JUL:H]. (B:217)
HOWDERSHELL, Ralph M. / 1897-1952. (B:217)
HOZEK, Anna. [BR:13 MAR 1977:Ar]. (B:194, no stone)
HUEY, David R. / 1857-1935. (16:15)
HULFISH, David Nicholas. In Memory of / DAVID NICHOLAS HULFISH / 1884-1961 / Interment / Ivy Hill Cemetery[1]. (25:14)
HULFISH, Marianne Minnigerode Maigne. In memory of / MARIANNE / MINNIGERODE MAIGNE / wife of / THOMAS A. HULFISH, JR. / born July 24, 1906 / died Oct. 17, 1981 [BR:19 OCT:D]. (44:150)
HULFISH, Paul Barton. PAUL BARTON HULFISH / April 1, 1881 / Alexandria, Va. / April 19, 1967 / Atlanta, Ga. (25:13)
HULFISH, Susan S. In memory of / SUSAN SOUTHGATE / HULFISH / born July 8, 1944

---

[1] Virginia Irene Sullivan Bruch and Josephine Elizabeth Sullivan, comp., Beneath the Oaks of Ivy Hill (Alexandria: Jennie's Book Nook, 1982), p. 183, gives burial for David Nicholas Hulfish in Section R (West), born Feb. 1, 1884 in Alexandria, Va., died Sept. 27, 1961, son of Worth Hulfish and Virginia Cogan.

First Presbyterian Church Cemetery (1809)

/ died Mar. 26, 1979 / beloved wife of / THOMAS A. HULFISH, III. (44:150)
HULFISH, Thomas Andrew, Jr. In memory of / THOMAS ANDREW, JR. / son of / THOMAS A. & BETTY POLLARD / HULFISH / born Sept. 24, 1904 / died Jan. 14, 1976 [BR:17 JAN:D]. (44:150)
HULFISH, Virginia Cogan. VIRGINIA COGAN / wife of / WORTH HULFISH / 1854-1920. (25:14)
HULFISH, Worth. WORTH HULFISH / 1848-1930. (25:14)
HUNT, Sean P. (infant). [BR:14 JUL 1965:C]. (2:4, no stone)
HUNTER, Albert B. / 1888-1952. (16:23)
HUNTER, Cordelia Meeks. In memory of CORDELIA M. HUNTER / consort of JOHN HUNTER / Shipbuilder / who departed this life / September 21, 1815 / in the 63d year of / her age [AG:22/9/15:3; MR:funeral 22 SEP]. (42:50, broken tablet)
HUNTER, John C. / 1851-1919. (16:23)
HUNTER, Lois. [BR:27 FEB 1967:E]. (16:23, no stone)
HUNTER, Mary Elizabeth. MARY E. HUNTER / 1864-1936 [BR:17 OCT:C]. (16:23W)
HUNTER, Thelma Mary Pullman. Mother / THELMA PULLMAN / HUNTER / Aug. 6, 1902 / Dec. 14, 1985 [BR:17 DEC:D]. (B:205)
HUTCHENS, Infant (fetal). [BR:24 NOV 1964:C]. (2:1, no stone)
HYDE, John M. [BR:5 MAY 1949:D]. (1:6, no stone)
HYDE, Sarah M. Mother / SARAH McKEOWN HYDE / Sept. 9, 1874 / Oct. 15, 1960. (1:7)

I

IDEN, Capt. James. My work is done / Capt. JAMES IDEN / died / April 26, 1885 / aged 7[9?] years. (B:185)
IDEN, Laura. [BR:26 JUN 1941:D]. (43:185, no stone)
INSCOE, Thomas W. THOMAS W. INSCOE / Oct. 9, 1865 / Nov. 19, 1926 / his wife / MARY A. INSCOE / Sept. 30, 1862 / July 21, 1953 [BR:21 JUL:E]. (19:14)
IRWIN, James. JAMES IRWIN / of Belfast, Ireland / the faithful / Guardian of JOHN ADAM / died Sept. 5, 1822 [on Eliza Adam obelisk]. (41:14; FR:6, an elder in the church, died of fever at the age of 65 years)

J

JACOB, John Brevard / July 29, 1926 - April 11, 1988. (19:10)
JACOBS, Almira. ALMIRA / duaghter of / PRESLEY & ELIZABETH JACOBS / born / April 26, 1810 / died / Jany. 9, 1881 [AG:25/1/81:2, gives date 23 JAN 1881; AG:21/1/81:3, "Grave Robbers in Alexandria - Their Work Last Night"]. (44:130)
JACOBS, Elizabeth. In memory of / ELIZABETH / wife of PRESLEY JACOBS / who departed this life / Novr. 28th 1823 in the 46th / year of her age. (44:130)
JACOBS, Presley. In / memory of / PRESLEY JACOBS / died August 24th 1852 / in the 79th year / of his age. (44:130)
JAMES, Henry Bright. HENRY BRIGHT JAMES / 1875-1968 [BR:29 MAR:E] / JESSIE A. JAMES / 1884-1944 / EVERETT HOUGH / son of HENRY B. & JESSIE A. JAMES / 1903-1923 / <u>CRUMBAUGH</u> / ETTA L. CRUMBAUGH / 1890 Remember 1948 /

First Presbyterian Church Cemetery (1809)

EDWARD L. CRUMBAUGH / 1887-1978. (19:3)

JAMES, Jessie Armenta. [BR:9 SEP:1944:W]. (19:3, no stone)

JAMES, Mary R. [BR:17 JUN 1943:I]. (25:11?, no stone)

JAMIESON, Andrew. In memory of / ANDREW JAMIESON / a native of Scotland / who departed this life / on the 6th July, 1823 / in the 74th year of his age / *Mark the perfect man and behold the upright; / for the end of that man is peace. / Psalm 37 Ch. 37 V.* (41:28, tablet; Alexandria Wills, Bk. 3, p. 98)

[JAMIESON], "Little Bobbie." (44:131)

JAMIESON, Catharine Porter. CATHARINE PORTER / wife of / ROBERT JAMIESON, Obiit. 9th April 1843 / AET 38. (44:131)

JAMIESON, Catharine Porter. CATHARINE PORTER / daughter of / THOMAS & JULIA R. JAMIESON / died Oct. 13, 1861 / aged 5 years / & 8 days. [footstone: "Little / Katie"] (44:131)

JAMIESON, Elizabeth Jane Smith. ELIZABETH JANE JAMIESON / wife of / ROBERT JAMIESON / and daughter of / HUGH and ELIZABETH WATSON SMITH / all of Alexandria, Virginia / January 5, 1809 / September 29, 1890. (41:30, tablet)

JAMIESON, George W. GEORGE W. JAMIESON / 1835-1903 [AG:31/12/03:1, gives date 18 JUN 1903] / His wife / BETTIE W. STEWART / 1839-1910 [AG:31/12/10:1, gives date 5 MAY 1910] / ALICE J. / wife of / J. STEWART / JAMIESON / 1887-19[blank] / JOHN STEWART JAMIESON / 1867-1931 / his wife / ELEANOR BELL WILSON / 1868-1925 / WILLIS / 1870-1871 / CATHERINE S. / 1871-1872 / Children of / GEO. W. & BETTIE W. / JAMIESON. (44:159)

JAMIESON, John Jay / August 7, 1838 / January 21, 1899 / *A servant of God / where I am there shall / also my servant be.* / MARY SHERRARD / daughter of / J.J. and A.R. JAMIESON / Aug. 7, 1871 / Sept. 3, 1886 / *Because I live he shall / live also.* / BESSIE STEWART / daughter of / J.J. and A.R. JAMIESON / Sept. 12, 1873 / Dec. 1, 1891 / ANNA R. STEWART / wife of JOHN JAY JAMIESON / died Sept. 13, 1927. (B:210)

JAMIESON, Julia B. JULIA B. JAMIESON / wife of / THOMAS S. JAMIESON / born February 6th 1827 / died February 12th 1895. (44:131)

JAMIESON, Kate S. / died June 4th 1863. (44:131)

JAMIESON, Mary. In memory of / MARY / consort of / ANDREW JAMIESON / who departed this life / 12th July, 1824 / in the 55th year of her age [AG:13/7/24:3; Alexandria Wills, Bk. 3, p. 128]. (41:28, tablet)

JAMIESON, Mary. MARY JAMIESON / daughter of / ROBERT & CATHARINE P. / JAMIESON / 1831-1898 [AG:31/12/98:1, gives date 7 APR 1898]. (44:131)

JAMIESON, Robert. ROBERT JAMIESON / died / April 10, 1862 / in the 67th year / of his age. (44:131; Alexandria Wills, Bk. 8, p. 176, men. wife Elizabeth J. Jamieson)

JAMIESON, Robert Douglass. ROBERT D. JAMIESON / died December 22d, 1852.

JAMIESON, Thomas Sanford / born October 14th, 1827 / died November 24th, 1862. (44:131)

JANNEY, John / 1872-1929. (16:6)

JANNEY, Joseph T. JOSEPH T. JANNEY / 1832-1882 / his wife / EDITH H. / 1842-1913. (16:6)

JANNEY, Margaret / Jan. 20, 1878 / Nov. 5, 1939. (16:6)

JAVINS, J. Randolph. In memory of my / beloved husband / J. RANDOLPH JAVINS / born / Dec. -, 1835 / died Sept. 16, 1892 / *Asleep in Jesus, blessed / sleep.* (B:179)

First Presbyterian Church Cemetery (1809)

JENKINS, Ellen G. / 1892-1979. (15:11)

JENKINS, Ellen G. Regan / wife of / NORMAN B. JENKINS / 1856-1938 [BR:7 DEC:D]. (15:11)

JENKINS, Inez E. / 1890-1988. (15:11)

JENKINS, Norman B. / 1853-1942 [BR:13 OCT:D]. (15:11)

JEWETT, Joseph. Hope / Sacred / to the memory of / JOSEPH JEWETT / who departed this life on / the 23d of June 1859 in the / 69th year of his age. (44:165)

JOHNSON, Frankie. Our darling / FRANKIE / son of J.F. & CLARA / JOHNSON / born August 13th 1863 / died June 11th 1865. (44:156)

JOHNSON, William Austin / beloved son of / DORA L. SOUTHWORTH / 1907-1923. (14:15)

JOHNSON, William Reynolds. WM. REYNOLDS / son of / GEO. & ELIZBH. / JOHNSON / departed this life / Feb. 17, 1817 / aged 2 years, 7 months, 14 days. (41:26)

JOHNSTON, Annie Eliza. ANNIE ELIZA / daughter of / S.R. and MARY E. / JOHNSTON / born / Jan. 5, 1868 / died / July 16, 1868. (44:161)

JOHNSTON, Claudius Legrand. CLAUDIUS LEGRAND / son of / REUBEN and MARY C. JOHNSTON / died March 30, 1850 / aged 18 months & 12 days [AG:1/4/50:3]. (41:27)

JOHNSTON, Dennis McCarty, shipmaster. Died 17 JUL 1811 at the age of 46 years, funeral held 19 JUL 1811. He was buried in the MacKenzie lot (41:19?) of the Presbyterian grounds per <u>Brockett</u>, p. 110. (stone not found)

JOHNSTON, Elizabeth. In / memory of / ELIZABETH / wife of REUBEN JOHNSTON / who departed this life / September 19th 1838 / in the 60th year of her age. (41:27)

JOHNSTON, Emma K. <u>KIRCHNER</u> / Daughter / EMMA K. JOHNSTON / July 15, 1871 - Oct. 9, 1960 [BR:12 OCT:E] / JOHN H. JOHNSTON / 1871-1922 / daughter / ELIZABETH K. O'NEIL / 1869-1924 / WALTER L. O'NEIL / 1871-1930 / <u>KIRCHNER</u> / Father / JACOB F. / Jan. 10, 1831 - Nov. 8, 1921 / son / CHARLES D. / May 11, 1875 - Oct. 3, 1904 / Mother / ROSINA / July 13, 1842 - May 19, 1902 / daughter / ROSA D. / Dec. 29, 1879 - June 23, 1910. (15:15)

JOHNSTON, Francis Edgar. In memory / of / FRANCIS EDGAR / JOHNSTON / April 24, 1897 / March 2, 1978. (B:192)

JOHNSTON, Frankie M. In memory / of / FRANKIE M. JOHNSTON / born / Jan. 20, 1865 / died / Feb. 21, 1938. (B:193)

JOHNSTON, Frederick W. / 1860-1908. (44:161)

JOHNSTON, George. GEORGE JOHNSTON / born / July 27, 1829 / died / June 17, 1897 / HENRIETTA EGE, / wife of / GEO. JOHNSTON / May 21, 1836 / April 16, 1862 / HENRIETTA E. JOHNSTON / wife of / NATHANIEL C. MANSON / April 15, 1862 / Nov. 2, 1892 / Interred at Lynchburg, Va. (44:161)

JOHNSTON, Geo. Dennis / 1858-1912 [AG:31/12/12:1, gives date 27 SEP 1912]. (44:161)

JOHNSTON, Isobel G. ISOBEL GREGORY / wife of / GEO. JOHNSTON / Oct. 16, 1839 / Oct. 25, 1916. (44:161)

JOHNSTON, James Edgar. In memory / of / JAMES EDGAR JOHNSTON / born / June 6, 1860 / died / March 24, 1927. (B:193)

JOHNSTON, Margaret L. Hipkins. MARGARET L. HIPKINS / wife of / R.W. JOHNSTON / 1855-1901. (42:67)

JOHNSTON, Mary Ege. MARY EGE / wife of / S.R. JOHNSTON / born / Feb. 4, 1832 / died / Jan. 28, 1879 / ROBERT E.L. JOHNSTON, M.D. / 1865-1909 / SARA

First Presbyterian Church Cemetery (1809)

CAMPBELL WATTS / wife of / S.R. JOHNSTON / born May 25, 1854 / died March 30, 1931. (44:161)

JOHNSTON, Nina Maria. Our darling / NINA MARIA / infant daughter of / JAMES E. & FRANKIE M. / JOHNSTON / born Nov. 21, 1891 / died July 4, 1892. (B:193)

JOHNSTON, Rebecca Sims. REBECCA SIMS / wife of DENNIS JOHNSTON / 1785-1823 / DENNIS JOHNSTON / 1787-1852 [AG:2/8/52:2, gives date 22 JUL 1852] / ELIZA DALE / wife of / DENNIS JOHNSTON / 1790-1853 [AG:14/9/53:3, gives date 13 SEP 1853] / FRANCIS E. JOHNSTON / March 2, 1820 / March 16, 1862 / ANNA M. BURKE / wife of / FRANCIS E. JOHNSTON / Oct. 31, 1831 / Oct. 22, 1898 / JAMES A. JOHNSTON / 1814-1833 / JOHN F. JOHNSTON / 1860-1864 / WILLIAM S. JOHNSTON / 1809-1866 [AG:9/6/66:3, gives date 9 JUN 1866] / DENNIS JOHNSTON / 1816-1871 [AG:28/2/71:2, gives date 28 FEB 1871] / JANE A. JOHNSTON / 1811-1876 [AG:18/3/76:3, gives date 17 MAR 1876] / MARY A. JOHNSTON / 1813-1876 [AG:18/1/76:2, gives date 18 JAN 1876]. (B:192)

JOHNSTON, Reuben. In / memory of / REUBEN JOHNSTON / born in King George / County, Va. / on the 17th of January 1767 / died on the / 25th of September 1840 / *A just man* / _____ [AG:26/9/40:3; Alexandria Wills, Bk. 4, p. 263]. (41:27)

JOHNSTON, Samuel R. SAMUEL R. / son of / S.R. and MARY E. / JOHNSTON / born April 10, 1860 / died / Dec. 24, 1863. (44:161)

JOHNSTON, Samuel Richard. SAMUEL RICHARD JOHNSTON / born / March 16, 1833 / died December 24, 1899 / *An honorable man, a valiant soldier / a Christian gentleman / Lord who shall dwell in / Thy tabernacle or who shall / Rest upon thy holy lull / Even he that leadeth an / uncorrupt life and doeth / The thing which is right / and speaketh the truth / from his heart.* (44:161)

JOHNSTON, Watts King. WATTS KING / infant son of / S.R. and S.C.W. / JOHNSTON / died / Nov. 2, 1888 / *A member of Christ.* (44:161)

JOHNSTON, William Gregory. WILLIAM GREGORY / son of / GEO. & ISOBEL / JOHNSTON / born / Mch. 9, 1873 / died May 27, 1873. (44:161)

JONES, Edward Z. Father & Mother / EDWARD Z. JONES / born July 4, 1812 / died Nov. 26, 1866 / his wife / MARGARET JANE JONES / born Mar. 10, 1818 / died Aug. 17, 1871. (43:87a)

JOYCE, Mary / 1853-1899 [AG:30/12/99:1, gives date 13 APR 1899]. (B:192)

JUDKINS, Esther L. In memory of / ESTHER L. / wife of / Rev. WM. E. / JUDKINS / and daughter of / JAMES & SARAH / McKENZIE / born / Jan. 18, 1832 / and died / Jan. 10, 1889. (44:153)

JUDKINS, John McKenzie. JOHN McKENZIE / son of / Rev. WM. E. & ESTHER L. JUDKINS / died Novr. 18, 1869 / aged 4 years & 6 days. (44:153)

JUDKINS, Wallace Sanford. WALLACE SANFORD JUDKINS / son of / Rev. WM. E. & ESTHER L. / JUDKINS / Given by God / July 18, 1867 / Taken by God / April 11, 1876. (44:153)

JUDKINS, Rev. William E. Rev. WM. E. JUDKINS, D.D. / 1829-1923 / Seventy years a Minister / of Christ / Virginia Conference / M.E. Church South / In His Holy keeping / LEWIS MacKENZIE JUDKINS / 1869-1939 [BR:19 AUG, Richmond]. (44:153)

First Presbyterian Church Cemetery (1809)

K

KEENE, Estelle. [BR:28 AUG 1972:E]. (B:172:2, no stone)

KEENE, Hattie E. HATTIE E. / wife of / EDWARD L. KEENE / born / August 31, 1870 / died / Feb. 4, 1903 / At Rest. / EDWARD LEE KEENE / aged 10 years / PEARL ISABEL KEENE / aged 4 years / THERON RICE KEENE / aged 4 months / GEORGE FRANKLIN / aged 11 months / Children of / E.L. & H.E. KEENE / HATTIE ELLEN / daughter of / E.L. & H.E. KEENE / born May 16, 1892 / died June 16, 1909 / EDWARD L. KEENE / born / Nov. 23, 1860 / died / Oct. 14, 1938 [BR:15 OCT:C]. (B:175)

KEENE, Mary E. MARY E. KEENE / Jan. 9, 1899 / Aug. 25, 1972. (B:175)

KEENE, Newton and others. To the memory of / NEWTON and NANCY MOORE KEENE / of Alexandria, Va. / and their children / NEWTON KEENE, youngest son of NEWTON / and SARAH EDWARDS KEENE, born at Cherry Point / Northumberland Co., Va., Died Sept. 21, 1841 / aged 74 / NANCY MOORE KEENE, wife of NEWTON KEENE / eldest daughter of JOHN and AGNES DUNDAS / died NY, Sept. [9], 1850 / aged 62 / JOHN NEWTON KEENE, second son of NEWTON / and NANCY MOORE KEENE, Died Sept. 1836 / aged 24 / SARAH EDWARDS KEENE, daughter of NEWTON / and NANCY MOORE KEENE, Died Aug. 23, 1849 / aged 17 months, 11 days / NEWTON KEENE, youngest son of NEWTON / and NANCY MOORE KEENE, Died Sept. 16, 1842 / aged 16 / CHARLES KEENE, Eldest son of NEWTON and / NANCY MOORE KEENE / NANCY, eldest daughter of NEWTON and NANCY / MOORE KEENE, and wife of HENRY SMITH. (42:69, tablet)

KEENE, Samuel R. SAMUEL R. KEENE / Jan. 8, 1900 / Nov. 11, 1981 [BR:13 NOV:E]. (B:175:3)

KEITH, William. In / memory of / WM. son of / WM. & GEAN / KEITH / who departed this life / May 14th, 1815 / aged 3 years. (42:70)

KELLY, Charles Hopkins. CHARLES HOPKINS / son of / C.W. & LIDEY KELLY / born June 29, 1879 / died May 17, 1897 / LIDEY / beloved wife of / CHARLES W. KELLY / 1853-1924. (14:16)

KELLY, Charles W. C.S.A. Capt. Chas. W. KELLY / Kempers Battery / died Nov. 24, 1901. (14:15)

KELLY, Charles W. / born / March 28, 1843 / died Nov. 24, 1901 [second stone]. (14:16)

KELLY, Indianna. INDIANNA / daughter of / THOMAS & LUCY E. / KELLY / born April 20, 1872 / died Feb. 12, 1880. (42:56)

KELLY, Capt. John C. Capt. JOHN C. KELLY / 1779-1865 / ELLEN KELLY / 1812-1886 / PHILIP KELLY / 1835-1843 / J[ohn]. L. KELLY / died / July 22, 1895 / in the 49th year / of his age / At rest. [AG:22/6/65:2, gives date 20 JUN 1865; AG:31/12/86:3, gives date 6 MAR 1886; AG:31/12/95:1, gives date 25 JUL 1895]. (42:56)

KELLY, John Churchill. In memory of / our brother / JOHN CHURCHILL / beloved son of THOMAS L. / & LUCY E. KELLY / born Oct. 29, 1865 / died Nov. 30, 1923. (42:56)

KELLY, Lucy E. In memory of / our mother / LUCY E. / beloved wife of / THOMAS L. KELLY / born Feb. 24, 1849 / died Mar. 23, 1908. (42:56)

KELLY, Peter A. / November 9, 1914 / May 6, 1984 [BR:11 MAY:E]. (4:25)

KELLY, Thomas L. In memory of / our father / THOMAS L. KELLY / born Feb. 20, 1848 / died Feb. 3, 1921 / Member of Co. H. 17th Va. Regt. / From 1861 to 1865 / C.S.A.

First Presbyterian Church Cemetery (1809)

(42:56)
KELLY, Thomas Philip. In memory of / our brother / THOMAS PHILIP / beloved son of THOMAS L. / and LUCY E. KELLY / born Aug. 31, 1876 / died June 17, 1913. (42:56)

KENNEDY, Andrew Thomas [grave of]. Sacred / to the memory of / JAMES KENNEDY / a native of Ireland / and for many years a resident of Alexandria, D.C. / He was distinguished for piety / a love of letters and an elegant taste. / **He died in Philadelphia Octr. 15, 1820 in the 68th / year of his age / and was interred in the 2d Presbyterian burial / ground of that city** by his only son / ANDREW THOMAS / whose mortal remains are here deposited. He was born in Dublin July 1788 / and died on the 7th of April 1829. *Temperance and integrity marked his character / he bore his long protracted illness with great / fortitude and meek submission to / the devine will Beloved relatives / in life you enjoyed the confiding love of each / other and the esteem of all who knew you / & falling asleep in Jesus / the resurrection and the life / his promise remaineth for you that / though you are dead yet shall you live.* (41:38, tablet; Alexandria Wills, Bk. 3, p. 315, men. mother Susannah Kennedy, daughter Sarah Gird)

KENNEDY, Clarence E. CLARENCE E. KENNEDY / died Oct. 30, 1957 [BR:4 NOV:C] / wife / ELSIE KENNEDY / died Nov. 7, 1971 [BR:10 NOV:Hy] / JACOB L. RINKER / died July 16, 1959 / wife / HELEN RINKER / WINDSOR / EDWARD WINDSOR / 1866-1920 / wife / JULIA WINDSOR / died Aug. 24, 1963. (15:23)

KENNEDY, Eliza. ELIZA KENNEDY / died October 22nd 1853 / aged 72 years / *I shall be satisfied when I / awake with thy likeness.* (41:38; FR:6, cancer as cause of death)

KENNEDY, James. Erected / in memory of / JAMES KENNEDY / a native of Dumfries / Shire, Scotland / who departed this life / January 12 A.D. 1816 / in the 64th year of his / age. / *He was distinguished / for honesty & truth and / that hospitality characteris / tic of his country men / He has left / a widow and three chil / dren in tears / to lament his loss.* (41:28)

KENNEDY, John. Sacred / to the memory of / JOHN KENNEDY / a native of Scotland / and for many years / a citizen of Washington, D.C. / who departed this life / within the 79th year of his age / May 2nd 18[4]7. (41:38)

KENNEDY, Susannah. In / memory of / SUSANNAH / the wife of / JAMES KENNEDY / born July 25, 1760 / married May 12, 1780, and died May 30, 1845 / aged eighty four years ten months and eight days / *In the hope of a blessed / resurrection / Yet a little while and he / that shall come will come / and will not tarry / Hebrews 40 Chap 57 verse.* (41:38; Alexandria Wills, Bk. 4, p. 405)

KETLAND, Elmer Joseph / 1893-1953 [BR:7 OCT:D]. (16:20E)

KIDWELL, Ada Muir / 1864-1924. (19:5)

KIDWELL, Charles Ernest. In memory of / CHARLES ERNEST / son of / CHARLES H. & LUCRETIA / KIDWELL / born March 12, 1865 / died May 2, 1884. / *Blessed are the pure / in heart for they / shall see God.* (B:181)

KIDWELL, Emma V. Our darling / EMMA V. / infant of / CHAS. H. & MARGARET / KIDWELL / born Mar. 5, 1888 / died June 26, 1888. (B:181)

KILTON, George. GEORGE KILTON / departed this life the 18th / day of October 1803 aged / 31 years / Also his son GEORGE / died 3rd day of Novr. 1802 / aged 15 months & 13 days. (43:101)

KINCAID, John. Erected / to / the memory of / JOHN KINCAID / a native of Ireland / who

First Presbyterian Church Cemetery (1809)

/ departed this life / Janry. 30th, 1811 / aged 57 years / and / LUCY / his wife / who departed this life / April 18th, 1842 / aged 83 years. (41:24, tablet)

KING, Charles. CHARLES KING / 1838-1910 / *And whosoever liveth and / believeth in me shall / never die.* [AG:31/12/10:1, gives date 26 DEC 1910]. (17:1)

KING, Frank T. FRANK T. KING / son of / CHARLES & LAURA KING / died Sept. 15, 1941 / *Lead, kindly light, / Lead thou me on.* (17:1)

KING, Laura Virginia. LAURA VIRGINIA / beloved wife of / CHARLES KING / 1845-1926 / *I am the resurrection and / the life, saith the Lord.* (17:2)

KING, Louise Fletcher. LOUISE FLETCHER / beloved wife of / MARSHALL L. KING / November 15, 1929 / *Whosoever believeth in Him should / not perish, but have eternal life.* (17:2)

KING, Margaret Willoughby. MARGARET WILLOUGHBY / wife of / FRANK T. KING / died May 30, 1938 [BR:1 JUN:C] / *I heard the voice of Jesus say, / come unto me and rest.* (17:1)

KING, Marshall L. MARSHALL KING / son of / CHARLES & LAURA V. KING / 1873-1947 / *I trust in the mercy of God / for ever and ever.* [BR:2 AUG:C] (17:2)

KINZER, Anna Bolling. ANNA B. KINZER / born / May 20, 1857 / died / April 22, 1890 [AG:31/12/90:1, gives name Anna Bolling Kinzer]. (44:132)

KINZER, J. Louis. In memory of / I. LOUIS KINZER / born in Lancaster Co. Pa. / August 5, 1824 / died / in Alexandria, Va. / June 13, 1863. (44:132)

KINZER, Maggie C. MAGGIE C. KINZER / born / June 12, 1854 / died / Feburary 4, 1885. (44:132)

KINZER, Margaret G. MARGARET G. / wife of / I. LOUIS KINZER / born July 2, 1824 / died Jan. 11, 1888. (44:132)

KIRK, Unnamed. Infant daughter of / HARRY and LUNETTE KIRK / Jan. 4, 1927 - Jan. 7, 1927. (18:2)

KIRK, Unnamed. Infant son of / JOHN H. and EVELYN H. KIRK / December 1, 1950. (18:2)

KIRK, Adelaide Massey / 1860-1940 [BR:23 AUG:C]. (18:1)

KIRK, Harrison, Jr. / 1852-1913 / *The spirit shall return / unto God who gave it.* [AG:31/12/13:1, gives date 23 JUN 1913]. (18:1)

KIRK, Harry D. / 1882-1961 [BR:16 JUN:C]. (18:2)

KIRK, Jessie Cochran / 1882-1965 [BR:30 JAN:C]. (18:2)

KIRK, Lunette C. / 1896-1969. (18:2)

KIRK, Orlando H. / 1880-1963 [BR:22 MAR:C]. (18:2)

KIRKPATRICK, (Charles) Darrow / May 3, 1898 / Dec. 5, 1989. (18:15)

KIRKPATRICK, Eleanor Smith / April 1, 1902 / June 5, 1983 [BR:5 JUN:E]. (18:15)

KIRKWOOD, Peggy Jean. PEGGY JEAN / June 3, 1910 / July 23, 1970 / LEWIS H. / Aug. 13, 1905 / Mar. 5, 1968 [BR:8 MAR:C] / *In loving memory.* (17:26W:6 & 5)

KITE, David Millard. DAVID MILLARD KITE / 1851-1916 / his wife / ANNA MARY GIST / 1868-1930. (26:6)

KITE, D. Millard. D. MILLARD / son of / D.M. and M.G. KITE / 1894-1912 [AG:31/12/12:1, gives date 2 OCT 1912]. (26:6)

KITE, Mary Gist. MARY GIST KITE / Dec. 25, 1891 - May 14, 1959 [BR:16 MAY:G, cremation] / REBECCA B. KITE / Sept. 5, 1897 - Feb. 26, 1981. (26:6)

First Presbyterian Church Cemetery (1809)

L

LAMAR, Gasaway B. GASAWAY B. LAMAR / of Georgia / born October 3, 1798 / died October 5, 1874 / *His bow abode in strength and the arms / of his hands were made strong by the / hands of the mighty God of Jacob / and his rest shall be glorious* / HARRIET CAZENOVE / beloved wife of / GAZAWAY B. LAMAR of Georgia / and youngest daughter of / A.C. CAZENOVE / of Alexandria, Va. / born May 2, 1817 / died May 3, 1861. / *Thou art fairer than the children of men; / full of grace are thy lips, because God / has blessed thee forever.* (43:107, obelisk)

LAMB, William Herbert. WILLIAM HERBERT LAMB / Aug. 24, 1898 - Oct. 24, 1978 [BR:27 OCT:E] / and his wife / HARRIET BOOKER LAMB / June 15, 1907 - May 20, 1981. (19:9)

LAMBERT, James Arthur. JAMES ARTHUR / Oct. 26, 1891 / March 7, 1971 [BR:9 MAR:H&I] / KATHERINE CURTIN / April 20, 1885 / May 27, 1971. (13:13:3)

LAMMOND. Our children / ALEXANDER / born Jan. 19th 1833 / died Mar. 7th 1833 / EDWIN / born Feb. 5th 1834 / died Feby. 7th 1834 / CAROLINE / born July 29th 1837 / died May 29th 1838 / FRANCIS / born Nov. 15th 1841 / died April 3d 1844. (44:137)

LARMAND, Francis. Father / FRANCIS LARMAND / 1856-1917 / *At rest.* (26:7)

LARMAND, John William. JOHN WM. LARMAND / born / Sept. 3, 1883 / died / March 25, 1910. (26:7)

LARMAND, Medora N. Mother / MEDORA N. LARMAND / Jan. 19, 1912 / Aged 59 years / *At rest.* (26:7)

LATHAM, Lucy. [BR:1972:Co]. (14:19:4, no stone)

LATHAM, Wilburn Edward, Jr. W.E. LATHAM, JR. / 1875-1954 [BR:24 JUL:W]. (14:19)

LATHAM, William E. WILLIAM E. LATHAM / June 7, 1848 / Feb. 19, 1925 / his wife / ADA V. / Feb. 5, 1851 / Oct. 18, 1931. (14:19)

LATTA, John William, Jr. / May 21, 1933 / November 20, 1982. (18:20)

LEADBEATER, Lizzie J. LIZZIE J. LEADBEATER / wife of THOS. LEADBEATER / born Lancaster Co. Pa. / January 14, 1850 / died Alexandria, Va. / July 8, 1875 [AG:10/7/75:2]. (41:25)

LEADBEATER, Thomas. THOMAS LEADBEATER / July 25, 1848 / June 1, 1895 / JANET BOYD GREGORY / May 4, 1852 / April 30, 1929 [AG:31/12/95:1]. (41:25)

LEADBEATER, Thomas Boyd. THOMAS BOYD / son of / JANET GREGORY & / THOMAS LEADBEATER / born May 17, 1895 / died Sept. 14, 1914 [AG:31/12/14:1]. (41:25)

LEADBEATER, William Gregory. WILLIAM GREGORY LEADBEATER / November 25, 1882 / July 13, 1967. (44:141)

LEAKE, Agnes B. In memory of / AGNES B. LEAKE / who departed this life / Jan. 28, 1938 / *At rest.* (14:6)

LEAKE, Alfred P. Husband / ALFRED P. LEAKE / born / September 10, 1869 / died / December 28, 1905 / *At rest.* (14:6)

LEAP, Jacob. In memory of / Mr. JACOB LEAP / who died December / the 15th 1820, / in the 66th year of his age / *I know that my redeemer lives / And ever from the skies; / Looks down and watches all my dust / Till he shall bid it rise.* (41:42; Alexandria Wills, Bk. 2, p. 405)

LEATHERLAND, John W. In memory of / Father and Mother / JOHN W. LEATHERLAND

First Presbyterian Church Cemetery (1809)

/ born August 31, 1847 / died April 26, 1909 / ANNIE E. LEATHERLAND / born July 16, 1852 / died June 24, 1918. (B:216)
LEATHERLAND, Lawrence Campbell / 1883-1936. (B:216)
LEATHERLAND, Walter I. WALTER I. / son of / JOHN W. & ANNIE E. / LEATHERLAND / born May 6, 1879 / died May 13, 1922. (B:216)
LEDBETTER, Cathy Lynn. [BR:10 NOV 1965:C, infant]. (2:12, no stone)
LEDBETTER, William G. [BR:17 JAN 1967:E]. (44:142, no stone)
LEE, Ellen Dora Kelly. Mother / ELLEN DORA KELLY / wife of WILLIAM A. LEE / born 1871, died 1952. (42:56)
LEE, Thomas F. LEE / son / THOMAS F. / Aug. 31, 1906 / March 28, 1983 / mother / MARGARET T. / June 7, 1873 / Aug. 6, 1967 [BR:11 AUG:Mc, "colored"] / May 20, 1869 / THOMAS L. / Sept. 6, 1953. (42:81)
LEEF, Kate Thompson / died Jan. 22, 1938. (26:14)
LESTER, Emily Black / Oct. 30, 1916 / April 25, 1971 [BR:28 APR:D] / *A smile for everyone.* / [footstone] "Mom." (1:35)
LESTER, James / June 4, 1914 / June 10, 1979 / *A very special Person.* / [footstone] "Daddy." [BR:12 JUN:D]. (1:36)
LESTER, Marcus Randolph / Sept. 21, 1947 / Sept. 3, 1967 [BR:6 SEP:D] / *God took a Bouquet.* / [footstone] "Randy." (1:34)
LILLY, Dawn Marie. [BR:8 OCT 1965:C, infant]. (2:7, no stone)
LINDSEY, Belle Hill / April 9, 1890 / Sept. 25, 1981. (17:26)
LINDSEY, Mary. [BR:6 MAR 1963:E]. (13:5, no stone)
LINDSEY, Melville W. MELVILLE W. LINDSEY / born January 27, 1879 / died July 6, 1901 / EDITH G. LINDSEY PAXSON / born March 12, 1877 - died January 20, 1911 / FLORENCE L. LINDSEY / born August 31, 1893 - died July 12, 1929 / SAMUEL E. / 1855-1933 / ELLA D. / 1857-1941. (13:8)
LINDSEY, Noble. NOBLE LINDSEY / born / August 24, 1848 / died / December 25, 1900, / his wife / CATHERINE / 1853-1926. (13:5)
LINDSEY, Paul / Sept. 12, 1896 / March 5, 1962 [BR:7 MAR:Dl]. (17:26E)
LOGAN, Frances. In / memory of / FRANCES, the wife of / SAMUEL LOGAN / who departed this life / Oct. 19th 1812 / aged 31 years / also / SAMUEL LOGAN / her husband / departed this life / Octr. 10, 1817 / aged 55 years. (41:10)
LONG, Charlotte V. Smith / wife of A. RAYMOND LONG / 1904-1925. (18:14)
LOWE, Mark Clifford / March 20, 1900 / March 6, 1924. (19:15)
LUCKETT. No names. *The Lord is my shepherd.* (3:11)
LUCKETT, Catherine Tassa / (Kay) / October 7, 1919 / November 14, 1968 [BR:18 NOV:D]. (3:11:2)
LUCKETT, James Thornton / April 30, 1886 / May 7, 1945. (17:8)
LUCKETT, James Thornton, Jr. / December 27, 1910 / January 13, 1967 [BR:17 JAN:D]. (17:8)
LUCKETT, John Asbury / October 5, 1907 / April 30, 1918. (17:8)
LUCKETT, Minnie Scrivener / October 11, 1884 / December 30, 1963 [BR:3 JAN 1964:D]. (17:8)
LUNSFORD, Heaton P. / 1879-1932. (17:17)
LUNSFORD, Mary I. MARY I. / wife of / CHARLES D. LUNSFORD / born March 28, 1858 / died March 22, 1919 / C.D. LUNSFORD / 1855-1930. (17:17)

First Presbyterian Church Cemetery (1809)

LUNT, J.D. JOHN D.H. LUNT / born May 16, 1852 / died May 4, 1905 / LUCY LEE LUNT / born Oct. 21, 1861 / died May 22, 1956 [BR:25 MAY]. (25:17)
LUNT, Mary H. MARY H. / 1844-1910 / SAMUEL H. / 1846-1925 / HANNAH J. / 1849-1929. (25:16)
LYLES, Mary E. Beckley. Our devoted mother / MARY E. BECKLEY / wife of / RICHARD H. LYLES / died Dec. 6, 1919 / aged 79 years. / *I have fought a good fight / I have kept the faith, / Henceforth, there is laid / up for me a crown of / righteousness.* (43:123)
LYLES, Richard H. In memory of / RICHARD H. LYLES / beloved husband / of / MARY E. LYLES / died Jan. 20, 1911 / aged 71 years. (43:123)

M

MACRAE, A. Eliza Page / born / Sept. 14, 1828 / died / June 16, 1904 / *Whosoever believeth in / me shall never die.* (41:8)
MacINNES, John / died May 27, 1962 / aged 30 years / from Barra, Scotland / S/S. Margaret Bowater [BR:31 MAY:C]. (1:24)
[MAGUIRE?], Annie Elizabeth. ANNIE ELIZABETH / _____ / _____... (43:99)
MAIGNE, Florence English Davidson. In memory of / FLORENCE ENGLISH DAVIDSON / wife of / CHARLES MINNIGERODE MAIGNE / born June 9, 1882 / died June 19, 1942 [BR:22 JUN:C]. (44:145)
MANSON, Henrietta E. HENRIETTA E. JOHNSTON / wife of NATHANIEL C. MANSON / April 15, 1862 / Nov. 2, 1892 / interred at / Lynchburg, Va.
MARBURY, Elizabeth. In / memory of / ELIZABETH / daughter of / LEONARD and MARY W. / MARBURY / who departed this life / May 18th 1820 / aged 1 year 9 months and / 18 days. (42:50, broken)
MARBURY, Joseph Hatton. In / memory of / JOSEPH HATTON / son of / LEONARD and MARY W. / MARBURY / who departed this life / Nov. 12, 1824 / aged 2 years, 1 month / and 14 days. (42:50, broken)
MARBURY, Mary Wade Hunter. To perpetuate the memory of departed worth, a greatly bereaved husband has caused this / monument to be erected Beneath it in silent hope of a body beautified and glorious at the / resurrection of the Just are reposing all that remains of / MARY WADE / wife of Capt. LEONARD MARBURY / who departed this life Octr. 4th A.D. 1822 / in the 26th year of her age. (42:50, tablet; FR:6, died in "childbed")
MARK, Samuel. SAMUEL MARK / died / October 23, 1831 / ANN S. MARK / wife of SAMUEL MARK / died / April 8, 1870 / SARAH E. MARK / daughter of / SAMUEL and ANN S. MARK / died / December 14, 1858 / MARGARET LISLE / wife of V. NEWTON CARTER / daughter of S. & A.S. MARK / died / February 3, 1872 / LYDIA G. MARK / born / Feb. 20, 1820 / died / Sept. 6, 1892 / ELLEN M. MARK / born / Aug. 12, 1809 / died Dec. 7, 1892. (42:51)
MARSH, Barbara Ann. [BR:10 MAR 1966:E]. (2:10, no stone)
MARSHALL, Charles Bennett. CHARLES BENNETT MARSHALL / 1862-1915 / his wife / MARGARET L. HAYES / 1866-1949. (16:19)
MARSHALL, Maria J. MARIA J. MARSHALL / born Dec. 18, 1849, died March 9, 1926 / JOHN ARMISTEAD MARSHALL / born July 2nd 1849, died May 3rd 1913. (16:18)

First Presbyterian Church Cemetery (1809)

MARTIN, Infant. [BR:22 SEP 1966:C]. (2:11, no stone)
MARTIN, Helen Blake. HELEN B. MARTIN / 1895-1989 [BR:16 AUG:E]. (24:9:8)
MARTIN, John. JOHN MARTIN / born / Jan. 4, 1823 / died March 4, 1890 / *None knew him but / to love him* / SALLIE J. MARTIN / born 1850 / died [13 JAN] 1901 / *Rest sweet rest* / JOSEPH E. MARTIN / born 1852 / died [6 JAN] 1915 / *Gone but not forgotten* / SOPHIA / wife of / JOHN MARTIN / born 1831 / died [8 SEP] 1899 / *Faithful & true*. (B:208)
MARTIN, Keith L. KEITH L. / Dec. 21, 1910 / Mar. 30, 1981 / SUSIE L. / Jan. 31, 1915 / May 15, 1982. (14:9:1 & 2)
MARTIN, Madeleine L. / 1895-1914 [AG:31/12/14:1, gives date 3 SEP 1914]. (14:9)
MARTIN, Minnie C. / 1869-1929. (14:9)
MARTIN, William L. / 1864-1935. (14:9)
MASSEY, Margaret Robinson. MARGARET ROBINSON / wife of / REV. ALBERT MASSEY / 1881-1917. (26:5)
MASSIE, Fanny Ansley / born / Nov. 2, 1854 / died Nov. 12, 1920. (43:93)
MAUCK, Aubrey W. AUBREY W. / 1914-1964 [BR:7 NOV:E] / FRANCES L[ee]. MAUCK / 1913-1978. (1:40)
MAUCK, W. Thomas. [BR:12 DEC 1988:D]. (1:51, no stone)
MAXFIELD, Edward F. [BR:23 MAR 1942:D]. (13:10, no stone)
MAY, Adelaide Ursula Kirk / 1886-1916. (18:1)
MAYER, William Grover. [BR:11 JAN 1949:I]. (26:7, no stone)

McBURNEY, George. GEORGE [Jr.?] / son of / GEORGE & ALICE / McBURNEY / born April 20, 1887 / died Sept. 5, 1888. (18:4)
McBURNEY, George Raymond. GEORGE RAYMOND McBURNEY / May 1896 - Aug. 1921 / GEORGE McBURNEY / April 10, 1848 - Jan. 29, 1927 / ALICE D[ienette]. McBURNEY / Dec. 13, 1856 / Sept. 21, 1944 [BR:25 SEP:D]. (18:4)
McCALLISTER, Edward P. / Nov. 30, 1882 / July 15, 1947 [BR:17 JUL:D] / *Gone but not forgotten / by his wife*. (1:12)
McCLIESH, Archibald. Sacred / to the memory of / ARCHIBALD McCLEISH / died 25 Oct. 1831 / in the 34th year of his age. (42:55)
McCLEISH, Archibald. Sacred / to the memory of / ARCHIBALD McCLEISH / who departed this life / May 6, 1819 / in the 55th year of his age. (42:55)
McCLIESH, Catharine F. CATHARINE F. McCLIESH / beloved wife of / GEORGE McCLIESH / died April 21, 1869 / in the 67 year of / her age / *I shall be satisfied when I / awake with thy likeness*. (B:202)
McCLIESH, Elizabeth J. ELIZABETH McCLIESH / Holy and beloved daughter / of GEO. & CATHARINE McCLIESH / died June 14, 1851 / in the 11 year of her age [AG:18/06/51:2]. (B:202)
McCLIESH, George. GEORGE McCLIESH / died May 4, 1880 / in the 78 year of / his age / *As for me I will behold thy / face in Righteousness*. (B:202)
McCLIESH, James. In memory of / JAMES McCLISH [sic] / who departed this life / January 20th, 1815 / in the 55th year of his age. (42:55; AG:21/1/15:3, a native of Scotland, members of the St. Andrew's Society are respectfully invited to attend.)
McCLIESH, William. Sacred / to the memory of / WILLIAM McCLIESH / who departed this life / October 5th 1821 / in the 23rd year of his age. (42:55)

First Presbyterian Church Cemetery (1809)

McCOWAN, Nathalie M. Boush. In loving memory / of / NATHALIE M. BOUSH / wife of / ROBERT J.F. McCOWAN / October 13, 1961 [BR:17 OCT:C]. (16:8)

McCRACKEN, George. GEORGE McCRACKEN / born Sept. 29, 1843 / died June 8, 1925 / *Peaceful Sleep.* (B:171)

McCRACKEN, George K. [BR:23 FEB 1989:Mu]. (17:26W:7, no stone)

McCRACKEN, Isabella. ISABELLA / wife of / GEORGE McCRACKEN / born April 2, 1851 / died Oct. 13, 1922 / *Peaceful Sleep.* (B:171)

McCRACKEN, James Grafton. Our beloved son / JAMES GRAFTON / son of GEORGE & ISABELLA / McCRACKEN / born Jan. 17, 1878 / died July 6, 1896 / *Asleep in Jesus.* (B:171)

McCRACKEN, Margaret C. MARGARET C. / Dec. 26, 1902 / Oct. 16, 1970 / GEORGE K. Feb. 4, 1896 / Feb. 18, 1989 / *Peaceful Rest.* Ladies Auxillary, V.F.W. marker. (17:26:8)

McCULLOUGH, Mary Jaquelin. Beloved wife of / THOMAS ROUGIER McCULLOUGH / MARY JAQUELIN McCULLOUGH / *The Lord has been thy shelter / the Lord will be thy light.* / Aug. 23 / 1917 / Dec. 9 / 1984. (25:5:4)

McCURTIN, George R. / 1875-1906.

McGAUGHEY, Kate. In memory of / KATE McGAUGHEY / died / May 20, 1913 / aged 88 years. / Sacred / to the Memory of / WILLIAM HENRY / infant son of / JOHN & SARAH ANN / CLARVOE / who departed this life / January 24th, 1833 / aged 1 year, 5 months & 1 day. (43:110)

McGINNIS, Lawrence C. / Feb. 22, 1878 / Feb. 27, 1919. (14:6)

McGUIRE, Mary B. In memory / of / MARY B. McGUIRE / born Sept. 23, 1842 / died Feb. 14, 1911 / *Blessed are the pure in / heart for they shall see / God!* (B:186)

McGUIRE, Rev. William. In memory / of / REV. WILLIAM McGUIRE / born Dec. 1, 1824 / died June 26, 1887 / *They that be wise shall show / us the brightness of the / firmament and they that / turn away to righteousness / as the stars forever and ever.* (B:186)

McKENNA, Marion Greenaway / 1898-1927 [BR:died 4 MAR 1927, removed from Huntington WV, reinterred 10 AUG 1962]. (18:16)

McKENNEY, William B. / April 3, 1896 / April 11, 1976 / ESTHER BELLE / May 15, 1901 / July 17, 1982 [BR:21 JUL:D]. (1:1F and 1G)

McKENZIE, Alexander. ALEXANDER McKENZIE / son of / JAMES & MARGARET / McKENZIE / died July 2, 1876 / aged 76 years. (44:153)

McKENZIE, James. JAMES McKENZIE / born August 9th 1802 / died September 30th, 1859 / *He giveth his beloved sleep.* (41:19)

McKENZIE, James Alexander. JAMES / A. / McKENZIE / died / November 2nd 1848 / aged / 18 years 3 mos. 4 dys. [AG:4/11/48:3]. (41:19)

McKENZIE, Lewis. LEWIS McKENZIE / born / Oct. 15, 1810 / died / June 28, 1895. (44:153)

MacKENZIE, Margaret. MARGARET MacKENZIE / widow of the late Capt. / JAMES MacKENZIE / died / February 5th 1859 / aged 80 years. (44:153)

McKENZIE, Margaret Steel. Sacred / to the memory of / MARGARET STEEL / youngest daughter of / JAMES & SARAH E. / McKENZIE / born Oct. 29, 1835 / died November 21, 1839 / aged 4 years / 23 days. / *Suffer little children to come unto / me and forbid them not for of / such is the Kingdom of Heaven.* (41:19)

McKENZIE, Mary. To the memory of / MARY / infant daughter of / JAMES and SARAH E.

First Presbyterian Church Cemetery (1809)

/ McKENZIE / died / June 10, 1842 / aged 4 mos. 21 dys. (41:19)
MacKENZIE, Mary. MARY MacKENZIE / daughter of / JAMES & MARGARET MacKENZIE / died March 26, 1881. (44:153)
McKENZIE, Sarah Eveleth. In / memory of / SARAH E. McKENZIE / wife of / JAMES McKENZIE / died / July 22nd 1843 / in the 33rd year of her age / *Precious in the sight of the Lord / is the death of his Saints*. (41:19)
McKERNAN, Margaret / a native of Ireland / died in Alexa. Va. / Oct. 3rd, 1912. (B:211)
McKNEW, Goldsborough E. GOLDSBOROUGH E. McKNEW / born June 30, 1875 / died Feb. 8, 1907 / *Not lost, but gone before*. / his wife / MARTHA FRANCIS McKNEW / born June 9, 1879 / died Jan. 30, 1957 [BR:3 FEB:W]. (B:187)
McKNIGHT, Asenath L. Graves. [blank] / his wife / ASENATH L. GRAVES / Aug. 13, 1908 / June 25, 1988 [BR:12 JUL:G]. (19:2)
McKNIGHT, Catharine Piercy. CATHARINE PIERCY / wife of / JOHN McKNIGHT / born Jan. 7, 1780 / died Dec. 13, 1867 [AG:14/12/67:2]. (41:20, epitaph illegible)
McKNIGHT, Capt. Charles. In / memory / of / CHARLES McKNIGHT / born April 7th, 1774 / died / March 11th, 1853 / aged 78 years 11 months / & 4 days[1]. (41:20)
McKNIGHT, Charles Henry. CHARLES HENRY / son of / WILLIAM H. and / MARGARET J. McKNIGHT / born April 21, 1840 / died August 15, 1916. (41:20)
McKNIGHT, Elizabeth Chew. ELIZABETH CHEW / daughter of / WILLIAM H. and / MARGARET McKNIGHT / born April 2, 1833 / died November 16, 1911 / *He giveth his beloved sleep*. [AG:30/12/11:4]. (41:20)
McKNIGHT, John. In / memory of / JOHN McKNIGHT / born / July 2d, 1769 / died / February 7, 1834 / aged / 64 years 7 months & 5 days. [Note: the bible of the McKnight family is now in the possession of the Old Presbyterian Meeting house, and was printed by Mathew Carey of Philadelphia in 1802. John McKnight and Catharine Piercy were married by Rev. Mr. Swan on Tuesday, Oct. 29, 1799] (41:20; Alexandria Wills, Bk. 4, p. 81, men. wife Catharine)
McKNIGHT, Mary E. In memory of / MARY E. McKNIGHT / born Nov. 23rd 1810 / died Jan. 10th 1882. (41:20)
McKNIGHT, Susannah Evans. In / memory / of / SUSANNAH EVANS / 2nd wife / of / WILLIAM McKNIGHT / born / 19th of Septr. 1746 / died / Novr. 10th, 1836 / aged 90 years 7 months / & 22 days. (41:20)
McKNIGHT, William. To the memory of / WILLIAM McKNIGHT / who departed this life / on the 25th of July 1812 / in the 80th year of his age / MARTHA BRYAN / Wife of / WILLIAM McKNIGHT / departed this life / June 3, 1775 / Aged 30 years. (41:20, boxtomb)
McKNIGHT, William Henry. WILLIAM H. McKNIGHT / born Aug. 24, 1800 / died Dec. 29, 1887 / MARGARET [Jacobs] / wife of / WILLIAM H. McKNIGHT / born Jan. 28, 1802 / died Feb. 7, 1888 / *They also which / sleep in Jesus / will God bring / with him*. (41:20)
McKNIGHT, William Presley / born June 12, 1838 / died Oct. 24, 1927. (41:20)
McLEAN, Baby Girl / Dec. 12, 1969 [BR:14 DEC:T]. (B:191)
McNAIR, Henry / aged 8 years / 1850. (44:152)

---

[1] Sengel, p. 66, the family bible of Captain Charles McKnight was donated to the Meeting House by a descendant Miss Katherine Piercy Howard.

First Presbyterian Church Cemetery (1809)

MELVILLE, Hattie Hoof / 1893 - [blank]. (44:144)

MERRIAM, Sidney A., Jr. / Sept. 13, 1909 - Oct. 30, 1967 [BR:2 NOV:Gr] / wife EMILY. (26:5)

MILBURN, Joseph. JOSEPH MILBURN / a native of New Castle, England / but for many years an esteemed / citizen of Alexandria / was born July 4th 1759 / died 13th Oct. 1821 / leaving a motherless child to mourn / her irreparable loss. / *Blessed are the pure in heart for / they shall see God.* (42:62; FR:6, died of a malignant fever at the age of 63 years; Alexandria Wills, Bk. 3, p. 30, men. daughter Jane as wife of William Deakins)

MILBURN, Margaret. MARGARET MILBURN / wife of / JOSEPH MILBURN / died October 12th 1821. (42:62)

MILLS, Adaline Margaret. Dedicated / sacred to the / memory of ADALINE / MARGARET MILLS daughter / of WM. N. MILLS & ANN his wife / who departed this life on / 3rd day of Septemr. 1817 / aged ten years eight / months and el / even days. (41:41)

> *Wake up muse, condole the loss*
> *Of those that mourn this day*
> *Let tears distil on every face*
> *And every mourner pray.*
>
> *The tyrant death came marching in*
> *This day his power did she*
> *Out of this world this child did take*
> *Death laid its visage loss.*
>
> *No more the pleasant child is seen*
> *To please its parents eye*
> *The tender plant so fresh and green*
> *Is in eternity.*
>
> *The winching sheet doth bind its limbs*
> *The coffin holds it fast*
> *Today its seen by all its friends*
> *But this must be the last.* (41:41, tablet)

MILLS, Alonzo. ALONZO MILLS / died June 4, 1894 / his wife / GEORGEANNA DAVIS / died Feb. 7, 1898 / *May the souls of the / departed through faith / in thee rest in peace* / Mother and Father / GEORGE E. DAVIS / his wife / SARAH E. DAVIS. (43:102)

MILLS, Ann. Sacred / to the / memory of / ANN MILLS / wife of / W.N. MILLS / who departed this life / on 6th of Feb. 1831 / aged forty one years eight / months & 26 days / *Remember man as thou* _____ / *As thou art now* _____ / *And* _____ *wilt thou be / Thou* _____ *thyself follow me.* (41:42)

MILLS, William N. GULIELMI N. MILLS / nati tertio id mart MDCCLXXXIII / Hic Exanimum corpus requiesoit / Parentes amicos patria moue / amavit / exivitque vita /

First Presbyterian Church Cemetery (1809)

quarto non Oct. MDCCCLII [AG:5/10/52:3]. (41:42)

MINIS, Janet Davidson. In memory of / JANET DAVIDSON MINIS / born / October 21, 1874 / died / March 20, 1951 [BR:23 MAR:W]. (44:145)

MOFFETT, Capt. John. CAPT. JOHN MOFFETT / who departed this life / 18 Sept. 1842 / aged 48 years. (42:66)

MOFFETT, Matilda Ann. MATILDA A. MOFFETT / consort of / Capt. JOHN MOFFETT / who departed this life July 6th 1836 / aged 33 years. (42:66)

MONROE, Amanda E. / 1823-1895 [AG:31/12/95:1, gives date 11 SEP 1895]. (B:183)

MONROE, Daniel. Sacred to the memory / of / DANIEL MONROE / born July 18th 1792 / died July 23rd 1839 / *An affectionate husband and parent / a good and useful citizen.* (44:129, tablet)

MONROE, Daniel / 1855-1858. (B:183)

MONROE, Edwin. In memory of / EDWIN / son of / DANIEL and ELIZABETH MONROE / who departed this life / Dec. 2, 1861 / in the 36th year of his age. (44:129)

MONROE, Elizabeth. In memory of / ELIZABETH / wife of / DANIEL MONROE / who departed this life / April 5, 1872 / in the 79th year of her age. (44:129)

MONROE, James T. / 1824-1886. (B:183)

MONROE, Julia Anna / 1863-1911 [AG:30/12/11:4, gives date 27 NOV 1911]. (B:183)

MONROE, Kate Elizabeth. KATE E. MONROE / died / June 30, 1937 [BR:2 JUL:W]. (B:183)

MONROE, Slighter S. In memory of / SLIGHTER S. / son of / DANIEL and ELIZABETH MONROE / who departed this life / May 25, 1853 / in the 32nd year of his age [AG:27/5/53:2]. (44:129)

MONROE, Capt. Thomas. In / memory of / Capt. THOMAS MONROE / who in full prospects of a / blessed immortality fell / asleep in Jesus / September 10th 1839 / in the 50th year of his age. (43:96)

MONTGOMERY, Charles M. Beloved husband / CHARLES M. MONTGOMERY / Dec. 9, 1920 / Aug. 17, 1986. (17:18)

MONTGOMERY, Grace Carter / April 23, 1896 / August 22, 1963 [BR:24 AUG:E]. (15:25)

MOORE, Harry VanGuysling. HARRY V. MOORE / April 10, 1893 / Sept. 8, 1948 [BR:10 SEP:W]. (17:7)

MOORE, Marian Dienelt / 1905-1934. (16:4)

MOORE, Marion Hopkins. MARION HOPKINS / wife of / WILLIAM A. MOORE, JR. / August 31, 1876 / November 26, 1966 [BR:29 NOV:E]. (15:2)

MOORE, William A., Jr. / June 27, 1875 / April 4, 1950 [BR:7 APR:W]. (15:2)

MORRILL, William T. WILLIAM T. MORRILL / died June 11, 1862 / LAURA MASON / wife of / WILLIAM T. MORRILL / died Aug. 2, 1887 / WILLIAM / infant son of / WM. & MARY MORRILL / aged 3 days / MARY STANWOOD / wife of / WILLIAM MORRILL / died Sept. 18, 1870 / VIRGINIA MORRILL / died Sep. 6, 1861 / MARY S. MORRILL / died Dec. 26, 1861 / SARA MORRILL / born Dec. 1, 1830 / died Sep. 27, 1895 / CAPT. WM. MORRILL / died Sept. 2nd 1843 / agd 53 / *Blessed are the dead / that die in the Lord.* (43:96)

MORRIS, Helen Baker / *Heaven became a richer place.* / September 29, 1977. (3:16)

MORSE, Sarah "Sally." Erected / in memory of / SARAH / wife of / ORLANDO S. MORSE / born April 22, 1800 / died June 26, 1831 / also / VIRGINIA / daughter of / O.S. & SARAH MORSE / died July 10, 1831 / aged 7 months / and 11 days. (42:47)

First Presbyterian Church Cemetery (1809)

MOUNT, James Harry / June 28, 1890 / Sept. 30, 1959. (19:5)
MOUNT, Phillip Herbert. PHILLIP HERBERT MOUNT / 1892-1967 [BR:19 DEC:C] / his beloved wife / ESTELLE KIDWELL MOUNT / 1893-1971 [BR:24 FEB:C]. (19:5)
MOUNTAIN, Ralph Thomas, Jr. / June 9, 1947 / Oct. 29, 1986. (3:26)
MUIR, Eliza A. Green. ELIZA A. GREEN / wife of WM. H. MUIR / born Aug. 7, 1822 / died Jan. 27, 1861 / *And I heard a voice from heaven / saying unto me, write; blessed / are the dead which die in the / Lord.* (41:17)
[MUIR], Ethel. (25:15)
[MUIR], Esther. (25:15)
[MUIR], Helen. (25:15)
MUIR, James F. / 1846-1925. (41:17)
MUIR, John. Sacred / to the memory of / JOHN MUIR / who departed this life / February 12, 1815 / in the 45th year / of his age / *My glass is run and yours are running / remember death for Judgment's comeing. [sic]* / also / JAMES MUIR / son of JOHN and MARY MUIR / departed this life July / 11th 1814 / in the 5th year / of his age. (41:17, tablet)
MUIR, John A. JOHN A. MUIR / 1849-1925. (41:17)
MUIR, Mary. In memory of / MARY MUIR / (Relict of the late / JOHN MUIR) / who died May 24, 1841 / aged 61 years / *After a Christian experience / of 34 years she was able in lifes / Last struggle to exclaim / The Lord is the portion of / his people.* (41:17, table)
MUIR, Mary A. MARY A. MUIR / January 3, 1844 - May 17, 1923. (25:15)
MUIR, William H. WILLIAM H. MUIR / born / March 5, 1814 / died / Aug. 15, 1891 / *Comfort ye comfort / ye my people saith / your God. / He giveth power to / the faint and to them / that have no might he / increaseth strength / but they that wait / upon the Lord shall / renew their strength / they shall mount up / with wings as eagles / they shall run, and / not be weary, and / they shall walk, and / not faint.* (41:17)
MUIR, William M. [BR:29 AUG 1938:D]. (25:15, no stone)
[MUIR?], Willie / and / Mary. No dates. (41:17)
MUNDY, Mary Jane. Mother / MARY JANE MUNDY / widow of / DABNY MUNDY / born / March 28, 1845 / died / Dec. 10, 1923 / *Safe in the arms of Jesus.* (15:12)
MUNROE, Lamar / 1876-1921. (15:24)
MUNROE, Maude M. Jenkins. MAUDE M. JENKINS / wife of / LAMAR MUNROE / 1880-1974 [BR:8 FEB:D]. (15:24:2)
MUNSON, Charlotte E. / Sept. 29, 1900 / Jan. 13, 1965 / *Beloved Piano Teacher.* (1:43)
MURRAY, Catherine Ann. CATHERINE ANN MURRAY / wife of / JESSE MURRAY / born / April 11, 1846 / died / Jan. 15, 1929 / U.D.V. (3:1A)
MURRAY, Jesse / born / June 20, 1844 / died / Aug. 9, 1930 / U.C.V. (3:1A)
MURRAY, Margaret Lee. MARGARET LEE / daughter of / JESSE & CATHERINE / MURRAY / born Nov. 21, 1868 / died / March 27, 1934. (3:1A)
MYERS, Margaret. Sacred / to the memory of / MARGARET, wife of / JOHN MYERS / who departed / this life Aug. 25, 1821 / aged 29 years. (42:65)

N

NALLS, Dasie D. / March 15, 1893 / February 26, 1983 [BR:2 MAR:E]. (20:3:3)
NALLS, Jeanne L. / December 12, 1917 / August 6, 1967 [BR:10 AUG:E]. (20:3:4)
NARAMORE, Leonard J. / 1872-1936 / ANNIE FRANCIS / 1876-1930. (B:187)

First Presbyterian Church Cemetery (1809)

NASH, Capt. Charles F. CAPT. CHARLES F. / NASH / U.S. Coast Guard / 1857-1924. (B:183)

NASH, George Washington. In / memory of / GEORGE WASHINGTON / son of / ROBERT and JANE NASH / who departed this life / August 15th 1829 / in the 17th year / of his age. (42:59)

NASH, Louise R. / 1888 - 1891. (B:183)

NASH, Rebecca Monroe. REBECCA MONROE / wife of / CAPT. CHAS. F. NASH / died April 18, 1949 [BR:20 APR:D]. (B:183)

NASH, Robert. Gunsmith. In / memory of / ROBERT NASH / a native of / Dumfries, Scotland / who departed this life / July 15, 1814 / aged 36 years [AG:19/7/14:3]. (42:59)

NELSON, George Whaley. GEO. WHALEY NELSON / Dec. 10, 1809 / Jan. 8, 1864 / his wife / ELIZABETH ARMSTRONG / Sept. 25, 1812 / May 26, 1891. (43:108)

NEWELL, Joseph Hazell. JOSEPH HAZELL NEWELL / April 5, 1890 - March 10, 1973 / CORRINNE PEALE / July 18, 1891 - Dec. 25, 1974 / Joined in Holy Wedlock on Dec. 22, 1919 / *Joy be with you.* (44:133)

NEWTON, Charles H., Sr. / June 21, 1904 / July 12, 1977 [BR:17 JUL:D]. (26:18)

NEWTON, Evelyn P. / Feb. 19, 1906 / Aug. 27, 1973 [BR:30 AUG:D]. (26:18)

NEWTON, Harry Hammill. HARRY H. NEWTON / July 31, 1881 - May 17, 1956 [BR:18 MAY:W]. (26:18)

NEWTON, Henry. HENRY / June 10, 1910 / [blank] / ANNA F. / Nov. 26, 1907 / July 14, 1988. (3:8)

NEWTON, John Thomas. Sacred / to the memory of / JOHN THOMAS NEWTON / commodore U.S.N. / born in Alexandria, Va. / 20th May 1794 / died in Washington, D.C. / 28th July 1857 / *Entered the navy in 1809, was an / officer in active service during / the war of 1812 and died while / in the performance of his duty / and celebrated 48 years of his life / to the service of his Country.* (42:45, obelisk)

NEWTON, Joseph M. Sacred / to the memory of / JOSEPH M. NEWTON / died of Paralysis / June 28, 1883 / in the 73rd year / of his age. (42:45, footstone "J.M.N.")

NEWTON, Margaret Hammond. MARGARET H. NEWTON / Jan. 24, 1882 - Nov. 9, 1959 [BR:12 NOV:E]. (26:18)

NEWTON, William. Our Parents / Died / on the 26th / Decbr. 1814 / WILLIAM NEWTON / in the 52nd / year of his age / *The world passeth away / but he that doeth the will of / God abideth forever.* / Died on the 25th Feby. 1815 / JANE B[arr Stuart]. NEWTON / in the 39th / year of her age / *For the Lord shall be thine / everlasting light and the / days of thy mourning shall / be ended. / We are more than conquerors / through him that loved us. / For if we believe that Jesus died and rose again, even so / them also which sleep in Jesus will God bring with him.* (42:45)

NICHOLSON, Ann. In memory of / ANN NICHOLSON / who departed this life / October 26, 1812 in the / 29th year of her age. (41:32)

NICHOLSON, Eliza. Erected / to / the memory of / ELIZA NICHOLSON / daughter of HENRY and / PRECIOUS NICHOLSON / who departed this life / July 29th 1820 / in the 20th year / of her age / *Beneath this clod her dust remains / Free from all her anxious pains / Christ was her choice, she's gone on high / To reign with him eternally.* (41:32)

NICHOLSON, Henry. Erected to / the memory of / HENRY NICHOLSON / who departed this

First Presbyterian Church Cemetery (1809)

life / November the 14th 1821 / in the _6th year of his age / He was a native of Ireland but for / many years a respectable inhabitant of / this town / *Oh shade rever'd this frail immortal take / Tis all alas a sorrowing child can make, / On this faint stone to mark her parents worth / And claim the spot that holds the sainted earth.* (41:32, tablet; Alexandria Wills, Bk. 3, p. 35)

NICHOLSON, Mary. In memory of / MARY NICHOLSON / who departed this life / March 14th 1821 / in the 80th year / of her age / *Tender mother thy days are ended / All thy afflicted days below / Go by Angels gaurds [sic] attended / To the sight of Jesus go.* (41:32)

NICHOLSON, Precious Talbert. Sacred / to the memory of / PRECIOUS NICHOLSON / wife of HENRY NICHOLSON / who departed this life / the 15th of October 1802 / aged 34 years / *Do not mourn for me my friend / Or shake at death's alarms / Tis but the voice that ... [under soil].* (41:32)

NOLEN, Constance E. CONSTANCE E. NOLEN / March 28, 1922 / December 30, 1965 [BR:31 DEC:D]. (1:47)

NUGENT, John J. JOHN J. NUGENT / born October 7, 1866 / died September 10, 1953 / ANNIE V. NUGENT / born March 4, 1870 / died December 17, 1917 / DOROTHY NUGENT / born February 13, 1900 / died March 20, 1976. (17:15)

NUGENT, Mary Josephine Travers. MARY J. TRAVERS / wife of / THOMAS W. NUGENT / 1876-1960 [BR:30 AUG:D]. (17:14)

NUGENT, Thomas W. THOMAS W. NUGENT / 1874-1935. (17:14)

O

O'BRIEN, Rebecca M. To / the memory of / REBECCA M. O'BRIEN / who died Aug. 23 / 1812, aged 7 mos. / & / JOSEPH D. O'BRIEN / died Aug. 22, 1814 / aged 15 mo. / the children of DENNIS & NANCY / O'BRIEN. (41:3)

OGDEN, Kenneth W. KENNETH W. OGDEN / 1884-1925. (17:6)

OGDEN, William D. WILLIAM D. OGDEN / died March 31, 1917 / aged 59 years / his wife / WILHELMINA TUBMAN / 1859-1943. (17:6)

O'MEARA, Collin W. COLLIN W. / Aug. 6, 1871 / July 5, 1938 [BR:7 JUL:W] / ADA L. / Nov. 1, 1872 / Oct. 19, 1951. (14:3)

O'MEARA, Herbert W. / Sept. 27, 1901 / April 2, 1966 [BR:5 APR:C]. (14:19:3)

O'MEARA, James Thomas. JAMES T. O'MEARA / 1874-1936 [BR:6 MAY:C] / his wife / NELLIE FRENZEL / 1876-1957. (14:3)

[O'MEARA?], Marguerite / 1901-1902. (14:3)

ORRISON, Florence W. / 1857-1934. (13:9)

OWEN-JONES, Charlotte Cazenove. CHARLOTTE CAZENOVE OWEN-JONES / October 3, 1863 - April 17, 1951. (43:93)

OWEN-JONES, Percy. PERCY OWEN-JONES / September 13th 1851 / July 4th 1922 / *A priest forever.* (43:93)

First Presbyterian Church Cemetery (1809)

P

PAFF, Frederick. FREDERICK PAFF / 1837-1903 [AG:31/12/03:1, gives date 7 APR 1903] / his wife / LOUISA PAFF / 1837-1903 [AG:31/12/03:1, gives date 15 JUL 1903] / *Let not your heart be / troubled* / FREDERICK J. PAFF / 1867-1933 / GRACE C. / wife of / FREDERICK J. PAFF / 1869-1930 / CHARLES B. PAFF / 1871-1926 / LUCY THOMAS / wife of / CHARLES B. PAFF / 1870-1901 [AG:31/12/01:1, gives date 1 AUG 1901]. (14:5)

PAGE, John Ramsay. In memory / of / JOHN RAMSAY PAGE / eldest son of / WILLIAM & MARY PAGE / born / 28th of June 1832 / died / 24th of June 1848 / aged / 43 years 11 mos. & 27 days / *Blessed are the dead that / die in the Lord.* (44:138, footstone "J.R.P. / 1848")

PAGE, William. In memory / of / WILLIAM PAGE / born June 15th 1803 / died May 11th 1851 / *Blessed are the dead who die in / the Lord.* [AG:13/5/51:3]. (44:138, footstone "W.P.")

PASCOE. In memory of / Three Children of CHAs. and / HONORE PASCOE / WILLIAM died the 10th of Feby. 1805 / aged 3 years and 9 months / CHARLES, died the 23d of Oct. 1806 / aged 2 years and 7 months / WILLIAM, died the 12th of Augt. 1807 / aged 11 months / *Here lies three children sweet asleep, / Which brings fresh to our mind / That die we must, and come to dust / And leave this world behind. / Weep not for us our parents dear, / We are not dead but sleeping here / God took us home as he thought best / And now in heaven our souls doth rest.* (41:21)

PASCOE, Charles. Sacred / to the memory of / CHARLES PASCOE / a native of / Devonshire, England / who departed this life / Dec. 30, 1843, aged / 76. (41:21, footstone "C.P." and broken headstone no longer legible)

PASCOE, William. Sacred / to the memory of / WM. PASCOE / who departed this life / June the 10, 1833 / in the 23 year of his age / *Kind amiable and affectionate / he secured the confidence and / esteem of all who knew him / His end was peace, / he lived and died a christian.* (41:26)

PATTERSON, Clyde W. CLYDE W. / July 5, 1909 / [blank] / MILDRED S. / Aug. 10, 1912 / [blank]. (3:3)

PAUL, Nannie S. In memory of / NANNIE S. / wife of JOSEPH PAUL / born Dec. 25, 1842 / died Sep. 9, 1869 / and their son / T. STOWERS PAUL / died Oct. 8, 1869 / age 1 mo. (44:146)

PAYNE, Jessie C. Butts. JESSIE C. BUTTS / wife of ELISHA K. PAYNE / 1880-1909 / ELISHA K. PAYNE / April 30, 1876 / July 1, 1959 / and his wife / MYRTLE [Anne] B. PAYNE / May 2, 1880 / Aug. 4, 1962 [BR:7 AUG:H] [AG:21/12/09:1, gives date 7 MAY 1909]. (B:170)

PERDIKRAS, Harry. [BR:13 SEP 1968:D]. (1:50, no stone)

PERRY, Alexander D.F. In / memory of / ALEXANDER D.F. PERRY / who departed this life / June 6th 1831 / in the 74th year of his age / *Blessed are the dead who / die in the Lord.* (41:15; Alexandria Wills, Bk. 4, p. 15)

PERRY, Jane. In / memory of / JANE / wife of / ALEXr. PERRY / who died Feb. 4th 1823 / aged 65 years / *Her life ensured a saviour bliss / a crown of Joy and righteousness.* (41:15)

PERRY, Lillian Estelle Allen. LILLIAN ESTELLE ALLEN / wife of MILTON B. PERRY / died Nov. 9, 1897. (13:3)

First Presbyterian Church Cemetery (1809)

PICKETT, Janet Rowen. JANET ROWEN / Sept. 9, 1888 / Jan. 10, 1977 [BR:12 JAN:E] / GEORGE EDWARD / June 6, 1885 / Aug. 5, 1953 [BR:8 AUG:W]. (42:76)
PICKIN, James Richard. JAMES RICHARD / 1847-1918 / ALICE HENNING / 1856-1937 [BR:26 JAN:C] / CHARLES HENRY / 1856-1923 / MARGARET HENNING / 1858-1929 / CARRIE BRIGHT / 1884-1901 / CHARLES RICHARD / 1921-1929. (25:11)
PIERSON, Emma L. EMMA L. PIERSON / 1847-1927. (B:203)
PIERSON, Harriet S. / 1855-1941 [BR:22 FEB:W]. (B:203)
PIERSON, Henry W. / 1859-1940 [BR:30 SEP:W]. (B:203)
PIERSON, Susan E. SUSAN E. PIERSON / 1862-1925. (B:203)
PLASTER, David H. DAVID H. PLASTER / Nov. 30, 1823 - April 18, 1906 / MINNIE H. PLASTER / 1848-1910 / EDWARD H. GREGORY / Sept. 13, 1823 - Oct. 13, 1903 / JANE W. GREGORY / June 17, 1830 - June 30, 1904 / DAVID M. OGDEN, M.D., 1851-1910 / ELEANOR GREGORY OGDEN, 1863-1928. (15:4)
POMEROY, Edith V. Beloved Mother / EDITH V. POMEROY / July 27, 1919 / April 12, 1973. (43:99)
POMEROY, Samuel S., Jr. Beloved husband & father / SAMUEL S. POMEROY, Jr. / Sept. 25, 1944 / April 29, 1974. (43:99)
POSS, Esther E. ESTHER E. / POSS / born / Nov. 19, 1845 / died / Mar. 11, 1898 / At rest. (43:126)
POSS, Harry Edward. HARRY E. POSS / 1871-1937 [BR:11 OCT:W]. (15:19)
POSS, John P. In memory of / my husband / JOHN P. POSS / born April 11, 1845 / killed June 16, 1888 / in the accident at / Pope Head on V.M.R.R. (43:126)
POSS, Louis B. / 1899-1988 [BR:12 SEP:E]. (15:19)
POSS, Marguerite A. MARGUERITE A. POSS / 1907-[blank]. (15:19)
POSS, Mary E. / 1873-1909 [AG:31/12/09:1, gives date 1 SEP 1909]. (15:19)
POSS, Mary V. MARY V. POSS / 1908-1922. (15:19)
POSS, Ruth Estelle. [BR:25 SEP 1962:E]. (15:19, no stone)
POWELL, Neville. In memory of NEVILLE POWELL / daughter of / DR. R.C. & MARY G. POWELL / born Jan. 24, 1883 / died April 8, 1886. (44:141)
POWELL, Dr. Robert Conrad. ROBERT CONRAD POWELL, M.D. / born Aug. 1, 1838 / died May 9, 1890 / his wife / MARY CRAUFORD GREGORY / born Jan. 12, 1847 / died Dec. 18, 1928 / WILLIAM GREGORY POWELL / born November 23, 1876 / died February 2, 1900. (44:141, tablet)
PRAYTOR, Willard Albert. WILLARD A. PRAYTOR / July 15, 1909 / March 17, 1960. (24:12)
PRESTON, James Truman / 1860-1936 [BR:9 OCT:W]. (19:16)
PRESTON, Kate Bradford / 1886-1977 [BR:4 FEB:D]. (19:16:1)
PRESTON, Laura Truman. LAURA TRUMAN PRESTON / 1889-1924. (19:16)
PRESTON, Laura Wood. LAURA WOOD PRESTON / 1861-1953. (19:16)
PRETTYMAN, David G. DAVID G. PRETTYMAN / departed this life / June 17, 1844 / in 53d yr. (42:102)
PRETTYMAN, Harriet Matilda. HARRIET MATILDA / daughter of DAVID & PRISCILLA / PRETTYMAN / died 21 January 1833, aged 10 years 4 mos. 2 days. (42:102)
PRETTYMAN, Harriet Virginia. In memory of / HARRIET VIRGINIA / daughter of ROBT. F. & / MARGARET V. PRETTYMAN / who died Oct. 7, 1848, / aged 4 ys. 8 mo. and 16 dys. (44:143, footstone "H.V.P.")

First Presbyterian Church Cemetery (1809)

PRETTYMAN, Lily Morgan. In remembrance of / LILY MORGAN / daughter of / ROBERT F. & MARGARET V. / PRETTYMAN / born Sept. 15, 1856 / died Oct. 7, 1944 [BR:9 OCT:W]. (44:143, footstone "L.M.P.")

PRETTYMAN, Margaret Virginia. In memory / of / MARGARET VIRGINIA / wife of / ROBERT F. PRETTYMAN / born April 23, 1824 / died March 13, 1870. (44:143)

PRETTYMAN, Margaret Virginia. In remembrance of / MARGARET VIRGINIA / daughter of / ROBERT F. & MARGARET V. / PRETTYMAN / born April 14, 1851 / died Nov. 17, 1934. (44:143, footstone "M.V.P.")

PRETTYMAN, Mary Esther. In remembrance of / MARY ESTHER / daughter of / ROBERT F. & MARGARET V. / PRETTYMAN / born July 19, 1854 / died April 29, 1943 [BR:1 MAY:W]. (44:143, footstone "M.E.P.")

PRETTYMAN, Priscilla. PRISCILLA / wife of / DAVID G. PRETTYMAN / departed this life Aug. 9, 1856 / aged 70 years. (42:102)

PRETTYMAN, Robert F. In memory of / ROBERT F. PRETTYMAN / born / June 12, 1821 / died / Jan. 26, 1892. (44:143, footstone "R.F.P.")

PRICE, Emma J. Sister / EMMA J. PRICE / died Aug. 26, 1908 / in the 59th year of her age. (42:68)

PRICE, Frank. Brother / FRANK PRICE / born / Jan. 28, 1851 / died / March 2, 1906. (42:68)

PRICE, George E. Father / GEORGE E. PRICE / born / Sept. 3, 1806 / died / July 17, 1860. (42:68)

PRICE, Georgianna. In / memory of / GEORGIANNA / daughter of / GEORGE & MARY ANN / PRICE / who died / Aug. 28, 1836 / aged 10 months. (42:68)

PRICE, Harold Lindsey. [BR:22 JAN 1943:W]. (13:5, no stone)

PRICE, Mark Leslie. MARK LESLIE PRICE / born April 18, 1838 / died July 20, 1916 / C.S.A. / MARY FOSSETT PRICE / born Dec. 18, 1841 / died Aug. 30, 1925 / MARK L. PRICE / born Dec. 23, 1873 / died Sept. 26, 1953 [BR:28 SEP:W] / his wife / ALMA STOVER PRICE / born March 6, 1882 / died Nov. 20, 1964 [BR:21 NOV:C] / C. MARION PRICE / born Dec. 15, 1875 / died Nov. 5, 1943. D.A.R. marker. (17:5)

PRICE, Mary Ann. Mother / MARY ANN PRICE / born / Jan. 14, 1814 / died / April 30, 1890. (42:68)

PRICE, Samuel T. / Eleanor W. Price. No dates. (14:21)

PRITCHARD, Jeanette Curtin / July 21, 1889 / July 4, 1934. (13:13)

PROFFITT, Tammy M. [BR:4 DEC 1967:C]. (2:19, no stone)

PULLMAN, Mary Lightfoot. Mother / MARY LIGHTFOOT PULLMAN / wife of / GARBUTT PULLMAN / 1862-1951 [BR:5 JUN:Ch]. (B:206)

PULMAN, Charles O. CHARLES O. PULMAN / 1860-1925. (B:208)

PULMAN, Frances Potter. FRANCES POTTER / wife of / PETER PULMAN / 1822-1898 [AG:31/12/98:1, gives date 9 DEC 1898]. (B:208)

PULMAN, Leon O. LEON O. PULMAN / 1904-1911. (B:208)

PULMAN, Lucy V. Martin. LUCY V. MARTIN / wife of / CHARLES O. PULMAN / 1858-1884 [AG:31/12/84:3, gives date 15 MAR 1884]. (B:208)

PULMAN, Mary A. Martin. MARY A. MARTIN / wife of / CHARLES O. PULMAN / 1856-1897 [AG:31/12/97:1, gives date 12 AUG 1897]. (B:208)

PULMAN, Peter. PETER PULMAN / 1832-1906. (B:208)

First Presbyterian Church Cemetery (1809)

Q

QUANDER, Julia E. In memory of / JULIA E. QUANDER / died Sept. 6, 1862 / in the 15th year of her age. (44:153)

QUISENBERRY, Rebecca Paton. REBECCA PATON / wife of / WILLIAM P. QUISENBERRY / departed this life / September 5, 1850 / *She is not dead but sleepeth.* / WILLIAM PRATT QUISENBERRY / died June 1864 / LITTLE WILLEY / born September 1847 / died June 1848. (42:77; Alexandria Wills, Bk. 8, p. 204, will of William P. Quisenbury proved 8 JUL 1864)

R

RAMSAY, Allen Taylor. ALLEN TAYLOR RAMSAY / son of / G.W.D. RAMSAY / born Jan. 8, 1849 / died Aug. 8, 1900. (41:31)

RAMSAY, Col. Dennis. In memory of / DENNIS RAMSAY / who died / Sep. 1st, 1810 / aged 54 years. / JANE A[llen Taylor]. / his wife / died Nov. 24th 1848 / aged 80 years / ANTHONY RAMSAY / died Sep. 23rd 1814 / aged 22 years / WILLIAM RAMSAY / died Oct. 18th, 1822 / aged 35 years. (42:72)

RAMSAY, George W.D. Our Children / asleep in Jesus / G.W.D. and / WILHELMINA B. RAMSAY / GEORGE W.D. / Born Oct. 26, 1840 / Died Jan. 10, 1844 / WILHELMINA B. / Born Aug. 5, 1842 / Died / Jan. 14, 1844 / DOUGLAS B. / Born Aug. 22, 1857 / Died / May 19, 1858. (41:31, obelisk)

RAMSAY, George Washington Dennis. GEO. WASHINGTON DENNIS RAMSAY / son of / Col. DENNIS RAMSAY / of the Revolutionary Army / Grand-son of / WILLIAM RAMSAY / One of the founders of / Alexandria; / For Fifty eight Years an Elder / in the Presbyterian Church; / Born July 3, 1808, / Died May 2, 1900. / *Mark the perfect man and / behold the upright for the / end of that man is peace.* (41:31)

RAMSAY, George William. GEORGE WILLIAM / son of / GEO. WASHINGTON DENNIS / and / WILHELMINA BARTLEMAN / RAMSAY / born June 8, 1844 / died Jan. 5, 1926 / *Whosoever liveth and / believeth in me shall / never die.* / C.S.A. (B:212)

RAMSAY, Harriet M. Fawcett. HARRIET FAWCETT / wife of / GEO. WILLIAM RAMSAY / born Oct. 16, 1847 / died July 5, 1922 / *My trust hath been also / in the Lord, therefore / shall I not fall.* (B:212)

RAMSAY, Henrietta Fawcett. HENRIETTA FAWCETT / daughter of / GEO. WILLIAM & / HARRIET M. / RAMSAY / born March 24, 1891 / died Aug. 6, 1891. (B:212)

RAMSAY, John. In memory of / JOHN RAMSAY / who departed this life / on the 13th of Sept. 1821 / in the 60th year of / his age. / *I am the resurrection and the life; / he that believeth in me though he / were dead yet shall he live.* (41:8, tablet; Alexandria Wills, Bk. 3, p. 17)

RAMSAY, John. In memory of / JOHN RAMSAY / who departed this life / on the 18th of August 1842 / in the 31st year of / his age. / He was the only son and the youngest child of the late JOHN RAMSAY. / *He possessed...* (41:8, tablet, badly worn)

RAMSAY, Louise Hill. LOUISE / wife of / D. McC. RAMSAY / and daughter of / Dr. J.C. & F.E. HILL / born Dec. 12, 1859 / died Sep. 25, 1886 / *At rest in heaven* / WILHELMINA / born July 4, 1881 / died Dec. 16, 1881. (41:31)

First Presbyterian Church Cemetery (1809)

RAMSAY, Margaret Douglas. MARGARET DOUGLAS / daughter of / G.W.D. and WILHELMINA / RAMSAY / born Nov. 25, 1846 / died March 7, 1884 / *Blessed are the dead which / die in the Lord.* (41:31)

RAMSAY, Maud. MAUD / daughter of / GEO. WILLIAM & / HARRIET F. / RAMSAY / born Oct. 16, 1879 / died July 21, 1880.

RAMSAY, Robert T. ROBERT T. RAMSAY / who departed this life / December 24, 1857 in the 56th year of his age. (42:72)

RAMSAY, Wilhelmina. WILHELMINA / wife of G.W.D. RAMSAY / and daughter of / WILLIAM & MARGT. BARTLEMAN / born June 5, 1816 / died Feb'y 27, 1863 [AG:27/2/63:3]. (41:31)

RAMSAY, William. WILLIAM / son of / GEO. WILLIAM & / HARRIET F. / RAMSAY / born July 7, 1875 / died June 18, 1876.

RANDOLPH, Sarah Blair McGuire. SARAH BLAIR McGUIRE / Oct. 4, 1855 - Aug. 18, 1919 / wife of REV. CHARLES C. RANDOLPH / daughter of REV. WILLIAM and / MARIETTE ALEXANDER McGUIRE / *They shall see his face and his / name shall be in their foreheads.* / REV. CHARLES C. RANDOLPH / C.S.A. / April 18, 1846 - May 14, 1925 / son of Capt. CHARLES C. RANDOLPH / and MARY ANNE MORTIMER / *He that dwelleth in love dwelleth / in God and God in him.* (B:186)

RANNELLS, Grace E. Beloved NaMaw / GRACE E. RANNELLS / 1900-1987. (2)

RAY, Annie Harmon. ANNIE HARMON / wife of / Capt. P.H. RAY / U.S.A. / born / Jan. 31, 1848 / died Jan. 19, 1888. (42:80)

RAYNOR / Emma / 1886-1940. (14:16)

REARDON, John T. Sacred / to the memory of / JOHN T. REARDON / who departed this life / October the 1, 1843 / aged 39 years. (43:96)

REARDON, John Underwood. JOHN UNDERWOOD REARDON / September 1, 1937 [BR:3 SEP:C] / EDITH KIRK REARDON / November 30, 1951. (18:3)

REARDON, Lucy V. / 1900-1979. (17:19)

REARDON, Nora Underwood. NORA UNDERWOOD REARDON / wife of / WILLIAM M. REARDON / August 2, 1870 / April 2, 1955. [second stone] (17:19)

REARDON, William M. WILLIAM M. REARDON / born Nov. 20, 1838 / died Dec. 18, 1919 / NORA UNDERWOOD / REARDON / born Aug. 2, 1870 / died April 2, 1955. (17:19)

REARDON, William M. / November 20, 1838 / December 18, 1919. [second stone] (17:19)

REARDON, William M. WILLIAM M. REARDON, JR. / 1872-1911 [AG:30/12/11:4, gives date 29 MAR 1911] / LULIE C[layborne Cox]. REARDON / 1875-1944 [BR:2 DEC:W] / CATHERINE C. REARDON / 1906-1944 [BR:6 MAR:W]. (16:3)

REECE, Irene E. REECE / Mother / IRENE E. / 1892-1944 [BR:18 AUG:C]. (16:13)

REECE, John Calvin. JOHN CALVIN REECE / 1924-1988 [BR:8 APR:E, cremation] / his wife / MARY HAFERKAMP REECE / [blank] / their daughter / ELIZABETH ANNE REECE / [blank]. (16:13)

REECE, John Carl. JOHN CARL / son of / JOHN & MARY REECE / 1956-1971 [BR:2 NOV:E]. (16:13:4)

REECE, Thomas Holland. REECE / Father / THOMAS HOLLAND / 1889-1969. (16:13)

REED, Francis A. FRANCIS AVERY REED / born at Acton, Mass. July 2, 1834 / died at Alexa., Va., Aug. 23, 1895 / Past Grand Commander Knights Templar Virginia / *No further seen his merits to disclose / or part his frailties from their dread abode / There*

First Presbyterian Church Cemetery (1809)

they alike in trembling, hope repose / The bosom of his father and his God / Past Master Andrew Jackson Lodge No. 120 A.F. & A.M. / Grand Senior Warden Grand Lodge of Virginia / Past High Priest Mount Vernon Royal Arch Chapter No. 14. (B:172)

REED, Harrah Leonard. HARRAH LEONARD REED / 1881-1915. (16:7)

REED, Helen Vernon / died June 4, 1962 [BR:6 JUN:E]. (16:7)

REED, Marinda E. MARINDA E. / beloved wife of / FRANCIS A. REED / died July 29, 1898. (B:172)

REESE, Arthur Lady. ARTHUR LADY / son of / ROBERT M. & / REBECCA R. / REESE / born and died / July 19, 1902. (B:212)

REESE, Rebecca Ramsay. REBECCA RAMSAY REESE / wife of / ROBERT MILLER REESE / April 22, 1870 / July 19, 1955 [BR:21 JUL:W]. (B:212)

REESE, Robert Miller. ROBERT MILLER REESE / son of / HENRY & MARY ANNA REESE / Baltimore, Maryland / Feb. 11, 1862 / July 28, 1949. (B:212)

REYNOLDS, Elizabeth B. In / memory of / ELIZABETH B. / the beloved wife of / JOEL C. REYNOLDS / who died Feby. 19th 1842, aged 38 years / also CHARLES W. REYNOLDS / their son / aged 5 months. (41:26)

REYNOLDS, Grace A. Harvey. In memory of / GRACE A. HARVEY / beloved wife of / WILLIAM C. REYNOLDS / who died August 16, 1864 / aged 47 years. (41:26)

REYNOLDS, Oscar B. OSCAR B. / son of WM. C. & GRACE A. REYNOLDS / born April 1851 / died Oct. 1852. (41:26)

REYNOLDS, Sarah. SARAH, the wife of / WILLIAM REYNOLDS / departed this life / Novr. 15th 1811 / in the 37 year of her age. / In the same grave / lies 4 of her children. (41:26)

REYNOLDS, William. Sacred / to the memory of / WILLIAM REYNOLDS / who died / 22nd August 1830 / in the 74th year of his age / *With love & affection / his children reverence / the memory of their Father.* (41:26)

REYNOLDS, William C. In memory / of / WILLIAM C. REYNOLDS / who was born in Alexandria, / Va., July 25, 1805 and died / on the 24 September 1865 / in the 61 year of his age / *With humble resignation to Gods / will, and a blessed hope of a glo- / rious resignation, he could say / All the days of my appointed time / will I wait until my change came.* (41:26; Alexandria Wills, Bk. 3, p. 363, men. daughter Elizabeth as daughter of George Johnston)

RHODES, Fern W. In memory of / FERN W. RHODES / August 3, 1894 / October 22, 1976 [BR:25 OCT:E]. (3:20:2)

RHODES, George Floyd. In memory of / GEORGE FLOYD RHODES / February 27, 1892 / September 11, 1944. (13:11)

RHODES, Geraldine E. In memory of / GERALDINE E. RHODES / Feb. 15, 1918 / July 2, 1990 [BR:6 JUL:E]. (3:20)

RICHARDS, Jane. Sacred / to the memory of / JANE / consort of / Dr. JOHN RICHARDS / who departed this life / Aug. 30, 1840 / aged 72 years [AG:1/9/40:3]. (43:116)

RICHARDS, Dr. John. To the memory / of / JOHN RICHARDS / died July 23, 1843 / aged 76. (43:116; Alexandria Wills, Bk. 4, p. 352)

RICKETTS, David. Sacred / to the memory of / DAVID RICKETTS / for many years a greatly esteemed / member and ruling elder of the / First Presbyterian Church in this / town who departed this life / Novr. 1st 1831 / in the 66 year of his age / *Few men have lived with so little of / the worlds hate, few have died with / so much of its regards. / He was an*

First Presbyterian Church Cemetery (1809)

Israelite indeed in whom / was no guile. (41:6)
RICKETTS, Elizabeth. Sacred / to the memory of / Mrs. ELIZABETH / relict of the late / DAVID RICKETTS / of Alexandria, Va. / who departed this life / July 8, 1853 / in the 86 year / of her age. (41:6) [epitaph illegible, and stone is in poor condition]
RICKETTS, Mary Barr. Sacred / to the memory of / MARY RICKETTS wife of JOHN THOMAS RICKETTS / who departed this life / Sept. 29th A.D. 1820 in the 66th year of her age / *Mrs. Ricketts was long time a member of / the First Presbyterian Church in / this town, always consistent and / uniformly loved by all that knew / her. She lived in the full and blessed / hope of a glorious immortality / beyond the grave.* (41:6)
RIDDLE, Joseph H. Owner of section 41, lot 40. (no stone)
RILEY, Terrence. TERRENCE RILEY / born at / New Baltimore / on the Hudson, N.Y. / July 13, 1807 / died in Fairfax Co., Va. / April 21, 1880 / MARY ELIZABETH BIERS / daughter of / SARAH DENINGTON / & WM. R. BIERS / wife of / TERRENCE RILEY / Dec. 31, 1825 / Aug. 4, 1897. (43:103)
RIMPELEIN, Joseph. JOSEPH / Jan. 16, 1893 / April 8, 1963 [BR:11 APR:D] / ANNA / Sept. 26, 1896 / March 21, 1975. (1:28 & 27)
RIPPON, Goldie M. / 1886-1965 [BR:1 JAN:Pu]. (17:17)
RITTENOUR, Frederick H. / March 23, 1877 / Nov. 14, 1948. (16:2)
RITTENOUR, Grace Prout / wife of / AVERY A. RITTENOUR / 1877-1907 [AG:31/12/07:1, gives date 2 APR 1907]. (16:1)
RITTENOUR, Richard D. RICHARD D. RITTENOUR / 1880-1928. (16:1)
RITTENOUR, Russell W. RUSSELL W. RITTENOUR / Jan. 27, 1886 / Feb. 7, 1937 [BR:10 FEB:H]. (16:2)
ROBBINS, Marie A. [BR:23 JAN 1978:D]. (16:11, no stone)
ROBBINS, Robert Oscar. ROBERT O. ROBBINS / 1882-1964 [BR:3 FEB:E]. (26:16:4)
ROBERTS, Audrey L. AUDREY L. ROBERTS / 1904-1914 / *An angel band in heaven / incomplete / God took our darling to / fill the vacant seat.* (15:21)
ROBERTS, Averiett F. AVERIETT F. ROBERTS / 1874-1930. (17:11)
ROBERTS, Erven J. ERVEN J. ROBERTS / 1876-1928 / *Mizpah*. (15:21)
ROBERTS, George W. GEORGE W. ROBERTS / 1878-1922. (17:11)
ROBERTS, Harry Willard. [BR:31 MAY 1956:C]. (17:11, no stone)
ROBERTS, Joseph T. JOSEPH T. ROBERTS / 1844-1933 / SALLIE CLEVELAND / beloved wife of JOSEPH T. ROBERTS / 1852-1927. (17:11)
ROBERTS, Leslie. [BR:1 JUN 1973:C]. (17:11:2, no stone)
ROBERTS, Minnie B. MINNIE B. ROBERTS / 1881-1972 / *Mizpah*. (15:21E)
ROBERTS, Richard Light / Apr. 13, 1925 / Aug. 27, 1927. (42:80)
ROBERTSON, Mary A. Sanderson. MARY SANDERSON ROBERTSON / 1888-1968 [BR:29 NOV:D] / wife of / GEORGE WILLIAM ROBERTSON / 1882-1955 / *She lived her life so very fine / Because she loved our God Devine.* (1:13)
ROBEY, David E. DAVID E. ROBEY / 1873-1964 [BR:21 DEC:E] / MARIAN CLARK / son of / DAVID E. & ORENE / ROBEY / 1917-1928 / ORENE SIMPSON / wife of / DAVID E. ROBEY / 1878-1922. (18:5)
ROBEY, Earl S. EARL S. / Sept. 13, 1904 / Aug. 4, 1969 / ADA M. W. / July 26, 1902 / [blank]. (3:17)
ROBEY, Gary W. Baby Robey / GARY WINIFIELD / Feb. 12, 1949 / son of / BEVERLY and WILLARD / ROBEY. (1:15)

First Presbyterian Church Cemetery (1809)

ROBEY, Hazel V. HAZEL V. ROBEY / 1906-1985. (B:216)
ROBEY, Willard Allen, Jr. / May 20, 1925 / June 19, 1975. (1:16)
ROBEY, Willard A. / US Navy / 1925-1975 [second marker]. (1:15)
ROBINSON, Editha Roland / August 24, 1895 / July 12, 1980. (B:191)
ROBINSON, Frances Johnston Virginia. FRANCES JOHNSTON ROBINSON / D.A.R. marker [BR:13 JUN 1942:W]. (B:191)
ROBINSON, John R. ROBINSON / Father / JOHN R. / 1853-1919. (26:5)
ROBINSON, Mary M. ROBINSON / Mother / MARY M. / 1864-1935. (26:5)
ROBINSON, Susanna. Sacred / to the memory of / SUSANNA ROBINSON / consort of / JAMES ROBINSON / who departed this life / September 25, 1829 / aged 49 years. (42:68)
ROBINSON, Thomas W. THOMAS W. ROBINSON / son of / GEORGE H. & MARY PAYNE ROBINSON / 1857-1925 / his wife / FRANCES JOHNSTON ROBINSON [also D.A.R. marker] / daughter of / FRANCIS E. & ANNA BURKE JOHNSTON / 1861-1942. (B:191)
ROBINSON, Thomas Wilfred / May 20, 1896 / May 18, 1970 [BR:22 MAY:E]. (B:191)
ROBINSON, William Stanleigh. WM. STANLEIGH ROBINSON / 1883-1957 [BR:17 OCT:W] / beloved husband of / LOUISE IRWIN ROBINSON / 1882-1962 [BR:27 APR:E]. (16:4)
ROCKWELL, Ralph Thomas. RALPH THOMAS / son of / SELDEN W. & JESSIE M. / ROCKWELL / born Oct. 3, 1881 / died Jan. 11, 1902. (41:25)
RODGERS, George H. In memory of / GEORGE E. RODGERS / 1843-1910 / *Gone but not forgotten.* [AG:31/12/10:1, gives date 21 DEC 1910]. (B:216)
RODGERS, Joseph F. [BR:2 SEP 1937:C]. (24:11, no stone)
RODGERS, Joseph W. JOSEPH W. / Aug. 18, 1881 / Sept. 20, 1948 [BR:22 SEP:W] / LULA E. / June 7, 1884 / Dec. 26, 1962 [BR:29 DEC:C]. (B:216)
RODGERS, Susan J. In memory of / SUSAN J. / wife of / GEORGE H. RODGERS / 1855-1904 / *Rest sweet rest.* (B:216)
ROGERS, Matilda Agnew. MATILDA AGNEW / wife of / WALTER G. ROGERS / 1872-1948. (15:5)
ROGERS, Millie Anne. [BR:2 JAN 1938:C]. (24:11, no stone)
ROGERS, Park Agnew. PARK AGNEW / son of / W.G. & M.A. ROGERS / 1907-1909. (15:5)
ROGERS, Walter G. WALTER G. ROGERS / 1869-1935. (15:5)
ROLLINS, James Herrell. JAMES HERRELL / July 4, 1877 - March 31, 1956 / MARIE ADAM / Nov. 19, 1886 - Jan. 19, 1978 / JAMES HERRELL, JR. / Sept. 23, 1910 - June 20, 1921 / JOHN LEE / July 20, 1912 - June 20, 1921. (16:11)
ROSS, Armstead Johnson. ARMSTEAD JOHNSON / July 10, 1874 / May 31, 1947 / NANNIE CORDELIA / May 26, 1879 / Nov. 14, 1944. (16:20)
ROSS, George Andrew. GEORGE ANDREW / ROSS / born in Alexandria, Va. / Aug. 18, 1875 / died Lewiston, Me. / June 22, 1943. (42:74)
ROSS, John Gaston. JOHN GASTON ROSS / January 16, 1908 / March 5, 1916. (16:20)
ROUNSEVAL, Andrew. In / Memory of / ANDREW ROUNSAVEL / who departed this life / Octr. 12th 1826 / aged 65 years / He was a native of / New Jersey [AG:12/10/26:3]. (44:127; Alexandria Wills, Bk. 3, p. 258, men. wife Elizabeth)
ROUNSEVAL, Nathaniel. In / Memory of / NATHANIEL ROUNSAVEL / who departed this

First Presbyterian Church Cemetery (1809)

life / Jan. 31t 1826, / aged 40 years. (44:127)
ROURK, Norris J. NORRIS J. ROURK / born Aug. 11, 1870 / died Jan. 14, 1918 / MARY J. ROURK / born April 2, 1858 / died Feb. 23, 1939 [BR:24 FEB:C]. (17:7)
ROWDON, Jennifer Brooke. Our Little Flower / JENNIFER BROOKE / ROWDON / Oct. 31, 1979 - Mar. 2, 1980. (18:11)
ROWDON, Robert Eric. ROBERT ERIC / Jan. 2, 1950 / [blank] / SUZANNE MARIE / June 7, 1950 / [blank] / STACEY SUZANNE / April 21, 1977 - Nov. 23, 1977 [BR:26 NOV:E, cremation]/ *A ray of shunshine that brightened our lives.* (18:11)
ROWEN, Mary Evelyn. MARY EVELYN / Sept. 23, 1864 - Feb. 5, 1937 / wife of / THOMAS B. ROWEN / Nov. 19, 1862 - Aug. 20, 1953. D.A.R. Marker. (42:76E)
ROYSTER, William A. WILLIAM A. ROYSTER / July 18, 1892 - June 13, 1963 [BR:17 JUN:D] / EDNA M. [Baader] ROYSTER / July 4, 1894 - May 10, 1964 [BR:12 MAY:D]. (B:182)
RUDD, Harry Webster / Nov. 5, 1881 / Sept. 1, 1956 [BR:4 SEP:W]. (18:8)
RUMNEY, John B. JOHN B. RUMNEY / 1788-1854 / ELOUISA / his wife / 1798-1849. (43:86a, Celtic cross)
RUMNEY, Martha Bryan McKnight. MARTHA BRYAN / widow of / JOHN RUMNEY / and daughter of / JOHN and CATHARINE B. / McKNIGHT / born Alexandria, Va. / May 7, 1802 / died Boston, Mass. / Dec. 12, 1891. (41:20)
RUTHERFORD, Margaret W. / April 9, 1906 / Oct. 9, 1965 [BR:13 OCT:E]. (15:26)
RUTHERFORD, Norris. [BR:20 JUL 1991]. (15:26, no stone)
RUTHERFORD, Oscar T. OSCAR T. RUTHERFORD / March 25, 1900 / Jan. 21, 1951. (15:26)
RUTHERFORD, Sarah Mark. Sacred / to the memory of / SARAH MARK / daughter of _____ SARAH RUTHERFORD / who departed this life / 6th day of Decr. 1830 / aged 13 years, 1 month & 21 days. (42:51)

S

SACRES, David. DAVID SACRES / born / July 24, 1860 / died Oct. 4, 1933 / *At rest.* (15:12)
SACRES, Mary Eliza Mundy. MARY E. SACRES / Oct. 6, 1873 / July 20, 1942 [BR:21 JUL:H&I] / *At rest.* (15:12)
SANFORD, Elizabeth M. [no dates] (41:19)
SANFORD, Frances Ann. In / memory of / FRANCES ANN / daughter of / THOMAS and ESTHER / SANFORD / who departed this life / on the 28th October 1840 / in the 26th year of / her age. (41:19)
SANFORD, Thomas. THOMAS and ESTHER / SANFORD / our / father / and / mother. No dates. (41:19; FR:6, Thomas was an elder of the church, died at the age of 72 years, funeral held [13] JAN 1852; FR:6, Esther died at the age of 74 years, funeral held in JUN 1852; Alexandria Wills, Bk. 6, p. 122)
SANTMIRE, Eston E. ESTON E. SANTMIRE / Aug. 15, 1896 - April 14, 1974 [BR:17 APR:C] / JULIA L. SANTMIRE / July 27, 1901 - July 12, 1959 / *What we keep in memory is / ours unchanged forever.* [BR:14 JUL:C, gives Julia Margaret Santmire]. (17:25E)
SAUNDERS, Dr. Addison H. ADDISON H. SAUNDERS, M.D. / died April 13th A.D. 1857,

First Presbyterian Church Cemetery (1809)

aged 46 years. (44:167)
SAUNDERS, Ellen Moore. Sacred / to the memory of / ELLEN wife of / Dr. A.H. SAUNDERS and daughter / of THOMAS A. MOORE who was / born 13th of August 1813 and / died November 21st 1855 in / the 42nd year of her age. (44:167)
SAUNDERS, Jacquelyn F.D.V. JACQUELYN / FAIRFAX DAVIS VINCENT / SAUNDERS / 1922-1983 [BR:5 MAY:Ba, cremation]. (25:8)
SAUNDERS, James Berkeley. Our dear brother / JAMES BERKELEY / son of the late Dr. A.H. & / ELLEN M. SAUNDERS / died June 19, 1882 / It is the Lords mercy that / we are not consumed because / His compassion faileth not / Gentle, kind and loving / he sleeps well. / C.S.A. (44:167)
SCHAFER, Abbie Isabella. ABBIE ISABELLA / daughter of / WILLIAM L. & EFFIE L. / SCHAFER / born Sept. 16, 1896 / died Oct. 19, 1910 / *Peaceful sleep.* (B:171)
SCHAFER, Effie Lee. SCHAFER / EFFIE LEE / 1872-1946 / WILLIAM L[ewis]., SR. / 1870-1959 [BR:29 JUN:W]. (B:171)
SCHLEIF, John H. SCHLEIF / JOHN H. / 1897-1988 / ESTELLE / 1891-1969. (3:6)
SCHON, Jean J. JEAN J. SCHON / 16 Feb. 1912 / 25 Dec. 1977. (4:8)
SCHREINER, Charles. My husband / CHARLES SCHREINER / born Aug. 23, 1862 / died April 10, 1905 / *At rest.* (14:2)
SCHREINER, Marian E. MARIAN E. SCHREINER / 1894-1933. (14:2)
SCOTT, Delia. DELIA SCOTT / died July 3, 1917. (B:204)
SCOTT, Jane. In memory of / JANE SCOTT / died August 17, 186[6] / in the 75th year of her age. (44:129)
SCOTT, Mrs. Margaret Ann. American War Mothers marker. [BR:15 FEB 1952:C]. (43:126)
SCOTT, Norvell Otey. NORVELL / OTEY / SCOTT / Capt. / U.S. Army / World War I & II / 1899-1977. (42:61)
SCRIVENER, James Raymond. JAMES RAYMOND / June 6, 1888 / Sept. 23, 1946 / ADDIE LINDSEY / Jan. 7, 1889 / Nov. 3, 1972. (17:25)
SEAMAN, Bleecker Provoost. BLEECKER PROVOOST SEAMAN / July 17, 1896 - May 10, 1970 / New York, N.Y. / FLORENCE CANN SEAMAN / April 7, 1897 - July 12, 1983 [BR:15 JUL, cremation] / Savannah, Ga. (16:26W)
SEAMAN, Lieut. Bleecker Provoost, Jr., U.S.N. / Born Savannah, Georgia, June 9, 1919 / died February 16, 1945 over Japan / Flight leader, U.S. Navy Fighter Pilot / *He stands in the unbroken line of patriots who have dared to die / in a way that humbles the undertakings of most men. / He is a portion of the loveliness which once he made more lovely.* [BR:20 OCT 1962, urn containing ashes interred under stone.] (16:26W)
SHANNON, Rosa. [BR:13 JUN 1957:C]. (14:6, no stone)
SHATTUCK, Alice DeK. ALICE DeK. SHATTUCK / died March 20, 1907. (43:109)
SHATTUCK, Lucious Holman. LUCIOUS H. SHATTUCK / died June 12, 1877. (43:109)
SHEARS, Rev. G. Charles. REV. G. CHARLES SHEARS / 1886-1928 / his wife / MARIAN A. LINDSEY / 1886-1958 [BR:15 APR:W] / WALLACE ROBBINS LINDSEY / September 12, 1922 / October 16, 1985 / MARY LINDSEY / April 13, 1881 / March 3, 1963 / NOBLE LINDSEY / born / August 24, 1848; / died / December 25, 1900, / his wife / CATHERINE / 1853-1926. (13:5)
SHEPARD, Charlotte B. Cazenove. Sacred to the memory of / CHARLOTTE B. SHEPARD / consort of WILLIAM BIDDLE SHEPARD / of North Carolina / and daughter of / ANTONY CHARLES CAZENOVE / of Alexandria, District of Columbia / the deceased

First Presbyterian Church Cemetery (1809)

/ departed this life / after a long and painful illness / on Wednesday the 23d day of / March A.D. 1836 / in the 24th year of her age. / *I heard a voice from / heaven, saying unto me, Write, / Blessed are the dead which / die in the Lord from hence- / forth; yea, saith the spirit, / that they may rest from their / labours and their works do follow them.* (43:104)

SHERWOOD, Joseph T. Husband / in memory of / JOSEPH T. SHERWOOD / born / Feb. 8, 1826 / died / July 2, 1906. (B:213)

SHILLIBAR, John. In memory / of / JOHN SHILLABAR / and ELIZABETH / his wife / who departed / this life, the former in / 1839, the latter in 1852 [AG:29/5/1839:3, gives death of Jonathan Shillabar on 28 MAY 1839]. (42:61)

SIDES, William H. Farewell / in memory of / my husband / WILLIAM H. SIDES / who was killed at Round Hill / December 25, 1874 / aged 23 years. (44:154, epitaph illegible)

SIMPSON, Carlin Lee. CARLIN LEE / Oct. 2, 1869 - July 3, 1941 [BR:7 JUL:W] / MAUDE MAY / Mar. 11, 1885 - Nov. 9, 1922. (18:6)

SIMPSON, George Lawrence. GEORGE LAWRENCE SIMPSON / 1843-1907 [AG:31/12/07:1, gives date 20 APR 1907] / his wife VIRGINIA ROBBINS SIMPSON / 1861-1944 [BR:21 MAR:W] / GEORGE ROBBINS SIMPSON / 1882-1934 / FRENCH C. SIMPSON, U.S.A. / 1887-1940. (25:2)

SIMPSON, John W. / Nov. 25, 1907 / Oct. 26, 1990 [BR:30 OCT:E]. (18:8:3)

SIMPSON, Margaret E. / July 16, 1910 / April 17, 1977 [BR:21 APR:E]. (18:8:4)

SIMPSON, Sarah E.R. SARAH E.R. SIMPSON / died / July 25, 1910 / *We shall sleep, but not forever.* (25:2)

SINCLAIR, John L. JOHN L. / 1861-1931 / ANNIE M. / 1861-1951 [BR:11 NOV:R] / HUGH H. / 1895-1951 [BR:16 NOV:R] / WILLIAM H., JR. / 1926-1926 / ALICE G. / 1890-1963 [BR:3 AUG:Ma] / CHARLES C. / 1889-1978. (19:17)

SIPPLE, Charles Oliver. CHARLES OLIVER SIPPLE / Sept. 24, 1837 / June 16, 1924 / C.S.A. (16:15)

SIPPLE, Mary L. / wife of / C.O. SIPPLE / 1849-1910 [AG:31/12/10:1, gives date 4 JUL 1910]. (16:15)

SIPPLE, Samuel S. Sacred / to the memory of / SAMUEL S. SIPPLE / who departed this life / August 7th 1845 / aged 45 years. (42:64, epitaph illegible)

SKIDMORE, John W. JOHN W. SKIDMORE / 1818-1865 / MARIA [L.] SKIDMORE / 1820-1893 [AG:30/12/93:2, gives date 6 SEP 1893] / JESSE SKIDMORE / 1790-1854 / his wife / SARAH BOYD / 1789-1865 / ANDREW F. SKIDMORE / Co. E. 17th Va. / C.S.A. / Killed at Yorktown / 1826-1862 / EMILY G. SKIDMORE / 1826-1911 [AG:30/12/11:4, gives date 3 AUG 1911]. (13:3)

SLATTERY, Grace. [BR:18 JAN 1968:C]. (1:10, no stone)

SLAYMAKER, Infant son. [BR:19 MAR:1937:W]. (44:160, no stone)

SLAYMAKER, Amos B. AMOS B. SLAYMAKER / born in / Lancaster Co., Pa. / June 20, 1835 / died in / Alexandria, Va. / October 30, 1894 / He was a resident of / Virginia 43 years. (44:160)

SLAYMAKER, A.H. In memory / of / A.H. SLAYMAKER / born / June 19, 1822 / died Dec. 3, 1889 [AG:31/12/89:2]. (44:139)

SLAYMAKER, Archie Clark. [BR:9 MAR 1939:W]. (44:160, no stone)

SLAYMAKER, Edmund H. EDMUND H. / son of A.H. & F.M. / SLAYMAKER / died July 3d, 1854 / aged 16 months. (44:139)

First Presbyterian Church Cemetery (1809)

SLAYMAKER, Edmund Witmer. EDMUND WITMER / son of / AMOS B. & ELIZABETH J. / SLAYMAKER / born / June 4, 1863 / died / Dec. 11, 1897.
SLAYMAKER, Elizabeth Faith. ELIZABETH FAITH / daughter of / ALEX. E. & MARY E. / SLAYMAKER / died June 14, 1919 / aged 37 years. (44:165)
SLAYMAKER, Faithful Mary. In memory / of / FAITHFUL MARY / wife of A.H. SLAYMAKER / died July 30, 1865 / aged 36 years. (44:139)
SLAYMAKER, Faithful Mary. FAITHFUL MARY / daughter of A.H. & F.M. SLAYMAKER / died July 26, 1858 / aged 14 months. (44:139)
SLAYMAKER, George Witmer. GEORGE WITMER / son of A.H. & F.M. / SLAYMAKER / died Sept. 7, 1865 / aged 7 mos. & 13 / days. (44:139)
SLAYMAKER, [S.] Hannah. In memory / of HANNAH / wife of A.H. SLAYMAKER / born / Feb. 10, 1831 / died / April 13, 1889. (44:165)
SLAYMAKER, Mary E. In memory / of / MARY E. / wife of / A.E. SLAYMAKER / died April 20, 1884 / aged 26 years / also JAS. GRAHAM / aged 8 mos. / A[lexander]. E. SLAYMAKER / died April 20, 1936 / aged 79 years. (44:165)
SLAYMAKER, Mary E. [BR:23 JUL 1964:E]. (44:160, no stone)
SLAYMAKER, Sarah Florence. SARAH FLORENCE / beloved wife of / AMOS B. SLAYMAKER / born August 27, 1846 / died January 25, 1918 / *Blessed are the dead that / die in the Lord.* (44:160)
SLAYMAKER, Willie. WILLIE / son of A.H. & F.M. / SLAYMAKER / died Sept. 17, 1863 / aged 4 years, 1 / month & 13 days. (44:139)
SMALLING, Walter Raymond / June 3, 1920 / May 15, 1977 / *He who binds to himself a joy / does the winged life destroy: / But who kisses the joy as it flies / lives in eternity's sunrise.* [second stone] WALTER R. SMALLING / U.S. Army / World War II / 1920-1977. (44:138)
SMITH, Ann. ANN, the wife of ROBT. SMITH / departed this life August 12th / 1806, in the 24th year of her age / also their son GEORGE died July / 14, 1808, aged 4 years, 6 m. and 9d. (41:12)
SMITH, Augustine Jaquelin. AUGUSTINE JAQUELIN / 1828-[Sept.] 1903 / ELIZABETH BEDINGER SMITH / 1829-1902 [AG:31/12/02:1, gives date 20 MAY 1902] / *Because I live ye shall live also.* / HOBBS / ELON ST. CLAIR HOBBS, JR. / born November 15, 1903 / died September 29, 1946 / ELON ST. CLAIR HOBBS / born August 24, 1863 / died November 10, 1948 / ANNA MORGAN HOBBS / born September 27, 1873 / died June 30, 1972 / EVELYN JACQUELINE / HOBBS / born September 27, 1905 / died March 25, 1983 / ELIZABETH ST. CLAIR / HOBBS / born September 21, 1900 / died January 26, 1991 / AUGUSTA LOUISA SMITH / daughter of / AUGUSTINE JAQUELIN / and ELIZABETH BEDINGER / SMITH / born November 26, 1866 / died November 29, 1934 / CHARLES MAGILL SMITH / son of / AUGUSTINE JAQUELIN / and ELIZABETH BEDINGER / SMITH / born in Winchester, Va. / November 25, 1873 / died in Alexandria, Va. / August 29, 1900. (25:25)
SMITH, Charles G. CHARLES G. SMITH / 1826-1904 / his wife / HELEN / 1843-1906. (15:1)
SMITH, Charlotte E. Rossiter. CHARLOTTE E. ROSSITER / beloved wife of / COURTLAND H. SMITH / born Sep. 14, 1854 / died March 1, 1880. (42:44)
SMITH, Clifton Hewitt. C.S.A. / CLIFTON HEWITT SMITH / Captain / and A.A.G. / died Jan. 27, 1902. (43:86)

First Presbyterian Church Cemetery (1809)

SMITH, Clifton Hewitt. CLIFTON HEWITT SMITH / second son of / FRANCIS LEE and SARAH GOSNELL SMITH / born August 19, 1841 / died January 27, 1902 / *Because I live, ye shall live also.* / *Whose memory is precious to me.* (43:86, tablet)

SMITH, Courtland Hawkins. COURTLAND HAWKINS SMITH / beloved son of / FRANCIS L. and SARAH G. SMITH / August 29, 1850 / July 22, 1892 / *Gifted - Honored - Loved / and / mourned.* / *Entered Into Rest.* (42:44)

SMITH, Edwin Hiner / June 8, 1900 / Nov. 23, 1974 [BR:25 NOV:C]. (4:7/20)

SMITH, Eleanor Eltinge. ELEANOR ELTINGE SMITH / died / In the faith of Christ and in / the communion of His church / May 30, 1871 / *The life with Christ / Brief life is here our portion / Brief sorrow; short-lived care / The life that knows no ending / The tearless life is there.* (41:37)

SMITH, Eliza Williams. In Memory / of / ELIZA WILLIAMS, / Beloved daughter of / Rev. GEORGE A. and OPHELIA / SMITH / Born Sept. 28, 1829 / Died Jan. 26, 1909 / *Blessed are they that wash their / robes, that they may have Right / to the tree of life and may enter in / through the gates into the city.* (41:37)

SMITH, Elizabeth W. No dates. (41:30)

SMITH, Florence C. Windsor. FLORENCE C. WINDSOR / wife of ROBERT L. SMITH / 1873-1924. (18:14)

SMITH, Francis Lee. FRANCIS LEE SMITH / third son of FRANCIS LEE SMITH / and SARAH GOSNELL SMITH / born October 6, 1845 / died August 25, 1916 / soldier-lawyer-Patriot / Christian / *Numbered with thy saints / in Glory everlasting.* (42:44)

SMITH, Francis Lee. FRANCIS LEE SMITH / born Novr. 25, 1808 / died May 10, 1877 / *The memory of the just is Blessed.* / Erected / with / Love and Gratitude / by / his Wife / and Children / *An humble christian / a devoted husband, and / father, a zealous patriot / a faithful friend; the ardent / advocate of truth, justice / and mercy, the earnest / counsellor of peace, and / goodwill among men.* (42:44, obelisk)

SMITH, Francis Lee. FRANCIS LEE SMITH / beloved son of COURTLAND H. / & CHARLOTTE E.R. SMITH / born Sep. 24, 1876 / died July 7, 1877. (42:44)

SMITH, Rev. George A. In memory / of / Rev. GEORGE A. SMITH / aged 87 / *In Christ / looking for that blessed hope / and the glorious appearing / of the great God our Saviour / Jesus Christ.* No dates. [AG:31/12/89:2, gives date 28 JUN 1889]. (41:37)

SMITH, Hugh. No dates. (44:136)

SMITH, Hugh. No dates. (41:30)

SMITH, Hugh. *Blessed are the dead who die in the Lord.* / To the memory of / HUGH SMITH / born at Knutsford, Eng., May 23, 1769 / died at Alexandria, Oct. 22, 1856 / and / ELIZABETH WATSON SMITH, his wife / born at Omagh, Ireland / March 19, 1773 / died at Alexandria March 13, 1854 / and / JOHN WATSON SMITH, their son / born February 8, 1811 / died July 20, 1819. (41:30, obelisk; FR:6, gives John W. Smith died of dysentery at the age of 8 years and 5 months; Alexandria Wills, Bk. 7, p. 134, men. daughter Elizabeth P. Jamieson)

SMITH, Hugh Goodwin. In / memory of / HUGH GOODWIN / SMITH / died Aug. 6th 1821 / aged 7 months & / 14 days. (43:94)

SMITH, Isabella Keitley. ISABELLA KEITLEY / daughter of / Rev. GEORGE A. & OPHELIA / SMITH / 1839-1922. (41:37)

[SMITH], James Hawley / 1855-1933. (18:15)

SMITH, James Sanford. In memory / of / JAMES / SANFORD / SMITH / born April 1st,

First Presbyterian Church Cemetery (1809)

1838 / died August 9th / 1844. (44:136)
[SMITH], Jane Elizabeth / 1860-1957 [BR:31 JUL:G]. (18:15)
SMITH, LaRouche Jaquelin. C.S.A. / L. JAQUELIN SMITH / Lieut. Col. / of Artillery / Jos. E. Johnston's / Army / died Feb. 19, 1895. (43:86)
SMITH, LaRouche Jaquelin. L. JAQUELIN SMITH / eldest son of / FRANCIS LEE and SARAH GOSNELL SMITH / born October 2, 1837 / died February 19, 1895 / *Where I am, there shall also my servant be.* / *Our souls do have him in remembrance.* (43:86, tablet)
SMITH, Margaret Vowell. MARGARET VOWELL SMITH / eldest daughter of / FRANCIS LEE SMITH / and / SARAH GOSNELL VOWELL SMITH / born March 2, 1839 / died March 18, 1926. (42:44)
SMITH, Mary Ellen. MARY ELLEN / daughter of / ROBT. & SARY SMITH / was born Nov. 11 / 1809 / died July 16 / 1811. (41:12)
SMITH, Mary Jaqueline. MARY JAQUELINE SMITH / died Sept. 7, 1884 / daughter of FRANCIS L. / and SARAH G. SMITH / *Blessed are / the pure in heart / for they shall see God.* (42:44)
SMITH, Norma C. SMITH / NORMA C. / 1904-1981. (18:15)
SMITH, Ophelia A. In memory / of / OPHELIA A. SMITH / wife of / Rev. GEORGE A. SMITH / aged 79 / *Not dead but sleepeth.* / *Until the day break and / the shadows flee away* [AG:6/8/79:2, gives death 5 AUG 1879]. (41:37)
SMITH, Robert. In memory of / ROBERT SMITH / who departed this life / March 6th, 1815, aged / 30 years. (41:12)
SMITH, Robert L. ROBERT L. SMITH / 1866-1906 / CHARLIE E. SMITH / 1893-1914. (18:14)
SMITH, Sarah Gosnell Vowell. SARAH GOSNELL SMITH / daughter of / JOHN CRIPPS and MARY JAQUELIN VOWELL / and wife of FRANCIS LEE SMITH / born October 6, 1813 - Died March 16, 1902 / *Sanctified through the truth.* / *Pure in heart, wise in counsel / patient in tribulation - gentle, gracious and full of / charity - just and devoted in every relation of life - an humble follower of Christ - / she is not dead, but risen. / Jesus Thou Prince of Life. / Thy chosen cannot die; / Like Thee they conquer in the strife, / to reign with Thee on high.* (42:44)
SMITH, Sarah Keightley. SARAH KEIGHTLEY SMITH / died March 24, 1862 / *Whosoever liveth and believeth in me, shall / never die / Death is swallowed up in victory / Thanks be unto God who hath given us / victory through our Lord Jesus Christ.* (41:30, boxtomb; Alexandria Wills, Bk. 8, p. 191)
SMITH, Sary. SARY, wife of ROBT. SMITH / departed this life / Decr. 17th, 1812 / aged 25 years. (41:12)
SMITH, Thomas. THOMAS SMITH / born / May 27, 1791 / died Feb. 22, 1844 / ELIZA G. SMITH / in her 16th year / SARAH K. SMITH / in her 3d year. (43:94)
SMITH, William Apollos. WILLIAM / APOLLOS / Aug. 17, 1874 - Dec. 11, 1940 / his wife / KATHRYN FISHER / Dec. 28, 1872 - Feb. 26, 1940 [BR:28 FEB:W]. (25:1)
SMITHERS, William B. / 1853-1917 / his wife / SUSANNA E. SMITHERS / 1862-1945 / her neice / ANNIE L. LEWIS / 1867-1943 [BR:7 SEP:C]. (14:22)
SMOOT, Julia F. Dean. JULIA DEAN SMOOT / 1921-1983 [BR:16 DEC:C] / EDWARD M. DEAN / 1888-1962 / MARY I. / wife of / EDWARD M. DEAN / 1879-1941 / CHARLES A. DEAN / 1865-1954 / MARY E. / wife of / CHARLES A. DEAN / 1867-

First Presbyterian Church Cemetery (1809)

1917. (16:8 & 9)

SOLBACH, Bertie Sipple / Oct. 1, 1879 / Feb. 12, 1972 / U.D.C. (16:15)

SPENCER, James LeRoy. JAMES SPENCER. No dates [BR:15 MAY 1962:D]. (1:19)

SPITTLE, Lloyd. [BR:17 MAR 1941:C]. (15:18, no stone)

STEELE, Sarah Jane. To the memory of / two sweet babes / SARAH JANE / died 1827, aged 3 / years & 6 months / daughter of J.H. & J.A. STEELE / also / MARY CATHARINE / died April 8th 1849, aged 1 yr. 3 mos. & 7 / days. (41:17)

STEUART, Amelia R. AMELIA R. STEUART / died / May 11, 1868 / *Asleep in Jesus.* (42:60)

STEUART, Elias James Ramsay. In / memory of ELIAS JAMES / RAMSAY / son of JAS. M. & ELIZABETH / STEUART / who died 21st Sept. / 1821 / aged 15 mo. / & 22 days. (42:60)

STEUART, Eliza Catherine. In memory of ELIZA CATHERINE STEUART / daughter of JAMES M. / & ELIZABETH STEUART / died 14 AUG 1819, aged 1y 18d. (42:60)

STEUART, Elizabeth. Sacred / to the memory of / our mother [name not included] / who fell asleep in Jesus / November 26th 1854 / aged 59 years / sacred / to the memory of / JAMES M. STEUART / who departed this life May 4th 1849 / aged 67 years [AG:28/11/54:3]. (42:60)

STEUART, James Montgomery. JAMES M. STEUART / died October 7, 1880 / *Loved and mourned.* (42:60)

STEUART, James M. Sacred / to the memory of / JAMES M. STEUART / who departed this life May 1st 1819 / aged 67 years, in the full hope of a blissful / immortality. / *Blessed are the dead which die in the Lord. / Tis a long _____ beautiful rest / when all sorrow has passed from the _____ / And the...* (42:64)

STEUART, Lizzie / died / February 28, 1865 / *Blessed are the pure / in heart for they shall / see God.* (42:60)

STEUART, Mary. MARY STEUART / died / April 1, 1891 / *Precious in the sight of / the Lord is the death of / his saints.* (42:60)

STEUART, Sarah Ann. SARAH A. STEUART / died / April 24, 1900 / MARY EMMA BROWN / died / September 1, 1899. (42:60)

STEUART, Thomas. In / memory of / THOMAS / a twin son of / JAMES M. & ELIZABETH / STEUART / who departed this life 20th August 1829 / aged 1 year / *Mourn not for me, I am / with my Saviour and / my God.* (42:60)

STEUART, William. WILLIAM STEUART / died June 9, 1871 / *I know that my / Redeemer liveth.* (42:60)

STEWART, Elizabeth. Sacred / to the memory of / Our Mother [no name] / who fell asleep in Jesus / November 25th 1854, aged / 50 years. / *She walked with God / Thou art gone yet we are keeping / Treasured in our hearts thy name, / Walking, sleeping, smiling, weeping / Thou art with us still the same. / Yes, the bank at last a river / All our happy dreams are o'er / For until we meet in Heaven, / You and we can meet no more.* (42:64)

STEWART, Elizabeth Ward. In memory / of / ELIZABETH / widow of ROBT. STEWART / who died Nov. 12, 1863 / in the 80 year of her age / the deceased was the daughter of WM. and ALICE WARD / was born in Brunswick, Nova Scotia, April 6, 1784 and came to Va. with her parents when a child. (43:114)

STEWART, Elizabeth Ann. In memory of / ELIZABETH ANN STEWART / daughter of WM. and / SARAH ANN STEWART / who departed this life / April 21, 1816, aged / 4 years

First Presbyterian Church Cemetery (1809)

and 5 months / *Weep not for me my parents.* (42:64)
STEWART, Elizabeth Eleanor. *Of such is the / Kingdom of God.* / In memory of / ELIZABETH ELEANOR / daughter of JAS. M. & / ELIZABETH STEWART / who departed this life / 21st July 1816, aged / 18 mo. & 10 days. (42:60)
STEWART, John A. JOHN A. STEWART / died / March 14th 1837 / ELIZA D. STEWART / died / July 11, 1860 [AG:15/3/37:3; AG:12/7/60:3, gives date 11 JUL 1860 for ELIZA DUNLAP STEWART]. (41:23)
STEWART, John W., 1805-1885 [AG:31/12/85:2, gives date 6 NOV 1885] / MARGARET SANFORD / his wife / 1817-1887 / *Precious in the sight of the / Lord is the death of his / saints.* (B:210, obelisk)
STEWART, Mary Jane. MARY JANE STEWART / died Nov. 18, 1909. (41:23)
STEWART, Thomas Tretcher Montgomery. In memory of / THOMAS TRETCHER / MONTGOMERY STEWART / who departed this life / Sept. 14th 1822 / aged 9 yrs. 5 mo. & 24 days / *He was a good dutiful and / affectionate child. / Young children unto Jesus came / His blessing to entreat / and I may humbly do the same / Before his mercy seat. / For when their feeble hands were spread / And bent each Infant knee / Forbid them not the Saviour said / And so he says of me.* (42:60)
STEWART, William. In memory of / WILLIAM STEWART / who departed this life / July 12th 1824 / aged 57 years. (42:64)
STEWART, William Dunlap. WM. DUNLAP STEWART / Past Master of Alexa. / Washington Lodge / No. 22, A.F. & A.M. / 1825-1896 [AG:31/12/96:1, gives date 29 SEP 1896]. (41:23)
STOKES, Horace C. HORACE C. / May 19, 1876 / Oct. 5, 1905 / NETTIE H. / Oct. 9, 1874 / March 18, 1961 [BR:21 MAR:H]. (B:187)
STONE, Joseph Leslie. JOSEPH LESLIE / [blank] / his wife / JANE FRANCES DUNN / October 4, 1919 / April 4, 1984. (18:20)
STOUTENBURGH, Cornelia H. White. CORNELIA H. / wife of / ABRAM STOUTENBURGH / and daughter of / THOS. M. WHITE / died Sept. 12, 1888. / *Waiting the resurrection.* (43:112)
STOVER, Lyda A. LYDA A. STOVER / 1875-1923. (17:22)
STRATTON, Alexander K. ALEXANDER K. STRATTON / 1874-1948. (15:6)
STRATTON, Mary Agnew. MARY A. STRATTON / 1874-1961 [BR:27 OCT:A]. (15:6)
STRAUB, Anna D. [BR:13 JAN 1965:G]. (B:214, no stone)
STRAUB, Archie L. [BR:18 JAN 1965:G]. (B:214, no stone)
STRAWTHER, Cassius L. CASSIUS L. STRAWTHER / May 25, 1910 / April 15, 1984. (42:74:4)
STROMER, Bernard A. / (Stramer) / born May 29, 1913 / died June 27, 1986 [BR:1 JUL:E]. (4:21)
STUART, Charles Edward. CHARLES EDWARD STUART / born / May 18, 1850 / died / April 16, 1889 / ELIZABETH McCARTY / infant / daughter of / CHA'S. E. & RUTH Y. / STUART / MARY FRANCES / daughter of / RUTH Y. & the late / CHA'S. E. STUART / born Jan. 14, 1878 / died Sept. 25, 1889 / *Of such is the Kingdom of heaven.* (B:194, obelisk)
STUART, Charles Edward. CHARLES EDWARD STUART / August 29, 1881 / June 20, 1943. (B:194)
STUART, Dorothy Sanders. DOROTHY SANDERS STUART / July 13, 1890 / December 12,

First Presbyterian Church Cemetery (1809)

1980 / *Beloved by all.* (B:194)
STUART, Harriot E. HARRIOT E. STUART / 1823-1896. (B:189)
SULLIVAN, William L. SULLIVAN / WILLIAM L., SR. / May 26, 1901 / October 13, 1986 / MILDRED C. KELLER / March 18, 1899 / July 29, 1983. (3:3)
SWAIN, _____. _____ / son of GEORGE and / MARY SWAIN, died / July 30, 1830 aged / Aged [sic] 11 months. (42:55)
SWAIN, Atha K. ATHA / KATE / SWAIN / Virginia / 73 U.S.N.R.F. / World War I / June 13, 1858 / November 8, 1947. (B:172)
SWAIN, George. In memory of / GEORGE SWAIN / born August 27, 1792 / died March 12, 1871. (42:55)
SWAIN, George William. GEORGE WILLIAM / son of / B.H. and F.B. / SWAIN / born / Nov. 8, 1896 / died / Jan. 19, 1897. (B:172)
SWAIN, Lizzie. A tribute / to the memory of / LIZZIE / wife of / STEPHEN SWAIN / who fell asleep May 3d 1853 / in the 29th year of her age / *She shall rise again.* (44:152, footstone)
SWAIN, Mary Violett. In memory of / MARY VIOLETT / wife of / GEORGE SWAIN / born Sept. 22, 1800 / died July 22, 1869. (42:55)
[SWAIN?], Rose. Here lies / our little / Rose. (44:152)
SWAIN, Stephen. STEPHEN SWAIN / entered / into rest / Dec. 15, 1897 / in the 80th year / of his age. (44:152, footstone)
SWIFT, Mary Donaldson Harper. Here rests / all that was mortal of / MARY D. HARPER / relict of WM. R. SWIFT / who died April 30, 1870 / in the 83d year of / her age. (44:142; Alexandria Corporation Court Wills, Bk. 1, p. 2)

T

TALBOT, Thomas. Departed this life / April 9th, 1852 / THOMAS TALBOT / aged about 47 years. / He served in the Flori / da & Mexican wars. (44:155)
TALIAFERRO, Edmonia B. / 1825-1907 [AG:31/12/07:1, gives date 12 OCT 1907]. (25:23)
TALIAFERRO, Marian M. Marian M. / wife / JOHN C. TALIAFERRO / died Oct. 3, 1872. (B:197)
TALIAFERRO, William Hay. WILLIAM HAY / TALIAFERRO / Feb. 10, 1895 - Dec. 21, 1973 / his wife / LUCY E. GRAVES / July 25, 1895 - Dec. 22, 1984. (19:1)
TATSAPAUGH, Charles. In loving memory of our / brother / CHARLES / son of / _____ TATSAPAUGH / born Oct. 13, 18__ / died May 9, 1883. (42:68)
TATSAPAUGH, Susanna V. In loving memory of our / mother / SUSANNA V. / wife of / P. TATSAPAUGH / born June __, 1802 / died Dec. 8, 1883. (42:68)
TATSAPAUGH, William. WILLIAM TATSAPAUGH / son of / R.F. and S.V. TATSAPAUGH / born Feb. 14, 1864 / died Oct. 3, 1908. (B:204)
TAYLOR, _____. _____ TAYLOR / who departed this life / July 21, 1825 in the 60th year of his age. (44:128)
TAYLOR, Arabella H. [BR:8 MAR 1938:W]. (25:22, no stone)
TAYLOR, Henry I. HENRY I. / 1904-1991 [BR:22 FEB:G] / *In God's care.* / KATHRYN E. / 1904-1947. (16:5)
TAYLOR, Dr. Julian. In memory of / JULIAN TAYLOR / born in Alexandria, / Virginia / February 15, 1829 / died in the city / of Paris / December 16, 1852 / HARRIET C.

First Presbyterian Church Cemetery (1809)

TAYLOR / born / February 24, 1827 / died / May 15, 1893 / *She was as tender / As infancy and grace.* (41:22)
TAYLOR, Robert J. ROBERT I. TAYLOR / born February 1778 / died October 4, 1840 / aged 62 years 8 months / *Mark the perfect man / and behold the upright / for the end of that man / is peace.* (41:22, obelisk; Alexandria Wills, Bk. 4, p. 263B)
TAYLOR, Rosalie Allen. Sacred / to the memory of / ROSALIE ALLEN / infant daughter of / H. ALLEN & ANN E. TAYLOR / born July 9th 1846 / died August 10th 1847. (41:22)
TAYLOR, Susan C. In memory / of / SUSAN C. TAYLOR / died Jany. 11, 1884 / in the 68th year / of her age. (44:165)
TAYLOR, Vincent. Sacred / to the memory of / VINCENT TAYLOR / who departed this life / July 2[1], 1835 / in the 60th year of his age [AG:29/6/35:3, gives date 26 JUL 1835]. (44:128)
TAYLOR, William P. WILLIAM P. / son of / W.P. & L.I. TAYLOR / June 12, 1911 / July 28, 1911 / *Of such is the kingdom of Heaven.* (16:4)
TAYLOR, William P. / 1875-1917. (16:5)
TAYLOR, William R. WILLIAM R. TAYLOR / 1837-1912 [AG:31/12/12:1, gives date 13 MAR 1912] / his wife / ANNIE M. / 1842-1919. (16:5)
TEPPER, Shirley / married surname is / Dutch Protestant / July 13, 1914 / June 27, 1979 [BR:2 JUL:E]. (4:13)
THOMAS, Amadeo L. / born Dec. 17, 1862 / died Jan. 27, 1937. (43:112)
THOMAS, Anna P. / born / Jan. 28, 1862 / died / Mar. 28, 1941 [BR:31 MAR:G]. (43:112)
THOMAS, Edgar A., Jr. / Sept. 27, 1953 / April 8, 1977. (4:23)
THOMAS, George I. Father / GEO. I. THOMAS / born Dec. 16, 1807 / died Nov. 20, 1874. (43:111)
THOMAS, John J. JOHN J. THOMAS / U.S.N. / born Nov. 15, 1852 / died June 23, 1884. (43:90)
THOMAS, Maria A. Mother / MARIA A. THOMAS / born Oct. 2, 1811 / died Aug. 25, 1890. (43:111)
THOMAS, M. Armantine Landry. Mother / M. ARMANTINE LANDRY / wife of / J.W. / THOMAS / died Aug. 23, 1866. (43:112)
THOMAS, Marian Maverick. MARIAN MAVERICK / wife of / AMADEO L. THOMAS / died March 26, 1892. / *I shall be satisfied / when I awake with / thy likeness.* (43:112)
THOMAS, Mary Jemima. Sacred / to the memory of / MARY / daughter of GEORGE & MARIA THOMAS / who departed this life on Friday Morning, May 17, 1839 / aged 3 years 5 months & 4 days. [AG:21/5/39:3, gives date 18 MAY 1839]. (43:111)
THOMAS, Richard A. Carrington. RICHARD A. CARRINGTON / infant son of / GEORGE I. & MARY E. THOMAS / died June 28, 1869 / aged 6 mos. & 22 days. (43:111)
THOMAS, William Enocha. Father / WILLIAM ENOCHA THOMAS / May 14, 1876 - April 29, 1954 / *Forever with the Lord.* (42:74)
THOMAS, William P. WM. P. THOMAS / died / June 18, 1852 / in his 60th year / MARY ANN THOMAS / died / July 14, 1836 / in her 36th year / Erected by / their youngest son / WILLIAM H. THOMAS. (42:66)
THOMPSON, James. To the memory of / JAMES THOMPSON / who departed this life Augt. / 28th 1848 in the 38th year / of his age. / *I heard a voice from Heaven / saying unto me, write, from / henceforth blessed are the dead / which die in the Lord even so / saith*

First Presbyterian Church Cemetery (1809)

the spirit for they rest / from their labours. / Rev. 14.13. / Hear what the voice from heaven / declares / To those in Christ who die / Released from all their earthly / cares / They... (44:168)

THOMPSON, Samuel. SAMUEL / son of / JOHN & SABINA / THOMPSON / departed this life / June 27th 1824 / aged 8 months & 5 days / *Happy infant early blest, / Rest in peaceful slumbers rest / Early rescued from the cares / which increase with growing / years.* (44:129)

THOMSON, James Dempsey. JAMES DEMPSEY / 1874-1878 [AG:5/8/78:3, gives date 1 AUG 1878] / ANNA DEMPSEY / 1876-1878 / children of / A.H. & S.D. THOMSON. (44:136)

THOMSON, Anna Dempsey. ANNA D. / daughter of / A.H. & S. McK, / THOMSON / born Aug. 30, 1876 / died Aug. 27, 1878. (44:136)

THOMSON, James Dempsey. JAMES D. / son of A.H. & S. McK. / THOMSON / born Feb. 5, 1874 / died July 30, 1878. (44:136)

TOBY, Nancy. Sacred / to the memory / of / NANCY, wife of Wm. I. TOBEY / who died December 12th / 1821, aged 23 years / *A soul prepar'd needs no delays, / The summons comes the saint obeys, / Swift was her flight & short the road, / She clos'd her eyes and saw her God. / The flesh rests here till Jesus comes, / and claims the treasure from the tomb.* (41:2)

TOMLIN, Agnes. [BR:19 JUL 1978:D]. (16:22:8, no stone)

TOPPING, Judith M. Minish. JUDITH M. MINISH / wife of / WILLIAM R. TOPPING / Oct. 17, 1858 - Apr. 6, 1948 / *At rest.* (15:21)

TOPPING, Thomas H. / August 5, 1868 / August 31, 1948 / *At rest.* (15:21)

TOPPING, William R. Father / WILLIAM R. TOPPING / 1869-1914 [AG:31/12/14:1, gives date 1 JAN 1914] / *Eternal rest grant to him / O Lord / and let perpetual light / shine on him.* (15:21)

TOWNSEND, Dr. George H. GEORGE H. TOWNSEND / Feb. 4, 1869 - Jan. 9, 1965 / Past Master, Federal Lodge / No. 1, F.A.A.M. - 1909 / Commander / Washington Commandery No. 1, K.T., 1917 / Washington, D.C. [BR:9 JAN:D]. (1:42)

TOWNSEND, Ida F. [BR:11 JAN 1966:D, died 10 MAR 1958]. (1:41, no stone)

TRAVERS, Alonza H. ALONZA H. TRAVERS / born Nov. 24, 1848 / died May 17, 1915 / his wife / MARY A. TRAVERS / born March 16, 1849 / died Aug. 26, 1912. (17:14)

TRAVERS, Lucretia. In memory / of LUCRETIA / beloved wife of / JAMES A.M. TRAVERS / born Dec. 27, 1837 / died Sept. 27, 1888 / *As a wife devoted / As a mother affectionate / As a friend ever kind / and true.* (B:174, footstone "L.T.")

TRAVERS, Sallie. SALLIE TRAVERS / *Resurgam.* No dates. (17:14, tablet)

TRETCHER, Eleanor. Sacred / to the memory of / ELEANOR TRETCHER / *This is dutifully erected / by an affectionate daughter. This lady was a na / tive of England and / thrice crossed the line / with her husband. / She departed this life / three weeks before him / after a short illness on / the 24th September 1813 / age 51 years.* (42:60)

TRETCHER, Capt. Thomas. Sacred / to the memory of / Capt. THOMAS TRETCHER / *this is dutifully erected / by an affectionate dau / ghter. This gentleman / was a native of England / and accompanied the / celebrated Cook in / his last Voyage around the / World. He departed / this life after a lingering / complaint on the 15th of / October 1813, aged / 53 years.* (42:60)

TRIPLETT, Alberta Welborne Davidson. In memory of / ALBERTA WELBORNE

First Presbyterian Church Cemetery (1809)

DAVIDSON / wife of / WILLIAM WIRT TRIPLETT / 1876-1923. (44:145)
TRIPLETT, Elizabeth D. ELIZABETH D. TRIPLETT / died Feb. 6, 1880 / ELLEN M. TRIPLETT / died April 19, 1883. (26:17)
TRIPLETT, George W. GEORGE W. TRIPLETT / died Nov. 24, 1852 / JANE R. TRIPLETT / died Oct. 24, 1878. Another monument reads: GEORGE W. TRIPLETT / his wife / JANE RICHARDS DALE, / of "Round Hill," / Fairfax Co., Va. (26:17)
TRIPLETT, George William. GEORGE WILLIAM TRIPLETT / Aug. 10, 1845 - May 6, 1929. (26:17)
TRIPLETT, Richard C. RICHARD C. TRIPLETT / died Jan. 26, 1908. (26:17)
TROTTER, Bertram T. [BR:4 AUG 1979:E]. (4:16:7, no stone)
TRUCKENMILLER, Margaret E. Deike. MARGARET DEIKE / TRUCKENMILLER / 1895-1958 [BR:15 SEP, cremation]. (24:13)
TRUCKENMILLER, Kenneth Royal. [BR:1973:E]. (no stone, no location given)
TRUMBLE, Edward. EDWARD TRUMBLE / 1878-1916. (16:22)
TUBMAN, Julia Frances / 1838-1908 [AG:31/12/08:1, gives date 17 JAN 1908]. (25:2)
TURNER, Capt. Charles W. In memory of / CHARLES W. TURNER / who departed this life / in New Orleans / on the 4th of May 1845 / aged 37 years / *The memory of the just is blessed.* (41:27; Alexandria Wills, Bk. 4, p. 397, men. wife Jane Williams Turner)
TYLER, Esther M. [BR:2 JUN 1944]. (44:141, no stone)

U

UHLER, Alfred G. ALFRED G. UHLER / 1845-1919 / his wife / LUCY L. BROWN / 1858-1945 / LUCY B. UHLER / BRIGGS / 1896-1979 / MARGARET S. / 1890-1892 / KATHARINE / 1893-1895 / THERON RICE / 1898-1899 / JOHN ANDREW / 1901-1902 / Children of / A.G. & L.L. UHLER / WILLIAM M. UHLER / 1872-1924 / his wife / ELIZA G[arnett]. KEMPER / 1872-1941 [BR:4 JUL:W] / EDWARD K. UHLER / 1906-1983 / his wife / LUCILE A. BUNN / 1905-1971 [BR:3 DEC:Co] / S.H. VA. [Virginia] U. / McCLOSKEY / 1909-1990 [BR:28 JUN:E]. (13:4)
UNDERWOOD, Oliver. OLIVER UNDERWOOD / April 30, 1835 / February 29, 1924. (17:19)
UPTON, Julian E. / Nov. 13, 1901 / Aug. 19, 1967 [BR:22 AUG:D]. (3:3:1)
URIE, Arthur T. Sacred / to the memory of / ARTHUR T. URIE / who departed this life / September 6th 1831 / in the 32d year of his age. (43:98)
URIE, James. Erected / to the memory of / JAMES / son of / ARTHUR T. URIE / departed this life / September 27th 1838 / in the 13th year of his age. (43:98)

V

VAZQUEZ, Antonio. A Papa / ANTONIO VAZQUEZ / March 22, 1894 / August 24, 1975. (4:7)
VEITCH, Alexander. Owner of section 42, lot 48. (no stone)
VEITCH, Dr. Harrison R. Owner of section 43, lot 93. (no stone)
VERNON, Ernest David, 1873-1947 [BR:30 JUN:C, died 27 JUN]. (43:99)
VERNON, Robert Lee. [BR:12 JUL 1950, died 10 JUL]. (43:99, no stone)

First Presbyterian Church Cemetery (1809)

VIA, Louisa V. [BR:died 27 APR 1949:D]. ("One grave section," no stone)

VINCENT, Ellalee F.D. ELLALEE FAIRFAX DAVIS VINCENT / 1926-1959 [BR:19 JAN:C]. (25:6A, cross)

VINCENT, Frances Smith. FRANCES S. DAVIS / VINCENT / 1901-1955 [BR:29 SEP:C]. (25:9)

VINCENT, John Truxton / 1895-1956 [BR:11 DEC:C]. (25:6A, cross)

VIOLETT, Ann. Sacred / to the memory of / ANN VIOLETT / who died April 10, 1836 / aged 66 years. (41:27)

VIOLETTE, Elsie A. ELSIE VIOLETTE / 1962 [BR:12 FEB:C]. (18:19)

VIOLETTE, T. Hager / 1907-1929. (18:19)

VIOLETTE, Thomas / 1875-1931. (18:19)

VIOLETTE, William J. / 1905-1931. (18:19)

VIPPERMAN, Infant Son. [BR:2 JUL 1965:C]. (2:3, no stone)

VOWELL, Charlotte. In / memory of / CHARLOTTE / daughter of the late / Col. ARCHIBALD ORME / of Montgomery County, Md. / and wife of / THOMAS VOWELL / of this city / In early life she devoted herself to the ser / vice of her Redeemer and subsequently her / path was as the light shining more and more / unto the perfect day till on the 10th April 1840 / she sweetly fell asleep in Jesus / aged 72 years, 14 days / The adjoining grave (north) contains the / remains of her sister / ELIZA VOWELL / who died in the Lord on the / 1st day of January 1817. (42:61, tablet)

VOWELL, Elizabeth. To the memory / of / ELIZABETH / wife of / THOMAS VOWELL / born Oct. 14, 1801 / died Dec. 29, 1883. (42:61)

VOWELL, Eliza King. ELIZA KING / daughter of / JOHN D. and MARGARETTA / VOWELL / died on the 4 Nov. 1832 / in the 4 year of her age. (43:97)

VOWELL, John Cripps. [first stone] JOHN CRIPPS VOWELL / Born in London, England / Aug. 12, 1767 / Died in Alexandria, / Dec. 9, 1852. / Sacred / to the memory of / MARY JAQUELINE / beloved wife of / JOHN C. VOWELL / of Alexandria; and daughter / of AUGUSTINE J. SMITH of / Shooter's Hill, Middlesex County, / Va., born Febry. 12, 1773, died / Oct. 31, 1846, ripe in years. / and in the full assurance of / a blessed immortality / OUR MOTHER / Her record is on high / Job. 16 Chap. 19 Ver. / Calm on the bosom of thy God / Fair spirit rest thee now; / Ev'n while with us, thy footsteps tread, / His soul was on thy brow. (42:44, obelisk; Alexandria Wills, Bk. 6, p. 178)

VOWELL, John Cripps. [second stone]. Sacred / to the memory of / JOHN C. VOWELL / born in / London, England / Augt. 12th 1767 / died in Alexandria, Va. / Dec'r 9th 1852. / Those that be planted in the house of the / Lord shall flourish in the courts of our God. / Life's duty don as well is the day. / Light from its land the spirit flies; / while heaven and earth combine to say / How blest the righteous when he dies. (42:44, boxtomb)

VOWELL, Margaretta. MARGARETTA / daughter of / JOHN D. and MARGARETTA / VOWELL / died on the 2 Dec. 1832 / in the 6 year of her age. (43:97)

VOWELL, Mary Jaqueline. [second stone] Sacred / to the memory of / MARY JAQUELINE VOWELL / beloved wife of / JOHN C. VOWELL / and daughter of / AUGUSTINE SMITH of Shooter's Hill / born in / Middlesex Co., Va. / Feby. 12th 1773 / died in Alexandria, D.C. / Oct. 30th 1846 / The sun shall be no more thy light by / day; neither for brightness shall the moom give light unto thee; but the Lord / Shall be unto thee an everlasting light / and thy God thy glory. / Isaiah Chap. 60 V. 19. (42:44, boxtomb)

First Presbyterian Church Cemetery (1809)

VOWELL, Thomas. THOMAS VOWELL / born Oct. 24, 1769 / died October 15, 1845 / For forty-six years an Elder / in the Presbyterian Church / *Thy prayers and thine alms / are come up for a memorial / before God.* (42:61; Alexandria Wills, Bk. 4, p. 410, men. wife Elizabeth)

W

WALKER, Addie L. [BR:28 SEP 1938:W]. (15:3, no stone)
WALKER, Champe. CHAMPE / beloved son of / JAMES W. & OCTAVIA / WALKER / 1859-1903 / *A loving son and / devoted brother.* [AG:31/12/03:1, gives date 21 OCT 1903]. (15:3)
WALKER, Mary. Sacred / to the memory of / MARY, wife of / ROBERT WALKER, who departed / this life August 25th 1821 / aged 23 years. (42:65)
WALLACE, James Bruce / Captain / United States Navy / 1916-1989 [BR:APR:E]. (14:22W)
WALLACE, Kevin Gene. [BR:6 MAR 1967, died 3 MAR:C]. (2:14, no stone)
WALLACE, Robert Bruce. ROBERT BRUCE WALLACE / 1886-1924. (14:22)
WALLACE, Robert Bruce. ROBERT BRUCE WALLACE / 1946-1947. (14:22)
WALLER, Constance Gardner Cazenove. CONSTANCE GARDNER CAZENOVE / wife of ROBERT E. WALLER / October 10th 1855 / June 10th, 1885. (43:107, obelisk)
WARD, Alice. In / memory of / ALICE WARD / consort of the late / WILLIAM WARD / born Feb. 13th 1755 / died Dec. 30th 1844. (stone not found)
WARD, Charles E. In memory of / Father & Mother / CHARLES E. WARD / 1850-1921 / JANE E. WARD / 1852-1919. (44:159)
WARD, John W. JOHN W. / son of / CHARLES E. & JANE E. / WARD / born Oct. 30, 1879 / died July 13, 1890 / *Asleep in Jesus.* (44:159)
WARD, Samuel. Sacred / to the memory of / SAMUEL WARD / who departed this life / Sept. __, 1821 / ___ears. (42:71)
WARDEN, Philip L. / Nov. 3, 1912 - Dec. 30, 1890. (18:18:4)
WARDEN, Thomas E. To my husband / THOMAS E. WARDEN / born Sept. 27, 1857 / died Aug. 20, 1885. (B:205)
WARFIELD, Marshall Gordon. MARSHALL GORDON WARFIELD / Oct. 20, 1882 - Sept. 26, 1907 / ANDREW A. WARFIELD / 1850-1917 / JANE E. WARFIELD / 1851-1918 / ALLEN A. WARFIELD / 1876-1959. (14:7)
WARING, Francis. [BR:13 JUL 1940:D]. (13:10, no stone)
WASHINGTON, Edith Garland / Oct. 22, 1893 - Feb. 4, 1977. (14:10)
WASHINGTON, Juliette Brown / Sept. 23, 1891 - March 23, 1985 [BR:27 MAR:I]. (14:10:6)
WASHINGTON, Mason. Combined stone. MASON / 1838-1915 / LELIA DEW / 1858-1936 [BR:B, died 28 NOV / ROBERTA BAILEY / 1886-1922 / GEORGIA LEE / 1894-1928 / MASON DEW / 1888-1980 [BR:29 JUL:I] / EDITH GARLAND / 1893-1977 / JULIETTE BROWN / 1891-1985. (14:10)
WASHINGTON, Mason. [BR:1937]. (14:10, no stone)
WASHINGTON, Mason Dew / Jan. 30, 1888 - July 27, 1980. (14:10)
WATSON, Hadlai Frank. HADLAI FRANK / 1888-1973 [BR:29 DEC:C] / NELLIE DUNCAN / 1884-1962 [BR:10 DEC:C] / *Together / In my Father's house.* (14:12)
WATTLES, Alvin M. ALVIN M. WATTLES / Nov. 12, 1911. Second stone, different date. (16:16)

First Presbyterian Church Cemetery (1809)

WATTLES, Nannie G. NANNIE G. WATTLES / April 5, 1914. Second stone. (16:16)

WEIR, Ella F. [BR:25 DEC 1964:Harrison Funeral Home, St. Michaels MD]. (16:12, no stone)

WEIR, Paul. PAUL WEIR / 1879-1952 / LILLIAN HAMMILL WEIR / 1884-1935 / HAMMILL / WILLIAM R. HAMMILL, SR. / 1902-1969 / HELEN HANNA HAMMILL / 1908-1976 / WILLIAM RANDOLPH HAMMILL, JR. / 1936-1978 / CLIFFORD E. CAGLE / 1896-1951 / CAROLINE H. CAGLE / 1909-1972 / PAUL E. HAMMILL / 1876-1955 / DAISY V. HAMMILL / 1876-1965. (16:12)

WEISBAND, William W. WILLIAM W. WEISBAND / Virginia / 1st Lt. Signal Corps. / World War II / Aug. 28, 1908 - May 14, 1967 [BR:18 MAY:E]. (1:1I)

WELBORNE, David. My Father / DAVID WELBORNE / died June 9th, 1827 / aged 47 years. (44:145)

WELCH, John P., Jr. / 1916-1918. (15:16)

[de] WENDT-WRIEDT, Adolph J. Touners. A.J.T. WENDT-WRIEDT / 1874-1954 [BR:10 OCT:Richmond VA]. (1:3)

WENDT-WRIEDT, Lillie A. / 1900-1979. (1:2)

WENZEL, Infant. [BR:21 OCT 1967:C]. (2:12, no stone)

WEST, Dorothy V. DOROTHY V. / daughter of / GEO. C. & MABEL B. / WEST / born July 12, 1912 / died Aug. 10, 1917. (26:8)

WEST, Linwood M. / Sept. 23, 1908 / April 7, 1968 [BR:10 APR:C]. (3:10)

WEST, Martha McAden. [BR:15 NOV 1940:D]. (15:9, no stone)

WESTCOTT, John. In memory of / JOHN WESTCOTT / merchant of this place / who departed this life November / 25th 1813 in the 72nd year / of his age./ He was a native of Cumberland County, / New Jersey, was an officer in the New / Jersey line during the revolutionary / war, was an upright citizen, and / honest man / also in memory of / JAMES D. WESTCOTT who died August 5th / 1799, aged 19 months and SARAH / WESTCOTT who died April 25th 1800, aged / 2 days both interred in this place, chil / dren of JAMES D. WESTCOTT and ANNIE / his wife, of Cumberland County, New / Jersey. (42:58, tablet; D.A.R. marker)

WESTON, Edwin. [BR:28 AUG 1967:D, cremation]. (2:17, no stone)

WHALEY, Carl Orrison / died Nov. 29, 1933. (13:7)

WHALEY, Cecile M. [BR:26 SEP 1967:E]. (13:7, no stone)

WHITE, Edna Vada. EDNA VADA / daughter of / J.H. & E.H. / WHITE / June 29, 1927 / Nov. 4, 1929. (26:8)

WHITE, Elizabeth DeDier. Mother / ELIZABETH DeDIER WHITE / 1881-1945. (17:13)

WHITE, Neida. [BR:29 DEC 1973:W]. (17:13, no stone)

WHITE, Walter C. WALTER C. / son of / R.C. & MARY ANNE WHITE / died May 28, 1870 / aged 14 years & 4 months. (44:155)

WHITING, Edith Douglass. In / memory of / EDITH DOUGLASS WHITING / daughter of / MARGARET D. and FAIRFAX E. / WHITING / who died May 2d 1846 / aged 22 months & 5 days. (44:135)

WHITTON, Elizabeth Ann / October 8, 1981. (14:12)

WHITTON, George. Father / GEORGE WHITTON / Feb. 16, 1857 - March 13, 1921 / EDITH MARGARET / Sept. 3, 1899 - Dec. 12, 1959 [BR:15 DEC:C] / mother / MARGARET ELIZABETH / Sept. 27, 1867 - Sept. 26, 1943 / ALICE HALSALL / Feb. 19, 1894 - Nov. 5, 1983 [BR:8 NOV:E] / GEORGE WHITTON, JR. / Oct. 6,

First Presbyterian Church Cemetery (1809)

1895 - July 28, 1898 / FLORENCE SAUTER / April 6, 1898 - Dec. 11, 1905 / ELEANOR WHITTON DAVIS / March 14, 1908 - March 1, 1981 / JAMES HAYDEN DAVIS / May 27, 1906 - Jan. 2, 1982. (18:21)
WHITTON, Robert Goodacre / Jan. 31, 1906 / April 17, 1986. (14:12)
WILBAR, George Harrison. Sacred / to the / memory of / GEORGE HARRISON / son of / JOHN T.O. and SARAH / WILBAR / who died Octr. 5th 1831 / aged 3 years and 6 months. / *Farewell my beloved, / the almighty's comin' and / To the Angel of death has been given / then go my dear boy / to the saviours right hand / For of such is the kingdom of / heaven.* (41:15)
WILDT, Charles. CHARLES / son of / E.C. & H.M. WILDT / 1908-1924. (17:16)
WILDT, Edmond C. / 1878-1952 [BR:15 DEC:H]. (17:16)
WILDT, Henrietta M. / 1878-1968 [BR:22 JAN:H]. (17:16)
WILKINS, Helen Wood. HELEN WOOD WILKINS / born Feb. 15, 1883 / died Mar. 11, 1971 [BR:13 MAR:D]. (17:21)
WILKINSON, Bland Addison. Mother of / MARY JACQUELIN McCULLOUGH / BLAND ADDISON WILKINSON / *Lo, I am with you alway [sic], even / unto the end of the world.* / Oct. 10 / 1890 / June 28 / 1986. (25:5)
WILLIAMS, Bertha. BERTHA WILLIAMS / 1884-1952 [BR:22 MAY:W] / Devoted friend of / the families of / MORRIS HORNER / EDWARD R. ROWLEY / LLEWELLYN POWELL. (41:25)
WILLIAMS, Caroline C. Greenaway / 1876-1955. (18:16)
WILLIAMS, Dallas Charles. [BR:19 JUN 1978:C]. (2:16, no stone)
WILLIAMS, Fannie. FANNIE / wife of / ROBERT WILLIAMS / died Dec. 3, 1889 / aged 58 years / *At rest.* (B:205)
WILLIAMS, John Wesley. [BR:6 MAY 1964:E]. (1:8, no stone)
WILLIAMS, Robert A. ROBERT A. WILLIAMS / 1845-1892 / *Rest.* / MARY MAXFIELD / 1862-1935 / *Rest.* / E.F. MAXFIELD / 1871-1942 / MARGARET D. WILLIAMS / 1884-1911 [AG:30/12/11:4, gives date 16 MAR 1911] / *Faithful and true.* / ROBT. A. WILLIAMS / 1889-1891 / HARVEY WILLIAMS / 1891-1891 / HARVEY W. MAXFIELD / 1896-1912 / GEO. E. MAXFIELD / 1899-1912 / CHAS. F. BRENNER / 1881-1957 / FRANCIS A. BRENNER / 1914-1961 / KATIE W. HARDING / 1877-1970. (13:10)
WILLIAMSON, Ida Mary. IDA MARY / Oct. 5, 1885 / May 15, 1984 [BR:18 MAY:E] / WHITFIELD H. / Aug. 2, 1888 / Dec. 13, 1951. (16:21)
WILSON, Caroline A. / 1877-1934. (24:14)
WILSON, Deborah A. [BR:10 MAR 1966:E]. (Isle between 1 & 2, no stone)
WILSON, Harley P. / 1873-1934. (24:14)
WILSON, Margaret. This Marble is to / Perpetuate the memory / of MARGRET WILSON. / the Beloved wife of / ISAAC WILSON. / whose Spirit returned / to God who gave it, on the / 18th of Feb: A.D. 1827 aged / 39 Years and 11 months. / *she was the pride of Husbd. / children & intam'te friend / How unsertent is life; today / we are big with hope. To / morrow may close our eyes in death. / Happy are those that die in the / Lord ; for they shall wave a Crown / of Glory, forever more.* (41:9)
WILSON, Mary. Our Mother / MARY WILSON. No dates. (44:137)
WILSON, Mary E. In memory of / MARY E. / wife of / ROBERT I.T. WILSON / born March 3, 1808 / died June 28, 1864. (41:6)

First Presbyterian Church Cemetery (1809)

WILSON, Mary R. MARY R. WILSON / 1832-1910 / DAVID R. / 1830-1881 / children of MARY E. RICKETTS / ROBERT I.T. WILSON / FRANCES ALLEN / 1843-1934. (41:6)
WILSON, Robert I.T. In memory of / ROBERT I.T. WILSON / born June 8, 1804 / died Dec. 22, 1875. (41:6)
WINDSOR, James H. JAMES H. WINDSOR / 1831-1888 / HENRIETTA W. DAVIS / 1858-1884. (18:14)
WINDSOR, Julia. [BR:29 AUG 1963:C]. (15:23, no stone)
WINDSOR, Mary L. / 1836-1916. (18:14)
WINDSOR, Mary Adeline Smith / April 15, 1886 - Feb. 10, 1959. (18:15)
WINDSOR, Mary A. Newman. MARY A. NEWMAN / daughter of / R.W. & S. WINDSOR / born April 27, 1821 / died Nov. 27, 1890. (43:103)
WINDSOR, Richard W. RICHARD W. WINDSOR / born Nov. 15, 1788 / died March 22, 1850 [AG:25/3/50:3]/ BEHETHELDON / wife of R.W. WINDSOR / born Sept. 22, 1799 / died Dec. 25, 1833 [AG:2/1/34:3] / *Asleep in Jesus* / RICHARD W[arden]. WINDSOR / born Dec. 18[33] / died July 23, 1852 [AG:24/7/52:2] / EMELINE WINDSOR / died May 30, 1843 / THOMAS R. WINDSOR / ____ / KATE KULP / daughter of / R.W. WINDSOR / born June 6, 1832 / died May 3rd 1860 / WINDSOR KULP / born Oct. 28, 1856 / died Nov. 1, 1866 [AG:5/11/66:2] / AMANDA F. WINDSOR / born [Nov.] 1819 / died Feb. 27, 1881 / SUSANNAH WINDSOR / born Aug. 10, 1817 / died Sept. 23, 1832. (43:103)
WISE, George. GEORGE WISE / born / in Alexandria, Va. / Nov'r. 3, 1778 / died / April 3, 1856 / MARGARET / wife of / GEORGE WISE / born in Ireland / Oct. 31, 1793 / died Jan. 2, 1887 / CHARLES J. WISE / son of / GEORGE & MARGARET WISE / born July 24, 1830 / died May 9, 1898. (44:132; Alexandria Wills, Bk. 7, p. 69)
WISE, George K. In / memory of / GEORGE K. WISE / who departed this life / June 5th, 1819 / in the 44th year of his age. (41:2; FR:5, gives his age as 38 years)
WISE, George P. 1806-1867 / GEORGE P. WISE / and / 1807-1871 / SINAH A. / his wife / *Even so them also which / sleep in Jesus will God / bring with him.* / 1874-1918 / CAROLINE M. WISE / *Behold I am alive / for evermore.* / 1869-1887 / CLAUDE NEWTON WISE / son of / GEORGE and IDA V. / WISE / *And the dead in Christ / shall rise first.* / 1840-1923 / GEORGE WISE / 1847-1927 / IDA V. WISE. (13:2, obelisk)
WITBECK, Adelaide S. Reardon. In memory of / ADELAIDE S. / wife of JAMES H. WITBECK / and youngest daughter of JOHN T. / and E.P. REARDON / died June 19, 1869 / in the 32d year of her age. (43:96; headstone not legible, footstone "A.S.W.")
WITHERSPOON, Marvin E. MARVIN E. / 1915-1988 [BR:25 JAN:E] / MIRIAM R. / 1908-[blank]. (4:23)
WITMER, Edmund F. No dates. (two stones, 44:139)
WITMER, Elizabeth Anna. In memory of / ELIZABETH ANNA / wife of / G.K. WITMER / died at Liberty / Bedford Co., Va. / January 31st 1864 / aged 37 years. (44:139)
WITMER, Elizabeth F. ELIZABETH F. WITMER. No dates. [BR:5 OCT 1950:W]. (44:139)
WITMER, George K. GEORGE K. WITMER / born / August 10, 1822 / died / March 6, 1901. (44:139)
WITMER, Isabella F., no dates. (44:139)

First Presbyterian Church Cemetery (1809)

WITMER, Isabella Fleming, no dates. (44:139)
WOLF, James G. [BR:died 26 DEC 1966:C]. (14:1, no stone)
WOLFFORD, Edgar Bruce. EDGAR B. / WOLFFORD, SR. / Aug. 7, 1892 / Aug. 24, 1942 [BR:26 AUG:W]. (13:11)
WOLFFORD, Frank P. / July 4, 1889 / Sept. 28, 1934. (13:11)
WOLFFORD, Jean / Oct. 19, 1917 / Sept. 11, 1918. (13:11)
WOLFFORD, Jennie P. JENNIE P. / Dec. 29, 1868 / Oct. 20, 1952 / DAVID J. / Aug. 27, 1856 / Jan. 20, 1949 [BR:22 JAN 1949:W]. (13:11)
WOLFFORD, Vivian R. / July 6, 1896 / May 23, 1956 [BR:26 MAY:W]. (13:11)
WOLFORD, Anna. [BR:7 DEC 1939:W]. (13:11, no stone)
WOLFORD, Claude H. CLAUDE H. / July 4, 1896 - Mar. 8, 1987 [BR:11 MAR:W] / EVELYN W. / Aug. 3, 1900 - Feb. 2, 1990. (13:11)
WOOD, Arabella Foote. ARABELLA FOOTE WOOD / born / Feb. 8, 1837 / died / March 22, 1900 / *Blessed are the pure / in heart for they shall / see God.* (43:117)
WOOD, Clayton E., Jr. / (Doc) / April 14, 1928 / February 24, 1968 [BR:8 MAR:D]. (3:26)
WOOD, C.W. C.W. WOOD / 1853-1930 / his wife / MARY E. / 1865-1931 / their daughter / ESTELLE / 1889-1929 / ALLENSWORTH / GEORGE W. ALLENSWORTH / born Feb. 23, 1891 - died Jan. 21, 1923. (16:24)
WOOD, Edna D. WOOD / EDNA D. / Nov. 5, 1891 / Jan. 23, 1982 [BR:27 JAN:E] / M[assey]. RAYMOND / Jan. 7, 1894 / April 12, 1962 [BR:16 APR:C] / EVELYN S. / Nov. 22, 1914 / Feb. 19, 1922. (14:8)
WOOD, Ruth Louise. [BR:4 JUN 1940:C]. (43:126, no stone)
WOOD, William Douglas. WILLIAM DOUGLAS WOOD / 1850-1933 / SELINA TUBMAN WOOD / 1852-1920. (17:21)
WOOD, Willie A. WILLIE A. / daughter of / WM. D. & SELINA T. WOOD / born April 21, 1884 / died Sept. 11, 1895 / *Jesus, lover / of my soul.* (17:21)
WOODEN, Lucy / 1856-1929. (14:21)
WOODHOUSE, Anna Maria Saunders. To my wife / sacred / to the memory of / ANNIE M. / daughter of / Dr. ADDISON H. & E.M. SAUNDERS / & wife of WM. M. WOODHOUSE / born Jany. 1st 1836 / died Nov. 17th 1859 / aged 23 years, 10 months & / 17 days.
WOODY, Ruth. RUTH / beloved wife of / LAWRENCE W. WOODY / born / Sept. 8, 1875 / died Jan. 25, 1899. (B:213)
WOOLLS, William. In memory of / WILLIAM WOOLLS / born in Alexandria, Va. / March 20, 1790 / died in Alexandria, Va. / March 22, 1874 / Aged 84 years. (42:55)
WORSHAM, Ollie Virginia. OLLIE V. WORSHAM / Oct. 12, 1875 / Feb. 16, 1943. (42:53)
WRIGHT, Daniel. DANIEL WRIGHT / died June 20, 1829, aged 56 years. (42:79)
WRIGHT, Harriet Lownds. HARRIET LOWNDS / WRIGHT / died May 20, 1849 / aged 74 years. (42:79)
WRIGHT, James B. Father / JAMES B. WRIGHT / 1848-1919 / *Sweet Rest.* (17:10)
WRIGHT, Robert L. ROBERT L. WRIGHT / Dec. 27, 1884 - Nov. 13, 1950 / MAE R. WRIGHT / Feb. 19, 1883 - June 26, 1980 / *Loved in life, in death remembered.* (17:10)

First Presbyterian Church Cemetery (1809)

Y

YOCHUM, John C. [BR:15 MAY 1961:W]. (15:12, no stone)

YOUNG, Elizabeth Conrad. Sacred / to the memory of / ELIZABETH CONRAD YOUNG / relict of General ROBERT YOUNG / born 22 October 1777 / died 1 March 1840. (42:53)

YOUNG, John. Departed this life / May 24th 1813 / Mr. JNo. YOUNG / aged 38 years. (41:18)

YOUNG, Robert. Sacred / to the memory of / Gen'l ROBERT YOUNG / born 27 December 1768 / died 27 October 1824 / *Frank, upright and generous, liberal / in prosperity; patient in adversity and / sickness; a tender husband and parent / a faithful friend and accomplished / Gentleman and a sincere Christian.* (42:53, obelisk)

First Presbyterian Church Cemetery (1809)

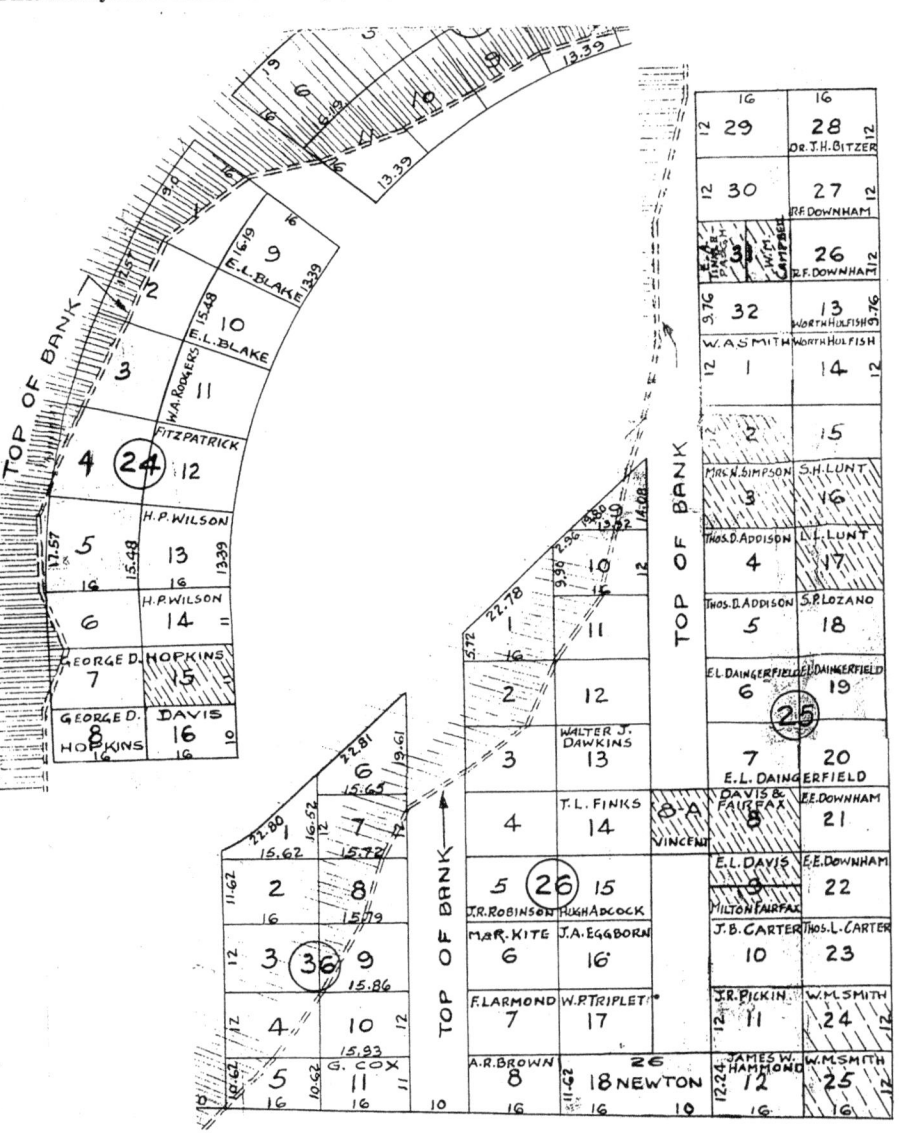

Plans

First Presbyterian Church Cemetery (1809)

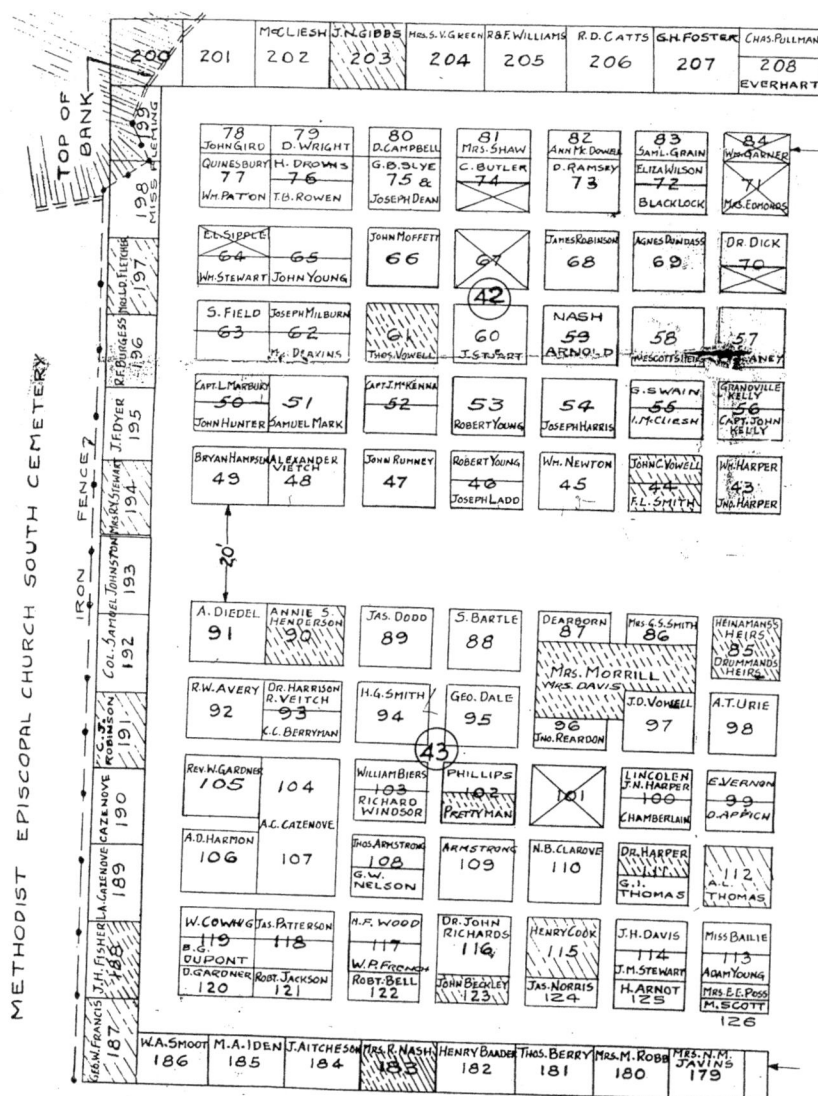

First Presbyterian Church Cemetery (1809)

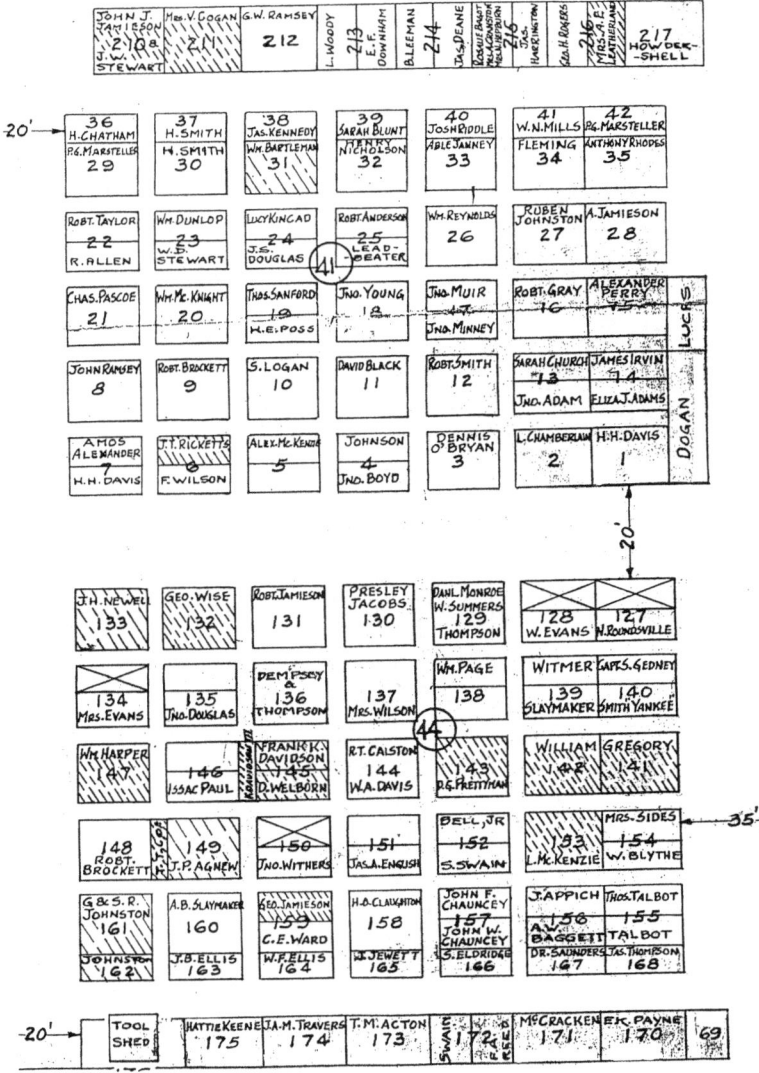

First Presbyterian Church Cemetery (1809)

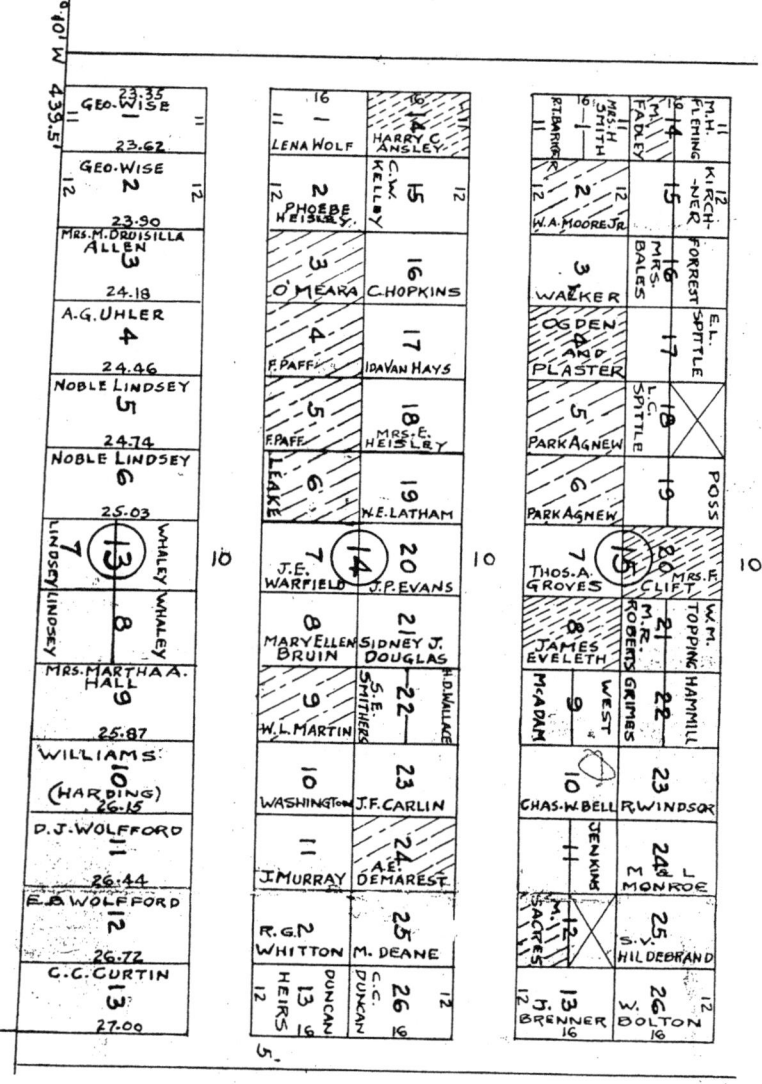

First Presbyterian Church Cemetery (1809)

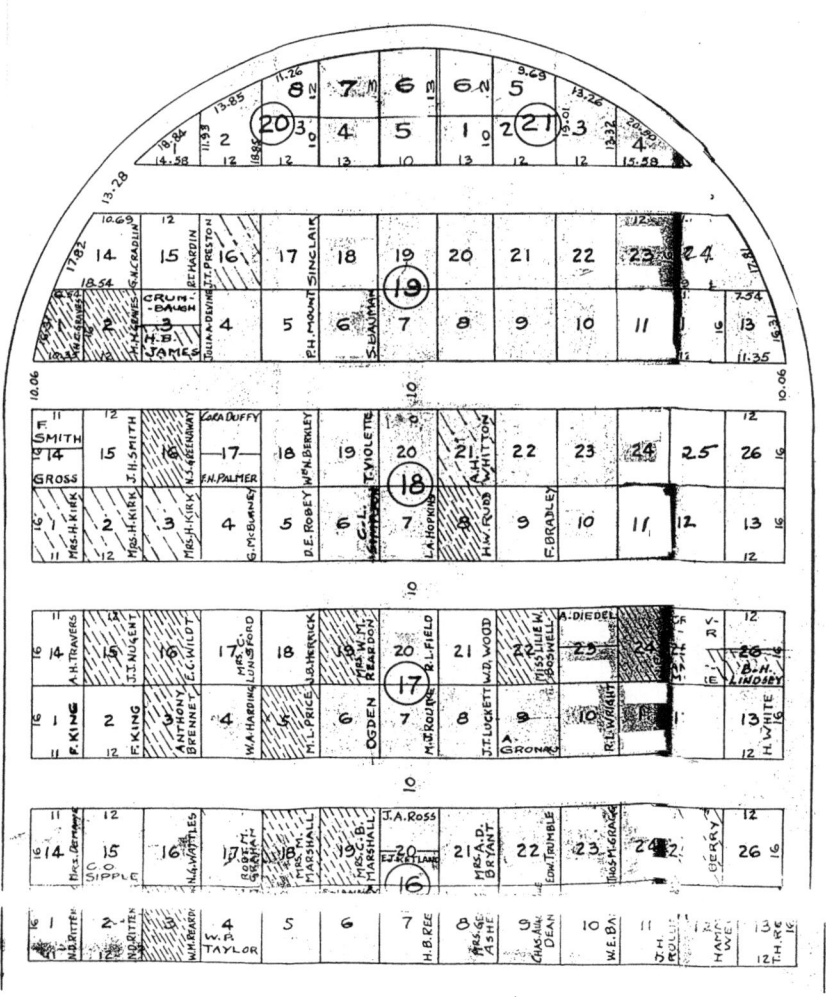

First Presbyterian Church Cemetery (1809)

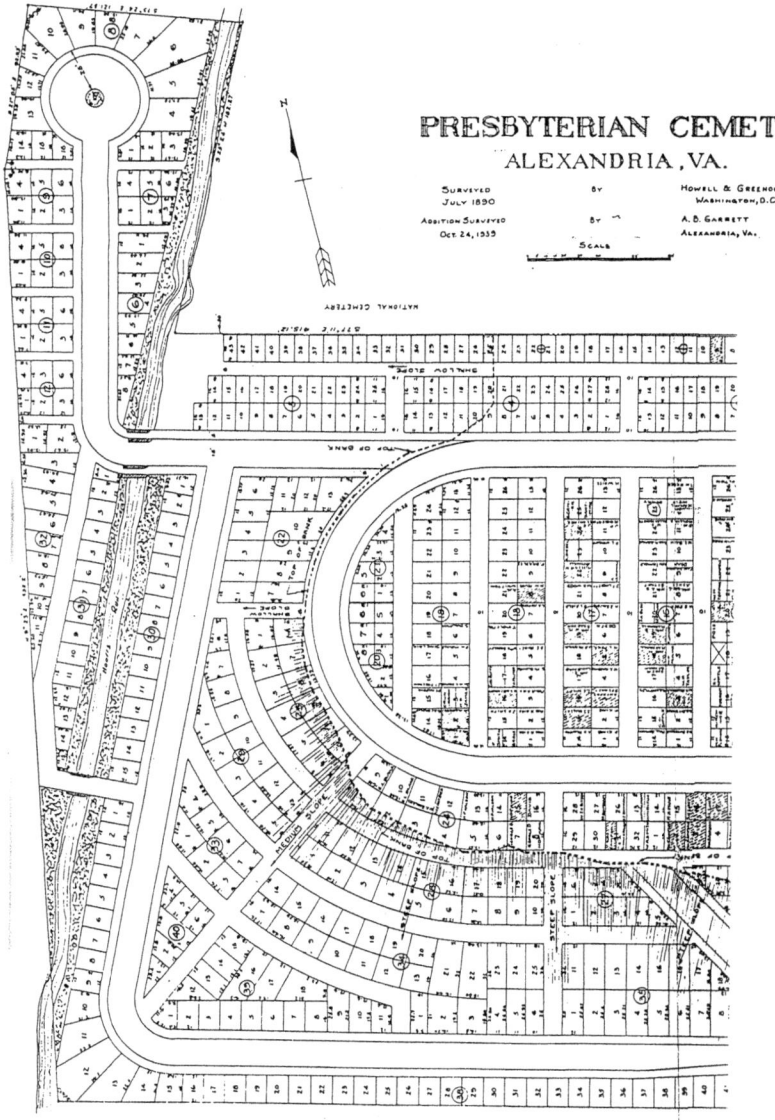

First Presbyterian Church Cemetery (1809)

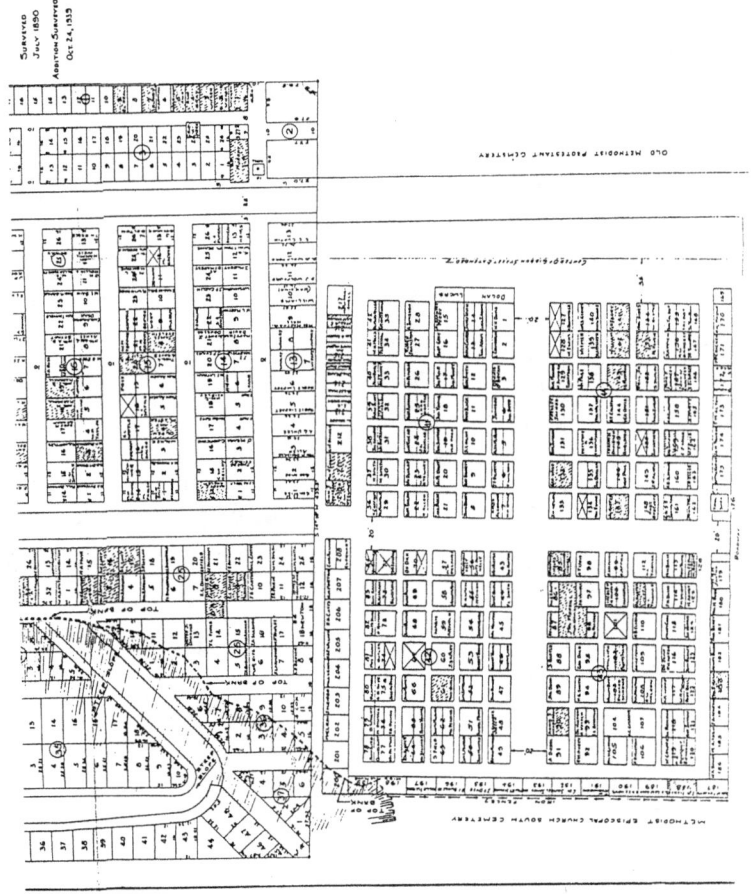

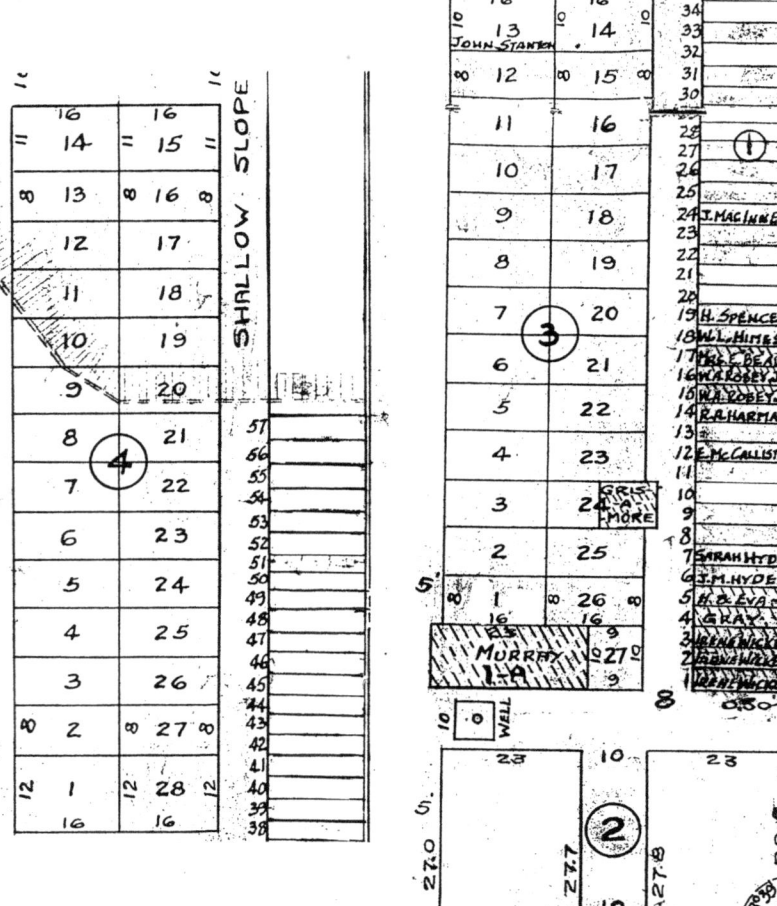

First Presbyterian Church Graveyard (1773)
(Now Known as the Old Presbyterian Meeting House)
South Fairfax Street

In 1927, an article which appeared in the Alexandria Gazette, announced discovery of church records in the attic of the home of the late Louis Bell, and included a compilation of names of persons which were thought to have been buried in the graveyard of the First Presbyterian Church of Alexandria[1]. The author has discovered that a small number of the names which appeared in the newspaper list were people who are in fact now buried in the "new" cemetery located off Wilkes Street and Hamilton Lane. In such cases, these names are not included in the list being presented here.

The list below is derived from the above 1927 article, has been supplemented with information gleaned from the graveyard, and is made from the record of funerals kept by Rev. Dr. Muir (implied in the above newspaper article), entitled: Register of Baptisms, Marriages, and Funerals During the Ministry of the Revd Doctr James Muir in the Presbyterian Church of Alexandria, D.C. A subsequent record containing like information is on microfilm (reels 440) at the Alexandria Library, Lloyd House, and covers a small portion of the years 1818-1861. It sometimes appears in Muir's register that the date recorded is actually a date of interment, and as such may have occurred without a funeral. Though unlikely that each funeral held by Rev. Muir equated to a burial in this graveyard, the record of funerals provides a starting point in identifying the doubtless many unmarked graves.

The location of the original Muir record is unknown, but an early transcript of it done all in one hand was restored by a chapter of the Daughters of the American Revolution in 1953 and is kept by the church at 316 South Royal Street. A photocopy of the record is located in the Archives Division of the Virginia State Library in Richmond. For most entries the cause of death is extracted from Muir's record, but on occasion it also has been found in a death notice in the newspaper.

According to an engraving on the face of the existing church building, the congregation of the First Presbyterian Church of Alexandria was founded in 1772. The first house of worship was erected in 1774[/5], and after it was destroyed by lightning on July 26, 1835, it was rebuilt on the same lot between 1836 and 1837. The church building was occupied in the twentieth century by a different congregation and is now known as the Old Presbyterian Meeting House. The flounder house which was the original manse and which now is used as the church office dates from 1787.

The parcel of land on which stands the flounder house, education building, cemetery, and

---

[1] Alexandria Gazette (Alexandria, 1 JAN 1927), "Record of the First Presbyterian Church Dating Back to 1794," Sect. A, p. 2.

First Presbyterian Church Graveyard (1773)

sanctuary, was obtained on July 12, 1773, when Richard Arell and his wife Eleanor conveyed a parcel measuring 88 feet 33-1/2 inches by 246 feet 10 inches (comprising the south half of Alexandria city lots 90 and 91) to Reverend William Thom[1] for the purposes of the Presbyterian Church.

It is obvious that the churchyard now contains but a small portion of the monuments once erected. Attached to the north wall of the brick wall surrounding the graveyard is found an inscription as follows:

1732-1932
In this church yard rest the remains of many of the comrades
in arms, intimate friends and fellow masons of George Washington.
Among them sleeps an unknown soldier of the Revolutionary Army.
To these, as a memorial, the wall around this sacred enclosure was
erected with funds subscribed by members of the Society of the Sons
of the Revolution throughout the nation under the direction of a
special committee from the society in the District of Columbia.

Some mention of the church and graveyard is to be found in Mary Gregory Powell's, The History of Old Alexandria, Virginia (Richmond: William Byrd Press, Inc., 1928), pages 99-113; hereafter referred to as Powell.

For each stone which has been located, the number of the row and lot are included in parenthesis, i.e. "(B:9)," and correspond to the map included in this section.

Because the building and graveyard were in extreme disrepair prior to the current congregation, it is certain that many of the monuments no longer rest in their original position. It has been indicated that with addition of a new education building in 1957 some graves in the Old Meeting House graveyard were disturbed.

Wesley E. Pippenger
Alexandria, Virginia

---

[1] Fairfax County Deeds, Bk. L No. 1, p. 215, Will Bk. C, p. 175, and records of William R. Sengel give surname "Thom,' yet Alden, p. 84, provides the surname transcribed as "Thorn;" complete transcript of his will dated 6 AUG 1773, prov. 20 SEP 1773, is found in Pennsylvania Genealogical Magazine, Vol. XXIX (1975), pp. 62-3; an obituary for both Mrs. Mary Thom and Rev. William Thom of Alexandria, appeared in the Pennsylvania Gazette (Philadelphia, 8 SEP 1773): *On Thursday the 5th of August last, departed this life at Alexandria, Va., Mrs. Mary Thom, and on the Sabbath following [i.e. 8 AUG 1773], the Rev. William Thom. They both died of an ardent fever and were decently intered in the burial ground of the Presbyterians in that Town. Mr. Thom, the son of a worthy clergyman, entered into the sacred office of the ministry in the 21st year of his age and was removed by death in the 23rd year of his age.*

First Presbyterian Church Graveyard (1773)

Unknown

Unknown Soldier. *Here lies a soldier of / the revolution whose identity / is known but to God / His was an idealism / that recognized a supreme / being that planted / religious liberty on our / shores that overthrew / despotism that established / a peoples government / that wrote a consitution / setting metes and bounds / of delegated authority / that fixed a standard of / value upon men above / gold and lifted high the / torch of civil liberty / along the pathway of / mankind. / In ourselves his soul / exists as part of ours / his memory's mansion.* (J:12, table].

A

ADAMS, Anne. Died at the age of 44 years, funeral held 4 JUN 1797.
ALEXANDER, Mrs. [Ann (Ricketts)]. Consort of Mr. AMOS ALEXANDER, died Monday morning, 16 JAN 1804 [AG:17/1/04:3] of consumption, aged 34 years.
ALLISON, Robert. Merchant, funeral 14 JUN 1801, died of consumption, aged 56 years.
ARELL, David. Died in 1792, between 15 AUG 1789 and 17 APR 1792 [Brockett[1], p. 96; Fairfax County Wills, Bk. F, p. 79].
ARELL, H. Died of consumption, aged 77 years, funeral 13 JUL 1796.
ARELL, Samuel. Died in 1795, between 1 NOV 1794 and 20 DEC 1795 [Brockett, p. 96; Fairfax County Wills, Bk. G, p. 130].

B

BADEN, [John Baptist?]. Died of consumption, aged 36 years, funeral 16 DEC 1796.
BAILLIE, Robert. Funeral 19 AUG 1804, aged 60 years.
BALFOUR, Mrs. _____. Died of decay, aged 60 years, funeral 9 DEC 1800.
BALFOUR, James. Died of decay, aged 65 years, funeral 13 DEC 1802.
BARBER, _____. A child, funeral held 15 JAN 1799.
BARTLEMAN, George. Died of a bowel complaint, aged 8 months, funeral held 23 JUN 1806.
BLACK, Dr. Robert. Died Sunday, 27 MAR 1803 [AG:28/3/03:3] of bilious fever, aged 27 years, funeral held 28 MAR 1803.
BLUNT, Washer. Mr. Blunt, superintendant of the Alexandria alms-house died of decay, aged 68 years, 30 OCT 1806 [AG:31/10/06:3].

---

[1] F.L. Brockett, The Lodge of Washington, A History of the Alexandria Washington Lodge, No. 22, A.F. and A.M. of Alexandria, Va. (Alexandria: George E. French, Publisher, 1876); hereafter referred to as Brockett.

First Presbyterian Church Graveyard (1773)

BOGUE, Mrs. Judith. Died of dropsy, aged 40 years, funeral 3 SEP 1799. Lot marker 13.

To the Memory of
JUDITH BOGUE, spoufe of JOHN
BOGUE of Alexandria who died
3rd September 1799, Aged 40 Years.

Her turn induftrious and hèr maternal care;
enhanced to me her worth, and to the four fhe bore.
In all hèr dealings just & in her friendship firm;
She died in peace & hope unaw'd by death tho grim.

Take warning of your end & live not as the throng.
Knowing that time is short, eternity how long;
Our friend has baid [sic] the debt we owe & all muft pay.
Peace guard the hallow'd place where now her afhes lay.
M.H.
Memento Mori. (F:4, tablet)

BRENT, Nancy. Died of consumption, aged 21 months, funeral held 13 JUN 1796.

C

C____, S____. Footstone "S.C." (H:11)

CAREY, Miss Mildred. Died of consumption, aged 38 years, funeral held 11 SEP 1799.

CARLYLE, Children. Ann, George Fairfax, Hannah, Rachel and William (see below).

CARLYLE, John. Here lies the body of / Major JOHN CARLYLE / son of / Dr. WILLIAM and RACHAEL MURRAY CARLYLE / born in Dumfriesshire, Scotland, 1720. / died in Alexandria, Virginia, [September] 1780. / One of the first trustees of Alex- / andria, 1748, appointed Commissary / of the Virginia Forces, 1754. / Erected by the / Alexandria Chamber of Commerce. (G:3, table with metal plaque; by his will, John Carlyle requested burial at the Presbyterian Church[1])

CARLYLE, Sarah Fairfax. Wife of John Carlyle, and daughter of William Fairfax. Stone illegible, but has been partially preserved in several sources[2]: *To the Memory of / Mrs. Sarah Carlyle / Wife of Coll^{o.} John Carlyle, Merch^{t.} in Alexandria / and Daughter of the Honble. Wm. Fairfax Esqr. / Coll^{r.} of his Majestys Customs on South Potomack / President of the Honble. Council in Virginia / Who died in Child-bed of her seventh Child / The 22^d of Jan^{ry.} 1761 / Aged 30 Years 22 Days / She was amiable thru Life as a / Dutiful Child Loving Wife / Affectionate Parent Indulgent Mistrefs / Faithful Friend Sincere Christian / and is thence justly lamented / by All who knew her / Our Life is short but to extend*

---

[1] Fairfax County Wills, Bk. D, p. 203, prov. 17 OCT 1780, "and as to my Body, I desire it be intered under the Tombstone in the enclosed ground in the Presbyterian Yard near where my first wife [Sarah] and children are intered."

[2] Sengel, p. 64; citing Timothy Alden's, A Collection of American Epitaphs and Inscriptions (New York: S. Marks, 1814), Vol. 5, p. 85; James D. Munson, Col. John Carlyle, Gent. (Northern Virginia Regional Park Authority, 1986), p. 89, probable epitaph written out.

First Presbyterian Church Graveyard (1773)

that span / to vast eternity in virtue's work / ----- / Nigh her lie Five of her Children / Rachel Ann William George-Fairfax and Hanah. (G:4, tablet now illegible)

CAZENOVE, Paul Charles. In memory of PAUL CHARLES / CAZENOVE / child of ANTONY / CHARLES & ANNE CAZENOVE / who departed this life / January 3, 1801, Aged / 13 Months & 10 days. (Q:11, footstone)

CHARLES, Mary. Died of consumption, aged 33 years, funeral held 27 AUG 1796.

CLIFFORD, Mrs. Funeral held 21 FEB 1805. Rev. Dr. Muir's record of funerals indicates that Mrs. Clifford *belonged to another denomination.*

COMPTON, William. Died of flux, aged 45 years, funeral held 4 SEP 1797.

COOKE, Julia Ellen. Died of flux, aged 9 days, funeral held 16 JUL 1796.

CRAIG, Mary. Died of consumption, aged 1 year, funeral held 10 JUL 1797.

CRAIG, Mrs. Joanna. Consort of SAMUEL CRAIG, died of fever 21 OCT 1806 [AG:22/10/06:3], aged 50 years, funeral held 22 OCT 1806.

CRAIG, Samuel. Merchant, funeral held 24 JAN 1808, aged 45 years. [Alexandria Wills, Bk. C, p. 32, proved 9 FEB 1810, men. wife Joanna, and neice Mary Grace Craig Hall]

CRAIK, Dr. James. In Memory / of / JAMES CRAIK / Chief Physician and Surgeon / of the / Continental Army / Born ..... 1727 / Near Dumfries, Scotland / Died February 4, 1814 / [at his residence in Fairfax county] Near Alexandria, Virginia [in the 84 year of his age]. [Note: This is a modern monument. Many years ago it was claimed that the remains of Dr. JAMES CRAIK lie near the wall of a dwelling house adjacent to the Presbyterian grave yard, the monument (a table stone) disappeared during the Civil War.] (T:11)

CRANDELL, Mrs. ____. Died of consumption, aged 28 years, funeral held 18 AUG 1797.

CRANDELL, Mrs. Mary. Died of consumption, aged 46 years, funeral held 19 JAN 1800. Mrs. MARY CRANDELL, The amiable consort of Mr. THOMAS CRANDELL, Born at / New Port, Rhode Island / Dec. 20th, 1753, Died 16th Jan. 1800. (stone not found)

CRANDELL, John. Died of fever, aged 25 years, funeral held 4 OCT 1803.

CRANDELL, Samuel. In memory of SAMUEL CRANDELL / Born November / 11th 1780, died September / 23, 1801. (stone not found)

CREEK, William. Died of dropsy, aged 33 years, funeral held 13 MAR 1796.

CR[E]IGHTON, Dr. Robert. Died of consumption, aged 67 years, funeral held 20 NOV 1801. Sacred / To the memory / of / ROBERT CRIGHTON, Esq. M.D. / *A Native of Scotland / He served Professionally in Braddock's Army / and after the defeat of that ill-fated Officer / went to the Island of Jamaica where he / resided for Forty Years and until declining / health induced him to come to America / in search of relief.* It was in Alexandria, / after a painful illness, Death arrefted him / on the 18th Day of November A.D. 1801 / in the sixty seventh Year of his Age. / *Much regretted by his friends & Acquaintances. / This monument whilst it exprefses the / attachment of his Widow reminds thofe / by whom it may be observed. / He was appointed unto Man once to die / and after death the Judgment.* (M:10, tablet)

CUSHING, Captain ____. Captain Cushing of Salem, Massachusetts, died Wednesday morning of fever [7 SEP 1796], aged 30 years, funeral held 9 SEP 1796 [AG:10/9/96:3].

D

DAVEY, David "Davey." Tavernkeeper, died of fever, *at half past ten o'clock* in the morning, 17 JAN 1807 [AG:17/1/07:3], aged 50 years, funeral held 18 JAN 1807. [Alexandria

First Presbyterian Church Graveyard (1773)

Wills, Bk. B, p. 403, men. wife Elizabeth]

DAVEY, Mary. Consort of Davey Davey, died 30 JAN 1806 in the 51st year of her age [AG:31/1/06:3, mentions burial in the Presbyterian burying ground].

DELIA of Mr. Patten. Died of consumption, aged 40 years, funeral held 14 FEB 1803.

DOUGLASS, Daniel. Died of bilious fever, age 35y, funeral held 7 SEP 1803. Here / lies the Body of / DANIEL DOUGLASS / who departed this life / Sept' 7th 1803 / aged 37 years [AG:9/9/03:3]. (N:11, epitaph illegible, footstone)

DOUGLASS, Mary. Died of old age and after a lingering illness, 26 SEP 1806 [AG:26/9/06:3], age 81y, funeral held 27 SEP 1806.

DOUGLASS, Sarah. Wife of JAMES DOUGLASS, died of consumption [10 OCT 1807], aged 40 years, funeral held 11 OCT 1807 [AG:10/10/07:3].

DUFFEY, _____. A child, died of consumption at the age of 1 year, funeral held 25 OCT 1801.

DUFFEY, Mrs. _____. Died in child birth, aged 40 years, funeral held 7 MAR 1808.

DUNBAR, Silas. Died of fever, aged 17 years, funeral held 28 OCT 1806.

DUNDAS, Edward. Died of croup, aged 1 year and 11 days, funeral held 26 SEP 1806.

DUNLOP, John. Died after a lingering illness, aged 50 years, funeral held 2 NOV 1806.

DYKES, Elizabeth. Died of [gravel?], aged 6 months, funeral held 19 SEP 1798.

E

EMACK, _____. A child, died of dropsy in the head, aged 1 year, funeral held 26 JUN 1798.

ERBY, Lawrence. Died at the age of 2 years, funeral held 7 APR 1806.

F

FAW, Mrs. [Mary Ann]. She "died by herself," apparently committing suicide, funeral held 20 JAN 1805.

FINLAY, David. Sacred to / the Memory of / DAVID FINLAY / a native of Scotland, who departed this life / on the ___ day of November, 17[97] / [epitaph illegible] / BUT / ___. [Note: Surname is "Lindsay" according to newspaper, yet stone indeed reads "Finlay."] (O:6, grey tablet)

FLEMING, Andrew. Died of fever, aged 6 years and 5 months, funeral held 2 OCT 1805.

FLEMING, Ann. Died of a bowel complaint, aged 9 momths, funeral held 18 JUL 1807.

G

GILLIES, Dr. James. Died the morning of 24 AUG 1807 of decline, aged 49 years, funeral held 25 AUG 1807. Late vice-president of the St. Andrew's Society [AG:25/8/07:3].

GILMAN, Laura Ann. Funeral held 18 AUG 1807. LAURA ANN GILMAN / Died / August 18th, 1807 / Aged / Nine Months & 18 Days. (S:9, footstone)

GRAHAM, David. Died of fever, aged 45 years, funeral held 8 OCT 1803.

GREENAWAY, Rebecca. Mrs. Rebecca Greenaway, widow of Capt. JOSEPH GREENAWAY, died 9 MAR 1797 [AG:11/3/97:3], of fever, aged 38 years, funeral held 10 MAR 1797.

First Presbyterian Church Graveyard (1773)

H

HALL, Mrs. (Mary) Grace Craig, died in child birth, age 18 years, funeral held 10 MAR 1798. Sacred to the Memory / of / Mrs. GRACE HALL / Confort of Mr. Wm. I. Hall/ Born in Antrim in Ireland. / Cut off in the Bloom of Youth on the 10th day of March / 1798 / Having juft attained her Eighteenth year. / *To the fummons of her God, / She submitted with a degree of fortitude / Seldom equalled, Perhaps never excelled. / Had Heaven delayed its call for a length of years / Still would the demand have been thought too soon / by him to whom she was United / And who erects this tribute of love / In remembrance of her transcendent virtues / And worth, and that, at a future day, it may / direct an Infant Daughter she has left / to trace this Hallowed Spot / Drop a tear on her grave and lament her lofs.* (O:7, tablet; see Sengel[1], p. 94)

HALL, John Shepard. Died at the age of 1 year and 9 months, funeral held 5 DEC 1804.

HALLODAY, Mary. M.H. / Mementomore. / In Memory of MARY / HALLODAY, wife of JAMES / who died the fecond of / July 1786, Aged 57 years / *fhe was a loving wife, a kind / mother, mistrefs and neighbour.* (B:9)

HAMILTON, Mrs. Susannah. Died 20 OCT 1807 [AG:21/10/07:3], of fever, aged 60 years, funeral held 22 OCT 1807.

HANNAH, Alexander. Died of old age, aged 74 years, funeral held 22 NOV 1803.

HARPER, Edward. Drowned at the age of 7-1/2 years, funeral held 22 AUG 1797.

HARPER, Rosalie H. A child, died at 8 months, funeral held 21 JUL 1803 [Powell, p. 112].

HARPER, Capt. John, Sr.. Died of old age, aged 76 years, funeral held 7 MAY 1804. In memory of Capt. JOHN HARPER, born Oct. 1728, died 1804 [monument covered by walls of the church near the original grave location of Rev. Dr. James Muir, and close to the current bell tower; Fireside Sentinel, Vol. V, No. 8, p. 103; Alexandria Wills, Bk. B, p. 25, men. last wife Mary, and lists children].

HARPER, Robert. Died Sunday morning, 11 MAR 1804, aged 20 years [AG:12/3/04:3], of consumption, funeral held 12 MAR 1804.

HARPER, Sophia. Sophia, daughter of the late JOHN HARPER, died 11 JAN 1807 [AG:12/1/07:3], of consumption, aged 44 years, funeral held 12 JAN 1807.

HEPBURN, Agnes. Died of old age, aged 87 years, funeral held 8 JUN 1814. Erected in memory / of / AGNES, the late wife of / WILLIAM HEPBURN / who departed this life / 7th June 1814 / *She was distinguished for simplicity of / manner and unfeigned piety. Having lived / in the fear of God she died in peace, / in her eighty seventh year.* [AG:9/6/14:3]. (L:8, table)

HUBBOLD, John. Died of pleurisy, aged 40 years, funeral held 9 MAR 1804.

HUNTER, Alexander. Died of decline, aged 82 years, funeral held 27 JUN 1798.

HUNTER, George. Died of intemperance, aged 56 years, funeral held 15 FEB 1798.

HUNTER, John. Died 4 SEP 1826 in his 67th year and was "buried in the Presbyterian graveyard" [Brockett, p. 130].

HUNTER, William, Jr. Relieve the Distressed / *Nemo me impune lacessit* / Sacred to the Memory of / WILLIAM HUNTER, Jun. / Born in Galfton, Scotland. / January 20, 1731 / *The Characteriftics of his life were / Unbounded Benevolence and Friendfhip.* / He Died

---

[1] William Randolph Sengel, Can These Bones Live? Pastoral Reflections on the Old Presbyterian Meeting House of Alexandria, Virginia Through its First Two Hundred Years (Kingsport Press, 1973); hereafter referred to as Sengel.

First Presbyterian Church Graveyard (1773)

in ALEXANDRIA / November 19, 1792 / *Beloved Efteemed and Lamented* / *The ST. ANDREWS SOCIETY OF / ALEXANDRIA / Whofe Founder he was and Among / whom he Rifided Until removed by / Death Erect this Monument Af a Tribute / of Gratitude and Refpect*. (M:6, lot marker 10, tablet; AG:22/11/92:3)

HUNTER, William. Died of fever, aged 54 years, funeral held 18 OCT 1803.

J

JAMIESON, George. A child, died in 1804.

JAMIESON, Charles. Died of jaundice at the age of 59 years, funeral held 9 JUL 1804.

JANNEY, Margaret[1]. Died of bilious cholic at the age of 49 years, funeral held 10 APR 1810 [stet]. In memory of / MARGARET JANNEY / wife of ABEL JANNEY / who departed this life / February [stet] the 9th, 1810. (S:11)

L

LADD, Joseph Brown. [same stone with Sarah]. In memory also of / Doctor JOSEPH BROWN LADD, / the eldest son of WILLIAM and SARAH LADD / who departed this life, / in Charleston, S.C., November 2, 1786, aged 22 years. Studious in infancy, he was a favourite of the muses, and highly promising in his profession of physick. His writings, published under the signature of Arouet, display genious, which riper years might have led to eminence. *How fair thy beauties and the early dawn! / The sun beheld them glorious in the morn; / But, ere his beams had pierc'd the noontide shade, / On earth's cold lap the wither'd rose laid. / On what great springs his spirit mov'd / Let those, with tears, who knew him, tell; / He liv'd, and he was all-belov'd, / He died, and all-lamented fell. / Arouet* (M:5, table; Powell, p. 107, indicates Ladd lies nearby Grace Hall.)

LADD, Mrs. Sarah Gardner. In Memory of Sarah Ladd, the amiable consort of William Ladd and daughter of BENONI GARDNER, Esq. late of Newport, R.I. She died at Alexandria, 30 OCT 1807, in the 74th year of her age. Exemplary and endearing in all the relations of life, she possessed the respect and esteem of an extensive acquaintance. Her mourning children have erected this monument as a small testimony of their filial duty, reverence, and affection. (M:5, table; AG:31/10/07:3; Powell, p. 110; this transcript taken from Alden, p. 87)

LADD, Capt. William. In memory of WILLIAM LADD, / who was born in the town of Little Compton, state of Rhode Island, / 30th October 1736, / and died, on a visit to his children at Alexandria, December 4th, 1800. Probity, benevolence, and patriotism characterized his life and gained him the esteem and confidence of society. On the day of his country's alarm, he volunteered in her cause and therein freely sacrificed the fruits of his honest industry. After being repeatedly elected to the legislature of his native state, he was called to seat in that convention, which ratified the favourite object of his wishes, the federal constitution. Truth was his guide, integrity his solace, and he found the reward of his virtues in the regard of his friends and in the hope of immortality. (M:4, boxtomb; AG:6/12/00:3, indicates burial at the Presbyterian church on December 5,

---

[1] Jane Farrell Burgess, Genealogy of the Janney Family in America (Rockville: 1990), p. 88, Margaret Wilkes Janney who died May 16, 1814 was the wife of Abel Janney who was born c.1755 and died at September 20, 1816.

First Presbyterian Church Graveyard (1773)

    1800)
LONG, Rebecca. Died of fever at the age of 45 years, funeral held 10 JAN 1796.
LONG, Samuel. Died after a short illness at the age of 26 years, funeral held 30 JUN 1806.
LOWE, Mrs. [Margaret]. Died of fever at the age of 45 years, funeral held 5 OCT 1803, leaving 5 children.
LUMSDEN, John. A child, died of flux at the age of 1 year 4 months, funeral held 14 NOV 1799.

M

MADDEN, Nancy. Died of fever at the age of 18 years, funeral held 13 SEP 1803.
MASTERSON, Sarah. Died of cancer of the breast at the age of 56 years, funeral held 29 JUN 1803 [Alexandria Wills, Bk. A, p. 160].
MATHESON, Kenneth. Merchant, died of fever at the age of 30 years, funeral held 17 SEP 1803.

MaCR[A]E, Mrs. Eliza. Died in 1798.
McCRAE, Infant "of James." Died of consumption at the age of 18 months, funeral held 3 SEP 1801.
Mc[C]RAE, Capt. John. Died 6 AUG 1808, after a short but severe illness, in his 35th year [AG:8/8/08:3].
McCRAE, Rebecca. Died of croup at the age of 2 years, funeral held 7 MAY 1808.
McCOLLOCH, Mrs. Died of consumption at the age of 37 years, funeral held 30 MAY 1804.
McDOUGALL, _____. Funeral held 7 MAY 1802.
McFADEN, James. Died of consumption at the age of 38 years, funeral held 24 APR 1799.
McFADEN, Nancy. Died at the age of 1 year and 2 months, funeral held 12 JUL 1799.
McKAY, Elizabeth. Died of cancer at the age of 19 years, funeral held 6 MAR 1805.
McKENZIE, John. Died of scarlet fever at the age of 26 years, funeral held 13 JUN 1796.
McKNIGHT, Charles. Funeral held 3 AUG 1807.
McLEOD, _____. Died at the age of a few months, funeral held 10 JUN 1800.
McLEOD, John. Died of flux at the age of 2 years and 6 months, funeral held 1 JUL 1796.
McLEOD, John. Died of scarlet fever at the age of 8 years, funeral held 1 JUN 1796.
McRAE, Nancy. Died of flux at the age of 3 years, funeral held 11 JUL 1797.

MEASE, Robert. Died 7 MAR 1803 of "decline" at the age of 57 years, funeral held 10 MAR 1803 [AG:9/3/03:3].
MILLAR, Mrs. _____. Died of consumption at the age of 33 years, funeral held 18 SEP 1797.
MITCHELL, James. In Memory / of / JAMES MITCHELL / From Glasgow / Who departed this life / June the 19th, 1787. / Aged 37 Years [AG:21/6/87:2]. (B:1, footstone "J.M. / 1787")
MITCHELL, Capt. William. Died of "decline" at the age of 42 years, funeral held 28 DEC 1802 [Alexandria Wills, Bk. A, p. 147].
MONROE, Mrs. _____. Died in child birth at the age of 28 years, funeral held 20 JAN 1800.
MOODY, Mrs. Elizabeth. Died of fever at the age of 25 years, funeral held 22 OCT 1803.
MUIR, Elizabeth. Sacred / to the memory of / ELIZABETH / widow of the late / JAMES MUIR, D.D. / Pastor of the First Presbyterian church / in this town. She was a native of the Island / of Bermuda, and for more than forty years a resident of this place and

First Presbyterian Church Graveyard (1773)

departed this / life in the full and blessed hope of the Gospel, / aged 65 years. / March 1st 1831 / *Precious in the sight of the Lord is the death of his saints.* This monument has been erected / by her three surviving children. (I:10, boxtomb)

MUIR, Elizabeth. Funeral held 15 SEP 1799. In memory of / ELIZABETH MUIR, infant child of Rev. James MUIR, D.D., died September 14th, 1799, aged 10 months. / *Sleep, sweet babe, / Summer Isles she saw / O'er the ocean She Flew, / But Columbia / brought her to slumber here.* (stone not found; Powell, p. 110)

MUIR, Frances Wardlaw. FRANCES WARDLAW MUIR / 179[1] / Died 7 months old / *Of Such is the Kingdom of Heaven.* (I:9, lot marker 27)

MUIR, Rev. James. Sacred to the memory / of departed worth. *Reposing beneath this monument / in the assured hope / of a Glorious Resurrection / are the mortal remains / of the / late Revᵈ JAMES MUIR, D.D. / For 31 years and 3 months the faithful Minister / of an affectionate people. / Amiable and unobtrusive in his manners / Kind and benevolent in his disposition; / Dilgent and unwearied in the discharge / of his pastoral duties. / He died as he lived / an illustrious example of the excellancy of / that faith once delivered to the saints. / Dr. Muir was a native of Scotland, / but having emigrated to the United States in / his thirty third year, he continued therein, / respected and beloved by all who knew him / until translated by death August 8th 1820, / in the 64th year of his age into that better / world where the wicked cease from troubling and / the weary are at rest / "And I heard a voice from Heaven saying unto me / write blessed are the dead which died in the Lord from / henceforth; yea, saith the spirit, that they may rest / from their Labours; and their works do follow them." / Rev. XIV.13.* (H:12, tablet)

[Note: The Rev. James Muir was buried beneath the pulpit of the old church, below where the mural tablet on the north wall is placed. When the present church was built, his tombstone was then removed to the northwest corner of the lot near the remains of his wife and children. On page 46 of Sengel, it is learned that the Rev. died at "Bel Air" which was later renamed "Colross." AG:9/8/20:2]

N

NICHOLA[S], Gen. Lewis. Died of old age on 9 AUG 1807 [AG:10/8/07:3], aged 90 years, funeral held August 10, 1807 [Alexandria Wills, Bk. C, p. 218, gives the will for Brig. Gen. Lewis Nicholas of the U.S. Army, prov. 16 MAY 1809].

NIVEN, Duncan. Died suddenly at the age of 40 years, funeral held 17 MAY 1806.

P

PATTEN, Elizabeth C. Died of teething at the age of 3 years and 22 days, funeral held 12 DEC 1802.

PATTEN, Susan. Died of fever at the age of 3 years and 3 months, funeral held 17 MAR 1801.

PATTON, Mary. Mary Patton, wife of Mr. THOMAS PATTON, died of consumption, 31 OCT 1808 [AG:1/11/08:3], at the age of 34 years, funeral held 2 NOV 1808.

PERRY, Daniel F. Master Dan F. Perry, son of Mr. ALEXANDER PERRY, died 19 AUG 1808. The death was occasioned by falling into a kettle of boiling soap [AG:20/8/08:3].

PITTMAN, ____. Found dead in bed at the age of 3 months, funeral held 7 MAR 1807.

First Presbyterian Church Graveyard (1773)

POMERY, John. Died at the age of 2 months, funeral held 2 APR 1797.
PORTER, James. Died of hives at the age of 2 years, funeral held 5 SEP 1799.
PORTER, Thomas. Died of fever at the age of 44 years, funeral held 1 MAY 1800 [AG:1/5/00:3].
POWELL, _____. Died of the measles at the age of 1 year, funeral held 13 JUN 1802.

R

RICKETTS, Sarah [Pennington]. Died of consumption at the age of 59 [sic] years, funeral held 7 MAY 1802. In Memory of / SARAH RICKETTS, / Wife of JOHN RICKETTS, / late of Cecil County / Maryland, / Born December 29th, 1743 / departed this life May 6th, / 1802, Aged 58 Years, 4 / Months and 7 Days. (A:5, footstone)
RIDDLE, Bushrod Washington. Died at the age of 1 year, funeral held 4 NOV 1804.
RIDDLE, Joseph. Died of a bowel complaint at the age of 1 year, funeral held 4 AUG 1800.
RIDDLE, Joseph. Died of hives at the age of 1 year, funeral held 31 AUG 1808.
RIDDLE, Joshua. Died at the age of 6 months, funeral held 13 DEC 1800.
RUSSELL, Hannah Throckmorton. Died of croup at the age of 1 year and 2 months [sic], funeral held 14 OCT 1804. HANNAH THROCKMORTON / Daughter of / James & Ann Ruffell / died Octr 13th 1804 / Aged 20 months & 7D. (D:12)
RUSSELL, James. Died of fever at the age of 38 years, funeral held 30 OCT 1808 [Alexandria Wills, Bk. C, p. 113].
RUSSELL, Mrs. Ann (Nancy). Died of consumption at the age of 36 years, funeral held 27 MAR 1807. In memory / of Mrs. ANN RUSSELL / born 17th December 1772 / died 26th March 1807 / Erected / by her surviving Husband / *To res___* / *of* / *his affection & resp[ect]* / *In her ___ was the law of ___* / *She looked well to the ways of her* / *household, and ate now the bread of ___* / *Her children arise up and call her blefsed;* / *her husband also, and he praises her* / *Favour is deceitful and beauty is vain* / *but a woman that deareth the Lord* / *she shall be praised.* (E:12, tablet)

S

SANFORD, Lawrence. Died of a bowel complaint at the age of 9 months, funeral held 29 JUN 1808.
SIMMS, _____. Died of small pox at the age of 9 months, funeral held 24 AUG 1800.
SIMMS, _____. Died of the measles at the age of 2 years, funeral held 9 JUL 1802.
SIMMS, Mrs. Margaret. Wife of Thomas Simms, died in childbed on 28 DEC 1797 [AG:29/12/97:3].
SIMMS, Nancy Neville. Died at the age of 2 days, funeral held 15 SEP 1808.
SIMMS, Thomas. Died at the age of 46 years, funeral held 7 APR 1808.
SMITH, Stillborn "of Thomas." Buried 26 SEP 1802.
SMITH, Alexander. Died at the age of 19 months, funeral held 5 NOV 1796.
SMITH, Mary. Died of teething at the age of 1 year and 9 months, funeral held 2 OCT 1798.
SMITH, Mrs. [Mary]. Died Saturday, 4 FEB 1797 [AG:7/2/97:3], in child birth, aged 28 years, funeral held 6 JAN 1797. Erected to the memory of / MARY the wife of / HUGH SMITH / who departed this life / Feb. 1st, 1797 / in the 29th year of her age / and to MARY ANN / their only child who died / Octr 2^d, 1798, / aged 21 months. / Near

First Presbyterian Church Graveyard (1773)

to this place are also interred the remains of THOMAS WILLIAM / the eldest son of / HUGH & ELIZABETH SMITH / who died Oct' 21, 1801 / aged 3 years / and of MARY their daughter / who died Aug. 11th, 1807 / aged 1 year. (R:11, boxtomb)

SMITH, Rebecca (Mrs. Thomas). Died of fever at the age of 44 years, funeral held 14 SEP 1803. Erected / in the memory of / a beloved sister, / REBECCA SMITH / who departed this life / on the / 14th day of September 1803 / Aged 51 Years. (H:8, table)

SMITH, Thomas. Died of stoppage at the age of 45 years, funeral held 7 SEP 1803. Erected / by a friend to / the Memory of / THOMAS SMITH / Who departed this Life / on the / 24th day of August, 1803 / Aged 45 Years. / A beloved son. (H:7, table; AG:26/8/03:3])

SMITH, William Henry. Died in 1808.

SPEAR, _____. Died of fever at the age of 29 years, funeral held 2 OCT 1803.

SPOONER, Capt. _____. Died of dropsy at the age of 40 years, funeral held 27 APR 1798.

STEELE, Margaret. Died of "disorders" at the age of 67 years on 26 MAY 1808, funeral 27 MAY 1808 at the house of Mr. ANDREW FLEMING [AG:27/5/08:3].

STEWART, John. Died at the age of 54 years, funeral held 12 SEP 1800.

STEWART, Mary. Died at the age of 1 year, funeral held 26 AUG 1799.

SWIFT, Ann Selina. Died of flux at the age of 1 year and 5 months, funeral held 19 JUL 1798.

SWIFT, Isaac Roberdeau. Died at the age of 3 years, funeral held 19 JUL 1797.

SWIFT, William Taylor. Died at the age of 1 day, funeral held 21 SEP 1808.

T

TAYLOR, Mrs. Maria "of Robert." Died in child birth at the age of 22 years, funeral held 6 NOV 1808.

TAYLOR, Jesse. Died of bilious fever at the age of 59 years, funeral held 15 OCT 1800.

TAYLOR, John Rose. Died of inflammation of the brain at the age of 3 months, funeral held 14 DEC 1807.

THOM[1], Mrs. Mary. In Memory of Mrs. MARY THOM, relict of the Rev. DAVID THOM, who departed this life, 5 August 1773, in the 56 year of her age. [stone not found; Sengel, p. 93; Alden, p. 84].

THOM[2], William. The Rev. WILLIAM THOM, their son, who was the first presbyterian pastor in Alexandria. He possessed a clear judgment, lively imagination, and extensive memory. These happy talents were improved by a liberal education. His life was a shining example of filial duty and affection, of sincere friendship, and of every amiable virtue. He entered into the ministry in the 21 year of his age, discovered a becoming zeal for religion in that sacred character, in performing the duties of his office was highly useful and acceptable to his congregation and, to their inexpressible sorrow, departed this life, 8 August 1773, in the 23 year of his age. [Sengel, p. 93; Alden, p. 84; stone not found, but may be B:7, inscription transcripts suggest both Thoms were listed on one stone; Fairfax County Wills, Bk. C, p. 175].

THOMPSON, Archibald. In Memory of / Mr. ARCHIBALD THOMPSON; / Who departed this life / July the 15th 1772 / Aged 41 Years / And alfo of / Mr. JOHN HEPBURN;

---

[1] Alden, p. 84, incorrectly cites surname as "Thorn," while Fairfax County Deeds, Bk. L No. 1, p. 215, and his will at Fairfax County Wills, Bk. C, p. 175, proved 20 SEP 1773, give the surname as "Thom."
[2] Ibid.

First Presbyterian Church Graveyard (1773)

/ who died December 10, 1787 / Aged 37 Years. (L:6)
TURNER, Mrs. [Francina (West)]. Died of "decay" at the age of 73 years, funeral held 1 DEC 1802.

U

ULAR, of Mrs. Sanford['s] family. Died of fever at the age of 18 years, funeral held 13 SEP 1803.

V

VEITCH, James Anthony. Died of fits at the age of 2 years and 9 months, funeral held 5 DEC 1807.
VOWELL, Charles. Died in 1801.
VOWELL, James Craik. Died of dropsy at the age of 3 months, funeral held 31 MAR 1800.
VOWELL, John G. Died at the age of 4 months, funeral held 8 APR 1799.
VOWELL, Mrs. Margaret Harper. Died of consumption at the age of 33 years, funeral held 26 JUL 1806. A monument raised by / the afflicted Husband of the / departed worth of / Mrs. MARGARET VOWELL, / daughter of JOHN HARPER, Esq. / Born August 20th A.D. 1775 / Died July 25th A.D. 1806 / The same lot contains the dust of four / Children who died in infancy / the eldest in her fifth year. / Her characteristick was an ardent mind, / which having received early impressions of / the religion of Jesus, was zealously bent, by / example and precept, to promote this glorious / interest. / *Here lies the heir of heavenly bliss, / Whose soul was fill'd with conscious peace; / A steady faith subdued her fear, / She saw the happy Canaan near; / Her mind was tranquil and serene; / No terrors in her look were seen; / Her Saviour's smile dispell'd the gloom / And smooth'd her passage to the tomb. / Let faith, like her's in joys to come, / Direct my walk, though dark as night; / Till I arrive at heaven, my home, / Faith be my guide and faith my light.* (Q:7, tablet; also see Sengel, p. 93)
VOWELL, Mary Harper. Died of consumption at the age of 34 years, funeral held 13 AUG 1805. Under this stone / are deposited the remains of / Mrs. MARY VOWELL, late wife of THOMAS VOWELL, junr. & daughter of the late Captain JOHN HARPER / who was born 28 of February 1772 / and died 19 August 1805 / aged 33 years, 5 months and 19 days. / In the same lot are deposited four infant children. / This Monument / is erected / by the surviving husband as a tribute of / love and afflicting remembrance. / *Here, in the just hope ablve the stars to rise, / The mortal part of MARY VOWELL lies; / In whom those beauties of a spotless mind, / Faith and good works, were happily combin'd. / Unblam'd, unequalled in each sphere of life, / The tenderest daughter, sister, parent, wife. / Sure in the silent sabbath of the grave / She tastes that tranquil peace she always gave. / Thy death, and such, oh reader, wish thine own, / Was free from terrors and without a groan. / Thy spirit to himself th' Almighty drew / Mild as the sun exhales th' ascending dew.* (P:7, boxtomb; also see Alden, p. 90.[1])
VOWELL, Mary Ann King. Died at the age of 4 years and 6 months, funeral held 3 SEP 1801.

---

[1] Timothy Alden, A Collection of American Epitaphs and Inscriptions with Occasional Notes (New York: Arno Press, 1977), Volumes IV and V, p. 90.

First Presbyterian Church Graveyard (1773)

VOWELL, Robert Harper. Died of dropsy at the age of 8 months, funeral held 25 SEP 1805.
VOWELL, Sarah. Died of an epidemic at the age of 9 years and 11 days, funeral held 21 APR 1808.
VOWELL, Sarah Wells. Died at the age of 7 months, funeral held 13 NOV 1797.
VOWELL, Thomas. Died at the age of 10 months, funeral held 17 OCT 1799.

W

WALES, Andrew. Died of "decline" at the age of 62 years, funeral held 23 NOV 1799.
WALES, Mrs. Margaret. Died of consumption at the age of 62 years, funeral held 3 MAR 1799.
WATSON, Andrew. Died of consumption at the age of 19 years on 9 AUG 1805 [AG:10/8/05:3], funeral held 10 AUG 1805.
WHITE, Elizabeth Anne. In Memory / of / ELIZABETH / ANNE WHITE, / the Wife of / JOHN WHITE, of / Alexandria, / who died the 23d of July, 1795 / in the 23d Year of her Age. (B:6)
WILBURN, Sarah. Died in 1793.
WILLIAMS, Mrs. ____. Died of consumption at the age of 40 years, funeral held 1 APR 1806.
WILSON, Bruce. Died at the age of 5 years, funeral held 1 JUL 1802.
WILSON, James. Merchant, died of fever on Tuesday evening, 9 JUL 1805, aged 38 years [AG:10/7/05:2], funeral held 9 JUL, Muir record gives month as June. His wife was Eliza Johnston Taylor, daughter of Jesse Taylor, Sr.
WILSON, Margaret. Died of consumption at the age of 56 years, funeral held 16 MAR 1808.
WILTON, Ann C. Died of worms at the age of 6 years, funeral held in NOV 1800.
WISE, George. Died at the age of 4 years, funeral held 4 DEC 1804.
WISE, John. Here lie the Remains of / JOHN WISE / Son of John & Elizabeth Wife, / of Alexandria; / who, in the 13th year of his age, / was fuddenly fummoned, / from this world, / to an infinitely better one, / on the 3d day of July A.D. 1790. / *Weep not, fond Parents, all your griefs difmifs; / I live, immortal, in the Realms of blifs.* (M:9, tablet; AG:8/7/90:3)

Y

YEATON, Mrs. [Sally]. Consort of Mr. WILLIAM YEATON, died the morning of 28 JUL 1803 [AG:29/7/03:3], aged 32 years, of consumption, funeral held 29 JUL 1803.
YOAST, John. Died at the age of 70 years, funeral held 8 MAR 1806.
YOUNG, James. Died of consumption at the age of 8 months, funeral held 13 JUL 1798.
YOUNG, James. Died from locked jaw at the age of 17 years, funeral held 20 OCT 1804.
YOUNG, Jenny. In memory of / JENNY YOUNG, Daughter of / JA^s and MARY YOUNG who / died aug^t 18th 1797, aged / 25 months and 25 days. / Also FRANCIS YOUNG, died / June 12th 1798, aged 18 / months and 25 days. (L:4)

Burials After the c.1809 Stoppage

Following is a list of persons found in the Muir record for funerals/burials which occurred after the c.1809 stoppage of further burials within the city boundaries. Though the 1927 newspaper article (previously presented herein) claimed many of these as probable burials at the graveyard, it is known that the source of the article was Rev. Dr. Muir's record of funerals. Since no monuments of any kind have been found for these persons in either cemetery, it is not known where the burial occurred, and it is more likely they were at the "new" Presbyterian burying ground off Wilkes Street and Hamilton Lane, rather than the graveyard on South Fairfax Street.

Per local historian T. Michael Miller, only a few exceptions to the c.1809 burial restriction are known. Exceptions which can be found here include: Margaret Janney (1810), Agnes Hepburn (1814), Rev. James Muir (1820), and Elizabeth Muir (1831).

ANDERSON, James. Funeral 7 NOV 1811, died of a rupture, aged 40 years.

BLACK, Esther Ann. Died of water in the head, aged 10 years, funeral held 23 OCT 1811.
BLOUNT, Polly. Died of decay, aged 20 years, funeral held 5 AUG 1811.
BOWEN, Samuel. Killed in battle in the War of 1812, funeral held 6 SEP 1814.

CHANDLER, Mrs. Mary Fowler. Mrs. MARY CHANDLER, relict of Mr. LEMUEL CHANDLER, and daughter of the late Mr. SAMUEL GARDNER FOWLER of Newport, R.I, died of consumption, aged 21 years, funeral held 17 FEB 1811 [AG:19/2/11:3].
CRAFFTS, Ann. Died of consumption, aged 25 years, funeral held 12 SEP 1814.
CRANDELL, Joseph. Died of consumption, 27 SEP 1813 [AG:28/9/13:3], aged 25 years, funeral held 27 SEP 1813. [Alexandria Wills, Bk. 1, p. 253, men. father-in-law McKenzie Talbott of Fairfax County]

DARLING, George. Shopkeeper, a native of Perth, Scotland, died 18 OCT 1813 [AG:19/10/13:3].
DENNETT, John L. Mr. Dennett, a native of Massachusetts, died after a short illness 29 MAR 1811, funeral at the dwelling of Mr. N. Hingston [AG:30/3/11:3], aged 26 years, funeral held 31 MAR 1811.
DUNLOP, Elizabeth. Died after a long illness, aged 54 years, funeral held 11 SEP 1812.

GULLATT, Mrs. Betsy. Betsy, the amiable consort of Mr. JAMES GULLATT, died 23 APR 1812 [AG:24/4/12:3], of decline, aged 30 years, funeral held 26 JUL 1812.

HALL, William James. William J. Hall, merchant, died of intemperance 17 APR 1810 [AG:18/4/10:3], aged 38 years, funeral held 16 APR 1810.
HARDING, Mrs. Mary. Mrs. Mary Harding, died 2 FEB 1812, aged 83 years, funeral at the home of Mr. JOHN HUGHES [AG:4/2/12:3].
HARPER, Joseph. Rope maker, died 31 NOV 1809 [AG:1/12/09:3], of palsy, aged 58 years, funeral held 1 DEC 1809.
HUNTER, Mrs. _____. Died of palsy, aged 52 years, funeral held 20 NOV 1809.

First Presbyterian Church Graveyard (1773)

IRWIN, Thomas. Merchant, died at the age of 40 years, funeral held 20 DEC 1814 [AG:20/12/14:3].

JANNEY, Abel. Merchant, died 13 APR 1812 [AG:14/4/12:3], aged 57 years.

JOHNSTON, Jane. Died of bilious fever at the age of 39 years, funeral held 2 DEC 1811.

KENNEDY, Dr. James, Jr. A native of Dumfrieshire, Scotland, died 6 JAN 1816 [AG:8/1/16:3], at the age of 63 years, funeral held 8 JAN 1816.

MARSTELLER, Mrs. Philip [Christiana D.]. Died of consumption, 7 JAN 1815 [AG:10/1/15:3], aged 41 years, funeral held 8 JAN 1815.

McCLEISH, Jane. Died of an inflammatory fever at the age of 15 years, funeral held 3 MAY 1813.

McDONALD, John. Died at the age of 26 years, funeral held 13 SEP 1812.

McGEHANNEY, Margaret. Died of fever at the age of 5 years and 5 months, funeral held 8 AUG 1813.

McKENZIE, Mrs. Ann. Late wife of Alexander McKenzie, died of an epidemic, 5 APR 1815 [AG:6/4/15:3], at the age of 43 years, funeral held 6 APR 1815.

McKINNEY, Mrs. S. Died of an epidemic at the age of 50 years, funeral held 3 MAR 1815.

NELSON, Mrs. [Fannie or Fame]. Died of pleurisy at the age of 56 years, funeral held 9 FEB 1812.

PIERCY, _____. Died at the age of 9 months, funeral held 8 SEP 1811.

RAMSAY, Jane "of John." Died of fever at the age of 9 years, funeral held 2 SEP 1811.

RICKETTS, Charles. *A young man possessed of every amirable quality*, died 29 DEC 1811 [AG:31/12/11:3], of pleurisy at the age of 28 years, funeral held 30 DEC 1811.

RICKETTS, E. "of Benjamin." Died in child birth at the age of 25 years, funeral held 30 DEC 1810.

RIDDLE, Infant of "Joshua." Died of a bowel complaint at the age of 6 months, funeral held 10 AUG 1811.

RIDDLE, Mrs. Sarah. Died in child birth at the age of 38 years, funeral held 25 APR 1810.

ROSE, Henry. Dr. Rose, died 4 FEB 1810 at Occoquan, Va., funeral from the house of ROBERT I. TAYLOR, buried 6 FEB 1810 [Brockett, p. 110; AG:6/2/10:3].

ROSS, Mrs. [Isabella]. Died at the age of 60 years, funeral held 7 SEP 1812. Muir record indicates she may have been buried in the Episcopal burying ground. [Alexandria Wills, Bk. 1, p. 223]

SCULL, William. Died 6 FEB 1813 of "old age," in his 76th year [AG:9/2/13:3], funeral held 6 FEB 1813 [Muir record gives month as March].

SHAW, Mrs. _____. Died of consumption at the age of 30 years, funeral held 13 MAR 1812.

SMITH, Mrs. _____ "of Alexander." Died at the age of 56 years, funeral held 12 FEB 1810.

TAYLOR, Jesse. A native of Ireland, and long a resident of this place, died 8 OCT 1812, aged 40 years. A merchant of Belfast who came to Alexandria from Williamsburg in 1799 [AG:15/10/12:3; AG:1/1/27:A2].

TOOMEY, Elizabeth. Died at the age of 30 years, funeral held 8 JUN 1814.

ZEPERNICK, Mrs. [Mariana]. Mother of ALEXANDER PERRY, died 20 MAY 1810, in the 79th year of her age [AG:21/5/10:3], funeral held 22 MAY 1810. [Alexandria Wills, Bk. C, p. 445]

FIRST PRESBYTERIAN CHURCH GRAVEYARD
(Now Known as Old Presbyterian Meeting House)

SOUTH FAIRFAX STREET

* = evidence of a marker
▦ = marker, but not legible
■ = marker, information included in this record
\+ = footstone only

Plan by Author

Trinity United Methodist Church Cemetery (1808)
(Formerly the Methodist Episcopal Church)
Wilkes Street

On December 15, 1808, members of the Methodist Episcopal Church of Alexandria purchased for $340 from Frederick Trytle and Mary his wife, along with Richard Lewis and Eliza his wife, a parcel of property at Spring Garden Farm which later would be used as a burial ground[1]. The size of the parcel measures approximately 130 feet wide by 369 feet long, and is used for the cemetery of what has been known since 1883 as the Trinity Methodist Church.

The earliest grave is that of John Lumsdon who died on September 6, 1806. It is unknown whether he was buried in this parcel prior to purchase as a burial ground, or he was reinterred from another location. Though there are recent burials, the cemetery is in disrepair.

Today's Trinity United Methodist Church was organized on November 20, 1774[2]. The first meeting house was built in 1791. A second church building was constructed by 1803 on the east side of the 100 block of South Washington Street, and the congregation later moved to 2911 Cameron Mills Road where a new building was occupied starting in 1941.

Initial information was extracted from Mrs. Carrie White Avery's genealogical notes as described in the Introduction of this volume. In addition, a review was made of a cemetery survey dated April 20, 1984 by Charles C. McNamara and Warren Mather, and an index dated February 1, 1985, both of which were prepared under the direction of Trinity United Methodist Church, 2911 Cameron Mills Road, Alexandria, Virginia 22302. Copies of these are on file at the Alexandria Library, Lloyd House.

For each tombstone which has been located at the time of this survey, the entry herein includes the row and section number, i.e. "R:3." Rows I and O were not used. If Avery's manuscript contained information about a tombstone which has not been found, that information is included in the list below with a notation "stone not found." Markers that are extremely eroded and cannot be transcribed are listed under the "Unknown" section immediately below.

Wesley E. Pippenger
Alexandria, Virginia

---

[1] Fairfax County Deeds, Bk. J No. 2, pp. 38-45.
[2] Fern C. Stukenbroeker, A Watermelon For God, A History of Trinity United Methodist Church, Alexandria, Virginia, 1774-1974 (Alexandria: 1974), p. ix.

Trinity United Methodist Church Cemetery (1808)

Unknown

____, ____. (Q:6)

____, ____. ____ / ____ beloved / ____ dear sister said / ____ took its flight / ___us I'm not afraid / ____ is even right. / ____ is erected by her / ____ is the last of / _ittle band. (B:5, broken remains)

____, ____. Sacred / in memory of / ____LT___ ... (Q:7, broken piece)

____, Mary Jones. To the / memory of / Mrs. MARY JONES / Consort ... / ... her hope / She died full of ____ / ____ hope, Oct' 27, 18[3]2 / aged 78 years. (E:7)

A

ABERCROMBIE, Robert. Sacred / to the memory of / ROBERT ABERCROMBIE / who was born on the 3rd / of March 1793, and departed / this transitory life on the / 14th of September 1822 / *Blessed are the dead which die in the Lord.* / *This languishing head is at rest / its thinking and aching are oe'r / His quiet immovable breast / is heav'd by affliction no more.* (R:5)

ADAMS, Leonard. Sacred / to the memory of / LEONARD ADAMS / Died December 23, 1833 / In the 75th year of his age / JOHN D. ADAMS / Died June 11th 1856 / In the 44th year of his age / Mrs. ANN ADAMS / wife of / LEONARD ADAMS / Departed this life / March 12th 1865 / In the 81st year of her age / *How blest the righteous when he dies, / when sinks a weary soul to rest; / How mildly beam the closing eyes.* (H:4)

ADAMS, Margaret. Gone to rest / Our beloved sister / MARGARET / Daughter of / LEONARD & ANN ADAMS / Died March 4, 1895 / Aged 76 years. (H:4)

ADAMS, Susanna. Gone to rest / Our beloved sister / SUSANNA / Daughter of / LEONARD & ANN ADAMS / Died Feby. 10, 1879 / Aged 69 years. (H:4)

ANDERSON, Eleanor. My mother / ELEANOR ANDERSON / Died June 28, 1860, / in the 75th year of her / age. / *Verily, verily, I say unto you, The / hour is coming, and now is, when the / dead shall hear the voice of the Son / of God: and they that hear shall live.* / John 5, Chap. 24, Verse. (J:3, footstone "E.A.")

ANDERSON, James H. My brother / JAMES H. ANDERSON, / Died May 27, 1861, / in the 57th year of his / age. / *We all do fade as a leaf.* (J:3, footstone "J.H.A.")

ANDREWS, Archibald. ARCHIBALD ANDREWS / Born / January 19th 1828 / Died / the 30th Oct' 1849 / *In his death his Father's / hopes have perished.* (G:1)

ARNOLD, Mary Ann. Sacred / to the memory of / MARY ANN / wife of / ALEX' ARNOLD / who fell asleep / Nov. 18th 1845 / in the 28th year of her age [AG:19/11/45:3]. (D:1)

ASHFORD, Ann Elizabeth. In / memory of / ANN ELIZABETH / wife of CRAVEN ASHFORD / born November 18th 1807 / died Nov. 14, 1837 [AG:18/11/37:3]. (C:6)

ASHFORD, Nicholas Darne. In Memory of / NICHOLAS DARNE. / Born April 8th 1840 / Died August 9th 1841 / AMELIA / Born September 24th 1846 / Died July 31st 1847 / ALEXANDER. / Born March 17th 1853 / Died August 21st 1853 / Infant Children of / C. & A.E. ASHFORD. / *Of such is the Kingdom of / Heaven.* (C:6)

ASHFORD, Samuel A. In Memory of / SAMUEL A. ASHFORD / Born November 10th 1844 / Died June 2nd 1865. / *Blessed are the pure in / heart for they shall see God.* (C:6)

Trinity United Methodist Church Cemetery (1808)

B

BAGGOT, Ellen. Gone to rest. / ELLEN / wife of / TOWNSEND BAGGOT / Born Feb. 12, 1806 / Died April 6, 1881 / *I know that my Redeemer / liveth.* (H:4)

BALANGER, Sally. In memory of / SALLY BALANGER / wife of / THOMAS BALANGER / who departed this life / August the 4th, 1849, in / the 66th year of her age. / *Blessed are the dead who die in the Lord.* (L:5)

BANGS, David B. Sacred / to the memory of / DAVID B. BANGS / who was born / in New York in 1789 / and departed this life / on the 27th of Octr 1846 / in the 57 year of his age. / *A kind husband, affectionate father / and a good citizen.* (N:5, footstone "D.B.B.")

BANGS, Margaret M. Sacred / to the memory of / MARGARET M. BANGS / our mother / Departed this life / March 9th 1871 / in the 75th year. / *A faithful Christian, wife / and friend.* (N:5, footstone "M.B.")

BENTER, Elizabeth. Sacred / to the / memory of / ELIZABETH, wife of / WILLIAM BENTER, / who departed this life on the 19 / day of October 1831 / aged 28 years / B'neath this clod her dust remains / Free from all her various pains. / Christ was her choice he's gone on high / To reign will her eternally. / also departed this life on the 11 / of November 1831 / JN^o ALEXANDER, son of / WILLIAM & ELIZABETH BENTER / aged 10 months & 10 days. (P:4, footstone "E.B")

BENTER, William, Sr. In memory of / WM. BENTER, SENR. / died on the 29th of August / 1823 in the 52 year of his age / Also / Mrs. ELIZABETH BENTER / Relict of WM. BENTER, SENR. / died on the 23 of November / 1848 in the 68 year of her age. / *Think O! ye who fondly languish, / O'er the grave of those you love. / While your bosom throb with anguish, / They are warbling hymns above. / Cease then, mourner, cease to languish, / O'er the grave of those you love. / Pain and death and night and anguish, / Enter not the world above.* (P:4)

BERKLEY, Elizabeth Woodward. ELIZABETH WOODWARD / wife of / WILLIAM N. BERKLEY / died / June 5, 1903 / aged 77 years. (L:2)

BERKLEY, Emily Pattison. Our mother / EMILY PATTISON BERKLEY / born / March 5, 1814 / died / Aug. 7, 1867. (L:2)

BERKLEY, George Pattison. Our brother / GEORGE PATTISON BERKLEY / born / June 10, 1842 / died Nov. 14, 1882. (L:2)

BERKLEY, William Norris. Our father / WILLIAM NORRIS BERKLEY / born / Nov. 25, 1814 / died / June 20, 1897. (L:2)

BLADEN, Rosier T. ROSIER T. BLADEN / 1861-1930. (P:4)

BONTZ, John W. JOHN W. BONTZ / 1861-1891 [AG:31/12/91:1, gives death 21 JAN 1891]. (F:5)

BONTZ, Ruth A. RUTH A. BONTZ / 1843-1913 [AG:31/12/13:1, gives death 26 FEB 1913]. (F:5)

BONTZ, William C. W.C. BONTZ / 1812-1882 [AG:31/10/82:3, gives death 30 OCT 1882]. (F:5, sign S33)

BRADLEY, C.C. C.C. BRADLEY / 1817-1900 [AG:31/12/00:1, gives death 26 APR 1900] / *An affectionate husband / a loving father, Kind / and charitable to all.* / ANN ELIZA BRADLEY / 1819-1910 [AG:31/12/10:1, gives death 22 JAN 1910]. (R:5)

BRADLEY, Elisheba Harris. In memoriam / Cheered by the sweet and blessed / hope of a glorious resurrection / fell gently asleep / April 28th 1867 / in the 69th year of her age / ELISHEBA HARRIS / Consort of / HARRISON BRADLEY. (Q:5)

117

Trinity United Methodist Church Cemetery (1808)

BRADLEY, Harrison. In memory of / HARRISON BRADLEY / who departed this life / March 21, 1872 / In the 79th year of his age / *He that overcometh shall inherit / all things and I will be his God / and he shall be my son. / Rev. 21C 7V.* (Q:5)

BRADLEY, Rev. John H. REV. JOHN H. / son of / C.C. & A.E. BRADLEY / 1839-1868 [AG:22/4/68:2, gives death 21 APR 1868] *Thy Saviour called / thee home.* / JAMES M. / son of C.C. & A.E. BRADLEY / 1847-1874 [AG:24/1/74:2, gives death 23 JAN 1874] / *A dutiful child, an / humble christian.* (Q:5, obelisk)

BRADLEY, Rose M. ROSE M. / Beloved Daughter of / CORA V. BRADLEY / Born April 22, 1898 / Died May 15, 1911. (E:3, statue)

[BREWIS], Our Baby / July 7, 1870. (P:2)

BREWIS, Thomas Anthony. THOMAS A. BREWIS / Born at Brenkley, near / Newcastle on Tyne, Eng / land, April 23, 1828 / Died April 27, 1870. (P:2)

BRIGHT, Ann. Sacred / to the memory of / ANN BRIGHT / Consort of JOHN BRIGHT / who died Novr 24th 1852 / aged 49 years & 21 days. / *Blessed are the servants, the / Lord when he cometh shall find watch / _____ unto all watch and pray.* (P:5)

BRIGHT, Araminta. In memory of / My Mother / ARAMINTA BRIGHT / Died March 29th 1881 / Aged 62 years. / *Blessed are the dead which / die in the Lord.* (P:5)

BRIGHT, Frances C. Sacred / to the memory of / FRANCES C. BRIGHT / Consort of JOHN BRIGHT / who died August 28th 1823 / in the 24 year of her age. / *O happy change and freed from care / In hope to dwell where blessed spirits / are.* (P:5)

BRIGHT, John. In memory of / JOHN BRIGHT / Born May 10th 1797 / Died Feb. 16th 1868. / *From early manhood he / Lived for Christ, and died / in full _____ hea / venly rest. / The path of the just is as / the shining light, that shineth more / and more unto the perfect day. / Prov. 5.18.* (P:5)

BROCK, Morgan Rives. MORGAN RIVES BROCK / July 21, 1874 / Dec. 31, 1936. (P:2)

BROOKS, Fanny. FANNY BROOKS / died Jany. 25th 1840 / in the 63rd year of her age / leaving a numerous family / to mourn her loss / this stone is erected by / her surviving children. / *Blessed are the dead who / die in the Lord.* (K:7)

BROOKS, William H. In memory of / WILLIAM H. BROOKS / born / in Norfolk, Va. / Dec. 8, 1837 / died / in Norfolk, Va. / Jan. 27, 1903. / *I saw the Holy City.* (C:3, footstone "W.H.B.")

BROOKS, William H., Sr. In memory of / WILLIAM H. BROOKS, SR. / born / October 11, 1815 / died / June 4, 1881. / *Requiescat in pace.* (C:3, footstone "W.H.B. Sr.")

BROWN, Charles P. In memory of / CHARLES P. BROWN / Born Nov. 6, 1868 / Died Aug. 7, 1888. / *At Rest.* (H:3)

BURCHELL, Edward. EDWARD BURCHELL / was born in Ireland / April 4th 1797 / Died March 23, 1866. / JOHN E.B. BURCHELL / son of / EDWARD and ANN BURCHELL / Was born Decr. 23 1825 / Died Sept. 6, 1837 / ANN / wife of / EDWARD BURCHELL / Was born in Virginia / March 22, 1787 / Died April 4, 1866. / *Arise, shine; for thy light is come, / and the glory of the Lord is risen upon thee.* (E:6, boxtomb)

BURRAGE, Georgie. GEORGIE / died July 9, 1864 / aged 1 year & 3 mos. / BENNY / died Oct. 10, 1843, aged 14 months / infants of THOMAS and / HANNAH BURRAGE / *Weep not for us / Our parents dear / we are not dead / but sleeping here.* (R:1)

Trinity United Methodist Church Cemetery (1808)

C

C____, T____. Footstone "T.C." (M:7)

CAMPBELL, Alcinda Fleming. ALCINDA FLEMING, / wife of / JOHN W. CAMPBELL / Born Oct. 29, 1815 / Died Dec. 19, 1880 / *Having the glory of God; / and her light was like unto / a stone most precious, even / like a jasper stone, clear / as crystal.* (N:4)

CAMPBELL, Ann. ANN CAMPBELL / wife of LOUDON CAMPBELL / died Nov. 30, 1825 / aged 48 years. / *Let sickness blast let death devour / If Heaven must recompense our pains / Perish the grass and fade the flow'r, / If firm the word of God remains.* (N:4)

CAMPBELL, Elizabeth. In memory / of / ELIZABETH / wife of WILLIAM CAMPBELL / who died June 6th 1853 / in the 69th year of her age [AG:8/6/53:3]. (P:3)

CAMPBELL, Hetty. HETTY / wife of LOUDON CAMPBELL / died Jan. 8th 1834 / in her 49th year. / *Blessed are the pure in heart / for they shall see God.* (N:4)

CAMPBELL, Capt. James. In / memory of / Captn JAMES CAMPBELL / a native of Scotland / who departed this life / March the 18th 1821 / in the 76th year of / his age. / *Blessed are the dead which die in / the Lord.* D.A.R. marker, "Naval Officer, 1775-1783." (Q:3)

CAMPBELL, John W. JOHN W. CAMPBELL / born / Dec. 22, 1815 / Died April 5, 1882. / *He that overcometh shall / inherit all things; and I / will be his God, and he shall / be my son. Rev. XXI.7.* (N:4)

CAMPBELL, Loudon. Sacred / to the memory of / LOUDON CAMPBELL / who departed this life / February 18th 1837 / in the 59th year of his age. / *I have fought a good fight / I have finished my course / I have kept the faith.* (N:4; Alexandria Wills, Bk. 4, p. 132)

CAMPBELL, Mary. In memory of / MARY / daughter of / JOHN [W.] & MARY A. CAMPBELL / died April 9th 1850 / aged 1 / mo. & 4 days. / *Suffer little Children / to come unto me and / forbid them not for as / such is the Kingdom of / Heaven.* (Q:3)

CAMPBELL, Mary Ann. Sacred / to the memory of / MARY ANN / wife of JOHN W. CAMPBELL / who departed this life / Octr 28th 1853 / in the 34th year of her age. / *And I heard a voice from heaven say / ing unto me Write, Blessed are the dead which die in the Lord for henceforth: Yea, saith the Spirit, that they / may rest from their labors and their works do follow them.* (Q:3, footstone "M.A.C.")

CAMPBELL, Rebecca. In Memory of / REBECCA, wife of / WILLIAM CAMPBELL / who departed this life / November 21, 1816 in / the 34th year of / her age. (P:3, footstone "R.C.")

CANNON, Mary Sincox. MARY CANNON / wife of / GRANDERSON CANNON / Died June 8, 1874 / aged 87 years. (G:3, replacement stone reads differently, to include years 1787-1874)

CANNON, Susanna. Sacred / to the memory of / SUSANNA CANNON / who for 27 years was a member of the / Methodist E. Church / Kind and unwearied as a friend / mild and affectionate as a mother / sincere and uniform a christian / She / in the joy and expection of a better / life calmly resigned her spirit and / slept in Jesus on the 29th of March / 1835, in the 72d year of her age. / *Her flesh rests in hope beneath / this stone erected by a filial love.* (N:5)

CARLIN, Elizabeth Harris. In memory of / Mrs. ELIZABETH / wife of Ge$^{o.}$ W. CARLIN / who departed this life on / the 27th day of Jan. 1853 / in the 65th year of her age. (L:3, footstone "E.C.")

CARLIN, George W. Sacred / to the memory of / GEORGE W. CARLIN / born on the 10th

Trinity United Methodist Church Cemetery (1808)

March / 1786, and died August / 25th 1843. / *For to me to live is Christ / and to die is gain.* (L:3, footstone "G.W.C.;" Alexandria Wills, Bk. 4, p. 363)

CAROLIN, Hugh. In memory of / HUGH CAROLIN / who died 27th of June 1843 / in the 66th year of his age. / *He was a native of Ireland and for the / last Forty years a highly respectable citizen / of Alexandria.* (N:6, tablet [broken], lot marker 137)

CAROLIN, Mercy Hawkins Latimer. Within this casement / lies the mortal remains of / MERCY CAROLIN / wife of HUGH CAROLIN / who departed this life / October 11th 1826 / in the 60th year / of her age. (N:6, tablet)

CARRELL, Elizabeth. In memory / of / ELIZABETH, / wife of / JAMES C. CARRELL / Who departed this life / December 6th 1853 / in the 46 year of her age / long to be remembered / by her friends and acquaintances. (L:5)

CARRELL, Leucinda. In memory / of / LEUCINDA / wife of / JAMES C. CARRELL / Who departed this life / March 15th 1830, / in the 28th year of her age / She is long / to be remembered. (L:5)

CARSON, Elizabeth. Sacred / to the memory of / ELIZABETH / consort of JOHN CARSON / who departed this life / April 21st 1851 / aged 62 years. (F:5)

CARSON, John. Sacred / to the memory of / JOHN CARSON / who departed this life / January 28th 1845 / aged 71 years. (F:5)

CARSON, Joseph C. Sacred / to the memory of / JOSEPH CARSON / Son of / JOHN & ELIZABETH CARSON / Died Sep. 29th 1854 / in the 35 year of his age [AG:30/9/54:3]. (F:5)

CARSON, Margaret. Sacred / to the memory of / MARGARET / Consort of GEO. W. CARSON / was born Jany. 8th 1816 / and departed this life Nov. 19th 1853 / in the 37th year of her age. / *Throughout her life she led an example / of Christian fortitude, her death was accom / plished with those qualities which ____ / ____ child of God. After suffering a long / and severe sickness, she at length breathed / out her spirit to be wafted on angels wings to / that God Who gave it birth.* / Also / HELEN SARAH / infant daughter of Margaret. (H:5)

CARSON, Mary Elizabeth. Sacred / to the memory of / MARY ELIZABETH / Daughter of JOHN and ELIZABETH / CARSON / who departed this life / July the 10th 1852 / in the 29th year of her age. (F:5, repaired)

CAWOOD, Daniel. DANIEL CAWOOD / Born / October 6, 1789 / Died / Feb. 12, 1872 / MARY, his wife / Born Jan. 20, 1800 / Died March 29, 1888. (K:3, footstone "D & M.C.")

CAWOOD, Delilah Robinson. Sacred / to the memory of / DELILAH ROBINSON / Consort of MOSES O.B. CAWOOD / who departed this life / April 9, 1854 / aged 53 years. / *Blessed are the dead which die in the / Lord from heaven henceforth, Yea the spirit / that they may rest from their labors and / their work will follow them. / A [damage] and devoted wife / And an affectionate mother / Sleep [damage] in Jesus / Rest [damage] everlasting life.* (D:4, repaired)

CAWOOD, Moses O.B. Sacred / to the memory of / MOSES O.B. CAWOOD / who departed this life in the / City of Alexandria, Va. on the / 29th day of January 1860 / in the 63rd year of his age. / *These are they which came out of great / tribulation, and have washed their / robes, and made them white in the blood of the Lamb. / Therefore are they before the throne of / God, and serve him day and night in / his temple: and he that sitteth on the / throne shall dwell among them. / They shall hunger no more, neither / Thirst any more; neither shall the / sun light on them, nor any heat. / For the Lamb which is in the*

Trinity United Methodist Church Cemetery (1808)

    midst / of the throne shall feed them, and / shall lead them unto living / fountains of waters: and God shall / wipe away all tears from their eyes. / Rev. 7.14.17 (D:4, repaired)

CHATHAM, James. In memory of / JAMES CHATHAM / born / December-1813 / died / April 8, 1885. / *Through much suffering / he is at Rest.* (B:6)

CHATHAM, Martha. Our Mother / MARTHA CHATHAM / Departed this life / Sept. 25, 1889 / Aged 74 years. / I've *anchored my soul in the / heaven of rest. / I'll sail the wide seas no more / The tempest may sweep o'er / the wild, stormy deep / In Jesus I'm safe evermore.* (B:6)

[CHAUNCY?], Fannie. FANNIE / Daughter of WM. & Va. E. [CHAUNCY?] / Died Feb. 1, 1873 / aged 18 months. / *She is Home.* (K:5)

CHAUNCY, Thomas A. C.S.A. / THOMAS A. CHAUNCY / Co. E. / 17th Va. Regt. / died / Jan. 4, 1874. (K:5, sign S44)

CHING, Grace. In memory of / Mrs. GRACE CHING / daughter of JOHN and / ELIZABETH SHEPHERD of / Devonshire, England and / wife of THOMAS CHING / and mother of SARAH / S., ELIZABETH M., THOMAS / S. and WILLIAM M. / Having hope of a glorio / us resurrection she died / in great peace March 7th / 1855 in Baltimore city at / the residence of her son-in- / law Rev. E.R. VEITCH, aged / 75 years. (J:5)

CHING, Thomas. [Alexandria Wills, Bk. 4, p. 179].

    In memory of
    THOMAS CHING
    a native of England, son
    of JOHN and ELIZABETH
    husband of GRACE, Father of
    SARAH S., ELIZABETH M., THO-
    MAS S. and WILLIAM M.

    In 1819 he emigrated to New
    York city and there resided
    about one year thence he
    came to Alexandria where
    in 1829 he became a nat-
    uralized citizen of the Uni-
    ted States, and here his use-
    ful and christian life clos-
    ed on the [blank] day of October
    1838 being in his 58th year. (J:5)

CHING, William Manning. In memory of / WILLIAM MANNING CHING / son of THOMAS and GRACE / who died near Portsm / outh, Va. June 1st 1846. (J:5)

CHIPLEY, Samuel N. Father / SAMUEL N. CHIPLEY / 1808-1887 [AG:24/12/87:2, gives date 23 DEC 1887]. (A:2)

CHIPLEY, Sarah M. Mother / SARAH M. CHIPLEY / 1807-1870 [AG:19/7/70:3, gives date 18 JUL 1870]. (A:2)

CLARK, Adeline Carlin. In memory of / ADELINE CARLIN / beloved wife of J.C. CLARK / Born Jan. 7, 1822 / Died July 10, 1888. / *Her toils are past, her work is done / And*

Trinity United Methodist Church Cemetery (1808)

she is fully blest. / She fought the fight, the victory won / And entered into rest. (A:3)

CLARK, Catharine Deagen (or Deager). In / memory of / CATHARINE / wife of / WILLIAM CLARK / and daughter of / GEORGE and FANNEY DEAGEN / who died / on the 14th of October / 1835 / in the 60th year of her age. (K:6)

CLARK, Harry C. In memory of / HARRY C. / Eldest son of J.C. and / ADELINE CLARK, / Departed this life / April 28, 1877 / in the 24th year of his / age. / *I heard the voice of harpers / harping with their harps; and / they sang as it were a new / song before the throne. / Rev. 14 Chap.* (A:3)

CLARK, John Curry. In memory of / JOHN CURRY CLARK / Born March 27, 1820 / Died April 28, 1901. / *The earth shall soon dissolve like snow / The sun forbear to shine; / But God who called me here below, / Will be forever mine.* (A:3)

CLARK, Joseph. C.S.A. / JOSEPH CLARK / Kemper's Battery / died / Aug. 11, 1896. (E:3)

CLARK, William. In / memory of / WILLIAM CLARK / who died / on the 12th day of February / 1832 / in the 63d year of his age. (K:6)

CLOWES, Thomas. In memory of / THOMAS CLOWES / of Loudon [sic] County, Va. / died in Alexandria, Va. / April 22, 1868 / aged 51 years & 8 days. (D:6, footstone "T.C.")

COLEMAN, Caroline Carolin. In memory of / CAROLINE / wife of / JAMES P. COLEMAN / who departed this life / March 2nd 1879 / Aged 70 years. (M:6)

COLEMAN, Caroline Victoria. In / memory of / CAROLINE VICTORIA / born August 1, 1835 / died October 26, 1837 / aged 26 months and 23 days / also / ALICE OPHELIA / born June 6, 1840 / died Aug. 5, 1841, aged 13 months / & 23 days / children of JAMES P. & CAROLINE COLEMAN. (N:6)

COLEMAN, James Prater. In memory of / JAMES P. COLEMAN / who departed this life / Oct. 22, 1870 / Aged 72 years. (M:6)

COLEMAN, Joseph H. C.S.A. / JOSEPH H. COLEMAN / Secret Service / died / Feb. 16, 1894. (M:6)

COLEMAN, Samuel S. C.S.A. / SAMUEL S. COLEMAN / Co. E / 17th Va. Regt. / died June 26, 1886. (M:6, sign S12)

COLLINGSWORTH, Thomas W. THOMAS W. COLLINGSWORTH / 1844-1919 / his wife / VIRGINIA A. NOLAND / 1842-1917. (D:5)

COLVIN, Miranda M. Chipley. My mother / MIRANDA M. / wife of / COLUMBUS T. COLVIN / 1848-1921. (A:2)

COX, Charles F. CHARLES F. COX / died / Mar. 30, 1889 / aged 68 years / CHARLES E. / FANNIE. (E:5)

COX, Sarah G. In / memory of / SARAH G. COX / daughter of / PETER P. & SARAH / COX / was born Feb. 21, 1807 / and died June 18th 1819. (N:4, broken)

CRAVEN, John. In memory of / JOHN CRAVEN / Born in England / June 15, 1808 / Died in Alexandria, Va. / Mar. 29, 1883. / *I am the resurrection and the life; / He that believeth in me though / he were dead yet shall he live; / And whosoever liveth and / believeth in me shall never die. / John XI.25.26.* (F:2, footstone "J.C.")

CRAVEN, Mary E. Nalls. In memory of / MARY E. NALLS / wife of / JOHN CRAVEN / Died July 19, 1904 / In her 86 year. / *Thou shall come to thy grave / in a full age, like as a shock / of corn cometh in in [sic] his / season, and thou shall take / thy rest in safety.* / Job V.26 & XI.18. (F:2, footstone "M.E.N.C.")

CRAVEN, Virginia A. In memory of / VIRGINIA A. / daughter of the late / JOHN CRAVEN / Died April 18, 1884 / aged 35 years. (F:2, footstone "V.A.C.")

CREIGHTON, Sarah Cornelia. In / memory of / SARAH CORNELIA / CREIGHTON / who

Trinity United Methodist Church Cemetery (1808)

died 27 Apl. 1835 / aged 2 years, 10 mo⁺ / 18 days. / *Short was thy stay / But ____tly long / To endear thee / To our hearts.* (J:1, footstone "S.C.")

CROOK, Agnes. In / memory of / AGNES CROOK / who departed this life / on the 5th day / of November 1840 / in the 66th year / of her age. (D:1, footstone "A.C.")

CROOK, Bernard. In Memory of / BERNARD CROOK / who departed this life / Sept⁺ 28th 1819 in the / 54th year of his age. (D:1, footstone "B.C.;" Alexandria Wills, Bk. 2, p. 324)

CROSS, John Reid. Departed this life / December the 5, 1832 / JOHN REID CROSS / son of / REID & SARAH CROSS / aged 5 years, 1 month and 25 days / *Dear parents don't la / ment for me / For ___ sweet / cont__.* (Q:1, footstone "_.C.")

CROSS, Mary. Departed this life / October the 24, 1820 / MARY CROSS / consort of / REID CROSS / aged 33 years / *Blessed are the dead / who die in the Lord.* (Q:1, broken footstone "M.C.")

CROSS, Reid. Sacred / to the memory of / REID CROSS / born February 7th 1788 / died February 16th 1851 / aged 63 years & 10 days. / *Blessed is the man who trusted / in the Lord, and whose hope the / Lord is.* (Q:1, footstone "R.C.;" Alexandria Wills, Bk. 5, p. 304, men. wife Sarah W.)

CROSS, Thomas R. [first stone] C.S.A. / THOMAS R. CROSS / Co. E / 17th Va. Regt. / died / Feb. 22, 1896. [second stone] THOMAS R. CROSS / Co. E / 17 Regt. / Va. Inf. / C.S.A. / Feb. 22, 1896. (Q:1, sign S17)

D

DARVELL, Henry. Sacred to the memory of / HENRY DARVELL / who departed this life Nov. the 11th / 1850 in his 83 year, He was for / ____ a native of Maryland / but for over fifty years a resident / of Alexandria, Va. He was beloved / and respected by all who knew him. *Blessed is the man that walketh not / in the counsel of the ungodly, nor stan / deth in the way of sinners, nor sitteth / in the seat of the scornful. / But his delight is in the law of the Lord; / and in his law doth he meditate day / and night.* Psalm 1. (R:6)

DAVEY, Mary. Sacred / to the memory of / MARY, wife of / THOMAS DAVEY, / who departed this life / May 2ᵈ 1832 / aged 51 years. (C:6)

DAVIES, Jane Elizabeth. Sacred to the memory of / JANE ELIZABETH / wife of / WILLIAM DAVIES / who departed this life on the / 22d of January 1833 / in the 26th year of her age. (C:3, boxtomb)

DAVIES, Mary. IN / memory of / MARY DAVIES / wife of WILLIAM DAVIES [of Williamsburg] / who departed this life / ____ / on the 30th of Sept. 1835 / Aged 57 Years. / *Blessed are the dead who die in the Lord.* (K:4; AG:2/10/35:3)

DAVIS, Aurelia. In memory / of / AURELIA / daughter of W. & M. DAVIS / Born Dec. 28, 1838 / Died July 13, 1881. / Also 4 infant children / and 2 grandchildren. (B:7)

DAVIS, Martena. In memory / of / MARTENA / wife of WILLIAM DAVIS / Born June 20, 1807 / Died Jan. 3, 1886. (B:7)

DAVIS, William. In memory / of / WILLIAM DAVIS / Born Feb. 28, 1807 / Died Aug. 31, 1886. / *I know that my redeemer / liveth.* (B:7)

DAVY, Susan. Sacred / to the memory of / SUSAN, / wife of THOMAS DAVY / Who departed this life / April 25, 1872 / In the 77th year of her age. (Q:5)

DAVY, Thomas. In memory of / THOMAS DAVY / born in Cornwall, England / Feby. 8,

Trinity United Methodist Church Cemetery (1808)

1791 / Died December 27, 1876 / in the 86th year of his age. / He had been a member of / the M.E. Church for / 63 years. / *Blessed are the dead which / die in the Lord.* (Q:5, repaired)

DAY, John F. Erected / by / The Bricklayers / Union No. 1, / Baltimore, Md. / To the memory of / JOHN F. DAY, / Son of / JOHN and ANN DAY, / Born Jan. 26, 1828 / Died Jan. 31, 1871. (L:5)

[DEETON?]. Place stone: "R.L.D. / A.B.D." (L:3)

DEETON, Ann Elizabeth. Sacred / to the memory of / ANN ELIZABETH / wife of / GEO. L. DEETON / who departed this life on the 1st day of December / A.D. 1840 / Aged 25 Years / Leaving a disconsolate husband and / three small children to mourn / their irreparable loss. / *Jesus has made a dying bed / Feel soft as downy pillows are / While on his breast I leaned my head / And breathed my life out sweetly there.* (L:3, footstone "A.E.D.")

DEETON, Christopher. Erected / to the memory / of / CHRISTOPHER DEETON / who was born / March the 10th 1775 / at Anderby Steeple / Northriding of Yorkshire / Old England / and died at Alexandria, D.C. / July 22nd 1827. (L:3, footstone "C.D.")

DEETON, George L., Jr. To the memory of / GEO. L. DEETON, Jr. / 2d son of GEO. L. & / ANN E. DEETON / Born June 7th 1837 / Died Sep$^{t.}$ 30th 1850. (L:3)

DEETON, Isabell Lambert. Sacred / to the memory of / ISABELL LAMBERT / wife of / CHRISTOPHER DEETON / born at North Alarton Co. of York / England, Nov. the 19th 1774 / died at Alexa. Va., May the 30th 1852. (L:3, footstone "I.L.D.;" Alexandria Wills, Bk. 6, p. 100)

DEETON, James H. To the memory of / JAMES H. DEETON / Born Aug. 5th 1839 / Died Feb. 24, 1844. / *Sleep gently oh dear / Boy, thy Mother lies / Close beside thee.* (L:3, footstone)

DEETON, Sarah E. SARAH E. / DEETON / 1835-1922. (L:3)

DORSEY, Henrietta Maria. In / memory of / HENRIETTA MARIA / infant daughter of / Rev. EDWARD DORSEY / who died Oct. 20th 1835 / aged 5 mos. (J:2)

DORSEY, Jane Prince Robbins. To the memory of / Mrs. JANE P. DORSEY / relict of / Rev. T.J. DORSEY, / who fell asleep in Jesus / on the morning of the 14th / March 1843, aged 58 years [AG:16/3/43:2]. (L:2, mismatched footstone is "H.M.D.")

DORSEY, Lucy J. To the memory / of / LUCY J. DORSEY / daughter of / Rev. T.J. and JANE PRINCE DORSEY / Born Aug. 15, 1836 / Died Feb. 23, 1908. / *Then are they glad because / they be quiet, so He bringeth / them to their desired haven. / Psalm 107.30 / O death, where is thy sting / O grave, where is thy victory / Thanks be unto God who giveth / us the victory through our / Lord Jesus Christ. / I. Cor. 15.55.57.* (L:2)

DORSEY, Rev. Thomas J. Sacred / to the memory of the / Rev$^{d.}$ THOMAS J. DORSEY / who died in Baltimore, June 3rd 1838. / in the 41st year of his age. / For 20 years a zealous and untiring / Minister of the gospel in the / Methodist E. Church / *Gone to God.* / In the same grave lies / MARY EMMA / infant daughter of the / Rev$^{d.}$ THOMAS J. and JANE P. DORSEY / who departed this life / April 9th 1835 / aged 14 months. (L:2)

DOVE, Mary P. Our father and mother / MARY P. / Wife of JILSON DOVE. / Died Jan. 21st, 1852; Aged 58 years. / Also / JILSON DOVE. / Died June 14th 1854 / In the 69th year / of his age. (Q:3, obelisk, lot marker: "J.D. / 69")

DREESE, Hester. Sacred / to the memory of / HESTER DREESE / who departed this life / April 27th 1842 / aged 45 years. / *Weep not for me my Children dear / I am not dead*

Trinity United Methodist Church Cemetery (1808)

but sleeping here / My debt is paid my grave you see. / Prepare in death and follow me. / This stone was erected / by her daughter / Mary E. Green. (P:4)
DUFFEY, George Nelson. C.S.A. / GEORGE N. / DUFFEY / Jan. 8, 1850 / Aug. 31, 1889 / Ordinance Dept. (G:22, three stones, sign S34)
DUFFEY, George S. GEORGE S. / DUFFEY / Mar. 13, 1877 / Jan. 27, 1893. (G:6)
DUFFEY, Mary S. MARY S. / DUFFEY / Aug. 24, 1852 / June 25, 1935. (G:6)
DUNCAN, Isabella. In remembrance of / my / beloved sister / ISABELLA / wife of / WILLIAM DUNCAN / died Aug. 31, 1887 / erected by her sister Elizabeth B. Taylor. (A:2, broken)

E

E[VANS?]. ANN VIRGINIA / born 1810, died 1811 / WILLIAM HENRY / born 1815, died 1816 / CATHARINE ELIZABETH / born 1816, died 1818 / Children of / SAMUEL & ELIZABETH / E[VANS?]. (E:2)
EVELETH, John. I give unto them / eternal life. / JOHN EVELETH / 1801-1863 / JULIA / daughter of / JOHN and JULIA / JULIA [Carolin] / wife of JOHN / 1811-1895 / WILLIAM SANFORD / son of / JOHN and JULIA [AG:31/12/95:1, gives date 4 AUG 1895; AG:23/7/52:2, gives date 22 JUL 1852 for Wm. S. Eveleth]. (N:6, obelisk)

F

FAW, Abraham. In memory of / ABRAHAM FAW / who departed this life on the / 26th day of June 1828 / in the eighty second year of his age. / What then if ____ would have / That ____ should ... (F:3, badly worn, broken by tree roots, footstone; Alexandria Wills, Bk. 3, p. 306, men. daughter Julianna M. Lowe, daughter Sophia Eliza as wife of Jacob Leonard)
FAW, Sarah. This silent stone in here / SACRED ERECTED / in the memory of / SARAH / the wife of ABRAHAM FAW / Who was Born March 28th 1764 / And Died August 28th 1818. / Blessed are the dead which die in the Lord / from henceforth; Yea, saith the spirit that they / may rest from their labors, and their works / do follow them. (F:3, broken footstone)
FITZHUGH, Rachel D. McCobb. Sacred / to the memory of / RACHEL D. FITZHUGH / Relict of / JOHN T. FITZHUGH / and Daughter of / JOHN & SARAH McCOBB / who departed this life / September 1', 1831 / aged 25 years. (Q:4)
FRYE, Margaret. In memory of / MARGARET FRYE, / widow of the late / REV. CHRISTOPHER FRYE / who departed this life / July 11th 1843 / in the 67th / year of her age. / I am the resurrection & the / life saith the Lord. (P:2)
FUGITT, Catharine. Sacred / to the memory of / CATHARINE FUGITT. / Consort of / GUSTAVOUS FUGITT / who was born / February 22nd 1800 / and departed this life / December 31st 1851 / in the 52nd year of her age. (D:1, footstone "C.F.")
FUGITT, Gustavus. In memory of GUSTAVUS FUGITT, / died June 17, 1868 / in his 77th year. (D:1, footstone "G.F.")
FUGITT, Joseph. Sacred / to the memory of / JOSEPH FUGITT / youngest son of / GUSTAVOUS & CATHARINE FUGITT / who was born / August 27th 1827 / and departed this life / October 20th 1844 / in the 18th year of his age. (D:1, footstone

Trinity United Methodist Church Cemetery (1808)

"J.F.")

FUGITT, Laura V. Mother / LAURA V. FUGITT / Died / Nov. 12, 1870 / Aged 20 years. (M:6)

FULMORE, Ann. This monument erected to / ANN, Consort of JOSEPH / FULMORE, who died / May 3, 1830 in the / 75th year of her age. (J:4)

G

G____, A. ... 1844 / ____ months & 11 days / ____ dear Child / the conflicts o'er, / the storm is hushed / will rise no more. (F:5, footstone "A.G.")

GIBBS, Theodore. Sacred / to the memory of / THEODORE GIBBS / who departed this life / February 4th 1830 / in the 39th year of his age. / *All you that come my grave to see / Prepare yourselves to follow me / Repent and turn to God in time / For I was taken in my prime.* (B:2, footstone "T.G.")

GRIFFITH, Kinzey. KINZEY GRIFFITH / died May 27, 1846 / aged 59 years. / ELIZABETH / wife of KINZEY GRIFFITH. / died Sept. 1, 1829 / aged 41 years. / GREENBURY. / son of / KINZEY & MARY ANN GRIFFITH / died April 30, 1862 / aged 23 years. / WILLIAM SMITH, / son of KINZEY & ELIZABETH GRIFFITH / died July 21, 1840 / aged 20 years. (N:5)

GRIGG, Careline. In memory of / CARELINE / wife of JOSEPH GRIGG, SR. / who departed this life / Septr 17th 1853 / in the 62nd year of her age. / *The winter of trouble is past, / The storms of afflictions are over, / Her struggle is ended at last, / And sorrow and death are no more.* (B:4, J.G. lot markers, footstone "C.G.")

GRIGG, Joseph, Jr. Our Leader / This stone was erected by / the choir of the Methodist / Episcopal Church / in memory of / JOSEPH GRIGG, JR. / who departed this life / on the 6th day of June 1852 / in the 38th year of his age. / *He died looking unto Jesus.* (B:4, broken, footstone "J.G.")

GRIGSBY, James. JAMES GRIGSBY / died June 10, 1822 / in his 28th year. (B:4, footstone)

GROSS, Nancy. In / memory of / NANCY / consort of / FREDRICK GROSS / who died on the 13 day of / July 1835, aged 18 years. / *She was a kind / an [sic] affectionate companion / and well beloved by / all her friends. / May her soul rest in peace / Amen.* (F:6)

GRUVER, Elizabeth Maria. In / Memory of / ELIZABETH MARIA / wife of / JOHN GRUVER, / who departed this life / Feb. 16, 1828, / in the 28, year of her age / *She's gone alas, too soon / But yet she's gone to rest / Her Saviour call'd her home / Because he thought it best.* (G:5, footstone)

GRUVER, John. Sacred / to the memory of / JOHN GRUVER / who departed this life / December 1st 1829 / in the 45 year of his age. / *One of the old defenders / of Baltimore / A patriot who loved his / country, and bravely / defended his native land.* (G:5, footstone)

GUEST, Rev. Job. In / memory of / REV^d JOB GUEST / Born February 13, 1785, / Died December 15, 1857 / In the 52nd Year / of his Ministry. / *Laborious and successful / in turning souls to Christ, he / now rests from his labors and / his works follow him. / With the tears of friends on / worth below his grave, the smile / of departed saints greet his / happy spirit in heaven.* (K:4, footstone "H. / E. / G.")

GUINN, David H. To / DAVID H. GUINN / who was stricken down in full bliss / of promise

Trinity United Methodist Church Cemetery (1808)

April 27th 1882 / To / ETHWALD / infant son of DAVID H. & ANNIE M. / GUINN / who died April 7th 1852 / *Tread highly 'round / This sacred spot / This hallow'd ground / Disturb it not.* (D:1)

H

HAINES, Lillie M.E. In memory of / LILLIE M.E. HAINES / Born June 3, 1865 / Died Jan. 19, 1883 / *Beloved by all who knew her* [AG:31/12/83:3]. (A:2)

HAMILTON, Alfred. In memory of / ALFRED HAMILTON / Died June 18, 1887 / aged 80 years. / *Resting in hope.* (Q:6)

HAMILTON, Catharine. CATHARINE HAMILTON / died / Feb. 3rd 1873 / aged 86 years / and 7 mo's. / *Dear is the spirit _____ / And since _____ / Oh, why should _____ / She is not lost but gone before.* (Q:6, repaired)

HAMILTON, Hannah Seaton. Sacred / to the memory of / HANNAH / wife of ALFRED HAMILTON / Daughter of GEORGE & LUCINDA / SEATON, who died May 2nd 1851 / aged 30 years & 9 days. / *Oh that my words were now written! oh that / they were printed in a book! That they were / graven with an iron pen and lead in the rock / for ever! For I know that my redeemer liveth, / and that he shall stand at the latter day / upon the earth: And though after my skin worms / destroy this body, yet in my flesh shall I see / God: Whom I shall see for myself, and mine eyes / shall behold. Job Chap. 19 V. 23.* (H:7)

HAMILTON, Philip. PHILIP HAMILTON / died / April 16th 1862 / in the 80th year of his age. / *Blessed are the pure in heart / for they shall see God.* (Q:6; Alexandria Wills, Bk. 8, p. 175, men. wife Catherine)

HARMON, F. Clark. F. CLARK HARMON / Born in Machias, Me. / April 2, 1817 / Died in Wash'n, D.C. / Jany. 2, 1879. (C:6)

HARMON, Lorenzo D. LORENZO D. HARMON / Born in Durham, Me. / April 19, 1814 / Died in Wash'n, D.C. / Dec. 13, 1889. (C:6, lot marker 161)

HARMON, Mary B. Stevens. MARY B. STEVENS / beloved wife of / LORENZO D. HARMON. / Born April 12, 1810 / Died Feb. 13, 1892. (C:6)

HARMON, Mary E. MARY ELLA ESPEY / Born April 4, 1849 / Died Jan. 15, 1920 / MARY E. HARMON / Born Jan. 13, 1877 / Died Aug. 12, 1877. (C:6)

HARPER, Sarah F. SARAH F. HARPER / died / June 21, 1911. (G:1)

HARRIS, Capt. James. In Memory of / Capt. JAMES HARRIS, / Died Nov. 14, 1865 / in the 73d, year of / his age. (K:3)

HARRIS, Lucy A. LUCY A. HARRIS / wife of the late Capt. J. HARRIS / Died Nov. 20, 1873 / aged 80 years. (K:3)

HASSMER, Judith Eleanor. In Loving Memory / JUDITH ELEANOR / HASSMER / Dec. 8, 1952 - Aug. 9, 1991. (R:2)

HAWKINS, Perry H. In memory of / PERRY H. HAWKINS. / and his wife / HANNAH C. / Died Feb. 9, 1867 / Aged 25 years. (C:5, footstone "P.H.H.")

HENDERSON, Ann Jeffries. Sacred / to the memory of / ANN JEFFRIES, / Consort of / GEORGE HENDERSON, / Who died July 10th 1840 / Aged 65 years. / *This is a mother's grave!, Tread softly here, / Where those to whom she being gave, / Shed the warm tear / To lay beneath the sod. / The dearest friend bestowed by God.* (F:6)

[HERRICK?], M_____ C. Headstone for infant, "M.C.H.," no dates. (H:6)

HERRICK, Mollie. MOLLIE / daughter of WM. T. & JANE E. HERRICK / Died June 8,

Trinity United Methodist Church Cemetery (1808)

1865 / Aged 5 years & 28 days. / *Of such is the Kingdom of / Heaven.* (H:6, obelisk)
HOCH, Marguerite Searles. MARGUERITE SEARLES HOCH / Feb. 5, 1890 - May 31, 1985 / ELLERY THORNLEY HOCH / Nov. 20, 1890 - Sept. 17, 1990. (R:2)
HODGE, Nancy Franklin. My mother / NANCY FRANKLIN / Wife of THOMAS HODGE / Died Mar. 4, 1880. (K:8)
HODGKIN, Robert. In memory of / Our Father / ROBERT HODGKIN / born / March 26, 1796 / died / March 27, 1876 / Aged 80 years / and 1 day / *He is not dead but / sleepeth.* / M.M. ROBERTA HODGKIN / died / April 26, 1872 / aged 36 / CLARA HODGKIN / died / Feb. 18, 1831 / aged 31. (R:6)
HOLLENSBURY, Fannie. FANNIE HOLLENSBURY / born / Feb. 22, 1818 / died / Feb. 13, 1894. (A:5, footstone "A.H.")
HOLLENSBURY, Harriet. HARRIET HOLLENSBURY / born / Sept. 16, 1816 / died / June 20, 1894. (A:5, footstone "H.H.")
HOLLENSBURY, John Wesley. JOHN WESLEY HOLLENSBURY / born / July 11, 1803 / died / Nov. 8, 1876. (A:5, footstone "J.W.H.")
HOSKINS, Moses. In / memory of / MOSES / the infant son of / JAMES O.C. & JANE E. / HOSKINS / died July the 12, 1838 / aged 11 months 25 days. (L:6)
HOUCK, Lonnie. LONNIE / son of / ALONZO & LAURA V. / HOUCK / Born May 30, 1867 / Died July 27, 1868. (N:6)
HOUCK, Oppelt. OPPELT / son of A.S. & L.V. HOUCK / born Mar. 11, 1877 / died Sept. 11, 1878. (N:6)
HOWARD, John. Sacred / to the memory of / JOHN HOWARD / who departed this life / December 17th 1821 / in the 33d year of his age. / *Our loss is great which / we will long deplore / But he has coquer'd / through Christ / and reach the / blessed shore.* (J:4, lot marker "J.H. 83," broken)
HUNTER, Charles Sidney. Sacred / to the memory of / CHARLES SIDNEY / eldest son of JOHN T. / & VIRGINIA HUNTER / who departed this life / Sept. 4, 1853 / aged 1 year & 1 mo. (B:7, fallen)
HUNTER, Elizabeth. ELIZABETH / wife of / ROBT. W. HUNTER / died Nov. 30, 1885 / aged 86 years. (R:1, footstone "E.H.")
HUNTER, Robert W. Died on the 22nd of September 1858 / ROBERT W. HUNTER, SR. / (Ship Builder) / in the 71st year of his age. / *But God will redeem my soul from the power of / the grave: for he shall receive me. / Psalms XLIX Ch. 15 v.* (R:1, tablet; Alexandria Wills, Bk. 7, p. 375, "Robert W. Hunter of Prince George County, Maryland")

J

J_____, C. [destroyed] / aged 46 years. Footstone "C.J." (Q:7)
JACKSON, Adele. *At Rest.* / ADELLE / daughter of / WARREN & CHRISTIANA / JACKSON. (L:7)
JACKSON, Christiana. Our Mother / CHRISTIANA JACKSON / died July 21, 1893 / age 70 years. / *Not on a downy couch she lay / But in her prison house of clay / Her body rest beneath the sod / Her spirit dwells above with God / I will dwell in the house of / the Lord forever. / Psalm XXIII.6.* (L:7)
JACOBS, Catharine. In / memory of / CATHARINE JACOBS / consort of / THOMAS JACOBS / who departed this life / May 27th 1829 / in the 52d year of her age. / *The last*

Trinity United Methodist Church Cemetery (1808)

26 years of her life / were devoted to the service of / God, her severe afflictions / (which she bore with christian / fortitude) worked but for her... [remainder under ground]. (N:3)

JACOBS, Catherine. In Memory of / CATHERINE, daughter of / THOMAS & CATHERINE / JACOBS, / who departed this life / January 5th 1815, in the / 16th year of her / age. (N:3)

K

KELL, Nancy. In memory of / Mrs. NANCY / Consort of ISAAC KELL / who died Sept[r] 11th 1820 / in the 32nd year of her age. / *Awake and sing ye that dwell / in dust. Isaiah 2C.19. / Thine eyes shall see the King in / his beauty. 33.17. / I will ransom them from the / Power of the grave; / I will redeem them from death: / O death, I will be thy plagues; / O grave, I will be thy destruction. / Hosea 13.14. / Taught by these doctrines I victorious rise / Faith points the way and hope unbars the skies / They tun'd my passions, taught them how to role / And sank this body but to raise the soul.* (D:2, footstone "N.K.")

KELL, Nancy. In / memory of / NANCY KELL / who died June 24th 1821 / in the 9th year of her age. / *Suffer the little children to come / unto me, and forbid them not. / Mark 10.14 / And God shall wipe away all / Tears from their eyes; and there / Shall be no more death, neither / shall there be any more pain. / Rev. 21.4 / No wonder then her course so swiftly ran / Like the young Eaglet, tow'ring to the sun / While friendly angels for her guidance given / ___ her admiring thro' the courts of heaven.* (D:2, footstone "N.K.")

KIRK, Barbara. BARBARA KIRK / died October / 21st 1813. (C:3, footstone "B.K.")
KRAMER, Emelia. EMELIA KRAMER / 1869-1882. (F:3)
KRAMER, Frederick. FREDERICK KRAMER / 1831-1894. (F:3)

L

LANPHIER, Elizabeth. Sacred / to the memory of / ELIZABETH LANPHIER / Born March 8, 1771 / Died June 6th 1853. (D:3, footstone "E.L.")
LANPHIER, Robert Going. Sacred / To the memory of / ROBERT G. LANPHIER / Born Sep. 18, 1765 / Died Aug. 27, 1846. / *There remaineth therefore at rest / the people of God.* (D:3, footstone "R.G.L.")
LAWSON, Robert M., Jr. ROBT. M. LAWSON, JR. / born / Decr. 25, 1877 / died / March 8, 1878. (P:2)
LEACOCK, L____. L____ / daughter of / MARY S. LEACOCK / died / Dec. 4, 1853 / aged 3 years / and 8 days. (D:5)
LEE, D. Lewis. D. LEWIS / son of CLAGETT & / HANNAH LEE / Born Feb. 7, 1856 / Died Oct. 29, 1888. / *Asleep in Jesus.* (G:7)
LEE, Mary Ann Jones. In memory of / MARY ANN, / Wife of / ALFRED H. LEE, M.D. / And Daughter of / NATHAN & ANN JONES, / of Phila. / Died March 27, 1844 / Aged 24 yrs. 6 mos. / & 8 dys. (M:1)
LEE, Nhia Chue / 1927-1982. (A:2)
LEVERING, Elizabeth. In memory of / ELIZABETH LEVERING / who departed this life /

Trinity United Methodist Church Cemetery (1808)

April 20th 1854 / in the 78th year of her age. (P:5)

LOCKWOOD, Cassandra Martha. *Hark they whisper, Angels say / sister spirit come away.* / Sacred / to the memory of / CASSANDRA MARTHA / Consort of AQUILA LOCKWOOD / who calmly fell asleep in Jesus on / the Morning of the 12th November / 1833, in the 42nd year / of her age. (M:4, obelisk)

LOCKWOOD, Harriet. HARRIET LOCKWOOD / died / June 27, 1854. (M:4)

LOGAN, William. In memory / of / WILLIAM LOGAN / died / April 8, 1887 / Aged 52 years. (M:7, fallen)

LONGDEN, John. In / memory of / JOHN LONGDEN / who died March 31, 1830 / aged 76. / *He was a good citizen, a kind / parent, an affectionate friend, / an honest man. / His descendants will long / cherish the remembrance of his / worth and virtue.* (P:1, footstone at headstone; Alexandria Wills, Bk. A, p. 173, men. his father Ralph Longden)

LOWE, Jane R. Sacred / to the memory of / JANE R. LOWE / daughter of JOHN F.M. and SOPHIA E. LOWE / Born July 27th 1835 / Died June 30th 1859. / *Without a grown or sigh or glance to show / A parting sprang the spirit from her pass'd / And they who awaked her in ____ / The very instant till the dying ____ / Her sweet face unto shadow dull and slow / closed o'er her eyes. / She lived in life a peacefull dove / She died as blossoms die / And now her spirit floats above / A seraphim in the sky. / Weep not she is not dead but sleepeth.* (F:3, footstone)

LOWE, Robert Steed. Sacred / to the memory of / R.S. LOWE / infant Son of JOHN F. / M. and SOPHIA E. LOWE / Born July 13th 1831 / Died July 4th 1832 [AG:6/7/32:3, gives date 3 JUL 1832] / Sacred / to the memory of / M[ercer]. L[loyd]. LOWE / infant son of JOHN F. / M. and SOPHIA E. LOWE / Born June 19th 1839 / Died March 7th 1840. / *Suffer the little children to come unto me / And forbid them not for of such is the / Kingdom of God.* / Mark 10th Ch. 14th V. (F:3, footstone)

LUGENBEEL, James W. JAMES W. LUGENBEEL / died / Sept.r 22nd 1857 / Aged 38 Years / *But God will / redeem my soul from / the power of the grave: / for he shall receive me.* / Psalm XLIX. XV. (R:5; Alexandria Wills, Bk. 7, p. 257, men. wife Martha Alice, and his unnamed father of Frederick County, Maryland)

LUMSDON, John. JOHN LUMEDON / departed this Life 6th / Sep.r 1806 in the / 38 year of his age. (L:2)

LUMSDON, Mary Ann. Erected by a friend / of MARY ANN, daut. of / JOHN & MARGERY LUMS / DON, who departed this / life November 2, 1828 / in her 22 year / *Pious she lived / With pure religion blest / Triumphant died / Let angels tell the rest.* (P:2)

LUNT, Agothian. AGOTHIAN LUNT / Died in California / June 13th 1855 / aged 24 years / *Far from the home that gave / him birth / His spirit passed away / from earth.* (N:3)

LUNT, Arthur. Sacred / to / the memory of / ARTHUR LUNT / died April 10th 1856 / aged 32 years / *None knew him but to love him.* (N:3)

LUNT, Elizabeth. Sacred / to the memory of / ELIZABETH LUNT / wife of EZRA LUNT / who departed this life / Aug. 28, 1828 / in the 39 year of her age. (N:3, "E.L.")

LUNT, Ezra. Sacred / to the memory of / EZRA LUNT / who departed this life / December 17th 1841 / in the 54th year of his age. (N:3, footstone "E.L.")

LYLES, Annas Isabell. ANNAS ISABELL / Daughter of / A.D. & E.A. LYLES / Died Aug. 3, 1889. / Aged 11 months. (A:2)

LYLES, Esther. To the / memory of / ESTHER, consort of / JAMES LYLES, / who departed July 14 / 1825, aged 30 years / wanting 15 days / Also her 3 children / who went before

Trinity United Methodist Church Cemetery (1808)

her, / the oldest 14 months old. (C:4)

LYLES, Mary Ann. In / memory of / MARY ANN, wife of / JAMES LYLES / who departed this life / Sep^t 12th 1815 / aged 23 years. (C:4, footstone "M.A.L.")

LYLES, James. Sacred / to the memory of / JAMES LYLES / who departed this / life on the 25th March / 1858 / Aged 79 years. (C:4, footstone "J.L.")

M

MACKALE, Mary E. In / Memory of / MARY E. MACKALE / who departed this life / August 29th 1814, in the / 16th year of her age. (H:3, footstone "M.E.M.")

MAJOR, Elizabeth Baden Crook. In / memory of / ELIZABETH BADEN / Youngest daughter of / BERNARD & AGNES CROOK / & wife of / JAS. J. MAJOR / who departed this life / August 4th, 1856 / in the 45th year of her age. / *Jesus can make the dying / bed. / As soft as downy pillows / feel.* (D:1, footstone "E.B.M.")

MAJOR, John. Sacred / to the memory of / JOHN MAJOR / who departed this life / August 16th 1834 / aged 52 years / also of / MARY, his wife / who departed this life August 21, 1849 / aged 64 years. (D:7, fallen)

MANDELL, Mary. Sacred / to the memory of / Mrs. MARY MANDELL / consort of / JOHN C. MANDELL / who was born 6th Sept. 1788 / and departed this life / on the 13th August 1834 / aged 46 years / *I am the resurrection and the / life saith the Lord, he that believeth / in me, though he were dead yet / shall he live.* (R:5)

MANGHER, Susan E. In memory of / SUSAN E. / Consort of JAMES B. MANGHER / and daughter of / W. and E. NOLAND / Born June 28, 1837 / Died June 13, 1866. (C:5, repaired)

MANSFIELD, Henry. In memory of / Our Father & Mother / HENRY MANSFIELD / Born Oct. 13, 1797 / Died Nov. 21st 1861 / LUCY MANSFIELD / Born Nov. 27th 1797 / Died Dec. 24th 1862. / *Sleep in Jesus.* / CHARLES E. MANSFIELD / Born Aug. 7, 1820 / Died Sept. 1, 1821 / ISABELLA MANSFIELD / Born July 18, 1825 / Died Sept. 19, 1826 / WILLIAM H. MANSFIELD / Born Dec. 16, 1829 / Died Oct. 22, 1830 / JANE E. MANSFIELD / Born June 22, 1831 / Died May 3, 1833 / GEORGE H. MANSFIELD / Born Jan. 2, 1836 / Died March 29, 1839 / CAROLINE R. MANSFIELD / Born Dec. 1, 1838 / Died Nov. 29, 1847 / Children of HENRY & LUCY MANSFIELD. (E:3, obelisk)

MARTIN, Thomas Littleton. Sacred to the memory of / THOMAS LITTLETON MARTIN / born in Northampton Co., Va. / May 12, 1791 / died in Washington City / May 6, 1835 / *For 21 years a citizen of Alexa. / Honest and inteligent, he was / esteemed by his fellow citizens / Humble and obedient he / enjoyed the _____ of God / His death was a triumph that _____ / Christ's blood.* (F:4)

MATHER, J. Warren. <u>MATHER</u> / June 4, 1911 / J. WARREN / Oct. 4, 1986. (R:2)

MATTHEWS, Rev. Lastley. This Stone is raised / in memory of / the Rev^d / LASTLEY MATTHEWS / who died April 23d / 1813 in the 57th Year / of his age / after traveling 27 Years / in the methodist / traveling connection. (K:2; Alexandria Wills, Bk. 1, p. 227)

MAY, Alice. In memory of / ALICE MAY / beloved wife of / EDWARD H. MAY / born / Dec. 31, 1830 / died / Sept. 19, 1896. / *Gone but not forgotten.* (P:6)

MAY, Edward H. To my husband / EDWARD H. MAY / Born June 20, 1827 / Died Nov. 21, 1886. / *But God will redeem / my soul from the power / of the grave for He shall /*

Trinity United Methodist Church Cemetery (1808)

receive me. (P:6, lot marker nearby: H. Carolin / 137)

McCOBB, John. Sacred / to the memory of / JOHN McCOBB / born in Phippsburg, Maine, February / 6th, 1778 / died May 20, 1818. (Q:4, tablet)

McCOBB, Parker N. In / memory of / PARKER N. McCOBB / son of / JOHN & SARAH McCOBB / who departed this life / June 1, 1826 in the / 11th year of his age. (Q:4)

McCOBB, Sarah. Sacred / To the memory of / Mrs. SARAH McCOBB / consort of / Mr. JOHN McCOBB / who departed this life / February 28th 1819 / in the 35th year of her age. (Q:4, tablet)

McCOBB, Sarah Weston. In memory of / SARAH WESTON / Daughter of THOMAS F. / and MARION L. McCOBB / who departed this life / August 9th 1848 / Aged 14 months. (Q:4)

McCORMICK, John. In memory of / JOHN McCORMICK / who departed this life / Aug. 8th 1850 / in the 61st year of his age. / *He was born in Loudoun Co., Va. and / was for many years a resident of / Baltimore, Md., but the last four / teen years of his life a useful and / greatly esteemed citizen of this / place. He was truly a good man. / As he lived univirsally [sic] respected / so died deeply lamented not / only by his own bereaved family / but by the entire community in / which he had lived.* (D:6)

McGUIRE, Capt. James. Sacred / to the memory of / Capt JAMES McGUIRE / who departed this life / on the 30th day of November 1850 / in the 78th year of his age. / *The greater portion of Capt. McGuire's / life was spent in the Town of Alexandria / where he filled different public offices / with great fidelity. Having the ____ / relatives, he devised his property for / the benefit of the POOR. / Blessed is he that considereth the ____ / Lord ____ / tremble.* (D:6, broken boxtomb, lot marker "J.M.")

McGUIRE, Lucy. In memory of / Mrs. LUCY McGUIRE / consort of / Mr. JAMES McGUIRE. / who departed this life / on the 19th of October 1831. / in the 54th year of her age. (D:6, boxtomb)

McNAMARA, Winfred. WINFRED McNAMARA / confort of JOHN McNAMARA / departed this life Auguft / 14th 1812, aged [damaged] & 6 M. (H:2)

McVEIGH, Cynthia Ariel Guest. Sacred / to the memory of / CYNTHIA ARIEL / wife of / JAMES HARVEY McVEIGH / and daughter of / Rev^d JOB GUEST / born Septr 22 / 1811 / died March 13, 1851 / *A faithful wife, / A fond and devoted Mother / A sincere and true friend.* / Our children / LUCY McVEIGH / born May 25, 1848 / died July 12, 1849. (L:4, obelisk)

McVEIGH, James H. In memory / of / JAS. H. McVEIGH. / 1806-1891 [AG:31/12/91:1, gives date 22 JUN 1891]. (L:4)

MEADE, Edith A. Our Mother / EDITH A. / wife of / ROBERT H. MEADE / born Jan. 26, 1850 / died April 2, 1885 / *Asleep in Jesus.* (E:3)

MERRIKEN, Elizabeth. My / ELIZABETH, / has here slept in Jesus / since 23rd of / February 1847 / JOSEPH MERRIKEN. (K:2)

MERRIKEN, Rev. Joseph. Here lies the body of / the Revd. JOSEPH MERRIKEN / who finished his course / gloriously triumphing over / death / March 4th 1848, Aged 38. / *He was a burning and shining light / This memorial / was placed here by those to whom / were devoteth as Pastor of the / Methodist Episcopal Church / in Alexandria / the last labors of his faithful ministry.* (K:2, broken; Alexandria Wills, Bk. 5, p. 36)

MIDDLETON, Ann. In / memory of / ANN MIDDLETON / who departed this life / Novr the

Trinity United Methodist Church Cemetery (1808)

4th 1832 / in the 60th year of her age. / *Blessed are the dead who die in the Lord.* (K:1, footstone "A.M.")

MIDDLETON, Elizabeth. Sacred / to the memory of / ELIZABETH MIDDLETON / who departed this life / December the 27th 1831 / in the 27th year of her age. / *Blessed are the pure in heart / for they shall see God.* (K:1, footstone "E.M.")

MILBURN, Alice. In / memory of / ALICE, wife of / GEORGE MILBURN / who died 25th Feb. 1833 / aged 34 years / Also / GEORGE, son of / GEORGE & ALICE MILBURN. / who died March 24th 1833 / aged 17 months. (P:3, footstone "A. & G.M.")

MILBURN, George. Sacred / to the memory of / GEORGE MILBURN / who departed this / Life 26th of August 1838 / Aged 43 Years. (P:3)

MILLS, Margery. Sacred / to the memory of / MARGERY / wife of Capt WILLIAM MILLS / who died Oct. 30th 1831 / aged 65 years / Also / WILLIAM / son of Capt. Wm. & MARGERY MILLS / who died Sep^t 19th 1830 / aged 33 years. / This stone was Erected by her / affectionate Daughter. (D:4, footstone "M.M. / W.M.")

MINNIY, Catharine C. In / memory of / CATHARINE C. / wife of / JOHN P. MINNIY / who died July 9th, A.D. 1836 / in the 38 year / of her age. (R:3, stone completely worn away)

MOORE, George. In Memory of / GEORGE MOORE / Son of / W. & M. MOORE / who died Sept^r / 16th 1812, aged 18 / M & 5 D. (H:2)

MORGAN, Catharine. Sacred / to the memory of / CATHARINE MORGAN, who departed this life / May 11th 1854 / in the 57th year of her age. / *Even so them also which die / in Jesus will God bring with him.* (H:6)

MOUNT, Ann Eliza. In / memory of / ANN ELIZA / Daughter of / THOMAS & SARAH / MOUNT, / who departed this life / Aug. 11, 1834 / aged 12 years, 8 mo. / and 18 days. (J:2)

MOUNT, Joseph S. Sacred / to the memory of / JOSEPH S. MOUNT / infant son of / THOMAS & SARAH / MOUNT / who departed this / life July 20th 1811 / aged 11 months / & 25 days. (J:2)

MOUNT, Sarah Smith. In / memory of / SARAH / wife of / THOMAS MOUNT / and daughter of / JOSEPH and MARY SMITH / who died Feby. 3d 1833 / in the 42d year of her age / Beside her / lie the remains of / SARAH PRITCHARD / daughter of / THOMAS and SARAH MOUNT / who died June 22d 1830 / aged 1 year wanting 1 day. (J:2)

MUIR, John. In memory of / JOHN MUIR / Born December 9, 1807 / Died August 22, 1865 / ELEANOR JOHNSON / Born October 6, 1864 / Died July 10, 1865. (D:7)

MUIR, Lydia. In memory of / LYDIA, / consort of JOHN MUIR / Mayor of Alex. / who died / April 29, 1853, aged 43 years. / For 27 years / a member of the M.E. Church / *She could say as life ebbed space / I would not live alway / No welcome the tomb. / Since Jesus hath lain there / I dread not his glory.* / NANNIE ROSZEL / daughter of J. & L. MUIR / died June 5, 1854. (D:7)

MUNRO, Julian. Departed this life / the 4th Octr 1822 / JULIAN MUNRO / Consort of ROBERT MUNRO / aged 40 years & 21 days. / *Blessed are the dead which die / In the Lord from hence forth / Yea, saith the spirit, that they / May rest from there labours; / And there works do follow them.* (C:2, broken footstone "J.M.")

MUNROE, Robert. In memory of / ROBERT MUNROE / died April 9th 1852 / aged 82 years. (C:2, footstone "R.M.")

Trinity United Methodist Church Cemetery (1808)

N

NALLS, Ann E. In memory of / ANN E. / wife of JAMES W. NALLS / born / Jan. 28, 1822 / died / June 22 / 1887. (A:1, broken)

NALLS, Eugenia. In memory of / EUGENIA / daughter of / J.W. & MARY A. / NALLS / who died 9th Jan. / 1852 in the 8th year / of her age. (A:1)

NALLS, James W. In memory of / JAMES W. NALLS / born / May 16, 1817 / died / Jan. 24, 1888. (A:1)

NALLS, Mary Ann. MARY ANN / Daughter of / JAMES W. and / MARY ANN NALLS / who died July 18, / 1848 / aged 18 days. (A:1, footstone "M.A.N.")

NALLS, Mary Ann. MARY ANN / wife of / JAMES W. NALLS / who departed this life / March 27, 1852 / aged 33 years. / *There the wicked cease from / troubling, and there the weary / be at rest.* (A:1, footstone)

NELSON, Lynwood, Sr. NELSON / Lynwood, Sr. / Sept. 11, 1890 / Mar. 23, 1963 / CARRIE N. / July 9, 1889 / Aug. 3, 1956. (G:7)

NEWMAN, Susanna Phillips Cawood. In / memory of / SUSANNA PHILLIPS / NEWMAN, sister of / MOSES O.B. CAWOOD / who departed this life / Oc^t 11th 1821 / in the 35th year of her age. / *She left this world triumphantly, / having made her peace with God / she's gone to reap the pleasure / of everlasting life.* (D:4, footstone "S.P.N.")

NEWTON, Ann. In memory of / ANN NEWTON / wife of / WILLIAM C. NEWTON / who departed this / life April 9th 1814 / aged 35 years. (R:3)

NIXON, Catharine Ellen. IN / memory of / CATHARINE / ELLEN NIXON / daughter of RICHARD & JANE / NIXON / who departed / this life Jan. 16th, 1840 / Aged 15 Months / and 4 days. (Q:6)

NOLAND, Elizabeth. In memory of / ELIZABETH / Consort of WILLIAM NOLAND / Born March 2, 1800, / Died June 4, 1869 / *A devoted wife and / affectionate mother.* (C:5)

NOLAND, [Reberter?]. [REBERTER?] / daughter of / ____ & ____ NOLAND / Born July 27, 1835 / Died July 16, 18[43]. (C:5, footstone "R.N.")

NOWLAND, Charles William. Sacred / to the memory of / CHARLES WILLIAM, the youngest Son of CHARLES / W. & SUSAN C. NOWLAND / born June the 28th 1849 / departed this life August the / 9th 1852, in the 4th year / of his age. / *Art thou gone my William dear / From sin and sorrow free. / Those two bright eyes in death are / closed. That often gazed on me. / Sleep on my babe in silent rest, Till Gabriel's trump shall blow / And I hope we'll meet again / On Canaan's happy shore.* (P:7)

NOWLAND, Thomas Seaton. Sacred / to / the memory of / THOMAS SEATON, / Son of CHARLES W. & SUSAN C. / NOWLAND, Who calmly fell / asleep in Jesus October 24th 1865 / In the 20th year of his age. / *His meek quiet spirit endeared / him many friends. / Sleep on my Son and take your rest, / God called you home he thought it best, / T'was hard indeed to part with thee, / But God's strong arm supported me. / Yet again I hope to meet you, / When the storm of life is fled / There in Heaven I hope to greet you / Where no farewell [damage] is bed.* (Q:5)

NUTT, James. Sacred / to the memory of / JAMES NUTT / of whom it may be truly said / that / He was an affectionate Husband / a tender parent / an honest benevolent and useful / citizen / while faithfully fulfilling the duties / of his country / He departed this life to the / great grief of all that knew Him / Sep^t 10th 1814 / in the 40th year of his age. (D:2, tablet)

Trinity United Methodist Church Cemetery (1808)

O

OGDEN, George A. GEORGE A. OGDEN / Co. E / 17 Regt. / Va. Inf. / C.S.A. / Sep. 18, 1895. (D:6, sign S42)

ORSBORN, Lawson. In Memory of / LAWSON ORSBORN / who departed this / life Sep^t. 28, 1817 / aged 35 years. / *Farewell dear & loving wife / Contented may you be / May you obtain eternal life / Prepare to follow me.* (C:5, footstone "L.O.")

P

PADGETT, Lucretia. Entered into / rest / June 21, 1889 / LUCRETIA PADGETT / in the 89th year of her age. (stone not found)

PATTERSON, Benjamin C. In / memory of / BENJAMIN C. PATTERSON / son of BENJAMIN and / SARAH PATTERSON / who departed this life / October 3rd 1810, aged / 7 months and 25 / days. (H:3, footstone "B.C.P.")

PATTERSON, Benjamin D. In Memory of / BENJAMIN D. PATTERSON / who departed this life / May 11, 1816 / aged 36 years. (H:3, footstone "B.D.P.")

PATTERSON, William. In Memory of / WILLIAM PATTERSON / who departed this / life February 16th / 1816 / in the 64th year of / his age. (H:3, footstone "W.P.;" Alexandria Wills, Bk. 3, p. 170, men. wife Mary)

PEAKE, Mary C. Zimmerman. In memory of / MARY C. / wife of B.F. PEAKE / and daughter of ADAM & SINAH E. ZIMMERMAN / Born Jan. 17, 1839 / Died April 25, 1871. (M:5)

PENN, Leonidas Rosser. LEONIDAS ROSSER / only son of W.L. & M.E. / PENN, died October 5th / 1854, aged 3 years & / 9 months / CHARLOTTE P[ierpont]., fifth / daughter of W.L. & M.E. / PENN, died June 30th / 1854, aged 8 months / WALTER ANN, third daughter of W.L. & M.E. / PENN, died May 24, 1847, aged 5 days. (C:3)

PENN, Mary Elizabeth Durr. In memory of / MARY E. DURR / wife of / WALTER L. PENN / born / May 7, 1815 / died / October 7, 1880. (C:3, footstone "M.E.D.P.")

PENN, Walter. In memory of / WALTER PENN / born in / St. Mary's Co., Md., 1777 / died in / Alexandria, Va., 1826. (C:3, footstone "W.P.")

PENN, Walter Lindsay. In memory of / WALTER LINDSAY PENN / born in / Fairfax Co., Va. / May 6, 1814 / died / April 1, 1885. (C:3, footstone)

PEYTON, Howard. HOWARD / eldest child of / MILLARD F. & ADA M. / PEYTON / died July 19, 1890 / aged 11 years. / *Jesus said suffer / little children to / come unto me.* (L:4)

PHILLIPS, Elizabeth. In / memory of / ELIZABETH / Daughter of / JOHN H. and ELLENOR / PHILLIPS / who departed this life / April 7th 1846 / Aged 67. (M:2, footstone "E.P.")

PHILLIPS, Ellenor. In / memory of / ELLENOR / Wife of / JOHN H. PHILLIPS / who departed this life / February 10th 1827 / Aged 67. (M:2, mismatched footstone "J.H.P." and footstone "E.P." is on ground)

[PHILLIPS?], G. Footstone "G.P." (M:2)

PHILLIPS, John H. (M:2, stone not found, see Ellenor Phillips above)

PLANT, Paschal, Sr. PASCHAL PLANT, SR. / 1830-1911 / MARY E. PLANT / 1840-1931 / HENRY <u>BLISH</u> / 1828-1887 / AMBROSE PLANT / 1875-1896 / MARIETTA PLANT / 1860-1912 / DAVID I. PLANT / 1871-1916 / PASCAL J. PLANT / 1866-1946.

Trinity United Methodist Church Cemetery (1808)

(H:1)
POINDEXTER, Robert J. ROBERT J. POINDEXTER / July 23, 1889 / March 1, 1965. (G:7)
POSS, Henry B. HENRY B. POSS / born June 26, 1841 / died August 11, 1900 / *At Rest.* / his wife / ALICE G. POSS / Oct. 8, 1851 - Aug. 21, 1915. [second stone] C.S.A. / HENRY B. POSS / Kemper's Battery / died / Aug. 12, 1900. [Note: these graves were removed to Ivy Hill Cemetery, where they are found in Section R (East)].
POSS, John W. JOHN W. POSS / born Aug. 11, 1873 / died May 6, 1911. [Note: this grave was removed to Ivy Hill Cemetery, where it is found in Section R (East)].
[POTTEN?], S. Footstone only, "S.P." (C:2)
POTTEN, John. Sacred / to the memory of / JOHN POTTEN / who departed this life / Sept$^{r.}$ 22nd 1835 / aged 72 years. (C:2, footstone "J.P." next to footstone "S.P." above; Alexandria Wills, Bk. 4, p. 91)
POTTEN, Sarah. This stone / is raised / to the memory of / SARAH POTTEN / Consort of / JOHN POTTEN / who left him on the 7th of Sep$^{t.}$ / 1829 / Passing through the gate of / death to join the / church triumphant in the 55th year of her age. (A:5)
PRESTON, Elisha C.D. In / memory of / ELISHA C.D. / PRESTON / who departed this life / June 2nd 1847 / Aged 30. (N:2, footstone "E.C.D.P.")
PRESTON, Thomas. Sacred / to the memory of / Mr. THOMAS PRESTON / who departed this life / the 6th April 1834 / in the 64th year of his age. / *He was an affectionate husband / a tender Father a sencire [sic] friend / & one who strove to serve his God. / Mark the perfect man & behold the upright, for the end of that man is peace.* (N:2, footstone "T.P.")
PRESTON, Thomas S. Departed this life on the / 14th Sep$^{t.}$ 1825, aged 18 / years, 7 months / THOMAS S. PRESTON / son of THOMAS and ELLEN / PRESTON. / *A dutiful son, an affectionate / brother, and sincere friend; / belov'd admir'd and esteemed / by all who knew him. / Here then repose the last remains / of one who living was beloved; / One free from earth's corrosive stains, / Whose conduct ev'ry virtue proved.* (N:2, footstone "T.S.P.")
PRICHARD, Julia Ada. JULIA / wife of / JOSEPH PRICHARD / died May 23, 1870 / aged 37 years / also her infant son / JAMES COLEMAN / died June 6, 1870 / aged 3 weeks. / *As a wife devoted as a mother affectionate / As a friend e'er kind and true; In life she exhibited all the grace of a christian; / In death her redeemed spirit r'turned to God who gave it.* (N:6)
PURSELL, Elizabeth. Sacred / to the memory of / ELIZABETH PURSELL, / consort of THOMAS PURSELL; / who departed this life, / in the full triumphs of the christian faith, / 17th Sep. 1835, / in the 35th year of her age. / Also their Infant Children, / MARY E. PURSELL, died 12. July 1832; / WM. C. PURSELL, died 28. June 1833; / & CHAS. W. PURSELL, died 8. July 1835 / *And of our fellowship below / With Jesus be so sweet, / Wh[damage] of rapture shall we know, / W [damage] nd his throne we meet.* (L:1, footstone "E.P." / "M.E.P." / "W.C.P." / "C.W.P.")

R

REARDON, Mary E. In, M / of / MARY E. REARDON / who departed this / life Oct$^{r.}$ 2nd 1811, / in the 2nd year / of her age. (J:3)
REESE, Harriet. Sacred / to the memory of / HARRIET / beloved wife of / SAMUEL REESE

Trinity United Methodist Church Cemetery (1808)

/ who departed this life / Aug. 24, 1843, in the 39 / year of her age. *After a long / and protracted illness of / 11 months which she bore / with christian fortitude / and resignation.* (H:7, footstone "H.R.")

REESE, Samuel. Sacred / to the memory of / SAMUEL REESE / who departed this life February / 17th 1853, in the 53d year. / *Blessed are the dead which die in the / Lord, from henceforth; yea, saith the spir / it, that they may rest from their / labors and their works do follow / them.* [remainder illegible] (H:7, footstone "S.R.;" Alexandria Wills, Bk. 6, p. 200)

REEVES, William C. In / memory of / WM. C. REEVES / born at Mount Holly, N.J. / January 17, 1800 / died Sep^t 9, 1834. (J:6)

REYNOLDS, David. In / memory of / DAVID REYNOLDS / who departed this life / Augt 30th 1821 / aged 54 years. / *His life ensur'd saviours bliss / a crown of Joy and righteous / ness.* (C:4, footstone "D.R.;" Alexandria Wills, Bk. 3, p. 16)

REYNOLDS, Phebe Veitch. Sacred / to the memory of / PHEBE / wife of WM. C. REYNOLDS / and daughter of / WM. and RACHEL VEITCH / who departed this life / February 13th 1842 / aged 37 years. / *In all the relations of life as daughter, / Wife and Mother... / ____ comfort them ____ life / and ____ illness her victory / and triumph was completed as her / last dying words in her weeping / Husband gave testimony, / I am going to my father and your / Father my God and yours.* (M:3, footstone "P.R.")

RICHARDS, John Z. In / memory of / JOHN Z. RICHARDS / who departed this life / August 25th 1824 / aged 8 months & 20 days. / *Sweet little babe take thy repose / distress'd thy Parents deep their / woes / to part with you our darling son / a trial great, God's will be done.* (E:1)

RICHARDS, Mary Ann. MARY ANN / Wife of / WM. C. RICHARDS / Died June 20th 1866 / in her 44th year / Also her infant / JOHN MORGAN / Born June 20th [1866], died July 4, 1866 / *Blessed are the dead / that die in the Lord.* (H:6)

RICHARDS, William Carlin. WILLIAM CARLIN RICHARDS / 1816-1901 / *With Christ which is far better. Phil. I.23.* (H:6; AG:31/12/01:1, gives date 7 SEP 1901)

RICHARDS, Willie F. WILLIE F. / son of W.C. & MARY A. / RICHARDS / Born Aug. 11, 1860 / Died March 2, 1877 / *Blessed are the pure in / heart.* (H:6, repaired)

RISTON, Dennis W. In memory of / DENNIS W. / Son of / J.H. & R.A. RISTON / Died May 27, 1863 / aged 17 yrs. 6 mos. / & 11 days. / *Sleep, Dennis, dear and take your rest / ...* (E:7, footstone "D.W.R.")

ROBBINS, D. Howell. Sacred / to the memory of / D. HOWELL ROBBINS, M.D. / Died Dec. 5, 1894 / aged 76 years. (L:2, broken, footstone "D.H.R.")

ROBBINS, Rev. Isaac. Sacred / to the memory of / Rev. ISAAC ROBBINS / born in Plymouth, Mass. / Went to his rest from / Alexa. on the 27th May / 1846, aged 75 years, 11 / months & 8 days. (L:2, footstone "I.R.;" Alexandria Wills, Bk. 4, p. 429)

ROBBINS, Mary Douglass. (L:2, stone not found; AG:9/3/55:3, gives death 20 FEB 1855; Alexandria Wills, Bk. 7, p. 12)

ROBBINS, Mary Howell. Sacred / to the memory of / MARY H. ROBBINS / Daughter of / Rev. ISAAC & MARY D. ROBBINS / aged 76 [AG:31/12/88:1, gives date 26 MAY 1888]. (L:2, broken, footstone "M.H.R.")

ROBERTS, Robert B. In Memory of / ROBERT B. ROBERTS / who departed this life / December 15th 1814, aged / 38 years & 9 months. (K:4)

RUDD, William. Erected / in memory of / WILLIAM RUDD / a native of England / who departed this life / August 30th, A.D. 1821 / in the 45' year of his age. / *Releas'd from*

Trinity United Methodist Church Cemetery (1808)

all his cares & woes / He rests in calm and sweet repose. (D:3)

RUNNELS, Abigail C. In / memory of / ABIGAIL G., wife of / JOHN H. RUNNELS / who departed this life / Dec. 23d 1818 / in the 31 year of her age. / Blessed from all the years _____ / She rest in calm and _____. (K:4)

RUPPLE, Elleanor M. Kane. In memory of / ELLEANOR M. KANE / beloved wife of / MICHAEL RUPPLE / Died Aug. 24, 1895 / In the 23rd year / of her age. / Gone but not forgotten. (G:7)

S

SCOTT, Elizabeth. Departed this life / April 27, 1825, / ELIZABETH SCOTT / wife of / CHARLES SCOTT / in the 56th year of her age. / Weep not for me my friends / Nor shake at death's alarms / It is the voice that Jesus sends / To call me to his arms. (L:5, footstone "E.S.")

SEATON, Adolphus. In memory of / ADOLPHUS SEATON / Died March 19, 1865 / in his 41st year / Gone before me O my brother / To the spirit land / fainly I look for another / In thy place to stand. / GEORGE B. / Son of JOHN A. & V.J. SEATON / Died May 1861 / aged 5 months. (H:7)

SEATON, George. Sacred / to the memory of / GEORGE SEATON / who departed this life / December 10th 1844 / in the 53 year of his age. (H:7, forced downward by tree roots; Alexandria Wills, Bk. 4, p. 387)

SEATON, George P. GEORGE P. / son of JOHN A. & V.J. SEATON / died May 18, 1861, aged 5 months. (H:7)

SEATON, Lucinda. In memory of / LUCINDA / wife of GEORGE SEATON / died March 15, 1865 / aged 67 years. / We only know that th_ _ust you_ and / that the same returnless tide which bore / thee for in us still glides on and we also / _____ mourn thee with it glide. / LUCINDA / [died] 1869. (H:7, broken by tree roots; Alexandria Wills, Bk. 8, p. 281)

SEATON, Sarah Ellen. Sacred / to the memory of / SARAH ELLEN SEATON / daughter of GEORGE & LUCINDA SEATON / who departed this life / October 5, 1847, aged 18 years & 8 months. [Lengthy epitaph illegible]. (H:7)

SHECKLE, Dedrick. In / memory of / DEDRICK SHECKLE / a native of / Prussia / who died June 25th 1829 / aged 80 years. (F:1, footstone "D.S.;" Alexandria Wills, Bk. 3, p. 310)

SHERWOOD, Charlotte. Sacred / To / the Memory of / CHARLOTTE / the loving & affectionate / Wife of / JOSEPH T. SHERWOOD / Who Died August 1, 1864 / Aged 50 years. / Her last words were I am going home. (A:5, footstone "C.S.")

SHIPLEY, Sarah Ann. SARAH ANN SHIPLEY / 1819-1877 / CHARLES H. McGLUE / 1846-1911. (Q:5)

SHIRLEY, Marion Middleton. IN / memory of / Mrs. MARION SHIRLEY / consort of / WILLIAM H. SHIRLEY / and daughter of / ELECTIUS & ANN MIDDLETON / who departed this life / on the 5th day of October 1833 / in the 26th year of her age. / why _____ / _____ fell asleep / _____ / _____ consoling while we weep. (K:1, footstone)

SIMPSON, Emma. In memory of / EMMA / infant daughter of / HENRY L. & JULIA A. / SIMPSON / died Sept. 8, 1850 / aged 2 years. / Of such is the kingdom / of heaven.

Trinity United Methodist Church Cemetery (1808)

(A:24)
SIMPSON, French Reid. Sacred / to the memory of / FRENCH REID / son of HENRY L. and JULIA ANN / SIMPSON / who departed this life / November 8, A.D. 1839, aged 7 years and 12 days. / ... / *The family above.* / *These feeble frames my power shall* / *And mould with Heavenly skill* / *I'll give them tongues to sing my praise* / *And hands to do my will.* (A:6, epitaph mostly illegible)

SIMPSON, French Reid. SIMPSON / FRENCH REID, / son of HENRY L. & JULIA A. / SIMPSON / born June 20, 1839 / died Feb. 16, 1899. (A:6, modern stone, sign S43)

SIMPSON, Henry L. HENRY L. SIMPSON / born August 20, 1805 / died / February 5, 1877 / ARTHUR / son of / H.L. & J.A. SIMPSON / Born Feb. 24, 1847 / Died Jan. 30, 1886 / WINFIELD M. / son of / H.L. & J.A. SIMPSON / Born April 12, 1852 / Died May 11, 1886 / *We shall meet again.* / JULIA A. / daughter of / REID & MARY CROSS, / wife of HENRY L. SIMPSON / Born Jan. 9, 1812 / Died April 1, 1899. (A:6, obelisk, top fallen and broken)

SIMPSON, Mary Alice. In memory of / MARY ALICE / daughter of HENRY L. / and JULIA A. SIMPSON / Died Nov. 22, 1862 / Aged 17 years. / *Y___ ___ / Till ___ / Shall call ___ / To the mansions above.* (A:6)

SIMS, Nancy. NANCY SIMS / wife of CHARLES SIMS / died April 4, 1860 / aged 86 years / *Rest, mother rest / wilt Thou be ___; thy hands / no more will labor here with / ours. / By that pure and silent stream / Shelter from the scorching beam; / Shepherd, Saviour, Guardian, Guide / Keep us ever near thy side.* (R:1)

SIPPLE, Anne Rosina. ANNE ROSINA / SIPPLE / Aug. 18, 1854 / July 9, 1950. (G:6)
SIPPLE, Bettie K. BETTIE K. / SIPPLE / Mar. 25, 1857 / Aug. 2, 1891. (G:6)
SIPPLE, Elizabeth D. ELIZABETH D. / SIPPLE / June 17, 1833 / Dec. 3, 1923. (G:6)
SIPPLE, Samuel S. SAMUEL S. / SIPPLE / Sept. 24, 1829 / Dec. 17, 1910. (G:6)

SKINNER, Elizabeth. Sacred / to the memory of / ELIZABETH SKINNER / Consort of / THOMAS L. SKINNER / who departed this life / March the 1st in the year 1843 / in the 61st year of her age. / *She was an affectionate wife and / a kind mother.* / *Blessed are the dead which die in the Lord.* (P:5, footstone "E.S.")

SLAUGHTER, Louis. Funeral marker, 1919-1984. (A:1, no stone)

SLOAN, Ann Rebecca. In Memory of / ANN REBECCA SLOAN / who departed this / life September 7th / 1815, aged 59 years / and 4 days. (F:2, footstone "A.R.S.")

SLOAN, John. In / Memory of / JOHN SLOAN / who departed this life / February 26th 1815 / aged 57 years, wanting 8 days. / *Prepar'd by grace to meet his / God / On that eventful day / He welcomes the celestial guard / That bears his soul away.* (F:2, footstone "J.S.;" Alexandria Wills, Bk. 2, p. 10)

SMITH. Our darlings / JULIA T. / born Dec. 16, 1876 / died July 15, 1877 / J. BERTA / born June 26, 1883 / died Aug. 15, 1885 / only daughters of / HESSELIUS & J. ROBERTA / SMITH. (N:2)

SMITH, Amanda Ann. IN / memory of / AMANDA ANN / wife of / DANIEL [H.?] SMITH / who died July 30, 1840 / aged 22 years & 27 days / Also her infant son / JAMES LEWIS / died [broken] ___ 1840 / [broken] months, 27 day / *And though after / my skin worms destroy this / body, yet in my flesh / Shall I see God.* / *Job 19th Ch. 26v.* (Q:7, broken and in poor condition)

SMITH, Hesselius. HESSELIUS SMITH / born / Dec. 22, 1838 / died / Oct. 2, 1906 / J. ROBERTA / wife of / HESSELIUS SMITH / born / Feb. 8, 1839 / died / Sept. 17, 1912. (N:2)

Trinity United Methodist Church Cemetery (1808)

SMITH, Joseph. In memory of / JOSEPH SMITH / who died / July 20th 1846 / aged / 85 years & 5 months. (P:2, footstone "J.S.;" Alexandria Wills, Bk. 4, p. 426)

SMITH, Martha Jane. In memory of / MARTHA JANE, daut. / of THOMAS & MARANDA / SMITH, who died Augt. / 13, 1830, aged 6 mon,s. (R:3)

SMITH, Mary. In memory of / MARY / wife of JOS. SMITH / who died / March 20th, 1847 / aged / 79 years & 11 months. (P:2, footstone "M.S.")

SMITH, Dr. Sidney W. In memory of / Dr. SIDNEY W. / son of JOS. and M. SMITH / who died / Nov$^r.$ 29th 1847 / aged / 45 years & 9 months. (N:2, footstone has been erroneously replaced at P:2)

SNOWDEN, Edgar. EDGAR SNOWDEN / born / Dec. 21, 1810 / died / Sept. 24th 1875 / LOUISA J. GRYMES / wife of / EDGAR SNOWDEN / Born March 30, 1814 / Died April 25, 1897 / *Blessed are the pure in / heart for they shall / see God.* / DR. HAROLD SNOWDEN / born / April 27, 1836 / died / May 4, 1901. / WILLIAM POWELL SNOWDEN / died / May 24, 1906 / LOUISA SNOWDEN / died / July 29, 1907 / ANNA SNOWDEN / died / July 27, 1872 / Aged 86 years. / OSMUND SNOWDEN / born / Oct. 3rd 1844 / died / May 16th 1897. (P:1)

SNOWDEN, Harold. HAROLD SNOWDEN / C.S.A. / He stood four square to / every wind that blew. No dates. (P:1)

SNOWDEN, Hubert. HUBERT SNOWDEN / born January 22, 1851. / died April 15, 1912 / *Lord who shall rest / upon thy holy hill? / Even he that leadeth an / uncorrupt life.* / EDITH ASHBY. / wife of HUBERT SNOWDEN / born January 8, 1856 / died July 30, 1937. / *Be thou faithful unto / death and I will give / thee a crown of life.* (Q:1)

SNYDER, Elizabeth. To the memory of / ELIZABETH / wife of MATHIAS SNYDER / who departed this life / November the 8th 1853 / in the 79 year of her age. (Q:2)

SNYDER, Mathias. To the memory of / MATHIAS SNYDER / who departed this life / February 19th 1850 / in the 72 year of his age / *Twas hard dear Father to part / with thee.* (Q:2)

SOLOMON, Ann. Sacred / to the memory of / ANN, / wife of SAMUEL SOLOMON / who departed this life / April 15th 1863 / in the 80th year of her age. / *I will behold thy face in righteousness / I shall be satisfied, when I wake, with thy likeness.* (M:5; Alexandria Wills, Bk. 8, p. 146, men. sister Lucretia Padgett)

SOLOMON, Samuel. In memory of / SAM$^L.$ SOLOMON / who departed this life / Jan$^y.$ 22nd 1851 / in the 62nd year of his age. / *I am the resurrection and the / life, saith the Lord.* (M:5; Alexandria Wills, Bk. 5, p. 308)

STEELE, Horatio Nelson. HORATIO NELSON STEELE / Jan. 14, 1806 - Dec. 3, 1862 / past master / Alexandria Washington Lodge No. 22. / A.F. and A.M. (G:6)

STEVENSON, Edgar. My husband / EDGAR STEVENSON / Died Oct. 4, 1889 / Aged 70 years. / *At Rest.* (P:7)

STILLARD, Jennie F. JENNIE F. STILLARD / January 10, 1904 / April 11, 1969. (F:7)

STOREY, Sarah E. Thompson. In / memory of / SARAH E. / Wife of / GEORGE D. STOREY / born / March 15th 1844 / died / June 8th 1863 / Daughter of the late / HENRY T. THOMPSON / Also her Infant daughter. (A:3)

SWAINE, Jane. Sacred / to the memory of / JANE / Consort of / J.G. SWAINE / Born June 6, 1811 / Died Nov. 9, 1844. (N:6)

SWAINE, Jane A. Sacred / to the memory of / JANE A. / Consort of / J.G. SWAINE / Born Sept$^r.$ 12, 1824 / Died July 3rd 1854. (N:6)

SWAINE, Julius G. In memory / of / JULIUS G. SWAIN / who departed this life / April the

Trinity United Methodist Church Cemetery (1808)

24th A.D. 1861 / Aged 50 years. / *We shall meet again.* (N:6)

SWAURTZ, Elizabeth. ELIZABETH SWAURTZ / was born September 15, 1834 / & departed this life July 6, 1854. / *My daughter sleeps.* (D:3, footstone)

T

T____, Henry W. HENRY W. / Son of / T.L. & M.E. T_[broken] / Born ____ 1842 / Died ____ 1855 / Aged 13 Years 4 mons. / and 28 days. / *Not dead but gone before.* Footstone "H.W.T." (E:3)

TAYLOR, Anna B. In memory of / ANNA B. / wife of JOHN T. TAYLOR / who departed this life / December 27th 1854 / aged 52 years. / *Precious in the sight of the Lord / is the death of his saints.* (A:4; Alexandria Wills, Bk. 6, p. 418)

TAYLOR, Annas Jane. In memory of / ANNAS JANE / wife of GEORGE B. TAYLOR / Died April 17, 1887 / Aged 60 years [AG:18/4/87:3, gives name Annie Taylor] / *One less at home / One more in Heaven.* (A:2)

TAYLOR, Arina. In memory of / ARINA TAYLOR / Relict of / ELIJAH TAYLOR / died May 21, 1880 / in the 95th year of her / age / *Blessed are the dead who / die in the Lord.* (Q:1, footstone "A.T.")

TAYLOR, Elijah. Sacred / to the memory of / ELIJAH TAYLOR / born / Jan. 19, 1781 / died in Washington / D.C., July 16, 1852 / *He was ___ an excellent citizen / sincere Friend ___ / a Christian in word and deed in his / Death, the Church mourn the loss / of one of her brightest ornaments.* (Q:1, footstone)

TAYLOR, Elizabeth Annas. In loving remembrance / of my niece / ELIZABETH ANNAS / daughter of GEORGE B. & / ANNAS JEAN TAYLOR / Born Aug. 6, 1865 / died May 10, 1895 / *I laid me down and slept / I awaked for the Lord / sustained me.* / Erected By Elizabeth B. Taylor. (A:2)

TAYLOR, Valentine M. VALENTINE M. TAYLOR / born / Nov. 8, 1840 / Died Nov. 6, 1886 / MARY VIRGINIA TAYLOR / born March 19, 1846 / died June 30, 1885. (A:4, footstone "V.M.T." / "M.V.T.")

THOMAS, E[lizabeth?]. ELI [damage], wife / of Hanfon THOMAS / died Oct. 30, 1813 / Aged 42 years. (N:4)

THOMAS, Margret. In Memory of / MARGRET THOMAS / who departed / this life February / 23d 1815, aged / 49 years. (H:4)

THOMAS, Thomas J. In memory of / THOMAS J. THOMAS / died March 26, 1862, / in the 36th year of / his age. (L:1, sign S29)

THOMAS, William Henry. Sacred / to the / memory of / WILLIAM HENRY THOMAS / died / March 19, 1857 / in the 39 year / of his age. / *Sleep loved one sleep, / Beneath the quiet sod; / With faith, and hope & prayer, / We gave thee up to God.* (H:4)

THOMAS, Winefred Rebecca. WINEFRED REBECCA THOMAS / born / Aug. 8, 1812 / died Nov. 14, 1896. (H:4)

THOMPSON, Elizabeth. ELIZABETH THOMPSON / born / April 12, 1791 / died Jan. 20, 1876. (C:3)

THOMPSON, Henry T. In memory / of / My Husband / HENRY T. THOMPSON / Born April 14th 1812 / Died April 14th 1860. (A:3)

THOMPSON, Peleg O. Sacred / to the memory of / PELEG O. THOMPSON / a native of the state of Maine / but for the last 4 years / a resident of this town / who departed this life

Trinity United Methodist Church Cemetery (1808)

/ Sept. 3rd 1852 / in the 24 year of his age. / *He was beloved by all who knew him / and has left many friends and rel / atives to mourn his loss.* (A:3)

THOMPSON, Virginia S. This tomb is raised to / the memory of / VIRGINIA S. THOMPSON / Who departed this life / October the 19th, 1834 / in the 8 year of her age. / *...me my Mother... / I am... / Is... / ...follow me.* (C:3, footstone "V.S.T.")

THORNTON, Beverly. Sacred / to the memory of / BEVERLY THORNTON / Only son of / MARY E. THORNTON / Died Nov. 5th 1859 / aged 3 years & 6 months / *The lovely bud so young / and fair. / Called hence early / bloom.* (P:7)

TORRES, Esther N. ESTHER N. TORRES, R.N. / May 4, 1915 / Oct. 6, 1981. (F:7)

TRAVERS, Ann. ANN ____IA / daughter of / THOMAS / & HENRIETTA A. / TRAVERS / departed this life / Sept. 9, 1849 / aged 9 years, 11 mo. and 11 days. (H:3; AG:11/9/49:3, gives death of Ann Travers, daughter of Capt. Thomas Travers.)

TRAVERS, Lucy Amelia. LUCY AMELIA / infant daughter of THOMAS / and HENRIETTA A. TRAVERS / Born Nov. 21, 1855 / Died Jan. 18, 1859 / Aged 3 years, 1 mo., 21 dys. / *Gem of our hearth our child pride, / Earth ____ / ____ / Our dear sweet child. / O can it be that o'er the grave, / The grass renewed shall early wave / Yet God forgot our child to save.* (H:3; AG:19/1/59:3)

TRIPLETT, Elizabeth. ELIZABETH TRIPLETT / Born Aug. 9, 1880 / Died Mar. 30, 1881. / ____ *suffer, we shall / also reign with him.* (K:7)

TRUNNEL. Note: the following Trunnel(l) family stones have been replaced with modern versions which lack information previously found.

TRUNNEL, Caroline. In / memory of / CAROLINE / consort of / ISAAC TRUNNEL / who departed this life / in the 23d year of her age / April 11th 1820. (G:3, replacement)

TRUNNELL, Mary Davi Sincox. MARY [DAVI] SINCOX TRUNNELL / [Mother of Susan Cannon Trunnell] / 1787-1874. (G:3)

TRUNNELL, Miriam Amanza. MIRIAM AMANZA TRUNNEL / [Daughter of Susan Cannon Trunnell] / 1870-1874. (G:3)

TRUNNELL, Susan Cannon. Sacred to the memory of / SUSAN CANNON TRUNNELL / widow of / SAMUEL TRUNNELL / died June 28, 1918 / in the 84 year of her age. (G:3, current stone gives birth date June 15, 1834)

TUCKER, Jane Rosalthe. Sacred / to the memory of / JANE ROSALTHE / wife of / J.E. TUCKER / died Nov. 8, 1853 / aged 26 yrs. 6m. & 22 d. (Q:7, stone badly worn and broken)

TURNER, Cecelia Lee. TURNER / Mother / CECELIA LEE / 1881-1947 / Father / GEORGE ROSSER / 1878-1946 / DEWITT C. / 1909-1932. (K:7)

TYLER, Thompson. In memory / of / THOMPSON TYLER / who departed this life / November ____ / in the 61 year of his age. (G:5)

U

UHLER, Martha Ann Veitch. Sacred / to the memory of / MARTHA ANN / Consort of / PETER G. UHLER / and last daughter of / WILLIAM and RACHEL VEITCH / who departed this life / July 25th A.D. 1843 / aged 24 years / and 24 days / and with her lies her / Infant Son. / *Requiescat in pace.* (M:3, footstone "M.A.U.")

Trinity United Methodist Church Cemetery (1808)

V

VEITCH, Rev. Eldrige Roberts. REV. ELDRIDGE ROBERTS VEITCH / Baltimore Conference / September 20, 1810 / February 10, 1867 / his wife / ELIZABETH MINNING CHING / July 15, 1882. (J:5)

VEITCH, Mary M.L. Johnston. In memory of / MARY M.L. VEITCH / second wife of WILLIAM, and / daughter of JOHN and MARY / M. JOHNSTON, / Born April 26th 1804 / Died July 6th 1857 / being in her 54th year. / *Lover and friend hast thou put / far from me, and mine acquaint / ances unto darkness.* / Psalms 88.18. (M:3, footstone "M.M.L.V.")

VEITCH, Rachel Page. In / memory of / RACHEL / wife of / WILLIAM VEITCH / and youngest daughter of / A. & W. PAGE / of Md. / who died August 19th 1836 / in the 55th year of her age. / *Weeping may endure for a night / but joy commeth in the morning.* (M:3, footstone "R.V.")

VEITCH, William. [Alexandria Wills, Bk. 7, p. 63].

> In memory of
> WILLIAM VEITCH
> son of JOHN and MARY of Prince
> George County, Maryland and
> Father of MARY, JAMES H., PHEBE
> SILAS, WILLIAM P., ELDRIGE R.,
> CHARLES W., ISAAC McK., MARTHA A.
> DANIEL A., & JOHN A.
> born November 3d 1775
> and died December 7th 1855, aged 80
> yrs. 1 mo. & 4 days.
>
> *For more than 50 years he was a citizen of Alexandria and during a period near ly as long, honorably connected with the interests of the city & Methodist Episco pal Church occupying important official positions in both, in the former, Councilman Superintendent of Police, & Mayor, in the latter, Class Leader, Trustee & Steward.*
>
> *Help Lord, for the godly man ceaseth, for the faithful fail from among the children of men. Psalms 17.15.* (M:3, footstone "W.V.")

VEITCH, William Page. In memory of / WILLIAM PAGE VEITCH / son of WILLIAM and RACHEL / Born November 3d 1808 / Died February 6th 1856 / being in his 49th year. / *I shall be satisfied, when I awake, / with thy likeness.* / Psalms 17.15. (M:3, footstone "W.P.V.")

VIOLETT, Robert G. My husband / ROBERT G. VIOLETT, / Died March 18, 1870, / in the 73d year of / his age. / *I am the resurrection and / the life; he that believeth in / me, though he were dead, yet shall he live.* / John II, Chapt. 25 verse. (J:3, footstone

Trinity United Methodist Church Cemetery (1808)
"R.G.V.")

W

W____, G____. Footstone: "G.W." (C:5)

WARING, Mary E. In / memory of / MARY E. / daughter of / ____ & MARY I. / WARING / who died / Dec. 4th, 1840 / in the 5th year / of her age. (G:4)

WATERS, Georgie A. In memory of / my sister / GEORGIE A. WATERS / Born Sept. 21, 1841 / died Dec. 20, 1861. (P:2)

WATERS, Thomas A. In memory of / THOMAS A. WATERS / born November 6, 1815 / died October 20, 1870. (R:2)

WATERS, William. In / memory of / WILLIAM WATERS / eldest son of / BENJ. & DORITHA WATERS / who departed this / life Dec. 7th 1835 in / the 24th year / of his age. (R:2)

WATKINS, Aurelia Henry. In / memory of / AURELIA HENRY / daughter of / DAVID G. and ELIZABETH / WATKINS / who departed this life / on the 8th day of November 1844 / aged 3 years, 9 months / and 7 days. (E:5)

WATKINS, James M. JAMES M. WATKINS / died / March 28th, 1853 / Aged 35 years & 21 da's. / The deceased was born in / Fairfax County, Va. / March / 7, 1818. / *My wife and Child ____ my heart / ____ kind / ____ are sorely to depart / And have you all behind / O Lord a Father to ...* (E:5)

WATKINS, Mary Elizabeth Benter. In memory of / MARY ELIZABETH / wife of W.T. WATKINS / and daughter of the late / JOHN WESLEY BENTER / died / in Alexandria, Va. / March 29th 1863 / aged 42 yrs. & 8 mo. (E:5, footstone "M.E.W.")

WATKINS, Sarah J. Biers. In memory of / SARAH J. / Wife of JAMES M. WATKINS / and daughter of W.R. and / SARAH BIERS / Born Nov. 16, 1822 / Died Oct. 29, 1860. / *Asleep in Jesus.* / Erected by John T. Watkins. (E:5)

WATKINS, William T. WILLIAM T. WATKINS / Born 1849 / Died 1871. (E:5, footstone "W.T.W.")

WEBESTER, Susanah. SUSANNAH / wife of / JAS. WEBESTER / died Apr. 14, 1858 / aged 67 years. (N:7)

WEDDERBURN, Dr. A.J. To the memory of / Dr. A.J. WEDDERBURN / born in Alexandria, Va. / March 11th 1812 / died July 5th 1859 / *Distinguished in his profession / as a physician and surgeon / he was no less beloved as a man / and / esteemed as a citizen / as husband, father, friend. / None knew him but to love him / none named him but to praise. / His talents, abilities and zeal / were acknowledged by all and / elevated him to the Professorship / of Anatomy in the Medical De / partment of the University of / Louisiana in NEW ORLEANS: / and the / MEDICAL FACULTY / of that Institution in testimony / of their respect for his memory / ERECTED THIS MONUMENT / over his remains.* (H:5, obelisk)

WEDDERBURN, Alexander John. ALEXANDER JOHN WEDDERBURN / born October 31, 1849 / died December 24, 1916 / his wife / JANE SARAH ADDISON / March 7, 1849 / June 18, 1930. (H:2)

WEDDERBURN, Alexander John. ALEXANDER JOHN WEDDERBURN / son of / Jane Sarah Addison / and / Alexander John Wedderburn / born December 10, 1873 / died March 20, 1948. (H:2)

WEDDERBURN, Ann. In / memory of / ANN WEDDERBURN / who departed this life /

Trinity United Methodist Church Cemetery (1808)

Nov. 13th 1836 / in the 70th year of her age. (H:2)

WEDDERBURN, Augustus. AUGUSTUS WEDDERBURN / son of / Jane Sarah Addison / and / Alexander John Wedderburn / born September 9, 1871 / died November 28, 1944. (H:2)

WEDDERBURN, George. GEORGE WEDDERBURN / son of / Jane Sarah Addison / and / Alexander John Wedderburn / born February 22, 1877 / died March 3, 1965. / *When the feeble implements of man / Deny me, I focus the transit of the / Imagination on infinity and discover / Worlds yet undreamed of* -- / *GEORGE WEDDERBURN.* (H:2)

WEDDERBURN, Mary Bernard. MARY BERNARD WEDDERBURN / daughter of / Jane Sarah Addison / and / Alexander John Wedderburn / born July 3, 1875 / died November 14, 1962. (H:2)

WEDDERBURN, Sarah Ann Johnson. SARAH ANN JOHNSON / Wife of / Dr. Alexander J. Wedderburn / June 13, 1815 - Oct. 12, 1890. (H:2)

WESTON, Rebecca. Sacred / to the Memory of / REBECCA, the amiable / consort of the late / Capt· WM. WESTON / who departed this life / May 22nd 1824 / in the 44th year of her age. (P:5)

WHEAT, Benoni. Sacred / to the memory of / BENONI WHEAT / born 18th Feb^y· 1787 / died 29 Oct^r· 1852 / In the 67 year of his age / *I have inclined my heart to perform / thy statutes always even unto the end / Ps. 119V 112Ch*. (R:4, dates correct though doesn't calculate correctly; Alexandria Wills, Bk. 6, p. 154, men. daughters Mary Ann Triplett and Martha Jane Carlin)

WHEAT, Harriet H. HARRIET H. / Daughter of / BENONI & MARY N. / WHEAT / Born March 9, 1813 / Died Jany. 14, 1879 / *I rest in peace*. (R:4)

WHEAT, James Solon. Departed this life / the 28th August 1850 / JAMES SOLON WHEAT / aged 7 months / 15 days. (R:4)

WHEAT, Mary Naphler. Sacred / to the memory of / MARY NAPHLER WHEAT / wife of BENONI WHEAT / who died 13th Sep^t· 1834 / in the 50th year of her age / *Blessed are they that keep his testimonies / and that seek him with the whole heart / Ps. 2V 119Ch*. (R:4)

WHEELER, Sarah. In / memory of / SARAH WHEELER / wife of SAMUEL WHEELER / who born Jany. 2d, 1776 / and died June 20th 1816, / *She had not attain'd / her 15th year when she sought / and obtain'd an evidence / of interest in the Redeemer, / his grace supported her / through afflictions of life / and enabled her to triumph / in death. / Seed sown by God to / ripen for the harvest*. (J:1, footstone "S.W.")

WHITMORE, Anna M. In loving memory of our / beloved sister / ANNA M. WHITEMORE / born Nov. 20, 1855 / died March 11, 1910. / *Asleep in Jesus*. (F:6)

WHITTLESEY, Elizabeth G. In loving / remembrance of / ELIZABETH G. / wife of LUMAN WHITTLESEY / born in Williamston, N.C. / November 24, 1806 / died in Alexandria, Va. / June 19th 1868. / *Oh sounds of sorrow; ____ / The ____ry thought wails in, / And __ailing calms o'er and o'er / Our mother, dear, is gone; / H____ aching void; there is no home / Where mother-feet were want to roam / When mother-life is risen; / We have no more an earthly home, / Our mother is in heaven*. (B:5)

WHITTLESEY, Luman. In loving / remembrance of / LUMAN WHITTLESEY / Born in Washington, Conn. / March 15th 1795 / Died in Alexandria, Va. / January 14th 1868 / *A kind husband, a loving / father, a faithful friend, an / humble Christian, an honest / man. / We thought we'd learned how / much the heart can bear. / Ere we went down him on / Jordan's side. / And saw him cross the solemn / waters there. / We never knew*

Trinity United Methodist Church Cemetery (1808)

sorrow till our / father died. (B:5)

WILCOX, Sophia. Sacred / to the memory of / SOPHIA WILCOX / Died September 4, 1865 / Aged 81 years. / *Blessed are the pure in heart for / they shall see God.* (H:4)

WILLIAMS, Laura Virginia. In / memory of / LAURA VIRGINIA / daughter of / W.A. & C.E. WILLIAMS / born 12 Sep^t 1829 / died July 25, 1831. (J:6, footstone "L.V.W.")

WILTBERGER, Louveteau Edwin. In Memoriam / LOUVETEAU EDWIN WILTBERGER / May 30, 1869 - Oct. 8, 1932 / his wife / ANNA REBECCA WILTBERGER / May 18, 1870 - Oct. 13, 1956. (R:3)

WINTERS, Frances. To our beloved mother / FRANCES WINTERS / Died Apr. 9, 1887 / Age 72 years. / *Asleep in Jesus.* (M:7)

WISEMILLER, Jacob. In memory of / JACOB WISEMILLER, / who was born in high / Germany in 1754 and / died Feb. 5th 1820 / aged 66 years. (F:1, footstone "J.W.")

WOOD, Alice. Sacred / to the memory of / ALICE WOOD / who departed this life / April 17th, 1833 / in the 77th year of her age. (C:1, footstone "A.W.")

WOOD, James P. JAMES PARSONS WOOD / Co. A / 1 Bn. Va. / Cavalry / C.S.A. / Feb. 18, 1906. (K:1)

WOOD, Mollie E. MOLLIE E. WOOD / Daughter of / JAMES P. / and / MARGARET M. / WOOD / March 10, 1847 / Sept. 5, 1908. (K:1)

[WOOD?], S.W. S.W. / 1813. (K:1, sign S40)

WOOD, Major William S. MAJOR WM. S. WOOD / died / Aug. 4, 1895. (K:1, sign S36)

WORTHAN, Mary A. Mother / MARY A. WORTHAN / Died / July 2, 1893 / Aged 77 years. (M:6)

WORTHAN, Mary Ann Paterson. Sacred / to the memory of / Mrs. MARY ANN WORTHAN / Consort of / WILLIAM R. WORTHAN / and daughter of / WILLIAM and SUSAN PATERSON / who departed this life on the / 4th of Decr 1839 in the 20th / year of her age. / Also / the infant Daughter of / WILLIAM R. & MARY ANN WORTHAN / who departed this life on the / 7th of Novr 1839 / *Jesus said suffer little children and forbid them not / to come unto me and of such is the Kingdom of Heaven. / Matthew 19c 14v.* (M:6)

WORTHAN, William A. Memorial / WILLIAM A. WORTHAN / born / May 19th 1845 / died / Nov. 29th 1863. / Erected by his boyhood friend / of Washington City. (M:6)

WORTHAN, William R. Father / WM. R. WORTHAN / Died / Oct. 11, 1884 / Aged 75 years. (M:6, lot marker 152 nearby)

WORTHAN, William R. Departed / this life / on the 23rd Septr 1843 / WILLIAM R. WORTHAN / beloved son of / WILLIAM R. & MARY ANN / WORTHAN / aged 1 year, 5 months / and 3 days. / *Make these little lambs to rest / and lay them in my breast. / Protection they shall find in me, / In me be ever blest.* (M:6)

WRIGHT, Helen M. (M:1, no stone)

WRIGHT, Richard M. (M:1, no stone)

Plan on the Following Page

Since no original documentation has been found for the cemetery layout, the author has used row numbers from previous surveys. Because lot or grave numbers have not been consistently recorded by previous surveys, none are used here. Instead, a grid comprising 8 sections is to be found on the following page. The length of each row section is approximately 16 graves.

Trinity United Methodist Church Cemetery (1808)

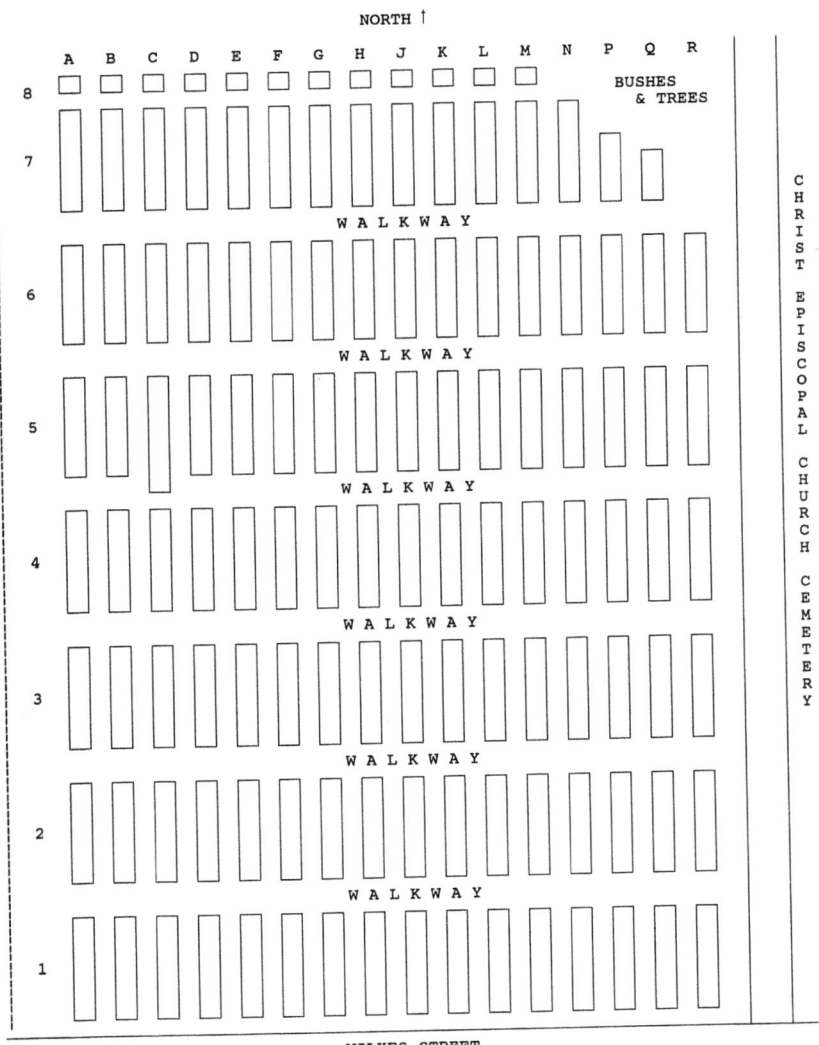

Plan by Author

Home of Peace Cemetery (1860)
South Payne Street

Initial data was provided by Ruth Sinberg Baker who also has shown that the Home of Peace Cemetery on South Payne Street is currently owned and maintained by the Hebrew Benevolent Society in association with the Beth El Hebrew Congregation of Alexandria[1]. A gate which marks the west entry of Section A is inscribed with the years 1858-1896; the first year of which commemorates establishment of the Hebrew Benevolent Society in Alexandria.

A newspaper article gives a claim without proof that the cemetery was opened on July 5, 1858, and that it later *contained about thirteen graves of soldiers who died in Alexandria during the Civil War and which were unmarked by tombstones*[2]. Despite this, Fairfax County land records show that on September 1, 1860[3], a parcel was purchased by the church trustees for the Union Cemetery of the Methodist Episcopal Church South. After assigning gravesite numbers, the M.E. Church South had, by October 9, 1860, conveyed gravesites 14 to 18 and 32 to 36 in the northeast corner to the Hebrew Benevolent Society as the starting point for Home of Peace cemetery. The next conveyance of adjacent gravesites 9 to 13 and 27 to 31 was made on January 20, 1864, and a subsequent one was made for the northern bounds of Section A on January 15, 1894. A small portion known as Section B was conveyed on January 21, 1911[4]. Additions were made in 1927 and 1929[5], and comprise what is known as Section C. Deed information as well as a plat of the Union Cemetery of the M.E. Church South has been provided to the author by Mr. Toivo E. Hedman.

When known, the location of the grave is indicated after an entry, and it contains the section and row numbers (and the plot number if available), i.e. "C:34:B." The map detail and numbering system were devised by the author as suggested by a grid map drawn in 1989 by Samuel Werth of Norfolk, Virginia.

Wesley E. Pippenger
Alexandria, Virginia

---

[1] Max Rosenberg and Arthur Marmar, <u>Temple Beth El, A Centennial History of Beth El Hebrew Congregation</u> (Alexandria, 1959), p. 1.
[2] <u>Alexandria Gazette</u> (Alexandria, 20 JUN 1881), p. 3, this source has been found unreliable.
[3] Fairfax County Deeds, Bk. C No. 4, p. 387, not recorded until November 8, 1860.
[4] Alexandria Corporation Court Deeds, Bk. 1190, pp. 1313-14, dated October 23, 1986.
[5] Alexandria Corporation Court Deeds, Bk. 94, p. 16; Bk. 97, p. 489.

Home of Peace Cemetery (1860)

<u>Unknown</u>

_____, "Unknown." Died January 11, 1919 / victim of Spanish influenza epidemic. (B:15:B)

ABBOTT, Julia. JULIA ABBOTT / beloved wife / of the late / SALOMON ABBOTT, / born Dec. 4, 1815. / died July 31, 1897. / *Our Mother / Gone but not forgotten / By her children.* (A:3:E)

ARNSTEIN, Jacob Solomon. Our Beloved / JACOB SOLOMON ARNSTEIN / September 6, 1990 / December 18, 1990. (C:42:B)

BAKER, Albert E. ALBERT E. BAKER / January 5, 1895 / March 29, 1972. (C:18:A)

BAKER, Matilda T. MATILDA T. BAKER / October 10, 1908 / January 22, 1984. (C:18:B)

BAUM, Jerome N. JEROME N. BAUM / Pennsylvania / Lt. Col. Medical Corps / World War II / Jan. 5, 1916 / March 29, 1962. (C:30:C)

BENDHEIM, Caroline. In memory of / CAROLINE. / beloved wife of / LEOPOLD BENDHEIM / born Feb. 22, 1830. / died Dec. 9, 1901 / *May her soul rest / in peace. / The Lord giveth / the Lord taketh away / Blessed be the name / of the Lord.* / In memory of / CHARLES BENDHEIM / beloved husband of / EDITH BENDHEIM / born / May 15, 1886 / died / April 30, 1934 / In memory of / EDITH S. BENDHEIM / born / Feb. 14, 1870 / died / Sept. 10, 1945 / Sacred to the memory of / LEOPOLD BENDHEIM / born / August 28, 1830 / died / October 22, 1903 / *Repose in peace, / beloved spirit, and / may we meet in eternity / Amen.* / SOPHIA BENDHEIM / Dec. 25, 1854 / March 19, 1930. (A:11)

BENDHEIM, David. DAVID BENDHEIM / born April 18, 1827. / At Gross Biberach / Hessen Darmstadt / Germany. / died April 3, 1904. / FANNY LAUER BENDHEIM / born Alten Constadt / Bavaria. / April 23, 1836. / died June 20, 1909 // SAMUEL BENDHEIM / born June 15, 1867 / died Sept. 24, 1945 / FANNY B. / wife of / SAMUEL BENDHEIM / died Aug. 6, 1936 / SARAH BENDHEIM / born Feb. 4, 1862. / died Feb. 12, 1890. / LEWIS BENDHEIM / born March 25, 1866 / died Nov. 25, 1948 / MINNIE B. / wife of / LEWIS BENDHEIM / died Aug. 26, 1936. (A:13)

BENDHEIM, Esther. Mother / ESTHER BENDHEIM / born / June 22, 1860, / died / Jan. 25, 1901. (A:5:E)

BENDHEIM, Leroy S., mayor (1955-1961), senator. <u>BENDHEIM</u> / LEROY S. / Feb. 12, 1906 / June 18, 1904 / ETHEL C. / Sept. 30, 1904 / [blank]. (A:12:C & D)

BENDHEIM, Moses. Father / MOSES BENDHEIM / born / Dec. 25, 1855 / died / June 21, 1918. (A:5:D)

BERG, Ethel M. ETHEL M. BERG / Dec. 9, 1909 / Aug. 11, 1990. (C:17:B)

BERG, Samuel. SAMUEL BERG / Sept. 2, 1904 / July 19, 1975. (C:17:A)

BERMANN, Rebecca W. <u>BERMANN</u> / REBECCA W. / March 4, 1880 / May 29, 1968 / FRED / Jan. 10, 1877 / April 4, 1963. (C:16:A & B, American Legion marker)

BERNHARD, Samuel. In memory of / SAMUEL BERNHARD / who departed this life / August 29, 1863. (A:20:E)

BERNHEIMER, Carrye T. CARRYE T. BERNHEIMER / born March 8, 1883 / died Feb. 15, 1955. (A:7:B)

Home of Peace Cemetery (1860)

BERNHEIMER, Esther. ESTHER BERNHEIMER / Beloved Mother of / HENRY _____ / BERNHEIMER / Died June 15, 1891 / Aged 72 yrs. & [5] mos. [AG:31/12/91:1]. (A:15:I)

BERNHEIMER, Harry. HARRY / son of / S. & J. BERNHEIMER / Born Oct. 29, 1881 / Died July 7, 1882. (A:17:14)

BERNHEIMER, Jeanette. JEANETTE. / wife of / SAMUEL BERNHEIMER / Born May 8, 1848. / Died / Jan. 2, 1907. / *Daughter, Wife, Mother, she was / best. / Heavenly Father give her / rest.* (A:15:H)

BERNHEIMER, Jona. JONA BERNHEIMER / 1870-1928. "Father" place stone. (B:9:A)

BERNHEIMER, Sammie. SAMMIE BERNHEIMER / son of / S. & J. BERNHEIMER / Born April 17, 1878 / Died May 22, 1879. (A:17:12)

BERNHEIMER, Samuel. SAMUEL BERNHEIMER, / Born April 13, 1845 / Died Dec. 15, 1885 / *Son, Husband, Father, he was best. / Heavenly Father give him / rest.* (A:17:G)

BERNHEIMER, Sydney. April 7, 187[3] - November 10, 1875 [AG:20/6/81:3]. (A:18:20)

BLOCH, Herman. BLOCH / HERMAN, / born July 17, 1868 - died Dec. 16, 1936 / HANCHEN / born Feb. 10, 1871 - died Nov. 4, 1957. Place stones "Wife" and "Husband." (B:4:A, B:4:B)

BLONDHEIM, Bertha. BERTHA / Beloved wife of / SIMON BLONDHEIM / died Oct. 27, 1890 / aged 49 years. / *May she rest in peace.* (A:18:E)

BLONDHEIM, Charles. Father / CHARLES / 1879-1937. (B:1:A)

BLONDHEIM, Cora. CORA BLONDHEIM / Nov. 11, 1869 / April 12, 1962. (A:18:B)

BLONDHEIM, Henry. HENRY / beloved son of / SIMON BLONDHEIM / died / July 25, 1901 / *At Rest.* (A:18:C)

BLONDHEIM, Lehman. BLONDHEIM / LEHMAN / Jan. 9, 1899 / Dec. 21, 1981 / LOUISE M. / July 29, 1899 / Oct. 25, 1986. (C:34:A & B)

BLONDHEIM, Sara F. Mother / SARA F. / 1888-1932. (B:1:B)

BLONDHEIM, Selig. In memory of / SELIG BLONDHEIM / Died Nov. 2, 1881 / Aged 84 years. (A:18:H)

BLONDHEIM, Seymour. BLONDHEIM / SEYMOUR / 1870-1939 / FLORENCE / 1876-1970. (A:17:A & B)

BLONDHEIM, Simon. SIMON, / Beloved Husband of / BERTHA BLONDHEIM / died Dec. 29, 1923. / Aged 89 years. / *May he rest in peace.* (A:18:D)

BLUMENFELD, Raymond. RAYMOND BLUMENFELD / Jan. 26, 1883 / Dec. 5, 1958. (C:5:A)

BLUMENFELD, Rena K. RENA K. BLUMENFELD / Nov. 3, 1881 / Jan. 6, 1959. (C:5:B)

BRAGER, Joseph, clothier. BRAGER / JOSEPH / beloved / husband of / ISABELLA / Born Sept. 2[2], 1823 / Died Sept 12, 1886 [AG:31/12/86:3] / _____ / ISABELLA BRAGER / Born / Oct. 19, 1836 / Died / March 8, 1906 / EMANUEL GOLDSMITH / beloved / husband of / IDA BRAGER / Aug. 29, 1855 / Dec. 5, 1932 / IDA BRAGER / beloved / wife of / EMANUEL GOLDSMITH / Nov. 24, 1864 / Mar. 14, 1946. (A:17, obelisk)

BREGMAN, Alfred. ALFRED BREGMAN / July 15, 1904 / May 22, 1971. (C:42:D)

BROWN, Abraham. In memory / of / ABRAHAM BROWN. / born / in Sulzbach, Bavaria, / Germany. / December 19, 1803 / died / In Alexandria, Va. / July 30, 1879 / Aged 75 years. / *Slumber in peace. / Amen.* (A:19:B)

BROWN, Isadore, merchant. In memory / of / ISADOR BROWN. / born / In Sulzbach, Bavaria / Germany. / died / October 26, 1906. / *Rest in peace.* (A:19:C)

Home of Peace Cemetery (1860)

CHAVKIN, Adele Jeanne. CHAVKIN / ADELE JEANNE / 1903-1973. (C:33:B)
CHAVKIN, Judith Blaz. Beloved Mother / JUDITH BLAZ CHAVKIN / June 1, 1939 - July 1, 1986 / *Remembering will have to do, / memories alone will get us through.* (B:1A:B)
COHEN, Abraham H. COHEN / ABRAHAM H. / 1885-1945. (C:7:D)
COHEN, Daniel. COHEN / DANIEL / Jan. 24, 1905 / Nov. 3, 1983. (C:12:B)
COHEN, Ida C. COHEN / IDA C. / 1896-1980. (C:7:C)
COHEN, Lenchen. Died in 1862, in the 28th year. (A:20:F; original stone A:20:G)
CRIM, George C., Jr. GEORGE C. CRIM, JR. / Sept. 12, 1935 / April 7, 1965. (C:13:A)

DIENER, Irving. IRVING DIENER / 1889-1962. (C:26:B)
DIENER, Minnie Weil. MINNIE WEIL / DIENER / 1894-1973. (C:26:A)
DREIFUS, Albert. DREIFUS / Father / ALBERT / 1872-1935. (A:10:B)
DREIFUS, Caroline. CAROLINE DREIFUS / Born January 22nd 1812 / Died June 16th 1881. (A:18:I)
DREIFUS, Estella. ESTELLA DREIFUS / wife / Jan. 25, 1889 - Oct. 27, 1965. (C:9:C)
DREIFUS, Hedwig. HEDWIG DREIFUS / wife of / JULIUS DREIFUS / March 31, 1871 / June 1, 1945 / *God love and Bless by Mother, / Who Loved God and all His / Creatures.* (A:14:F)
DREIFUS, Julius. JULIUS DREIFUS / born / Aug. 27, 1841 / died / Sept. 6, 1910 / *At Rest.* (A:14:G)
DREIFUS, Louis. LOUIS DREIFUS / husband / July 14, 1885 - Jan. 15, 1946. (C:9:D)
DREIFUS, Pauline. DREIFUS / Mother / PAULINE / 1870-1958. (A:10:C)
DREIFUS, Ray. Our Darling / RAY / daughter of / ALBERT & PAULINE / DREIFUS / Born Jan. 23, 1899 / Died April 3, 1901. (A:13:4)
DREIFUS, Rosa. ROSA / beloved wife of / JULIUS DREIFUS, / Born Oct. 12, 1844. / died May 6, 1897 / *Sleep mother dear and* ____ .... (A:14:H)
DREIFUS, Samuel. SAMUEL / beloved son of / JULIUS & ROSA DREIFUS / born Dec. 21, 1865. / died June 12, 1908 / *At Rest.* (A:14:I)
DREIFUS, Simpson. SIMPSON DREIFUS / Born June 22nd 1802 / Died December 22nd 1861. (A:19:K)

EICHBERG, Isaac, clothier, member of the Alexandria Common Council. ISAAC EICHBERG / 1830-1914 / his wife / BABETTE, / 1836-1916 / son / LOUIS, / 1867-1939. (A:2, obelisk)
EICHBERG, Rosa. EICHBERG / Mother / ROSA / 1874-1932. (C:4:D)
EICHBERG, Rudolph. EICHBERG / Father / RUDOLPH / 1871-1933. (C:4:A)
ETTINGER, Arnold A. ETTINGER. / ARNOLD A. / Mar. 25, 1867 - Feb. 13, 1942 / Beloved Husband, Father, and Grandfather / SABINE / May 17, 1872 - Oct. 18, 1963 / Beloved Wonderful Mother. (C:25:D & C)

FEDDER, Harry. HARRY FEDDER / Dec. 23, 1888 / April 19, 1961. (C:20:D)
FEDDER, Jennye B. JENNYE B. FEDDER / June 30, 1880 / Dec. 23, 1961. (C:20:C)
FEDDER, Stanley S. STANLEY S. FEDDER / Ltc. U.S. Army / World War II / Oct. 23, 1916 - July 28, 1975. (C:22:D)

Home of Peace Cemetery (1860)

FINE, A. Milton. A. MILTON FINE / Jan. 1, 1891 / Sept. 18, 1955. (C:24:C)
FINE, Hilda Wolf. HILDA WOLF FINE / May 4, 1898 / Nov. 3, 1974. (C:24:D)
FRANK, Harry. Father / HARRY FRANK / Nov. 26, 1864 - Jan. 7, 1957. (B:5:B)
FRANT, Estelle. FRANT / ESTELLE / July 19, 1895 / April 23, 1980 / ABRAHAM / March 5, 1892 / Sept. 29, 1979. (C:44:A & B)
FRIEDLANDER, Henry. HENRY FRIEDLANDER / born / March 1854. / died / Nov. 22, 1902 / KATHARINE A. BOYER / wife of HERMAN, [Friedlander] / died / Feb. 1, 1925 / HERMAN FRIEDLANDER / 1862-1944. (A:8:C, B & A, obelisk)
FUSFIELD, Emanuel. EMANUEL FUSFIELD / U.S. Army / 1924-1976. (B:2:A)

GENZBERGER, Hannah. HANNAH GENZBERGER / died / Jan. 14, 1909 / Age 75. / *Mother is gone but not forgotten.* (A:18:G)
GENZBERGER, Lee. In memory of / LEE GENZBERGER / died at Fredericksburg, Va. / Apr. 27, 1933, Age 65 yrs. (B:14:A)
GENZBERGER, Leopold. LEOPOLD GENZBERGER / born / March 8, 1821, / died / Oct. 5, 1901. / BETTIE MEYENBERG / wife of L. GENZBERGER / born in / Adelebsen / Germany / March 14, 1822. / died Aug. 17, 1905. [AG:30/12/05:1] / SIMON S. / son of / LEOPOLD & BETTIE / GENZBERGER / born / Aug. 19, 1865. / died / Oct. 1, 1898. / HANNAH / daughter of / L. & B. GENZBERGER / died / April 7, 1925 / SEGMOND GENZBERGER / died / June 28, 1915 / AMELIA / 1862-1956. (A:13, obelisk)
GENZBERGER, Lippman. In memory of / LIPPMAN GENZBERGER / born [Feb.] ___, 182[1] / died [Feb. 22], 188[4]. (A:18:F)
GENZBERGER, Michael. In memory of / MICHAEL GENZBERGER / died at Fredericksburg, Va. / Mar. 24, 1929, Age 62 yrs. / By his beloved brother LEE. (B:14:B)
GLADSTONE, Beatrice T. Seiff. BEATRICE T. SEIFF / GLADSTONE / May 30, 1910 - Oct. 15, 1991. (C:15:A)
GOLDBERG, Jack L. JACK L. GOLDBERG / October 11, 1930 / October 10, 1973. (C:33:A)
GOLDBERG, Tecla Scholl. TECLA SCHOLL / GOLDBERG / 1907-1977. (C:13:C)
GOLDWYN, Celestine Diener. CELESTINE DIENER / GOLDWYN / 1916-1988. (C:26:C)
GOLDWYN, Moe. MOE GOLDWYN / 1903-1964. (C:26:D)
GRUNEBAUM, Harry. In memory of / HARRY GRUNEBAUM, / born / Feb. 22, 1868. / died / Aug. 25, 1879. (A:17:14)

HABERMAN, Florence H. FLORENCE H. HABERMAN / Aug. 1, 1906 / April 19, 1968. (C:38:B)
HANDELSMAN, Amelia. HANDELSMAN / AMELIA / Dec. 22, 1885 / Sept. 24, 1966 / SAMUEL / Dec. 20, 1887 / April 8, 1961. (C:16:C & D, American Legion Auxiliary marker)
HENLY, Rosa. ROSA HENLY / 1865-1928. (B:6:C)
HERSCHMAN, Arthur. ARTHUR HERSCHMAN / Jan. 20, 1929 / May 29, 1991 / beloved / husband, father / and friend. (C:41:D)
HURWITZ, Mistie W. MISTIE W. HURWITZ / Aug. 27, 1941 - Mar. 8, 1992. / Wife,

Home of Peace Cemetery (1860)

  mother, grandmother / sister & friend. / *I will give to you / all the flowers / of my waking hours / all the words that rhyme / I will give to you love / without a season, / love without a reason / love that knows no time.* (B:7:C)
HUSS, Beckie. BECKIE HUSS / died October 9, 1918 / age 33 years / victim of Spanish influenza epidemic [AG:8/10/92:3]. (B:15:C)

JAFFA, MOSES. MOSES / July 6, 1868 / Feb. 8, 1956 / DILLA / Oct. 26, 1869 / Dec. 28, 1951 / HATTIE JAFFA / Aug. 28, 1893 - June 19, 1894. (A:4:C, D and E)

KAMENITZER, Ludwig. LUDWIG KAMENITZER / April 11, 1912 / Sept. 18, 1956 / *Beloved husband and Father* / *To live in hearts one leaves / behind is not to die.* (C:31:D)
KATZ, Aaron. AARON KATZ / born / June 26, 1863, / died / Jan. 30, 1923. / *At Rest.* (A:15:A)
KATZ, Stella. STELLA / beloved wife of / AARON KATZ, / born April 12, 1866, / died Sept. 1, 1911. / *At Rest.* (A:15:B)
KAUFMAN, Hannah. HANNAH / beloved daughter of / ___ & ___ / KAUFMAN / Born Nov. 21, 1875 / Died Mar. 19, 1879. (A:17:15)
KAUFFMAN, Isaac. ISAAC KAUFFMAN / Born the 4th of June / & died July 16th 1864 [AG:20/6/81:3]. (A:20:42)
KAUFMAN, Joseph. JOSEPH KAUFMAN. / born / June 6, 1838. / died / Nov. 5, 1902. / *At Rest.* (A:15:E)
KAUFMAN, Rosa. ROSA / beloved wife of / JOSEPH KAUFMAN. / Born May 2, 1842. / died June 6, 1893 / *Thy name is engraved / upon this marble / Thy image in our hearts.* (A:15:D)
KAUFMANN, Alexander. ALEXANDER KAUFMANN / beloved husband and father / June 8, 1874 - November 24, 1929. (C:3:A)
KAUFMANN, Jerome G. KAUFMANN / JEROME G. / Sept. 11, 1876 / Aug. 19, 1947. (C:11:D)
KAUFMANN, Joseph A. KAUFMANN / [separate stone] *To live in hearts we leave behind is not to die.* / JOSEPH A. KAUFMANN / husband, father, grandfather / February 23, 1906 - February 21, 1987. (C:3:C)
KAUFMANN, Minnie O. KAUFMANN / MINNIE O. / Sept. 27, 1887 / Aug. 28, 1965. (C:11:C)
KAUFMANN, Rebecca. REBECCA KAUFMANN / beloved wife and mother / January 24, 1875 - July 25, 1969. (C:3:B)
KLOSKY, Adele S. ADELE S. KLOSKY / 1908-1990. (C:42:C)

LATZ, Marcus. Born Mar. 10, 18[64] / Died Dec. 3rd, 1864 [AG:20/6/81:3]. (A:19:I)
LATZ, Marcus. MARCUS LATZ / December 5, 1864. (A:19:I) [Note: these two stones appear to mark the same grave, however the death date is clearly different as shown.]
LAUPHEIMER, Alexander. 10/17/188[1] - 7/21/[1881]. (A:17:17)
LAUPHEIMER, Henrietta. *Mother* / HENRIETTA LAUPHEIMER / Nov. 25, 1849 / Nov. 7, 1932. (A:9:D)
LAUPHEIMER, M. Wife of / M. LAUPHEIMER / Died July 29, 1879 / Aged 27 years

Home of Peace Cemetery (1860)

[AG:20/6/81:3]. (A:19:E)
LAUPHEIMER, Martha S. *Wife* / MARTHA S. LAUPHEIMER / Sept. 30, 1890 / April 25, 1970. (A:9:C)
LAUPHEIMER, Michael. *Father* / MICHAEL LAUPHEIMER / Oct. 20, 1844 / June 17, 1903. (A:9:E)
LAUPHEIMER, Sylvern. *Husband* / SYLVERN LAUPHEIMER / March 6, 1886 / July 22, 1949. (A:9:B)
LEMBERG, Rakhil. RAKHIL LEMBERG / 1907-1989. (C:25:B)
LETERMAN, Henrietta Strauss. HENRIETTA LETERMAN / born May 16, 1865, / died October 25, 1917. / *Her sweetness still lives on.* / LETERMAN. (B:3)
LEVINE, Abraham. LEVINE / Father / ABRAHAM / 1907-1970. (C:33:D)
LEVITAN, Hirsh. HIRSH LEVITAN / June 17, 1919 / January 5, 1990. (B:13:A)
LILIENTHAL, Rosa. In memory of / ROSA / daughter of / SAMUEL & JOHANNA / LILIENTHAL / Born Mar. 17, 1864 / Died May 14, 1864 [AG:20/6/81:3]. (A:19:32)
LINDHEIMER, Rudolph. LINDHEIMER / RUDOLPH / October 25, 1862. (A:20)
LINDHEIMER, Babetta. BABETTA / beloved wife of / SAMUEL LINDHEIMER. / died March 11, 1890 / in her 47th year. / *May she rest in peace* [AG:31/12/90:1, gives death of Balitti Lindheimer on 11 MAR 1890]. (A:16)
LINDHEIMER, Samuel. SAMUEL. / beloved husband of / BABETTA LINDHEIMER. / born Feb. 22, 1837. / died April 4, 1904. / *He taketh only that He gave.* (A:16)
LIPPMAN, Morris. LIPPMAN / MORRIS LIPPMAN. / 1862-1916 / IDA E. CRAMER / died Nov. 26, 1954 / wife of / JOHN J. CRAMER / died Dec. 3, 1957. (C:8)
LOVIN, Jenice. JENICE / Sept. 28, 1902 / Sept. 29, 1977 / MANFRED / March 9, 1892 / May 22, 1991. (A:4:B and A)

MARTZ, Helen E. HELEN E. MARTZ / August 12, 1906 / January 7, 1992. (C:47:D)
MARTZ, Samuel E. SAMUEL E. MARTZ / February 18, 1909 / [blank]. (C:47:C)
MINTZ, Abbey J. ABBEY J. MINTZ / Sept. 11, 1906 / July 18, 1990. (C:5:D)
MINTZ, Isadore. ISADORE MINTZ / May 17, 1878 / Aug. 7, 1951. (C:17:D)
MINTZ, Rose B. ROSE B. MINTZ / Dec. 2, 1907 / Jan. 3, 1989. (C:5:C)
MINTZ, Sadie B. SADIE B. MINTZ / Nov. 11, 1881 / Sept. 6, 1969. (C:17:C)
MORRIS, Moses A. MORRIS / MOSES A. / Feb. 8, 1870 / Aug. 7, 1944. (A:6:D)
MORRIS, Rosa W. MORRIS / ROSA W. / April 12, 1874 / May 14, 1969. (A:6:C)
MYERS, Harry. HARRY / son of / A. & C. MYERS, / Born Sep. 24, 1866 / Died July 21, 1868. (A:18:30)

OPPENHEIM, Benjamin M. BENJAMIN M. OPPENHEIM / 1891-1951 / Husband - father - grandfather. (C:27:C)
OPPENHEIM, Sara B. SARA B. OPPENHEIM / 1887-1960 / Wife - mother - grandmother. (C:27:B)
OSTROW, Irma Wolf. IRMA WOLF OSTROW / June 9, 1904 / March 1, 1992. (C:24:B)
OSTROW, Maxwell A. MAXWELL A. OSTROW / Sept. 20, 1898 / July 27, 1970. (C:24:A)

POLLACK, Joseph. JOSEPH POLLACK / 1898-1980. (C:25:A)

Home of Peace Cemetery (1860)

PRETZFELDER, Carline. PRETZFELDER / CARLINE / Apr. 4, 1888 - Oct. 2, 1889. (A:13:1)
PRETZFELDER, Madelin. PRETZFELDER / MADELIN / Jan. 30, 1884 - May 24, 1884. (A:13:3)
PRETZFELDER, Max. MAX / 1848-1925 / PRETZFELDER / RACHEL / 1862-1936. (A:12:A)
PRETZFELDER, Millard Lester. PRETZFELDER / MILLARD LESTER / Apr. 26, 1895 - Aug. 23, 1895. (A:13:2)
RONEY, Blanche W. RONEY / BLANCHE W. / Feb. 20, 1918 / Aug. 5, 1983. (C:43:D)
ROSE, Jacob. JACOB ROSE / born July 16, 1870 / died Aug. 21, 1934 / Father. (B:12:A)
ROSE, Sarah Anna. SARAH ANNA ROSE / born Sept. 4, 1872 / died Nov. 16, 1928 / Mother. (B:12:B)
ROSENBERG, Abraham S. ABRAHAM S. ROSENBERG / Aug. 15, 1897 - Sept. 15, 1976. (C:10:C)
ROSENBERG, Beatrice. *Innocence.* / BEATRICE / daughter of / SAMUEL & KATE / ROSENBERG / Born Aug. 9, 1915 / Died Aug. 15, 1919 / *She shall rise again.* (B:15:A)
ROSENBERG, Cecilia K. CECILIA K. ROSENBERG / 1902-1945. (C:10:D)
ROSENBERG, Kate. Mother / KATE ROSENBERG / 1878-1945. (C:12:D)
ROSENBERG, Maurice D. MAURICE D. ROSENBERG / 1909-1950. (C:12:C)
ROSENBERG, Samuel. ROSENBERG / SAMUEL / Jan. 12, 1879 - July 15, 1930 / Beloved Husband, Father and Grandfather. (C:14:D)
ROSENTHAL, Janette. Died June 3, 1865, otherwise illegible [AG:20/6/81:3]. (A:19:31)
ROSSIO, Fannie. FANNIE ROSSIO / Nov. 25, 1901 / August 6, 1992. (C:47:A)
ROTHSCHILD, Fannye. FANNYE ROTHSCHILD / 1873-1951. (A:19:B)
RUBEN, Moritz. RUBEN / To my husband / MORITZ RUBEN, / born / March 3, 1833, / died Nov. 5, 1893. / his wife / AMELIA, / born Oct. 25, 1820. / died Jan. 8, 1916 / SARA RUBEN / born / May 1, 1864 / died Sept. 13, 1940 / LEOPOLD RUBEN. / born / June 8, 1856. / died July 17, 1931. / DANIEL RUBEN / born / Sept. 28, 1858. / died Jan. 3, 1906. (A:16:F, obelisk)
RUBENSTEIN, Walter A. RUBENSTEIN / WALTER A. / Feb. 28, 1896 / Nov. 2, 1976. (A:6:B)

SALOMONSOHN, Max D. MAX D. SOLOMONSOHN / father / April 18, 1892 - Oct. 30, 1959. (C:9:A)
SALOMONSOHN, Victoria. VICTORIA SALOMONSOHN / mother / Sept. 2, 1892 - April 27, 1953. (C:9:B)
SALZINGER, Esther Ann. ESTHER ANN SALZINGER / June 1, 1913 - March 23, 1979 / Wife, mother, grandmother. (C:29:C)
SALZINGER, Ida T. IDA T. SALZINGER / born June 5, 1916 / died Nov. 7, 1953 / *A loving wife and / devoted mother.* (C:29:D)
SANGER, Morris. MORRIS SANGER / June 7, 1845 / October 26, 1862. (A:20:C, footstone "M.S.")
SCHNEIDER, Lawrence R. LAWRENCE R. SCHNEIDER / August 10, 1936 / July 12, 1974. (B:8:B)

Home of Peace Cemetery (1860)

SCHOLL, Fannie. FANNIE SCHOLL / May 26, 1881 / April 2, 1953. (C:13:B)
SCHOLL, Irving J. IRVING J. SCHOLL / January 26, 1902 / July 4, 1948. (C:13:D)
SCHWARZ, Isaac. ISAAC / beloved husband / of the late / LENA SCHWARZ. / born Feb. 9, 1834, / died Oct. 11, 1898. / *A kind loving husband / A devoted and / affectionate Father. / Loved and respected / in life / Honored and lamented / in death.* / LENA. / beloved wife / of / ISAAC SCHWARZ. / born / March 3, 1839. / died Dec. 9, 1893. / *A most devoted / Self-sacrificing wife / and mother. / A steadfast friend. / Faithful in the / Discharge of every / duty.* / SAMUEL / beloved son / of the late / ISAAC and LENA / SCHWARZ / born Oct. 25, 1867. / died Jan. 30, 1939. (A:16:A, obelisk)
SEIFF, Joanne Ellen. JOANNE ELLEN SEIFF / March 3, 1944 / November 16, 1948. (C:15:D)
SEIFF, Lazard. LAZARD SEIFF / February 13, 1909 / December 1, 1977. (C:15:B)
SEIFF, Marion Buxbaum. MARION BUXBAUM SEIFF / October 2, 1913 / August 5, 1970. (C:15:C)
SONDHEIMER, Leser. In Memoriam / LESER SONDHEIMER - July 8, 1871 / FLORA AUERBACH - April 11, 1872 / JANETTE ROSENTHAL - June 30, 1865 / M. IRISH - June 20, 1872 / IDA COHEN ... and others / Erected by / Hebrew Benevolent Society / 1985. (A:20:D)
STEIN, Caroline. CAROLINE / daughter of / _____ STEIN / Born Dec. 21, 1868 / Died Feb. 21, 1870. (A:18:24)
STEIN, Jacob. Died June 2, 1863 [AG:20/6/81:3]. (A:20:41)
STEIN, Simon. STEIN / SIMON / 1899-1982. (C:41:A)
STERN, Samuel. SAMUEL STERN / died February 2, 1919 / age 24 years / victim of Spanish influenza epidemic [AG:8/10/92:3]. (B:14:C)
STRAUSS, Henry, haberdasher, mayor (1891-1897). STRAUSS / HENRY / [footstone] Aug. 24, 1835 / Oct. 10, 1908. (A:15)
STRAUSS, Emma. STRAUSS / EMMA / [footstone] Dec. 22, 1846 / March 24, 1906. (A:15)

TORNER, Arie. ARIE TORNER / holocaust survivor / November 18, 1918 / February 14, 1991 / *The Good Person.* (C:41:C)
TRAUB, Morton M. TRAUB / [blank] / MORTON M. / June 18, 1924 / Dec. 29, 1990. (C:34:D)

WARREN, Clyde K. CLYDE K. WARREN / dad / Jan. 11, 1922 - Mar. 11, 1972. (C:35:D)
WASSERMAN, Jeanne R. Beloved / JEANNE R. WASSERMAN / March 6, 1901 / July 6, 1983. (C:14:B)
WASSERMAN, Stanley B. Beloved Son / STANLEY B. WASSERMAN / July 2, 1932 / May 18, 1991. (C:14:C)
WATERMAN, Inman H. INMAN H. / son of / SIMON & CAROLINE / WATERMAN [died April 23, 1863 per AG:20/6/81:3]. (A:11:H)
WATERMAN, Caroline. CAROLINE WATERMAN, / Born May 18th 1821 / Died Dec. 13th 1905. (A:11:F)
WATERMAN, Simon, shoe merchant. SIMON WATERMAN, / Born July 16th 1808 / Died Nov. 30th, 1882. (A:11:E)
WEIL, Albert. ALBERT WEIL / Beloved Husband of NAOMI / Sept. 13, 1889 - July 14,

Home of Peace Cemetery (1860)

1960. (C:28:A)

WEIL, Babette. BABETTE WEIL / Daughter of SIDNEY & MOLLIE [N.]/ Sept. 3, 1924 - Dec. 5, 1924. (C:28:D)

WEIL, Benedict. BENEDICT WEIL / Nov. 14, 1863 / July 2, 1945 / JULIA, / beloved wife of BENEDICT WEIL / Feb. 11, 1864 / Mar. 12, 1940 / SIGMUND HASGAL / March 1, 1855 / Jan. 18, 1938 / Our Mother / BABETTA, / wife of / ABRAHAM HASGAL / born at Endingen / Switzerland / March 5, 1823. / died April 18, 1905. (A:1, obelisk)

WEIL, Mollie N. MOLLIE N. WEIL / Beloved Wife of SIDNEY / April 25, 1901 - May 13, 1984. (C:28:C)

WEIL, Sidney. SIDNEY WEIL / Beloved Husband of MOLLIE / Dec. 15, 1896 - Nov. 14, 1990. (C:28:B, American Legion marker)

WEINBERG, Joseph. Died November 24, 1865 [AG:20/6/81:3]. (stone not found, and Ruth S. Baker notes that the remains may have been removed to another cemetery)

WESTHEIMER, Henry. HENRY WESTHEIMER / Died Aug. 10th 1865 / Aged 43 years [AG:20/6/81:3]. (A:19:J)

WHITESTONE, Melvin. Died 28 SEP 1992 at his home in Falls Church, age 85 [AG:1/10/92:11].

WHITESTONE, Robert P. <u>WHITESTONE</u> / ROBERT P., April 22, 1872 - Nov. 7, 1937 / ROSA S., May 12, 1865 - June 19, 1961. (C:6:C & D)

WOLF, Julius. JULIUS / born April 3, 1868 - died Sept. 12, 1935 / his wife / IDA BERNHEIMER / born July 28, 1873 - died July 4, 1936. (A:7:C & D)

WOLLBERG, Arthur. ARTHUR / beloved son of / NATHAN & ROSALIA / WOLLBERG / Born Oct. 11, 1877 / Died Sept. 22, 1924. (A:3:B)

WOLLBERG, Carrye. CARRYE [WOLLBERG] / 1880-1949. (B:11:C)

WOLLBERG, Nathan. NATHAN WOLLBERG / April 22, 1839 / May 12, 1909. (A:3:C)

WOLLBERG, Rosalia. In Memory / of / ROSALIA WOLLBERG / wife of / NATHAN WOLLBERG / Oct. 12, 1845 / Oct. 7, 1927. (A:3:D)

WOLLBERG, Sidney. SIDNEY [WOLLBERG] / 1872-1950. (B:11:B)

Home of Peace Cemetery (1860)
South Payne Street

EAST ↑

EAST ↑

SECTION C

Union Cemetery

ROADWAY

ROADWAY

SECTION B

Plan by Author

Home of Peace Cemetery (1860)
South Payne Street

EAST ↑

SECTION A

Plan by Author

Agudas Achim Cemetery (1933)
South Payne Street

Early history of Agudas Achim cemetery can be gleaned from Alexandria land records[1], wherein it is described that trustees Benjamin Abramson, Meyer J. Hoffman, M. Goldman, Jacob Shapiro and Jacob Appel were successful in "spirited bidding" at public auction on November 30, 1932, to secure for $250 a parcel measuring 100 feet by 140 feet which was located where the extensions of West and Jefferson streets intersect. About December 15, 1932, the Alexandria City Council passed resolution by authority of the mayor to execute a deed of conveyance to the Agudas Achim trustees. The deed is dated January 5, 1933.

About ten years later, an additional adjacent parcel was obtained from the City with the stipulation that the increase would be used for a chapel. The record which was signed November 26, 1943[2], shows that trustees Goodman Ruben, Dan Kerbel, Sidney Abramson, Sam Fagelson, Louis Goldman, Irving Byers, Albert Woolf and Dave Schrott obtained from the City of Alexandria, a 30 by 40 foot addition to the east of the original parcel, "to hold in trust for use by Agudas Achim congregation as long as it is used and maintained as a cemetery chapel without any manner of excavation." This condition was due in large to there being many unmarked graves in the area close to the defunct and desecrated Penny Hill cemetery, and the absence of an archaeological survey. At this time the trustees have no plans for a chapel, but have landscaped the area to accommodate private outdoor ceremonies. The cemetery is active.

Initial information herein was provided by Ruth Sinberg Baker, and it included a chart drawn in 1989 by Samuel Werth of Norfolk, Virginia. Mr. Allan Labowitz of the Agudas Achim synagogue at 2908 Valley Drive, Alexandria, provided assistance in obtaining information from land records.

A

ABRAHAM, David. ABRAHAM / DAVID - father / Oct. 1888 - Oct. 21, 1966 / MARY - mother / Oct. 1889 - May 29, 1965. (P:14 & 13)

ADEM, Maurice Samuel. MAURICE SAMUEL / ADEM / Mar. 25, 1905 - Jan. 10, 1951 / 18 ADAR 2 5665 - 3 SHEVAT 5771. (L:22)

APPEL, Jacob. JACOB APPEL / died March 5, 1947 / age 65 / father. (M:27, headstone and tablet)

---

[1] Alexandria Deeds, Bk. 112, p. 512.
[2] Alexandria Deeds, Bk. 204, p. 425.

Agudas Achim Cemetery (1933)

B

BERMAN, Samuel. SAMUEL BERMAN / 1909-1944. (N:18)

BIER, Ita. ITA BIER / April 22, 1891 / March 20, 1973. (P:23)

BIER, Moritz. BIER / MORITZ BIER / July 10, 1915 - Aug. 13, 1987 / MINNIE BIER / Oct. 2, 1905 - Jan. 15, 1988. (Q:24 & 23)

BLACKMAN, Blanche. Daughter / BLANCHE BLACKMAN / died / Mar. 3, 1936 / age 15. (N:13, headstone resembles a potted plant)

BLACKMAN, Fannie. BLACKMAN / Mother / FANNIE / 1899-1972 / father / HENRY / 1887-1945. (O:14 & 13)

BRANDT, Marvin J. MARVIN J. BRANDT / April 20, 1921 / October 19, 1989 / husband of / NORMA R. BRANDT. (O:21)

BREGMAN, Isadore. ISADORE BREGMAN / Oct. 21, 1898 - Nov. 26, 1945. (N:21)

BREGMAN, Sylvia. SYLVIA BREGMAN / Oct. 23, 1905 - June 7, 1976. (N:20)

BREN, Infant. BREN. No dates. (H:1)

C

CARB, Rosalyn. ROSALYN CARB / Feb. 20, 1935 / Oct. 3, 1985 / Beloved Wife and Mother. (K:22)

CHAMOT, Louis. CHAMOT / LOUIS / husband - father / grandfather / great-grandfather / 1892-1986 / beloved wife and mother / [RACHEL N., not in English] / March 1, 1967 / *We love you.* (P:18 & 17)

CHAPMAN, Isaac David. CHAPMAN / Isaac David / Beloved Husband / Daddy and Zadie / Dec. 20, 1907 / Feb. 10, 1989. (I:26)

D

DAITZ, Florence. FLORENCE DAITZ / Oct. 1, 1908 - July 20, 1972 / *Rest in peace.* (N:3)

DAITZ, Judith "Bobbie." JUDITH "Bobbie" DAITZ / Aug. 4, 1937 - Nov. 12, 1952 / *Loveliest of lovely things are they, on earth, that soonest pass away. / The rose that lives its little hour / is prized beyond the sculptured flower.* (N:1, enameled photograph on headstone)

DAITZ, Nathan. NATHAN DAITZ / Feb. 3, 1908 - Aug. 2, 1960 / *Rest in peace.* (N:2)

F

FAGELSON, Lillian. LILLIAN FAGELSON / 1906-1944. (M:13)

FAGELSON, Mary. MARY FAGELSON / Jan. 7, 1891 - Sept. 8, 1956 / Beloved and devoted / wife and mother. (M:15)

FAGELSON, Milton. MILTON FAGELSON / Sept. 18, 1889 - Aug. 30, 1958 / Beloved and devoted / husband and father. (M:16)

FAGELSON, Samuel N. FAGELSON / SAMUEL N. / died June 16, 1985 / TILA FAGELSON / died April 27, 1962. [separate stone] *Their sons were lucky / in their parents.* (M:18 & 17)

FAGELSON, Zalda. ZALDA FAGELSON / July 10, 1864 - May 16, 1943. (M:14)

Agudas Achim Cemetery (1933)

FINN, Melvin. FINN / MELVIN / Jan. 1, 1920 / Oct. 12, 1986 / HARRIET / Nov. 22, 1920 / [blank]. (Q:15 & 14)
FISCHER, Morris. MORRIS FISCHER / June 5, 1894 - May 11, 1964 / My devoted husband. (M:6)
FREEDMAN, Hannah. Our dear mother / HANNAH / FREEDMAN / 1863-1939. (N:12)

G

GERSTMAN, Aviva Alaina. AVIVA ALAINA / GERSTMAN / June 26 - Aug. 16, 1962. (O:8)
GLASS, Hyman Frank. GLASS / beloved husband, father and brother / HYMAN FRANK / Nov. 26, 1917 - Aug. 16, 1981. (Q:12)
GOLDBERG, Murray Joseph. MURRAY JOSEPH GOLDBERG / Aug. 16, 1905 - Nov. 16, 1969 / BEATRICE GOLDBERG / April 9, 1907 - Oct. 23, 1971. (P:27 & 26)
GORDON, Robert B. ROBERT B. GORDON / July 4, 1903 - Oct. 17, 1979. (Q:28)
GROSSMAN, William. GROSSMAN / [blank] / WILLIAM / Feb. 17, 1915 / Oct. 27, 1967. (O:20 & 19)

H

HIRSCH, Frances G. FRANCES G. HIRSCH / Beloved Wife, Mother, / Grandmother / July 13, 1919 / January 9, 1986. (M:2)
HOROWITZ, Fannie. FANNIE HOROWITZ / 1866-1952. (N:10)

I

IMMERMAN, Dr. Richard P. RICHARD P. IMMERMAN / March 4, 1952 - August 31, 1989. (O:6)

K

KATZ, Reuben. KATZ / REUBEN LIEB BEN TODROS / KOHEN TZEDEK / Loving Husband, Father, Grandfather, Greatgrandfather / Devoted friend to all who were / privileged to know him / Aug. 10, 1906 - Jan. 26, 1986. (L:1)
KATZ, Theodore. TODROS BEN REUBEN LIEB / THEODORE KATZ / Cpl. U.S. Army / March 7, 1930 - Sept. 1, 1950 / *Wonderful was thy love to me* / II Samuel I: 26. (M:1)
KATZELNIK, Henrietta. Beloved Wife, Mother, / Grandmother, Great-grandmother / HENRIETTA KATZELNIK / Oct. 23, 1890 - Dec. 26, 1968. (M:3)
KERBEL, Dan E. KERBEL / DAN E. / Nov. 30, 1902 / Dec. 4, 1981 / SHARA H. / Apr. 12, 1904 / Feb. 24, 1989 / *Loved by all who knew him*. (R:28 & 27)
KEISER, Lena. LENA KEISER / 1862-1937. (N:11)
KIRSCHBAUM, Samuel. SAMUEL KIRSCHBAUM / June 16, 1968 / 20 SIVAN 5728. (P:24)
KLEINMAN, Israel. Citation of honor / United States Army Air Forces / Corporal ISRAEL KLEINMAN / who gave his life in the performance of his duty / November 17, 1942 -

Agudas Achim Cemetery (1933)

age 24 years. (N:16)
KLEINMAN, Jacob. KLEINMAN / JACOB / May 4, 1884 / Oct. 17, 1947 / GITLA KLEINMAN / FAGELSON / Oct. 4, 1972. (O:16 & 15)
KLEINMAN, Joseph. KLEINMAN / [blank] / JOSEPH / May 21, 1911 / Nov. 25, 1963. (O:18 & 17)
KLINE, Gertrude. GERTRUDE KLINE / March 1894 - May 1988 / age 94 / WILLIAM KLINE / April 1890 - March 1952 / age 62. (M:9 & 8)
KOFFLER, Joseph Lionel. JOSEPH LIONEL / KOFFLER / Aug. 20, 1890 / Feb. 13, 1965 / Beloved Husband and Father / KOFFLER. (M:26, headstone and tablet)
KOFFLER, Mollie Appel. MOLLIE APPEL / KOFFLER / Mar. 15, 1902 / Feb. 19, 1987 / Beloved Wife and Mother / KOFFLER. (L:26, headstone and tablet)
KOFFLER, Sarah. SARAH KOFFLER / September 29, 1973 / 3 TISHRI 5734 / KOFFLER. (L:24, headstone and tablet)
KOHEN, Tzedek. 1906-1986. (L:2)
KOLATSKY, Dvora. Beloved mother / DVORA / KOLATSKY / Nov. 30, 1952. (O:9)
KRAMER, Edith S. EDITH S. KRAMER / Oct. 7, 1916 / March 16, 1987. (Q:22)

L

LEHMAN, Bernard. LEHMAN / BERNARD - father / Sept. 15, 1899 - Jan. 10, 1985 / IDA - mother / Sept. 14, 1900 - Mar. 4, 1962. (P:9 & 8)
LEVIN, Stanford M. STANFORD M. LEVIN / Aug. 3, 1936 - Nov. 28, 1983 / husband of / AMY ELIZABETH EVANS / father of / RENA FRANCES LEVIN / and / JOSEPH IRVIN LEVIN. (J:2)
LIEBERMAN, Bertha Bamdas. LIEBERMAN / BERTHA BAMDAS / Mar. 7, 1871 / July 11, 1939 / FELIX / Dec. 12, 1869 / Dec. 9, 1966. (N:15 & 14)
LONDON, Philip. PHILIP / LONDON / died Feb. 26, 1935 / age 65 / father. (G:1)
LONDON, Sarah. Beloved and devoted mother / SARAH LONDON / died August 1, 1945 - age 73 / beloved daughter and sister / MOLLY L. WEINER / died March 4, 1949 - age 54. (G:2 & 3)
LUDWIG, Benjamin J. BENJAMIN J. LUDWIG / December 17, 1920 / March 25, 1972 / beloved husband and father. (P:2)

M

MARCUS, Sally. Died 1944. (N:7)

P

POSNER, Gussie. POSNER / GUSSIE / April 30, 1952. (M:12)
POSNER, Harry. POSNER / HARRY / May 28, 1967. (M:11)
POSNER, Rose Goldstein. POSNER / ROSE GOLDSTEIN / August 16, 1983. (M:10)

S

SCHROTT, Baby. Baby / BABY SCHROTT / died / Aug. 7, 1936. (N:8)

Agudas Achim Cemetery (1933)

SHAPIRO, Charlotte D. CHARLOTTE D. SHAPIRO / July 15, 1927 / March 18, 1981 / beloved wife and mother. (K:8)
SHAPIRO, Isidore. ISIDORE SHAPIRO / Oct. 10, 1890 - Nov. 14, 1947 / beloved husband / and father / SHAPIRO. (M:25, headstone and tablet)
SHAPIRO, Rose Appel. ROSE APPEL SHAPIRO / July 8, 1906 - Feb. 6, 1991 / beloved wife / and mother / SHAPIRO. (M:24, headstone and tablet)
SHORT, Jessica Lauren. In loving memory of / JESSICA LAUREN SHORT / stillborn Oct. 20, 1989. (H:2)
SIEGEL, Esther. SIEGEL / ESTHER / 1896-1952 / JACOB / 1887-1960. (M:23 & 22)
SILVERMAN, Alan Jay. ALAN JAY SILVERMAN / March 25, 1947 / March 5, 1972 / SILVERMAN. (L:27, headstone and tablet)
SLOTKIN, Nat. SLOTKIN / NAT SLOTKIN / died June 4, 1968. (P:21)
STONE, Ida. IDA STONE / 1898 - June 14, 1966. (N:4)
STONE, Julius. JULIUS STONE / 1894 - Nov. 24, 1961. (N:5)

T

TEITELBAUM, Bertha G. BERTHA G. TEITELBAUM / June 13, 1907 / October 13, 1989 / beloved wife, sister / and friend. (P:6)
TEITELBAUM, Louis M. LOUIS M. TEITELBAUM / September 7, 1909 - November 22, 1969 / he loved his fellow man. (P:5)

W

WEINER, Pearl Appel. PEARL APPEL / WEINER / March 15, 1900 / June 27, 1979 / Beloved Wife and Mother / WEINER. (K:25, headstone and tablet)
WEINER, Louis Julius. LOUIS JULIUS / WEINER / March 17, 1899 / October 20, 1973 / Beloved Husband and Father / WEINER. (K:27, headstone and tablet)
WEINTRAUB, David D. DAVID D. WEINTRAUB / Aug. 17, 1912 / March 6, 1980 / beloved / husband & father. (Q:27)
WITKIN, Isadore B. ISADORE B. / WITKIN / March 29, 1959 / age 64 / beloved husband / and father. (N:25)
WITKIN, Mary. MARY / WITKIN / June 14, 1950 / age 72 / beloved mother. (N:27)
WITKIN, Max. MAX / WITKIN / Sept. 17, 1955 / age 83 / beloved father. (N:26)
WITKIN, Norman S. NORMAN S. / WITKIN / January 31, 1971 / age 46 / beloved husband / devoted father. (N:23)
WITKIN, Reichel. REICHEL / WITKIN / May 18, 1956 / age 74 / beloved mother. (N:24)

Agudas Achim Cemetery
South Payne Street

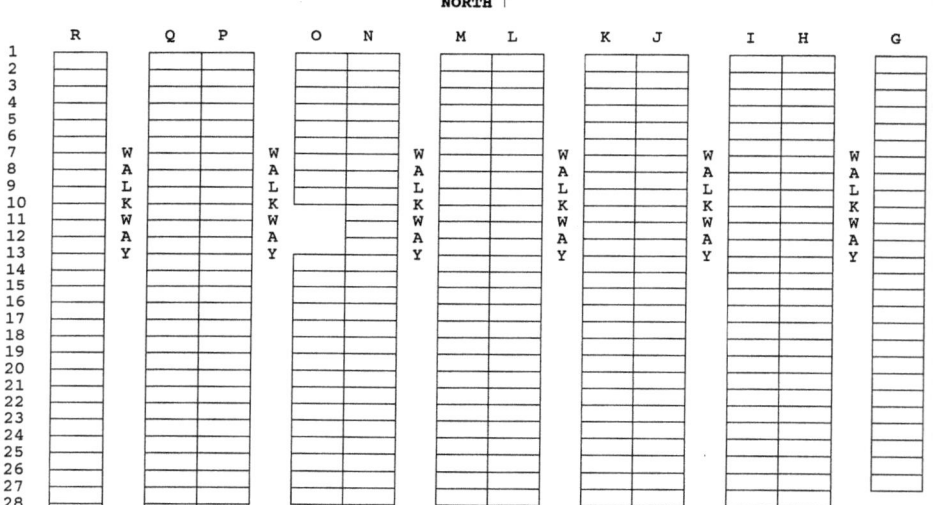

Plan by Author

Penny Hill Cemetery (c.1796)
South Payne Street

An early record of Penny Hill cemetery appears in the <u>Alexandria Gazette</u> of August 29, 1795, in which it is found that: *Francis Peyton, George Deneale, and James Keith, are appointed a Committee, to purchase a piece of ground for a general burying ground, containing not less than two acres, nor exceeding four acres--not nearer to any part of the town, than half a mile from the well line of Washington Ftreet.*[1] By July 1809, a request was made for job proposals to erect a fence surrounding the burial ground[2].

Less than a dozen headstones now provide evidence that Penny Hill cemetery was one quite active. For a number of years it was primarily a burial place for paupers and indigents.

A brief record of burials for the years, 1912-1976, has been provided to the Alexandria Library, Lloyd House by Mr. Walter Sanford. In recounting a mystical story about the disappearance of tombstones at the cemetery, Mr. Sanford shared that a Mr. Robey of the Rosemont neighborhood told him that as a little boy Mr. Robey remembered being in Penny Hill cemetery with his father and watched as workmen threw the tombstones down a well in the northwest corner of the graveyard[3]. As this ghastly sight unfolded while Mr. Robey was *still in knee pants*, it is thought that many of the tombstones were to have been removed between 1900 and 1910[4].

Some of the last burials at Penny Hill were said to have taken place along the south line which connects to Agudas Achim cemetery.

For additional information on Penny Hill, see <u>Tombstone Inscriptions of Alexandria, Virginia</u>, Volume 3, at pp. 43-45.

Wesley E. Pippenger
Alexandria, Virginia

---

[1] <u>Alexandria Gazette</u> (Alexandria, 29 AUG 1795), p. 3.
[2] <u>Alexandria Gazette</u> (Alexandria, 29 JUL 1809), p. 3. "NOTICE. -- Proposals in writing will be received by the Superintendant of Police, till the first day of August next, for fencing in the public burial ground at Penny-Hill-- the fence was to be fifteen hundred forty four feet, the posts to be locust or red cedar, and to be set not more than eight feet apart and not less than three feet in the ground, and to square not less than four inches-- there are to be three boards that will average twelve inches each, and a strip to be nailed on each post where the boards meet-- there are to be two gates not less than eight feet wide, and the gate posts to square not less than twelve inches and to be of white oak, locust or cedar-- the gates to be hung with hooks and hinges that shall be five feet long and a good padlock upon each gate. JOHN LONGDEN; Superintendant of Police."
[3] T. Michael Miller, <u>Memorandum of Record</u>, Alexandria Library, Lloyd House, File: Cemeteries (Penny Hill), dated September 13, 1991.
[4] Ibid.

Penny Hill Cemetery (c.1796)

Unknown

____, ____. A smooth stone tablet marker, no inscription. (8)

____, ____. ____ / ____ / and 1 day / *She was a loving wife, and / an affectionate mother / untill her death.* (10)

CARNE, [Susan]. IN Memory of / Suf^r CARNE who departed / this life 24 Octr 1804 in the / 36 Year of her Age / Alfo of / ____ who departed / ____ ec^r 1811, / 58th Year of his age. (9)

CARNE, William H. Sacred / to the memory of / WILLIAM H. CARNE / who departed this life / on the 17th of March 1836 / in the 35th year of his age / *possessed of the friendship / and an affectionate disposition / he was tenderly beloved and / his death is deeply regretted / by those who had long known him / and could appreciate his worth. / Though deep the slumber of the tomb / Though dark that bed of day / But shall he wake and ___ that ___ / For everlasting day.* [AG:18/3/36:3]. (11)

DUDLEY, Reuben. "On Thursday last, Reuben Dudley, an old colored man who had been an inmate of the alms house for some time past died, and on Friday his remains were buried in Penny Hill during a severe rain storm." [AG:26/11/89:3]

G____, K. H. Footstone "K.H.G." (12)

HALL, Francis. In / memory of / FRANCIS HALL / who departed this life / August 18th, 1845 / in the 70th Year / of his age. (7)

HARRIS, Joseph. In memory of / JOSEPH HARRIS / who died 8 Novr 1832 / aged 67 years [AG:13/11/32:3, body servant to Dr. James Craik]. (13)

HOTCHKISS, Harris. In memory / HARRIS HOTCHKISS / who died August 13, 1865 / Aged 59 Years. (1)

McCUBBIN, Edward, Jr. To / the memory of / EDW^d McCUBBIN, Junr / son of EDW^d & SUSAN McCUBBIN / who departed this life / August 27, 1837 / Aged 1 year 5 months & 21 days / *Wake up muse ___ the loss / of those that mourn this day / Let tears distill from every ___ / And every mourner pray /* .... (3)

MILLS, Rebekah. Sacred / [to th]e memory of / Mrs. REBEKAH MILLS / who departed this life / the 27th of August 1834 / in the 60th year / of her age / *Blessed are the dead which / die in the Lord, from henceforth; / yea, saith the spirit, that they / may rest from their labors / and their works do follow them.* [AG:2/9/34:3]. (5)

NELSON, William. Sacred / to the memory of / WILLIAM NELSON, / Died Aug. 14, 1869. / Aged 22 years. / ___ and take ___ / ___ he thought it had / Ever hard indeed, to part with thee / For Christ's strong arm supported me. / Erected by his sister / GEORGIANA NELSON. (6)

PARSONS, Mary Ann. In memory of / MARY ANN PARSONS / [broken]. (14)

RYE, John. In Memory of / JOHN RYE Who / depa'ted this life / January 27th, 1815 / Aged 23 years. (2)

Penny Hill Cemetery (c.1796)
South Payne Street

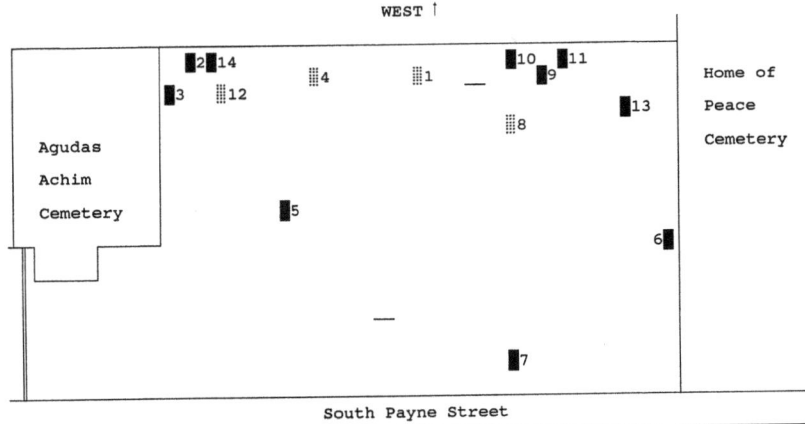

■ = headstone, information included in this work.

▦ = grave marker, little or no information.

Plan by Author

INDEX

()
  Catey 7
  Delia 102
  Isabella 7
  John 7
  Mary J. 116
  Sonny 7
  Ular 109
ABBOTT
  Julia 150
  Sallie M. 7
  Salomon 150
ABERCROMBIE
  Robert 116
ABRAHAM
  David 161
  Mary 161
ABRAMSON
  Benjamin 161
  Sidney 161
ACTON
  Eliza V. 7
  James H. 7
  John S. 7
  Mathew 7
  R. Cárlton 7
  Theodore M. 7
ADAM
  Anna 7
  Charles I. 7
  Eliza 44
  Eliza C. 7
  Jane 7
  Janet C. 7
  John 7, 44
  John G. 7
  Mary 7
  Mary A. 7
  Mary D. 7
  Robert 7
  Robert F. 8
  Thomas I. 7
ADAMS
  Ann 116
  Anne 99
  John D. 116
  Leonard 8, 116
  Margaret 116
  Sally 8
  Susanna 116
ADDISON
  Edward C. 8
  Eliza B. 8
  Jane S. 144, 145
  John D. 8
  Mary B. 8
  Thomas D. 8
ADEM
  Maurice S. 161
ADLER
  Berwin 8
  Edna O. 8
AGNEW
  Anne R. 8
  Augustus H. 8
  David S. 8
  Elizabeth H. 8
  John P. 8
  Laura B. 8
  Laura T. 8
  Mabel 8
  Margaretta L. 8
  Mary V. 8
  Matilda 69
  Matilda E. 8
  Minniehaha 8
  Park 8, 9
AITCHESON
  Alan C. 9
  Benjamin M. 9
  Caroline 9
  David D. 9
  Jessie O. 9
  John 9
  Mary C. 9
  Nannie A. 9
  S. Maude 9
  Sarah M. 9
ALDEN
  Timothy 100
ALEXANDER
  Amos 9, 99
  Ann R. 99
  Mariette 66
ALLEN
  Ada A. 9
  Ernest L. 9
  Lillian E. 62
  Mary D. 9
  William L. 9
  William W. 9
ALLENSWORTH
  George W. 87
ALLISON
  Robert 9, 99
ANDERSON
  Eleanor 116
  James 111
  James H. 116
  John 9
  Margaret 9
  Robert 9
ANDREWS
  Archibald 116
ANSLEY
  Anne W. 10
  Harrie C. 9
  Harriet F. 9
  Lewis M. 9
  Urquhart 9
APPEL
  Jacob 161
APPICH
  Barbara 10
  Barbara A. 10
  Caroline C. 10
  Christina 10
  David 10, 12
  Eve C. 36
  George D. 10
  Gertrude B. 10
  Gotlieb 10
  Gottlieb 10
  Jacob D. 10
  John A. 10
  Mary A. 12
ARCHER
  Caroline A. 12
ARCHIE
  Harry W. 10
ARELL
  David 99
  Eleanor 98
  H. 99

171

Richard 98
Samuel 99
ARMSTRONG
  Anthony G. 10
  Anthony W. 10
  Catherine 10
  Elizabeth 60
  George L. 10
  Jessie R. 10
  John T. 10
  Louise R. 10
  Lucy L. 10
  Marion E. 10
  Wayne E. 10
ARNOLD
  Alexander 116
  Amanda V. 10
  Annie L. 10
  Howard L. 10
  J. Raymond 10
  James B. 10
  Lucille W. 10
  Mary A. 116
ARNOTT
  Henry 11
ARNSTEIN
  Jacob S. 150
ARRINGTON
  Charles H. 11
  Emma C. 11
ASHBY
  F. Westwood 11
  Lucy 21, 37
  Margaret D. 11
ASHER
  George G. 11
  John 11
  Mildred M. 11
ASHFORD
  Alexander 116
  Amelia 116
  Ann E. 116
  C. 116
  Craven 116
  E. 116
  Nicholas D. 116
  Samuel A. 116
ASHTON
  Annie L. 17
  Henry 17
  Leetta E. 17
  Ouida W. 17
ATKINSON
  David W. 11
  Janet 11
  Roscoe 11
AUERBACH

Flora 157
AUMAN
  Edith F. 11
  Evelyn F. 11
  William R. 11
AUSTIN
  John 11
  Mariana 11
AVERY
  Carrie W. 5, 115
  Hattie E. 11
  Mary 11
  R.W. 11
  Richard W. 11
  Wesley 11
BAADER
  Caroline 11
  Carrie 11
  Charlie 11
  Edna M. 70
  Emma 11
  Henry 11
  Lizzie 11
  Mamie 11
  Rosa L. 12
BADEN
  John B. 99
BAGGETT
  A.W. 12
  Mary A. 12
BAGGOT
  Ellen 117
  Townsend 117
BAGOT
  Annie E. 22
  John C. 12
  Julia A. 12
  Mary R. 42
  Nellie E. 42
BAILLIE
  Robert 99
BAIN
  Fannie C. 12
  William E. 12
BAKER
  Albert E. 150
  Clara E. 12
  Evelyn P. 12
  Matilda T. 150
  Ruth S. 2, 149
  Selden S. 12
BALANGER
  Sally 117
  Thomas 117
BALFOUR
  () 99
  James 99

BANGS
  David B. 117
  Margaret M. 117
BARBER
  () 99
BARKER
  Mary E. 12
  Roger F. 12
BARLEY
  J.R. 12
BARNES
  Thelma C. 12
BARR
  Mary 68
BARTLE
  Andrew 12
  James 12
  Phebe A. 12
  Samuel 12
  Thomas 12
BARTLEMAN
  Ann E. 12
  George 99
  Isabella P. 12
  Margaret 12, 36, 66
  Margaret D. 12, 36
  Rebecca J. 12
  Wilhelmina 65, 66
  William 12, 36, 66
BARTON
  Virginia 21
BASCELL
  Louis A. 12
BASHFORD
  Maude 13
BAUM
  Jerome N. 150
BAUMANN
  David M. 13
BAYLISS
  Burt L. 13
  Stuart I. 13
  Tillie M. 13
BEACHUM
  Thomas W. 13
BEALL
  Eugene L. 13
  Florence M. 13
  James B. 13
BECKLEY
  Mary E. 53
BEDSWORTH
  Edmund M. 5

BELKOSKY
  John P. 13
  Margaret J. 13
BELL
  Elizabeth B. 13
  James E. 13
  Lewis V. 13
  Lizzie T. 13
  Louis 97
  Maggie C. 13
  Margaret A. 13
  Mary 13
  Mary G. 13
  Mary S. 13
  Robert 13
BENDHEIM
  Caroline 150
  Charles 150
  David 150
  Edith 150
  Edith S. 150
  Esther 150
  Ethel C. 150
  Fanny B. 150
  Fanny L. 150
  Leopold 150
  Leroy S. 150
  Lewis 150
  Minnie B. 150
  Moses 150
  Samuel 150
  Sarah 150
  Sophia 150
BENTER
  Elizabeth 117
  John A. 117
  John W. 144
  Mary E. 144
  William 117
BERG
  Ethel M. 150
  Samuel 150
BERKLEY
  Elizabeth W. 117
  Emily P. 117
  George P. 117
  Harold P. 13
  William N. 13, 117
BERMAN
  Samuel 162
BERMANN
  Amelia 150
  Fred 150
  Rebecca W. 150
BERNHARD
  Samuel 150
BERNHEIMER
  Carrye T. 150
  Esther 151
  Harry 151
  Henry 151
  Ida 158
  J. 151
  Jeanette 151
  Jona 151
  S. 151
  Sammie 151
  Samuel 151
  Sydney 151
BERRY
  Blanche D. 13
  Charles A. 13
  E. Louise 13
  Elizabeth 13
  John H. 13
  Margaret F. 13
  Thomas 13, 14
  Winifred M. 14
BERRYMAN
  Charlotte L. 14
  John 14
BEST
  John J. 14
  Martha E. 14
BIER
  Ita 162
  Minnie 162
  Moritz 162
BIERS
  Mary E. 68
  Sarah 14, 144
  Sarah D. 68
  Sarah J. 144
  W.R. 144
  William R. 14, 68
BIRCH
  J.F. 6
BITZER
  Ellen T. 14
  James H. 14
BLACK
  David 14
  Eliza 14
  Esther A. 111
  Helen A. 14
  Robert 99
BLACKLOCK
  Ann M. 14
  Eliza J. 14
  Elizabeth V. 14
  Nicholas F. 14
  Robert S. 14
  William R. 14
BLACKMAN
  Blanche 162
  Fannie 162
  Harry 162
  Henry 162
BLACKWELL
  Joseph H. 14
  Mary S. 14
BLADEN
  Rosier T. 117
BLAKE
  William J. 14
BLISH
  Henry 135
BLOCH
  Hanchen 151
  Herman 151
BLONDHEIM
  Bertha 151
  Charles 151
  Cora 151
  Henry 151
  Lehman 151
  Louise M. 151
  Sara F. 151
  Selig 151
  Seymour 151
  Simon 151
BLOUNT
  Polly 111
BLUMENFELD
  Raymond 151
  Rena K. 151
BLUNT
  Sarah 15
  Washer 99
BLYTHE
  Washington 15
BOGUE
  John 100
  Judith 100
BOLAND
  David S. 15
  Edward J. 15
BOLTON
  Helen P. 15
  Walter A. 15
BONTZ
  John W. 117
  Ruth A. 117
  William C. 117
BOSWELL
  Lillie W. 15
BOUSH
  Jane C. 19
  Mary A. 15
  Nathalie M. 55

Nathaniel 19
Samuel C. 15
BOWATER
   Margaret 53
BOWEN
   Samuel 111
BOWLES
   Elsie F. 15
   William E. 15
BOYD
   Charles W. 15
   Harry P. 15
   John T. 15
   Lillie M. 15
   Marie T. 15
   Martha A. 15
   Mary R. 15
   Minnie W. 15
   Richard T. 15
   Rose I. 22
   Sarah 72
   William R. 15
BOYER
   Katharine A. 153
BRADLEY
   A.E. 118
   C. James 15
   C.C. 117, 118
   Cora V. 118
   Elisheba H. 117
   Florence E. 15
   Harrison 117, 118
   Helen M. 15
   James M. 118
   John H. 118
   Rose M. 118
BRAGER
   Ida 151
   Isabella 151
   Joseph 151
BRANDT
   Marvin 162
   Marvin J. 162
   Norma R. 162
BREGMAN
   Alfred 151
   Isadore 162
   Sylvia 162
BREN
   Infant 162
BRENNER
   Addie C. 15
   Anthony 15
   Charles F. 15, 85
   Francis A. 85
   George E. 15
   John E. 15

Julia C. 15
Mary E. 15
Nellie A. 15
Sarah E. 15
BRENT
   Nancy 100
BREWIS
   Infant 118
   Thomas A. 118
BRIGGS
   Lucy B. 81
BRIGHT
   Ann 118
   Araminta 118
   Frances C. 118
   John 118
BROCK
   Morgan R. 118
BROCKET
   Andrew 16
   Annabela 15
   Elizabeth 16
   Robert 15, 16
   Walter 16
BROCKETT
   Albert D. 16
   Caroline E. 16
   Edgar L. 16
   Elizabeth L. 16
   Franklin L. 16
   Georgeanna S. 16
   Hattie N. 16
   Laura V. 16
   Robert 16
   Virginia E. 16
   Walter B. 16
BRODBECK
   Annie E. 16
   Eliza M. 16
   Jacob 16
   Mary A. 16
BROOK
   Elizabeth B. 131
BROOKS
   Fanny 118
   John T. 16
   William H. 118
BROWN
   Abraham 151
   Arthur R. 16
   Charles P. 118
   Edna H. 16
   Ella H. 16
   George R. 16
   Georgianna 16
   Isador 151

Leonard 16
Lucy L. 81
Mary E. 16, 76
Mary R. 16
William A. 16
BRUCH
   Virginia I. 43
BRUSH
   Mary P. 16
BRYAN
   Martha 56
BRYANT
   Arthur D. 17
BUNN
   Lucile A. 81
BURCHELL
   Ann 118
   Edward 118
   John E. 118
BURGESS
   Albert C. 17
   Amelia B. 17
   Benjamin F. 17
   Bennie 17
   Enock N. 17
   Eugene S. 17
   Jane F. 104
   Lillian E. 17
   Lillian L. 17
   Mary L. 17
BURKE
   Anna M. 47
BURRAGE
   Benny 118
   Georgie 118
   Hannah 118
   Thomas 118
BURROUGHS
   Ida M. 17
BUTLER
   Catherine 17
   Walter A. 17
BUTTS
   Jessie C. 62
BYERS
   Irving 161
CAGLE
   Caroline 17
   Caroline H. 84
   Clifford E. 84
CALDWELL
   Anthony 17
   Charles 17
   Hannah L. 17
CAMPBELL
   Alcinda F. 119
   Ann 119

Elizabeth 119
Hetty 119
Ida M. 20
James 119
Janet 7
John W. 119
Joseph F. 17
Loudon 119
Mary 29, 119
Mary A. 119
Rebecca 119
William 17, 119
CANNON
  Granderson 119
  Mary S. 119
  Susanna 119
CARB
  Rosalyn 162
CAREY
  Mathew 56
  Mildred 100
CARIGNAN
  Yvonne 2
CARLIN
  Elizabeth 119
  George W. 119
  John F. 17
  Martha J. 145
  Sarah V. 17
CARLYLE
  Ann 101
  George F. 101
  Hanah 101
  John 100
  Rachael M. 100
  Rachel 101
  Sarah 100
  William 100, 101
CARNE
  Susan 168
  William H. 168
CAROLIN
  Caroline 122
  Hugh 120, 132
  Julia 125
  Mercy 120
CARPENTER
  Annie L. 17
  Ralph 19
  Ralph L. 17
CARRELL
  Elizabeth 120
  James C. 120
  Leucinda 120
CARSON
  Elizabeth 120
  George W. 120
Helen S. 120
John 120
Joseph C. 120
Margaret 120
Mary E. 120
CARTER
  Claude 17
  Elisabeth J. 17
  Elizabeth 17
  J. Brooke 18
  J. Newton 17
  Margaret L. 17, 53
  Richard C. 18
  Sarah T. 18
  Thomas L. 18
  Thomas T. 18
  V. Newton 53
CARTWRIGHT
  Eliza 18
  Johnathan 18
CATTS
  Fannie A. 18
  Fannie D. 18
  J.H. 18
  Rosier D. 18
  Samuel R. 18
CAWOOD
  Daniel 120
  Delilah R. 120
  Moses O. 120, 134
  Susanna P. 134
CAZENOVE
  Anne 18, 101
  Anne H. 18
  Antony C. 18, 51, 71, 101
  Charlotte B. 71
  Charlotte L. 14
  Constance G. 83
  Eleuthera D. 18
  Frances A. 14
  Frances E. 18
  Harriet 51
  Harriot E. 18
  James O. 18
  Louis A. 14, 18
  Mary E. 18, 19
  Mary O. 18, 19
  Mary S. 18, 19
  Octavus A. 19
  Paul C. 101
  Paulina 33
  W.G. 18
  William G. 18, 19
CHAMBERLAIN
  Jacob 19
  Jane L. 19
  Luther 19
CHAMBERS
  W.W. 6
CHAMOT
  Louis 162
  Rachel N. 162
CHANDLER
  Lemuel 111
  Mary F. 111
CHAPMAN
  Isaac D. 162
  John S. 19
  Julia G. 19
  Mary L. 19
  William G. 19
CHARLES
  Mary 101
CHATHAM
  Fanny 19
  Henry 19
  James 121
  Jane 19
  Martha 121
  Mary 19
CHAUNCEY
  Frank 20
  John F. 20
  Mary C. 20
CHAUNCY
  Fannie 121
  Thomas A. 121
  Virginia E. 121
  William 121
CHAVKIN
  Adele J. 152
  Judith B. 152
CHESHIRE
  Andrew H. 20
  Victoria R. 20
CHINAULT
  Louis A. 20
CHING
  Elizabeth 121
  Elizabeth M. 121, 143
  Grace 121
  John 121
  Sarah S. 121
  Thomas 121
  Thomas S. 121
  William M. 121
CHIPLEY
  Miranda M. 122
  Samuel N. 121

Sarah M. 121
CHURCH
    Gilbert 20
    Jane 9
    Thomas 9
CLARK
    Adeline C. 121, 122
    Alta K. 20
    Catharine D. 122
    Clifton P. 20
    Edna M. 42
    Elizabeth W. 20
    Harry C. 122
    John C. 121, 122
    Joseph 122
    Laura 43
    Robert E. 20
    William 122
CLARVOE
    Annie G. 20
    John 55
    Mary 20
    Napoleon B. 20
    Sarah A. 55
    William H. 55
CLEVELAND
    Sallie 68
CLIFFORD
    () 101
CLIFT
    Florence H. 20
    Percy E. 20
CLOWES
    Thomas 122
CLYBURN
    Clifford L. 20
COAKLEY
    Lillian L. 18, 20
COE
    Martha B. 20
    Theodore I. 20
COGAN
    Albert C. 21
    Charles A. 20
    Edward 20
    Ella I. 20
    Ida M. 20
    John 20
    John A. 20
    John P. 20
    Katherine 20
    Mary V. 21
    Richard B. 20
    Virginia 43, 44
    Virginia B. 21
    Virginia M. 43
    William 21

William W. 21
COHEN
    Abraham H. 152
    Daniel 152
    Ida 157
    Ida C. 152
    Lenchen 152
COLEMAN
    Alice O. 122
    Caroline 122
    Caroline V. 122
    James P. 122
    Joseph H. 122
    Samuel S. 122
COLLINGSWORTH
    Thomas W. 122
    Virginia A. 122
COLVIN
    Columbus T. 122
    Miranda M. 122
COMPTON
    William 101
CONWAY
    Margaret 21
    Margaret A. 9
    Robert 9, 21
COOK
    Henry 21
    Hortense H. 21
    Hortensia H. 21
    Llewellyn M. 21
    Lucy A. 21
    Mary S. 21
COOKE
    Julia E. 101
COOPER
    Samuel 21
COPE
    C. Duane 21
    Fay G. 21
    Oliver W. 21
CORNELL
    Claudia M. 21
CORSA
    Mary F. 21
    Ralph W. 21
COX
    Charles F. 122
    Charles N. 21
    Ella L. 21
    Gilbert J. 21
    Lulie C. 66
    Meade E. 21
    Peter P. 122
    Rebecca B. 21
    Sarah 122

Sarah B. 21
Sarah G. 122
Thomas W. 21
CRADLIN
    George N. 21
    Lillie M. 22
    Rose I. 22
CRAFFTS
    Ann 111
CRAGG
    Mabel I. 22
    Mary V. 22
    Thomas M. 22
CRAIG
    Joanna 101
    Mary 101
    Mary G. 101, 103
    Samuel 101
CRAIK
    James 101, 168
CRAMER
    Ida E. 155
    John J. 155
CRAMLEY
    Helen S. 22
CRANDELL
    () 101
    John 101
    Joseph 111
    Mary 101
    Samuel 101
    Thomas 101
CRANE
    Elsie V. 22
    John A. 22
    Richard A. 22
    Richard E. 22
    Sarah A. 22
CRANSTON
    Annie E. 22
    John D. 22
CRAVEN
    John 122
    Mary E. 122
    Virginia A. 122
CREEK
    William 101
CREIGHTON
    Sarah C. 122
CRIGHTON
    Robert 101
CRIM
    George C. 152
CROOK
    Agnes 123, 131
    Bernard 123, 131

176

Elizabeth B. 131
CROSS
　　John R. 123
　　Julia A. 139
　　Mary 123, 139
　　Reid 123, 139
　　Sarah 123
　　Sarah W. 123
　　Thomas R. 123
CRUMBAUGH
　　Edward L. 22, 45
　　Etta L. 22, 44
CUMPSTON
　　Anna B. 22
　　Anna R. 22
　　E.H. 22
　　Wilhelmina B. 22
CURTIN
　　Benjamin F. 22
　　Christopher 22
　　Elizabeth J. 22
　　George R. 22
　　James E. 22
　　John T. 22
　　Katherine 51
　　Margaret H. 22
　　Willie 22
　　Willie L. 22
CUSHING
　　Capt. 101
DADE
　　Charles S. 7
　　Jane A. 7
DAINGERFIELD
　　Edward 22, 23
　　Edward L. 23
　　Francis L. 23
　　Henry 23
　　John B. 23
　　Margaret B. 23
　　Mary H. 23
　　Rebecca 23
　　Rosalie T. 23
　　S.V. 23
　　Sarah V. 23
DAITZ
　　Florence 162
　　Judith 162
　　Judith B. 162
　　Nathan 162
DALE
　　A. Caldwell 23
　　Eliza 23, 47
　　George 23
　　James 23
　　Jane R. 23, 81
　　Mary J. 23

　　Robert 23
　　Rosanna 23
DARLING
　　George 111
DARST
　　Florence W. 23
　　Thomas C. 23
DARVELL
　　Henry 123
DAVEY
　　David 101
　　Elizabeth 102
　　Mary 102, 123
　　Thomas 123
DAVIDSON
　　Alberta M. 23
　　Alberta W. 80
　　Ann E. 23
　　Eva T. 23
　　Faith H. 23
　　Florence E. 53
　　Francis J. 23
　　Francis K. 24
　　Jane W. 23, 24
　　William K. 24
DAVIES
　　Jane E. 123
　　Mary 123
　　William 123
DAVIS
　　Albert 24
　　Ann E. 24
　　Arthur G. 25
　　Aurelia 123
　　C. Randolph 24
　　Charles E. 24
　　Charlie 24
　　Charlotte V. 24
　　Constance G. 24
　　Edwin 24
　　Eleanor W. 24, 85
　　Eliza A. 24
　　Eliza K. 24
　　Ella L. 24
　　Emma M. 24
　　Esther 25
　　Frances D. 25
　　George 24
　　George E. 57
　　George O. 24
　　Georgeanna 57
　　Georgiana 24
　　Hannah A. 24
　　Henrietta W. 86
　　Henry W. 24
　　J. Hewes 24

　　James D. 25
　　James H. 24, 85
　　John H. 24
　　John R. 24
　　Josiah H. 24
　　Lillian B. 24
　　M. 123
　　Martena 123
　　Mary E. 25
　　Mildred B. 24
　　Ray O. 24
　　Sally M. 24
　　Sarah E. 24, 57
　　Sarah W. 24
　　Thomas V. 24
　　W. 123
　　William 123
DAVY
　　Susan 123
　　Thomas 123
DAWKINS
　　Alethea P. 30
　　Eva 30
　　Young P. 30
DAWSON
　　Christine N. 24
DAY
　　Ann 124
　　John 124
　　John F. 124
DEAGEN
　　Catharine 122
　　Fanney 122
　　George 122
DEAKINS
　　Jane 24
　　Jane M. 57
　　Joseph M. 25
　　William 57
DEAL
　　W.W. 6
DEAN
　　Charles A. 25, 75
　　Edward M. 75
　　Elizabeth W. 25
　　Elwood 25
　　Hannah 25
　　James F. 25
　　Jane 25
　　Joseph 25
　　Julia F. 75
　　Mary A. 25
　　Mary E. 75
　　Mary I. 25, 75
　　Mary J. 25
　　Mr. 5

177

William 25
William H. 25
DEANE
   Annie M. 25
   James 25
   James B. 25
   Joseph 5
   Margaret 25
DEARBORN
   Harriet 25
   Simon 25
DEBOGANDE
   Ada H. 25
DECAZENOVE
   Elizabeth A. 25
   Helga T. 25
   Infant 25
   Louis A. 25
DEEBLE
   Joseph H. 25
DEETON
   Ann E. 124
   Christopher 124
   George L. 124
   Isabell L. 124
   James H. 124
   Sarah E. 124
DEIKE
   Frederick 25
   Mary 25
DELANEY
   Catharine O. 25
   Dorothy D. 26
   Infant 25
   Martin 26
   Martin D. 25, 26
   Paul L. 26
   Sarah C. 26
DEMAINE
   Alice K. 26
   Charles W. 26
   Janie W. 26
DEMAREST
   Alma E. 26
   David T. 26
   Dorothy 26
   Henry E. 26
   Margaret C. 26
   Margaretta A. 26
DEMOLL
   Bessie S. 26
DEMPSEY
   Esther W. 26
   James 26
   Sarah M. 26
DENEALE
   George 167

DENINGTON
   Sarah 68
DENNETT
   John L. 111
DENNIS
   Alice V. 37
   Gordon M. 37
DETTERER
   Gladys K. 26
   Lewis A. 26
   Marguerite E. 26
DETWILER
   Richard W. 26
DEVINE
   Charles E. 26
   Charles J. 26
   Homer L. 26
   Julia A. 26
   Robert E. 26
DIBBLE
   Dorothy S. 26
DICK
   David 26
DIEDEL
   Adolph 26
   Carolina M. 26
   Caroline L. 26
   Charles 27
   Fannie E. 27
   Virginia 27
DIENER
   Irving 152
   Minnie W. 152
DIXON
   Fanny C. 20
   John A. 20
   Mary 27
   Mary J. 27
   Turner 27
   William P. 27
DODSON
   Emmitt O. 27
DOGAN
   Leonard 27
   Mary M. 27
DOLPHIN
   Dolly 27
DORSEY
   Edward 124
   Henrietta M. 124
   Jane P. 124
   Laura M. 17
   Lucy J. 124
   Mary E. 17, 124
   Thomas J. 124
DOUGLAS

Eliza K. 27
Harriet F. 27
J. Sidney 27
James 12, 27
James S. 27
John G. 27
Margaret 12
R.S. 27
Sallie W. 27
Stuart 27
V.T. 27
DOUGLASS
   Catharine 27
   Daniel 102
   Eliza C. 27, 28
   Helen 27
   J. Edwards 27
   James 27, 28, 102
   John 27
   Margaret 27, 28
   Mary 102
   R. Stuart 28
   Sarah 28, 102
   Thomas V. 28
DOVE
   Jilson 124
   Mary P. 124
DOWNHAM
   Belle H. 28
   E. Francis 28
   E.E. 28
   Esther M. 28
   Everlina U. 28
   Grace E. 28
   Harry A. 28
   Horace E. 28
   S. Maude 9
   Sarah M. 28
DOWNS
   Harvey C. 28
DREESE
   Hester 124
DREIFUS
   Albert 152
   Caroline 152
   Estella 152
   Hedwig 152
   Julius 152
   Louis 152
   Pauline 152
   Ray 152
   Rosa 152
   Samuel 152
   Simpson 152
DRISCOLL
   Harriette C. 28

        Theodore G. 28
DROWNS
    Harvey C. 28
    Ida V. 28
    John T. 28
    Marion L. 28
DUDLEY
    Edward L. 28
    Reuben 168
DUFFEY
    ( ) 102
    Charles W. 28
    Constance S. 28
    Cora 28
    Ella L. 28
    George N. 125
    George S. 125
    Josephine D. 28
    Mary S. 125
DUNBAR
    Silas 102
DUNCAN
    Amelia H. 29
    Clarence E. 28
    Elizabeth V. 14
    George M. 28
    Isabella 125
    James A. 28
    James E. 28
    Martha M. 28
    Virginia 28
    William 29, 125
    William A. 14, 29
    William H. 29
DUNDAS
    Agnes 29, 48
    Edward 102
    John 29, 48
    Nancy M. 29, 48
    Sophia M. 29
DUNLAP
    Ann 29
    James 29
    Mary 7
    William 29
DUNLOP
    Elizabeth 111
    John 102
DUNN
    Jane F. 77
DuPIGNAC
    Sarah P. 29
DURR
    Mary E. 135
DYER
    Ann M. 29
    Cordelia H. 29

    Francis 29
    Henrietta D. 29
    James W. 29
    John F. 29
    Lucy 29
    Margaret 29
    Margaret M. 29
    Rosalie H. 29
    Virginia 29
DYKES
    Elizabeth 102
EDELEN
    Eva D. 30
    Frances R. 30
    J. Steed 30
    James S. 30
    Philip R. 30
EDMONDS
    Edmund 30
EDWARDS
    Sarah 48
EGE
    Henrietta 46
    Mary 46
EGGBORN
    Anita R. 30
    Infant 30
    J. Armistead 30
    Margaret 30
EICHBERG
    Babette 152
    Isaac 152
    Louis 152
    Rosa 152
    Rudolph 152
ELDRIDGE
    Edward E. 30
    Elizabeth M. 30
    Georgie H. 30
    Joseph E. 30
    Lucinda A. 30
    Manchester 30
    Sybil H. 30
ELKINS
    Lucy D. 30
ELLIS
    Beverley C. 30
    Lula B. 30
    William F. 30
EMACK
    ( ) 102
EMERSON
    Ellen 30
    Ellen E. 30
    Eraslus? 30
    William D. 30
EMM

    Martha C. 30
ENGLISH
    Alberta M. 23
    Edwin 30
    Emily H. 30
    Francis C. 30
    Henrietta E. 30
    Horace L. 31
    James A. 30, 31
    John A. 30
    Maria S. 30, 31
    William 31
ERBECK
    Evelyn V. 31
ERBY
    Lawrence 102
ESPEY
    Mary E. 127
ESPOSITO
    Nance C. 31
ETTINGER
    Arnold A. 152
    Sabine 152
EVANS
    Amy E. 164
    Ann V. 125
    Catharine E. 125
    Catherine 31
    Elizabeth 125
    James D. 31
    Percy 31
    Samuel 125
    Susannah 56
    Victoria L. 31
    William H. 125
EVELETH
    Harriot M. 31
    James 31
    John 125
    Julia 125
    Julia C. 125
    Kate P. 31
    Sally S. 31
    William S. 125
EVERHARDT
    John D. 31
FADELEY
    Anna M. 31
    Milton M. 31
FAGELSON
    Gilta K.   162, 164
    Lillian 162
    Mary 162
    Milton 162
    Sam 161
    Samuel N. 162

179

Tila 162
Zalda 162
FAIRFAX
  Susanna 31
  Thomas M. 31
  William 100
FARRAR
  Dolly H. 31
  Rupert G. 31
FAW
  Abraham 125
  Mary A. 102
  Sarah 125
FAWCETT
  Harriet 65
FEAGAN
  Stella H. 31
FEDDER
  Harry 152
  Jennye B. 152
  Stanley S. 152
FENDALL
  Elizabeth 31
  Elizabeth M. 31
  Florence F. 31
  Mary L. 31
  Philip R. 31
  Robert Y. 31
FERNANDEZ
  Ricardo J. 32
FIELD
  Alice H. 32
  Alice V. 37
  Janet V. 37
  R. Lee 32
  Ruth S. 32
  Saidee M. 32
  Stephen H. 37
FINE
  A. Milton 153
  Hilda W. 153
FINKS
  Lucy L. 32
  Paul 32
  Robert E. 32
  Thomas L. 32
  Virginia 32
FINLAY
  David 102
FINN
  Harriet 163
  Melvin 163
FISCHER
  Morris 163
FISHER
  Elizabeth L. 32
  Isaiah 32

John H. 32
Kathryn 75
Sallie A. 32
Samuel P. 32
Thomas A. 32
FITZGERALD
  John F. 32
FITZHUGH
  John T. 125
  Rachel D. 125
FITZPATRICK
  Bernard W. 32
  Ruth L. 32
FLEMING
  Alcinda 119
  Andrew 32, 102, 108
  Andrew J. 32
  Ann 102
  Ann P. 32
  Catharine 32
  Catharine I. 39
  Edgar S. 32
  Eliza 32
  Grace I. 32
  Ida V. 32
  James 32
  James P. 32
  Mamie L. 32
  Maria A. 32
  Mary 32
  Mary L. 32
  Robert F. 32
  Thomas 32, 33
FLETCHER
  George E. 33
  Leila D. 33
  Louise 50
  Thomas W. 33
FOGLEMAN
  Lyman M. 33
FONES
  Albert R. 33
  Clarice T. 33
  Linwood B. 33
  Mary E. 33
  Mary F. 21
  Melvin M. 33
  S. Catherine 33
  Thomas R. 33
  Virginia B. 33
FOOTE
  Catharine R. 33
  F. 33
FORREST
  Dora 33
  James P. 33

FORTENEY
  Catherine 33
  Elizabeth 33
  Jacob 33
FOWLE
  Anne E. 33
  John 33
  John C. 33
  Paulina C. 33
FOWLER
  Mary 111
  Samuel G. 111
FOX
  Edward L. 28
  Mary V. 21
  Rebecca H. 28
FRANK
  Harry 153
FRANT
  Abraham 153
  Estelle 153
FREEDMAN
  Hannah 163
FREEMAN
  Ethel H. 33
FRENCH
  George E. 33, 99
  Virginia C. 33
  Willie P. 33
FRENZEL
  Nellie 61
FRIEDLANDER
  Henry 153
  Herman 153
  Katharine A. 153
FRINKS
  Alvin W. 34
  Marguerite J. 34
FRYE
  Christopher 125
  Margaret 125
FUGITT
  Catharine 125
  Gustavous 125
  Gustavus 125
  Joseph 125
  Laura V. 126
FULLER
  Harriet 9
FULLMORE
  Elizabeth C. 34
FULMORE
  Ann 126
  Joseph 126
FUSFIELD
  Emanuel 153

GARDNER
  Ann E. 34
  Benoni 104
  C. Cazenove 34
  Catherine C. 34
  Charles C. 34
  Dorsey 34
  Eliza C. 34
  Eliza F. 34
  Harriet C. 34
  Mary 34
  Paul 34
  Sarah 104
  William C. 34
  William F. 34
GARNER
  James A. 34
  William 34
GARNETT
  Frank M. 34
  Muscoe 35
  R.P. 34
  Sallie B. 34
GARRETT
  A.B. 5
GARST
  Paul E. 35
GAUSE
  Harriet D. 35
GAWLER
  Joseph 6
GEDNEY
  Emma E. 35
  Samuel 35
  Susan 35
  Susan A. 35
GENZBERGER
  Amelia 153
  Bettie M. 153
  Hannah 153
  Lee 153
  Leopold 153
  Lippman 153
  Michael 153
  Segmond 153
  Simon S. 153
GERBER
  Charles F. 35
  Julia B. 35
GERSTMAN
  Aviva A. 163
GIBBS
  Edward C. 35
  J. Norman 35
  Louise P. 35
  Margaret H. 35
  Theodore 126

GILLIES
  James 102
GILMAN
  Laura A. 102
GIRD
  John 35
  John H. 35
  Sarah 35, 49
GIST
  Anna M. 50
GLADSTONE
  Beatrice T. 153
GLANVILL
  Joseph 35
GLASS
  Hyman F. 163
GODFREY
  Courtney N. 35
GOLAS
  Janet L. 35
GOLDBERG
  Beatrice 163
  Jack L. 153
  Murray J. 163
  Tecla S. 153
GOLDMAN
  Louis 161
  M. 161
GOLDSMITH
  Emanuel 151
  Ida B. 151
GOLDWYN
  Celestine D. 153
  Moe 153
GOODMAN
  Nellie L. 35
GORDON
  Robert B. 163
GORHAM
  Michael J. 35
GOWAN
  Margaret M. 35
GRAHAM
  Alice H. 35
  Alice M. 35
  David 102
  Edythe M. 35
  John 19
  Mary C. 19
  Robert M. 35
GRAVES
  Asenath L. 56
  Clara E. 35
  Herbert C. 35
  Lucy E. 78
  Lucy M. 35
  Myrtilla M. 35

  Willard P. 35
GRAY
  Harrison B. 36
GRECHANIK
  Cynthia R. 36
  Walter 36
GREEN
  Eliza A. 59
  Henry 36
  Judith B. 36
  Linda M. 36
  Mary E. 125
  S. Virginia 36
GREENAWAY
  Coralie 36
  Irene C. 36
  Irene W. 36
  Joseph 102
  Mary C. 36
  Nevell S. 36
  Rebecca 102
GREENOUGH
  ( ) 5
GREGORY
  Boyd 36
  Charles N. 36
  Douglas S. 36
  Edward H. 63
  Isobel 46
  Jane W. 63
  Janet B. 51
  Julia 19
  Margaret D. 36
  Mary C. 63
  Mary D. 36
  Mary S. 36
  Peter M. 36
  William 36
  William B. 36
GRIFFITH
  Elizabeth 126
  Greenbury 126
  Kinzey 126
  William S. 126
GRIGG
  Careline 126
  Joseph 126
GRIGSBY
  James 126
GRILLBORTZER
  Esther D. 25
  Eve C. 36
  John A. 36
GRIMES
  Caroline H. 37
  Hunter F. 36
  Joseph S. 37

Mary A. 36
GRISAMORE
   Jesse W. 37
   Oscar L. 37
GRONAU
   Alice P. 37
   M. Alice 37
   Robert E. 37
GROSS
   Fredrick 126
   Ida B. 37
   Nancy 126
   W.B. 37
   W.F. 6
GROSSMAN
   William 163
GROTTO
   Wilhelmina N. 37
GROVES
   Mary E. 37
   Thomas A. 37
GRUNEBAUM
   Harry 153
GRUVER
   Elizabeth M. 126
   John 126
GRYMES
   Louisa J. 140
GUEST
   Cynthia A. 132
   Job 126, 132
GUINN
   Annie M. 127
   David H. 126, 127
   Ethwald 127
GULLATT
   Betsy 111
   James 111
GUTHRIE
   Louise D. 37
   N. Rawlins 37
HAAG
   Clara G. 37
HABERMAN
   Florence H. 153
HAINES
   Lillie M. 127
HALL
   () 103
   B.F. 37
   Francis 168
   George W. 37
   Grace 103, 104
   John S. 103
   Martha A. 37
   Mary G. 101
   R. Clifford 37

William J. 103, 111
HALLEY
   Esther 37
   William 37
HALLODAY
   James 103
   Mary 103
HALSALL
   Alice 84
HAMERSLEY
   Florence 37
   Florence A. 37
HAMILTON
   Alfred 127
   Catharine 127
   Catherine 127
   Hannah S. 127
   Philip 127
   Susannah 103
HAMMILL
   C. Perry 37
   Daisy V. 37, 84
   Edward 37
   Helen E. 37
   Helen H. 84
   Hunter A. 37
   J.H. 37
   Lucy A. 37
   Paul E. 37, 84
   Reuben C. 37
   Rita D. 37
   Rose 37
   Sophia H. 37
   William R. 37, 84
HAMMOND
   J.T. 38
   James W. 38
   Mary 38
   Sarah V. 37
HANDELSMAN
   Amelia 153
   Samuel 153
HANNAH
   Alexander 103
HANNOE
   Joseph 38
   Julia L. 38
HANNON
   Martha E. 14
HARDIN
   Annie E. 38
   Randolph T. 38
HARDING
   Claudia M. 38
   Claudia U. 38

   Helen L. 38
   Katie W. 85
   Mary 111
   William A. 38
HARMAN
   Richard A. 38
HARMON
   Aaron D. 38
   Allen C. 38
   Anne 38
   Annie 66
   Charles P. 38
   Elizabeth 38
   F. Clark 127
   Lorenzo D. 127
   Mary 38
   Mary B. 127
   Mary E. 127
   Mary H. 38
   Philippa 38
   Philippa A. 38
   Thomas D. 38
   William W. 38
HARPER
   Catharine F. 38
   Catharine I. 39
   Edward 103
   Ellen A. 38
   Emma D. 38
   F.S. 38
   Hannah A. 38
   Isabella 38
   Isabella F. 38
   Jane E. 39
   John 38, 103, 109
   Joseph 5, 111
   M.M. 39
   Margaret A. 39
   Margaret D. 39
   Maria A. 39
   Martha A. 39
   Mary 103, 109
   Mary A. 39
   Mary D. 78
   Mary L. 39
   Mary T. 39
   Robert 39, 103
   Rosalie H. 103
   Sally 38
   Samuel B. 39
   Samuel D. 39
   Sarah 38, 39
   Sarah F. 127
   Sophia 103
   Thomas P. 39
   Wells A. 39

William 39
William W. 38, 39
Willie 39
HARRELL
  Emma T. 39
  Roy B. 39
HARRINGTON
  Charles G. 39
  Edward B. 39
  Elizabeth L. 40
  John H. 40
  Margaret 40
HARRIS
  Gordon W. 40
  Irene C. 40
  James 127
  John W. 40
  Jordan W. 40
  Joseph 40, 168
  Laura 40
  Laura W. 40
  Lucy A. 127
  Lute M. 40
  Nick 40
  Samuel 40
HARRISON
  Albert R. 40
  Albert W. 40
  Alice R. 40
  Angeline C. 40
  Clara B. 40
  Elias 40
  Elizabeth V. 40
  Mary C. 41
  Mary N. 41
  Mary O. 40
  Thomas 40
HART
  Elizabeth B. 41
  John T. 41
  Nancy C. 41
  William A. 41
HARVEY
  Alva L. 41
  Grace A. 67
  Lillian E. 41
HASGAL
  Abraham 158
  Babetta 158
  Sigmund 158
HASSMER
  Judith E. 127
HAWKINS
  Hannah C. 127
  Perry H. 127
HAYES
  Margaret L. 53

HEDMAN
  Toivo E. 149
HEINAMAN
  Jacob 41
  Mary A. 41
HEISLEY
  Emeline 41
  Ferdinand F. 41
  George E. 41
  George W. 41
  Katherine H. 41
  Marie F. 41
  Phoebe 41
HENDERSON
  Alice V. 41
  Ann J. 127
  Anne M. 41
  Annie S. 41
  Archibald 41
  Archibald M. 41
  Emily 41
  Emily C. 41
  George 127
  Indiana B. 20
  James E. 41
  John A. 20
  John E. 41
  Julian F. 41
  Lois H. 41
  Paulina C. 41
  William A. 20
  William F. 41
HENDLEY
  John R. 42
  Mary R. 42
HENKEL
  James S. 42
  Nancy W. 42
  Oscar 42
HENLY
  Rosa 153
HEPBURN
  Agnes 29, 103, 111
  George E. 42
  John 108
  Nellie E. 42
  William 29, 103
HERBERT
  Ethel M. 42
  Linwood A. 42
HERRICK
  Doreen 42
  Edna M. 42
  James B. 42
  Jane E. 127
  M.C. 127

Mollie 127
William T. 127
HERRING
  Margaretta I. 42
HERSCHMAN
  Arthur 153
HICKS
  Gerald V. 42
  Vella H. 42
HIGGINBOTHAM
  James A. 42
HILDEBRAND
  Anna L. 42
  Edith J. 42
  Simpson V. 42
HILL
  F.E. 65
  J.C. 65
  Louise 65
HILLS
  Francis J. 42
  Mercy A. 42
  Samuel B. 42
HIMES
  Walter L. 42
HINES
  S.H. 6
HINGSTON
  N. 111
HINN
  William B. 42
HIPKINS
  Jennie E. 42
  Lewis 42
  Margaret L. 46
HIRSCH
  Frances G. 163
HOBBS
  Anna M. 73
  Elizabeth S. 73
  Elon S. 73
  Evelyn J. 73
HOCH
  Ellery T. 128
  Marguerite S. 128
HODGE
  Nancy F. 128
  Thomas 128
HODGKIN
  Clara 128
  M.M. 128
  Robert 128
HOEFT
  Infant 42
  John F. 43
HOFFMAN

Mabel S. 43
Meyer J. 161
HOGAN
  Anne 18
HOLBERT
  Infant 43
HOLLENSBURY
  Fannie 128
  Harriet 128
  John W. 128
HOLLOWAY
  Charles P. 43
HOLMES
  E.C. 43
  Mary H. 38
HOOFF
  Laura C. 43
  Laura W. 43
  Philip H. 43
  Wilson L. 43
HOOKES
  Jacob 43
  Mary A. 43
HOPKINS
  Aletha T. 43
  Benedict M. 43
  Frank E. 43
  Hildred T. 43
  Lawrence A. 43
HORNER
  Morris 85
HOROWITZ
  Fannie 163
HOSKINS
  James O. 128
  Jane E. 128
  Moses 128
HOTCHKISS
  Harris 168
HOUCK
  Alonzo 128
  Laura V. 128
  Lonnie 128
  Oppelt 128
HOWARD
  Beal 43
  Elizabeth 43
  John 128
  Katherine P. 56
HOWDERSHELL
  Amanda S. 43
  Bertha M. 43
  Clarence E. 43
  James E. 43
  Julian R. 43
  Ralph M. 43
  Virginia M. 43

HOWELL
  () 5
HOZEK
  Anna 43
HUBBOLD
  John 103
HUEY
  David R. 43
HUGHES
  John 111
HULFISH
  Betty P. 44
  David N. 43
  Marianne M. 43
  Paul B. 43
  Susan S. 43
  Thomas A. 43, 44
  Virginia C. 43, 44
  Worth 43, 44
HUNT
  Sean P. 44
HUNTER
  () 111
  Albert B. 44
  Alexander 103
  Charles S. 128
  Cordelia M. 44
  Elizabeth 128
  George 103
  John 44, 103
  John C. 44
  John T. 128
  Lois 44
  Mabel I. 22
  Mary E. 44
  Mary W. 53
  Robert W. 128
  Sophia 37
  Thelma M. 44
  Virginia 128
  William 103, 104
HURWITZ
  Mistie W. 153
HUSS
  Beckie 154
HUTCHENS
  Infant 44
HYDE
  John M. 44
  Sarah M. 44
IDEN
  James 44
  Laura 44
IMMERMAN

Richard P. 163
INSCOE
  Mary A. 44
  Thomas W. 44
IRISH
  M. 157
IRWIN
  Ann P. 32
  Grace 32
  James 5, 7, 44
  Mr. 5
  Thomas 112
  William H. 32
JACKSON
  Adelle 128
  Andrew 9
  Christiana 128
  Warren 128
JACOB
  John B. 44
JACOBS
  Almira 44
  Catharine 128
  Catherine 129
  Elizabeth 44
  Margaret 56
  Presley 44
  Thomas 128
JAFFA
  Dilla 154
  Hattie 154
  Moses 154
JAMES
  Everett H. 44
  Helen D. 27
  Henry B. 44
  Jessie A. 44, 45
  Mary R. 45
JAMIESON
  Alice J. 45
  Andrew 5, 45
  Anna R. 45
  Bessie S. 45
  Bettie W. 45
  Bobbie 45
  Catharine P. 45
  Catherine S. 45
  Charles 104
  Eleanor B. 45
  Elizabeth J. 45
  Elizabeth P. 74
  George 104
  George W. 45
  J. Stewart 45
  John J. 45
  John S. 45
  Julia B. 45

Julia R. 45
Kate S. 45
Mary 45
Mary S. 45
Mr. 5
Robert 45
Robert D. 45
Thomas 45
Thomas S. 45
Willis 45
JANNEY
  Abel 112
  Edith H. 45
  John 45
  Joseph T. 45
  Margaret 45, 104, 111
  Margaret W. 104
JAVINS
  J. Randolph 45
JENKINS
  Ellen G. 46
  Inez E. 46
  Maude M. 59
  Norman B. 46
JENNINGS
  Lula B. 30
JEWETT
  Joseph 46
JOHNSON
  Clara 46
  Eleanor 133
  Elizabeth 46
  Frankie 46
  George 46
  J.F. 46
  Sarah A. 145
  William A. 46
  William R. 46
JOHNSTON
  Anna B. 69
  Anna M. 47
  Annie E. 46
  Claudius L. 46
  Dennis 47
  Dennis M. 46
  Eliza D. 47
  Elizabeth 46
  Elizabeth R. 67
  Emma K. 46
  Frances 69
  Francis E. 46, 47, 69
  Frankie M. 46, 47
  Frederick W. 46
  George 46, 47, 67
  George D. 46
  Henrietta E. 46, 53

Isobel G. 46, 47
James A. 47
James E. 46, 47
Jane 112
Jane A. 47
John 143
John F. 47
John H. 46
Joseph E. 75
Margaret L. 46
Mary A. 47
Mary C. 46
Mary E. 46, 47
Mary M. 143
Nina M. 47
R.W. 46
Rebecca S. 47
Reuben 46, 47
Robert E. 46
S.R. 46, 47
Samuel R. 47
Sara C. 47
Tod J. 5
Watts K. 47
William G. 47
William S. 47
JONES
  Ann 129
  Edward Z. 47
  Margaret J. 47
  Mary 116
  Mary A. 129
  Nathan 129
JOYCE
  Mary 47
JUDKINS
  Esther L. 47
  John M. 47
  Lewis M. 47
  Wallace S. 47
  William E. 47
KAMENITZER
  Ludwig 154
KANE
  Elleanor M. 138
KATZ
  Aaron 154
  Reuben 163
  Reuben L. 163
  Stella 154
  Theodore 163
KATZELNIK
  Henrietta 163
KAUFFMAN
  Isaac 154
KAUFMAN
  Hannah 154

Joseph 154
Rosa 154
KAUFMANN
  Alexander 154
  Jerome G. 154
  Joseph A. 154
  Minnie O. 154
  Rebecca 154
KEENE
  Charles 48
  Edward L. 48
  Estelle 48
  George F. 48
  Hattie E. 48
  John N. 48
  Mary E. 48
  Nancy 48
  Nancy M. 29, 48
  Newton 48
  Pearl I. 48
  Samuel R. 48
  Sarah E. 48
  Theron R. 48
KEISER
  Lena 163
KEITH
  Gean 48
  James 167
  William 48
KELL
  Isaac 129
  Nancy 129
KELLER
  Mildred C. 78
KELLY
  Charles H. 48
  Charles W. 48
  Ellen 48
  Ellen D. 52
  Indiana 48
  John C. 48
  John L. 48
  Lidey 48
  Lucy E. 48, 49
  Peter A. 48
  Philip 48
  Thomas 48
  Thomas L. 48, 49
  Thomas P. 49
KEMPER
  Eliza G. 81
KENNEDY
  Andrew T. 49
  Clarence E. 49
  Elsie 49

James 35, 49, 112
John 49
Sarah 35
Susannah 49
KERBEL
   Dan 161, 163
   Dan E. 163
   Shara H. 163
KETLAND
   Elmer J. 49
   Eva V. 36
KIDWELL
   Ada M. 49
   Charles E. 49
   Charles H. 49
   Emma V. 49
   Lucretia 49
   Margaret 49
KILTON
   George 49
KINCAID
   John 49
   Lucy 50
KING
   Charles 50
   Fannie E. 27
   Frank T. 50
   Jane E. 14
   Laura V. 50
   Louise F. 50
   Margaret W. 50
   Marshall L. 50
KINZER
   Anna B. 50
   J. Louis 50
   Maggie C. 50
   Margaret G. 50
KIRCHNER
   Charles D. 46
   Elizabeth 46
   Emma 46
   Jacob F. 46
   Rosa D. 46
   Rosina 46
KIRK
   Adelaide M. 50
   Adelaide U. 54
   Barbara 129
   Evelyn H. 50
   Harrison 50
   Harry 50
   Harry D. 50
   Infant 50
   Jessie C. 50
   John H. 50
   Lunette 50
   Lunette C. 50

Orlando H. 50
KIRKPATRICK
   Charles D. 50
   Eleanor S. 50
KIRKWOOD
   Lewis H. 50
   Peggy J. 50
KIRSCHBAUM
   Samuel 163
KITE
   Anna M. 50
   D. Millard 50
   David M. 50
   Mary G. 50
   Rebecca B. 50
KLEINMAN
   Gitla 164
   Israel 163
   Jacob 164
   Joseph 164
KLINE
   Gertrude 164
   William 164
KLOSKY
   Adele S. 154
KOFFLER
   Joseph L. 164
   Mollie A. 164
   Sarah 164
KOHEN
   Tzedek 164
KOLATSKY
   D. Vora 164
   Dvora 164
KRAMER
   Edith S. 164
   Emelia 129
   Frederick 129
KULP
   Kate 86
   Windsor 86
LABOWITZ
   Allan 161
LADD
   Joseph B. 104
   Sarah 104
   William 104
LAMAR
   Gasaway B. 51
   Harriet C. 51
LAMB
   Harriet B. 51
   William H. 51
LAMBERT
   James A. 51
   Katherine C. 51
LAMMOND

Alexander 51
Caroline 51
Edwin 51
Francis 51
LANDRY
   M. Armantine 79
LANPHIER
   Elizabeth 129
   Robert G. 129
LARMAND
   Francis 51
   John W. 51
   Medora N. 51
LATHAM
   Ada V. 51
   Lucy 51
   Wilburn E. 51
LATTA
   John W. 51
LATZ
   Marcus 154
LAUPHEIMER
   Alexander 154
   Henrietta 154
   M. 154
   Martha S. 155
   Michael 155
   Mrs. 154
   Sylvern 155
LAWSON
   Robert M. 129
LEACOCK
   L. 129
   Mary S. 129
LEADBEATER
   Janet B. 51
   Lizzie J. 51
   Thomas 51
   Thomas B. 51
   William G. 51
LEAKE
   Agnes B. 51
   Alfred P. 51
LEAP
   Jacob 51
LEATHERLAND
   Annie E. 52
   John W. 51
   Lawrence C. 52
   Walter I. 52
LEDBETTER
   Cathy L. 52
   William G. 52
LEE
   Alfred H. 129
   Ann E. 34

Cassius F. 34
Clagett 129
D. Lewis 129
Ellen D. 52
Hannah 129
Margaret T. 52
Mary A. 129
Nhia C. 129
Thomas F. 52
Thomas L. 52
William A. 52
LEEF
  Kate T. 52
LEHMAN
  Bernard 164
  Ida 164
LEMBERG
  Rakhil 155
LEONARD
  Jacob 125
  Sophia E. 125
LESTER
  Emily B. 52
  James 52
  Marcus R. 52
LETERMAN
  Henrietta 155
LEVERING
  Elizabeth 129
LEVIN
  Amy E. 164
  Joseph I. 164
  Rena F. 164
  Stanford M. 164
LEVINE
  Abraham 155
LEVITAN
  Hirsh 155
LEWIS
  Annie L. 75
  Eliza 115
  Richard 115
LIBBY
  Lucy M. 35
LIEBERMAN
  Bertha B. 164
  Felix 164
LILIENTHAL
  Johanna 155
  Rosa 155
  Samuel 155
LILLY
  Dawn M. 52
LINDHEIMER
  Babetta 155
  Rudolph 155
  Samuel 155

LINDSEY
  Belle H. 52
  Catherine 52, 71
  Edith G. 52
  Ella D. 52
  Florence L. 52
  Marian A. 71
  Mary 52, 71
  Melville W. 52
  Noble 52, 71
  Paul 52
  Samuel E. 52
  Wallace R. 71
LIPPMAN
  Morris 155
LOCKWOOD
  Aquila 130
  Cassandra M. 130
  Harriet 130
LOGAN
  Frances 52
  Samuel 52
  William 130
LONDON
  Philip 164
  Sarah 164
LONG
  A. Raymond 52
  Charlotte V. 52
  Rebecca 105
  Samuel 105
LONGDEN
  John 130
  Ralph 130
LOVIN
  Jenice 155
  Manfred 155
LOWE
  Jane R. 130
  John F. 130
  Julianna M. 125
  Margaret 105
  Mark C. 52
  Mercer L. 130
  Robert S. 130
  Sophia E. 130
LUCAS
  John 38
LUCKETT
  Catherine T. 52
  James T. 52
  John A. 52
  Minnie S. 52
  Unnamed 52
LUDWIG
  Benjamin J. 164

LUGENBEEL
  James W. 130
  Martha A. 130
LUMSDEN
  John 105
LUMSDON
  John 115, 130
  Margery 130
  Mary A. 130
LUNSFORD
  Charles D. 52
  Heaton P. 52
  Mary I. 52
LUNT
  Agothian 130
  Arthur 130
  Elizabeth 130
  Ezra 130
  Hannah J. 53
  John D. 53
  Lucy L. 53
  Mary H. 53
  Samuel H. 53
LYLES
  A.D. 130
  Annas I. 130
  E.A. 130
  Esther 130
  James 130, 131
  Mary A. 131
  Mary E. 53
  Richard H. 53
MacINNES
  John 53
MACKALE
  Mary E. 131
MACRAE
  A. Eliza 53
MADDEN
  Nancy 105
MAGUIRE
  Annie E. 53
MAIGNE
  Charles M. 53
  Florence E. 53
  Marianne M. 43
MAJOR
  Elizabeth B. 131
  James J. 131
  John 131
  Mary 131
MANDELL
  John C. 131
  Mary 131
MANGHER
  James B. 131
  Susan E. 131

MANSFIELD
   Caroline R. 131
   George H. 131
   Henry 131
   Isabella 131
   Jane E. 131
   Lucy 131
   William H. 131
MANSON
   Henrietta E. 46, 53
   Nathaniel C. 46, 53
MARBURY
   Elizabeth 53
   Joseph H. 53
   Leonard 53
   Mary W. 53
MARCUS
   Sally 164
MARK
   A.S. 17
   Ann S. 21, 53
   Ellen M. 53
   Hortensia H. 21
   Lydia G. 53
   Margaret L. 17, 53
   Mary S. 36
   S. 17
   Samuel 21, 53
   Sarah E. 53
MARMAR
   Arthur 149
MARSH
   Barbara A. 53
MARSHALL
   Charles B. 53
   John A. 53
   Margaret L. 53
   Maria J. 53
MARSTELLER
   Christiana D. 5, 112
   Philip G. 5, 112
MARTIN
   Helen B. 54
   Infant 54
   John 54
   Joseph E. 54
   Keith L. 54
   Lucy V. 64
   Madeleine L. 54
   Mary A. 64
   Minnie C. 54
   Sallie J. 54
   Sophia 54
   Thomas L. 131
   William L. 54
MARTZ
   Helen E. 155

   Samuel E. 155
MASON
   Fannie C. 12
   Laura 58
MASSEY
   Albert 54
   Margaret R. 54
MASSIE
   Fanny A. 54
MASTERSON
   Sarah 105
MATHER
   J. Warren 131
   Warren 115
MATHESON
   Kenneth 105
MATTHEWS
   Lastley 131
MAUCK
   Aubrey W. 54
   Frances L. 54
   W. Thomas 54
MAVERICK
   Marian 79
MAXFIELD
   E.F. 85
   Edward F. 54
   George E. 85
   Harvey W. 85
   Mary 85
MAY
   Adelaide U. 54
   Alice 131
   Edward H. 131
MAYER
   Elizabeth B. 131
   William G. 54
McBURNEY
   Alice 54
   Alice D. 54
   George 54
   George R. 54
McCALLISTER
   Edward P. 54
McCLEISH
   Jane 105
McCLIESH
   Archibald 54
   Catharine F. 54
   Elizabeth J. 54
   George 54
   James 54
   William 54
McCLOSKEY
   S.H. 81
McCOBB
   John 125, 132

   Marion L. 132
   Parker N. 132
   Rachel D. 125
   Sarah 125, 132
   Sarah W. 132
   Thomas F. 132
McCOLLOCH
   Mrs. 105
McCORMICK
   John 132
McCOWAN
   Nathalie M. 55
   Robert J. 55
McCOY
   Roberta F. 32
McCRACKEN
   George 55
   George K. 55
   Isabella 55
   James G. 55
   Margaret C. 55
McCRAE
   Eliza 105
   Infant 105
   James 105
   John 105
McCUBBIN
   Edward 168
   Susan 168
McCULLOUGH
   Mary J. 55, 85
   Thomas R. 55
McCURTIN
   George R. 55
McDONALD
   John 112
McDOUGALL
   () 105
McFADEN
   James 105
   Nancy 105
McGAUGHEY
   Kate 55
McGEHANNEY
   Margaret 112
McGINNIS
   Lawrence C. 55
McGLUE
   Charles H. 138
McGUIRE
   James 132
   Lucy 132
   Mariette A. 66
   Mary B. 55
   Sarah B. 66
   William 55, 66
McKAY

Elizabeth 105
McKENNA
  Marion G. 55
McKENNEY
  Esther B. 55
  William B. 55
McKENZIE
  Alexander 5, 55, 112
  Ann 112
  Esther L. 47
  James 47, 55
  James A. 55
  John 105
  Lewis 55
  Margaret 55
  Margaret S. 55
  Mary 55
  Mr. 5
  Sarah 47
  Sarah E. 55, 56
McKERNAN
  Margaret 56
McKIGHT
  Elizabeth C. 56
McKINNEY
  S. 112
McKNEW
  Goldsborough E. 56
  Martha F. 56
McKNIGHT
  Asenath L. 56
  Catharine B. 70
  Catharine P. 56
  Catherine P. 56
  Charles 56, 105
  Charles H. 56
  John 56, 70
  Margaret 56
  Margaret J. 56
  Martha B. 56, 70
  Mary E. 56
  Susannah E. 56
  William 56
  William H. 56
  William P. 56
McLEAN
  Infant 56
McLEOD
  () 105
  John 105
McNAIR
  Henry 56
McNAMARA
  Charles C. 115
  John 132
  Winfred 132
McRAE

Nancy 105
McVEIGH
  Cunthia A. 132
  James H. 132
  Lucy 132
MEADE
  Edith A. 132
  Robert H. 132
MEASE
  Robert 105
MELVILLE
  Hattie H. 57
MERRIAM
  Emily 57
  Sidney A. 57
MERRIKEN
  Elizabeth 132
  Joseph 132
MEYENBERG
  Bettie 153
MIDDLETON
  Ann 132, 138
  Electius 138
  Elizabeth 133
  Marion 138
MILBURN
  Alice 133
  George 133
  Jane 57
  Joseph 25, 57
  Margaret 25, 57
MILLAR
  () 105
MILLER
  Anna 26
  T. Michael 111
MILLS
  Adaline M. 57
  Alonzo 57
  Ann 57
  Georgeanna D. 57
  John S. 7
  Margery 133
  Mary A. 7
  Rebekah 168
  William 133
  William N. 57
MINIS
  Janet D. 58
MINISH
  Judith M. 80
MINNIY
  Catharine C. 133
  John P. 133
MINTZ
  Abbey J. 155

Isadore 155
Rose B. 155
Sadie B. 155
MITCHELL
  James 105
  William 105
MOFFETT
  John 58
  Matilda A. 58
MONRO
  Julian 133
  Robert 133
MONROE
  () 105
  Amanda E. 58
  Daniel 58
  Edwin 58
  Elizabeth 58
  James T. 58
  Julia A. 58
  Kate E. 58
  Rebecca 60
  Robert 133
  Slighter S. 58
  Thomas 58
MONTGOMERY
  Charles M. 58
  Grace C. 58
MOODY
  Elizabeth 105
MOORE
  Ellen 71
  George 133
  Harry V. 58
  M. 133
  Marian D. 58
  Marion H. 58
  Mary E. 12
  Thomas A. 71
  W. 133
  William A. 58
MORGAN
  Catharine 133
MORRILL
  Laura M. 58
  Mary S. 58
  Sara 58
  Virginia 58
  William 58
  William T. 58
MORRIS
  Helen B. 58
  Moses A. 155
  Rosa W. 155
MORSE
  Orlando S. 58
  Sarah 58

Virginia 58
MORTIMER
  Mary A. 66
MOUNT
  Ann E. 133
  Estelle K. 59
  James H. 59
  Joseph S. 133
  Phillip H. 59
  Sarah 133
  Sarah P. 133
  Sarah S. 133
  Thomas 133
MOUNTAIN
  Ralph T. 59
MUIR
  Eleanor J. 133
  Eliza A. 59
  Elizabeth 105, 111
  Esther 59
  Ethel 59
  Frances W. 106
  Helen 59
  James 6, 59, 97, 103, 105, 106, 111
  James F. 59
  John 59, 133
  John A. 59
  Lydia 133
  Mary 59
  Mary A. 59
  Nannie R. 133
  William H. 59
  William M. 59
  Willie 59
MUNDY
  Dabny 59
  Mary E. 70
  Mary J. 59
MUNROE
  Lamar 59
  Maude M. 59
MUNSON
  Charlotte E. 59
  James D. 100
MURRAY
  Catherine A. 59
  Jesse 59
  Margaret L. 59
  Rachael 100
MYERS
  A. 155
  C. 155
  Harry 155
  John 59
  Margaret 59
NALLS

Amanda S. 43
Ann E. 134
Dasie D. 59
Eugenia 134
James W. 134
Jeanne L. 59
Mary A. 134
Mary E. 122
NARAMORE
  Annie F. 59
  Leonard J. 59
NASH
  Charles F. 60
  George W. 60
  Jane 60
  Louise R. 60
  Rebecca M. 60
  Robert 60
NELSON
  Carrie N. 134
  Elizabeth A. 60
  Fannie 112
  George W. 60
  Georgiana 168
  Lynwood 134
  William 168
NEWELL
  Corrinne P. 60
  Joseph H. 60
NEWMAN
  Susanna P. 134
NEWTON
  Ann 134
  Anna F. 60
  Charles H. 60
  Evelyn P. 60
  Harry H. 60
  Henry 60
  Jane B. 60
  John 39
  John T. 60
  Joseph M. 60
  Margaret H. 60
  Mary T. 39
  William 60
  William C. 134
NICHOLA[S]
  Lewis 106
NICHOLSON
  Ann 60
  Eliza 60
  Henry 60
  Mary 61
  Precious 60, 61
NIVEN
  Duncan 106
NIXON

Catharine E. 134
Jane 134
Richard 134
NOLAND 134
  E. 131
  Elizabeth 134
  Reberter 134
  Susan E. 131
  Virginia A. 122
  W. 131
  William 134
NOLEN
  Constance E. 61
NOWLAND
  Charles W. 134
  Susan C. 134
  Thomas S. 134
NUGENT
  Annie V. 61
  Dorothy 61
  Eleanor B. 35
  John J. 61
  Mary J. 61
  Thomas W. 61
NUTT
  James 134
O'BRIEN
  Dennis 61
  Joseph D. 61
  Nancy 61
  Rebecca M. 61
O'KEEFE
  Sandy 2
O'MEARA
  Ada L. 61
  Collin W. 61
  Herbert W. 61
  James T. 61
  Marguerite 61
  Nellie F. 61
O'NEIL
  Elizabeth K. 46
  Walter L. 46
OGDEN
  David M. 63
  Eleanor G. 63
  George A. 135
  Kenneth W. 61
  Wilhelmina T. 61
  William D. 61
OPPENHEIM
  Benjamin M. 155
  Sara B. 155
ORME
  Archibald 82

ORRISON
　Florence W. 61
ORSBORN
　Lawson 135
OSBURN
　Mary 40
OSTROW
　Irma W. 155
　Maxwell A. 155
OWEN-JONES
　Charlotte C. 61
　Percy 61
OWENS
　Marian F. 33
PADGETT
　Lucretia 135, 140
PAFF
　Charles B. 62
　Frederick 62
　Frederick J. 62
　Grace C. 62
　Louisa 62
　Lucy T. 62
PAGE
　A. 143
　A. Eliza 53
　John R. 62
　Mary 62
　Rachel 143
　W. 143
　William 62
PALMER
　Ella L. 28
PARSONS
　Mary A. 168
PASCOE
　Charles 62
　Honore 62
　William 62
PATERSON
　Mary A. 146
　Susan 146
　William 146
PATON
　John B. 27
　Mary J. 27
　Rebecca 65
PATTEN
　() 102
　Elizabeth C. 106
　Susan 106
PATTERSON
　Benjamin 135
　Benjamin C. 135
　Benjamin D. 135
　Clyde W. 62
　Mary 135

　Mildred S. 62
　Sarah 135
　William 135
PATTON
　Mary 106
PAUL
　Joseph 62
　Nannie S. 62
　T. Stowers 62
PAXSON
　Edith G. 52
PAYNE
　Elisha K. 62
　Jessie C. 62
　Myrtle B. 62
PEAKE
　B.F. 135
　Mary C. 135
PEALE
　Corrinne 60
PEARSON
　O.C. 6
PENN
　Charlotte P. 135
　Leonidas R. 135
　Mary E. 33, 135
　Walter 135
　Walter A. 135
　Walter L. 135
PENNINGTON
　Sarah 107
PERDIKRAS
　Harry 62
PERRY
　Alexander 106, 113
　Alexander D. 62
　Daniel F. 106
　Jane 62
　Lillian E. 62
　Milton B. 62
PEYTON
　Ada M. 135
　Francis 167
　Howard 135
　Millard F. 135
　Sophia M. 29
PHILLIPS
　Elizabeth 135
　Ellenor 135
　G. 135
　John H. 135
PICKETT
　George E. 63
　Janet R. 63
PICKIN
　Alice H. 63

　Carrie B. 63
　Charles H. 63
　Charles R. 63
　James R. 63
　Margaret H. 63
PIERCY
　Catharine 56
PIERPOINT
　Annie B. 20
PIERSON
　Emma L. 63
　Harriet S. 63
　Henry W. 63
　Susan E. 63
PITTMAN
　() 106
PLANT
　Ambrose 135
　David I. 135
　Marietta 135
　Mary E. 135
　Pascal J. 135
　Paschal 135
PLASTER
　David H. 63
　Minnie H. 63
POINDEXTER
　Robert J. 136
POLLACK
　Joseph 155
POLLARD
　Betty 44
POMEROY
　Edith V. 63
　Samuel S. 63
POMERY
　John 107
PORTER
　Catharine 45
　James 107
　Thomas 107
POSNER
　Gussie 164
　Harry 164
　Rose G. 164
POSS
　Alice G. 136
　Esther E. 63
　Harry E. 63
　Henry B. 136
　John P. 63
　John W. 136
　Louis B. 63
　Marguerite A. 63
　Mary E. 63
　Mary V. 63

191

Ruth E. 63
POTTEN
　John 136
　S. 136
　Sarah 136
POTTER
　Frances 64
POWELL
　() 107
　Llewellyn 85
　Mary C. 63
　Mary G. 98
　Neville 63
　Robert C. 63
　William G. 63
PRAYTOR
　Willard A. 63
PRESTON
　Elisha C. 136
　Ellen 136
　James T. 63
　Kate B. 63
　Laura T. 63
　Laura W. 63
　Thomas 136
　Thomas S. 136
PRETTYMAN
　David G. 63, 64
　Harriet M. 63
　Harriet V. 63
　Lily M. 64
　Margaret V. 64
　Mary E. 64
　Priscilla 64
　Robert F. 63, 64
PRETZFELDER
　Carline 156
　Madelin 156
　Max 156
　Millard L. 156
　Rachel 156
PRICE
　Alice 37
　Alma S. 64
　C. Marion 64
　Eleanor W. 64
　Emma J. 64
　Frank 64
　George E. 64
　Georgianna 64
　Harold L. 64
　Mark L. 64
　Mary A. 64
　Mary F. 64
　Samuel T. 64
PRICHARD
　James C. 136

Joseph 136
Julia A. 136
PRITCHARD
　Jeanette C. 64
PROFFITT
　Tammy M. 64
PULLMAN
　Garbutt 64
　Mary L. 64
　Thelma M. 44
PULMAN
　Charles O. 64
　Frances P. 64
　Leon O. 64
　Lucy V. 64
　Mary A. 64
　Peter 64
PUMPHREY
　R.A. 6
PURSELL
　Charles W. 136
　Elizabeth 136
　Mary E. 136
　Thomas 136
　William C. 136
QUANDER
　Julia E. 65
QUISENBERRY
　Rebecca P. 65
　Willey 65
　William P. 65
RAMSAY
　Allen T. 65
　Anthony 65
　Catharine 33
　D. McC. 65
　Dennis 65
　Douglas B. 65
　George W. 65, 66
　Harriet M. 65
　Henrietta F. 65
　Jane 112
　Jane A. 65
　John 33, 65, 112
　Louise H. 65
　Margaret D. 66
　Maud 66
　Robert T. 66
　Wilhelmina 65, 66
　Wilhelmina B. 65
　William 65, 66
RAMSEY
　George W. 65
RANDOLPH

Charles C. 66
Mary A. 66
Sarah B. 66
RANNELLS
　Grace E. 66
RAY
　Annie H. 66
　P.H. 66
RAYNOR
　Emma 66
REARDON
　Adelaide S. 86
　Catherine C. 66
　E.P. 86
　Edith K. 66
　John T. 66, 86
　John U. 66
　Lucy V. 66
　Lulie C. 66
　Mary E. 136
　Nora U. 66
　William M. 66
REECE
　Elizabeth A. 66
　Irene E. 66
　John C. 66
　Mary 66
　Mary H. 66
　Thomas H. 66
REED
　Francis A. 66, 67
　Harrah L. 67
　Helen V. 67
　Marinda E. 67
REESE
　Arthur L. 67
　Harriet 136
　Henry 67
　Mary A. 67
　Rebecca R. 67
　Robert M. 67
　Samuel 136, 137
REEVES
　William C. 137
REGAN
　Ellen G. 46
REYNOLDS
　Charles W. 67
　David 137
　Elizabeth 67
　Elizabeth B. 67
　Grace A. 67
　Joel C. 67
　Oscar B. 67
　Phebe V. 137
　Sarah 67

William 67
William C. 67, 137
RHODES
  Fern W. 67
  George F. 67
  Geraldine E. 67
RICHARDS
  Jane 67
  John 67
  John M. 137
  John Z. 137
  Mary A. 137
  William C. 137
  Willie F. 137
RICKETTS
  Ann 99
  Benjamin 112
  Charles 112
  David 67
  E. 112
  Elizabeth 68
  John 107
  John T. 68
  Mary B. 68
  Mary E. 86
  Sarah 107
RIDDLE
  () 112
  Bushrod W. 107
  Infant 112
  Joseph 5, 107
  Joseph H. 68
  Joshua 107, 112
  Mr. 5
  Sarah 112
RILEY
  Mary E. 68
  Terrence 68
RIMPELEIN
  Joseph 68
RINKER
  Helen 49
  Jacob L. 49
RIPPON
  Goldie M. 68
RISTON
  Dennis W. 137
  J.H. 137
  R.A. 137
RITTENOUR
  Avery A. 68
  Frederick H. 68
  Grace P. 68
  Richard D. 68
  Russell W. 68
ROBBINS
  D. Howell 137

Isaac 137
Marie A. 68
Mary D. 137
Mary H. 137
Robert O. 68
ROBERTS
  Audrey L. 68
  Averiett F. 68
  Erven J. 68
  George W. 68
  Harry W. 68
  Joseph T. 68
  Leslie 68
  Minnie B. 68
  Richard L. 68
  Robert B. 137
  Sallie C. 68
ROBERTSON
  Ella I. 20
  George W. 68
  Mary A. 68
ROBEY
  Ada M. 68
  Beverly 68
  David E. 68
  Earl S. 68
  Gary W. 68
  Hazel V. 69
  Marian C. 68
  Orene S. 68
  Willard 68
  Willard A. 69
ROBINSON
  Editha R. 69
  Frances J. 69
  George H. 69
  James 69
  John R. 69
  Louise I. 69
  Margaret 54
  Mary M. 69
  Mary P. 69
  Susanna 69
  Thomas W. 69
  William S. 69
ROCKWELL
  Jessie M. 69
  Ralph T. 69
  Selden W. 69
RODGERS
  George H. 69
  Joseph F. 69
  Lula E. 69
  Susan J. 69
ROGERS
  Matilda A. 69
  Millie A. 69

Park A. 69
Walter G. 69
ROLLINS
  James H. 69
  John L. 69
  Marie A. 69
RONEY
  Blanche W. 156
ROSE
  Henry 112
  Jacob 156
  Sarah A. 156
ROSENBERG
  Abraham S. 156
  Beatrice 156
  Cecilia K. 156
  Kate 156
  Maurice D. 156
  Max 149
  Samuel 156
ROSENTHAL
  Janette 156, 157
ROSS
  Armstead J. 69
  George A. 69
  Isabella 112
  John G. 69
  Nannie C. 69
ROSSER
  Cecelia L. 137
ROSSIO
  Fannie 156
ROSSITER
  Charlotte E. 73
ROTHSCHILD
  Fannye 156
ROUNSEVAL
  Andrew 69
  Elizabeth 69
  Nathaniel 69
ROURK
  Mary J. 70
  Norris J. 70
ROWDON
  Jennifer B. 70
  Robert E. 70
  Stacey S. 70
  Suzanne M. 70
ROWEN
  Mary E. 70
  Thomas B. 70
ROWLEY
  Edward R. 85
ROYSTER
  Edna M. 70
  William A. 70
RUBEN

Amelia 156
Daniel 156
Goodman 161
Leopold 156
Moritz 156
Sara 156
RUBENSTEIN
  Walter A. 156
RUDD
  Harry W. 70
  Sarah V. 17
  William 137
RUMNEY
  Elouisa 70
  John 70
  John B. 70
  Martha B. 70
RUNNELS
  Abigail C. 138
  John H. 138
RUPPLE
  Elleanor 138
  Michael 138
RUSSELL
  Ann 107
  Hannah T. 107
  James 107
RUTHERFORD
  Margaret W. 70
  Norris 70
  Oscar T. 70
  Sarah M. 70
RYAN
  James T. 6
SACRES
  David 70
  Mary E. 70
SALOMONSOHN
  Victoria 156
SALZINGER
  Esther A. 156
  Ida T. 156
SANFORD
  () 109
  Elizabeth M. 70
  Esther 70
  Esther W. 26
  Frances A. 70
  Lawrence 107
  Margaret 77
  Thomas 70
  Walter 167
SANGER
  Morris 156
SANTMIRE
  Eston E. 70
  Julia L. 70

SAUNDERS
  A.H. 14
  Addison H. 70, 71, 87
  Anna M. 87
  E.M. 87
  Ellen M. 14, 71
  Jacquelyn F. 71
  James B. 71
SAUTER
  Florence 85
SCHAFER
  Abbie I. 71
  Effie L. 71
  William L. 71
SCHLEIF
  Estelle 71
  John H. 71
SCHNEIDER
  Lawrence R. 156
  Lawrence T. 156
SCHOLL
  Fannie 157
  Irving J. 157
SCHON
  Jean J. 71
SCHREINER
  Charles 71
  Marian E. 71
SCHROTT
  Baby 164
  Dave 161
  Infant 164
SCHWARZ
  Isaac 157
  Lena 157
  Samuel 157
SCOTT
  Charles 138
  Delia 71
  Elizabeth 138
  Jane 71
  Margaret A. 71
  Norvell O. 71
SCRIVENER
  Addie L. 71
  James R. 71
SCULL
  William 112
SEAMAN
  Bleecker P. 71
  Florence C. 71
SEATON
  Adolphus 138
  George 127, 138
  George B. 138
  George P. 138

  Hannah 127
  John A. 138
  Lucinda 127, 138
  Sarah E. 138
  V.J. 138
SEIFF
  Beatrice T. 153
  Joanne E. 157
  Lazard 157
  Marion B. 157
SELLERS
  John 12
  Susan C. 12
SENGEL
  William R. 2, 5, 98
SEYMOUR
  Florence 151
SHANNON
  Rosa 71
SHAPIRO
  Charlotte D. 165
  Isidore 165
  Jacob 161
  Rose A. 165
SHATTUCK
  Alice D. 10, 71
  Lucious H. 10, 71
SHAW
  () 112
SHAY
  Henry J. 14
  Jane E. 14
  Mary J. 14
  Orland K. 14
  Orlando E. 14
  Samuel 14
  Virginia 14
SHEARS
  G. Charles 71
  Marian A. 71
SHECKLE
  Dedrick 138
SHEPARD
  Charlotte B. 71
  William B. 71
SHEPHERD
  Elizabeth 121
  Grace 121
  John 121
SHERWOOD
  Charlotte 138
  Joseph T. 72, 138
SHILLIBAR

Elizabeth 72
John 72
SHIPLEY
  Sarah A. 138
SHIRLEY
  Marion 138
  William H. 138
SHORT
  Jessica L. 165
SIDES
  William H. 72
SIEGEL
  Esther 165
  Jacob 165
SILVERMAN
  Alan J. 165
SIMMS
  () 107
  Margaret 107
  Nancy N. 107
  Thomas 107
SIMPSON
  Arthur 139
  Carlin L. 72
  Emma 138
  French C. 72
  French R. 139
  George L. 72
  George R. 72
  Henry L. 138, 139
  John W. 72
  Julia A. 138, 139
  Margaret E. 72
  Mary A. 139
  Orene 68
  Sarah E. 72
  Virginia R. 72
  Winfield M. 139
SIMS
  Charles 139
  Margaret 107
  Nancy 139
  Rebecca 47
SINCLAIR
  Alice G. 72
  Annie M. 72
  Hugh H. 72
  John L. 72
  William H. 72
SIPPLE
  Anne R. 139
  Bettie K. 139
  Charles O. 72
  Elizabeth D. 139
  Mary L. 72
  Samuel S. 72, 139
SKIDMORE

Andrew F. 72
Emily G. 72
Jesse 72
John W. 72
Maria L. 72
Mary D. 9
Sarah B. 72
SKINNER
  Elizabeth 139
  Thomas L. 139
SLATTERY
  Grace 72
SLAUGHTER
  Louis 139
SLAYMAKER
  A.H. 72
  Alexander E. 73
  Amos B. 72, 73
  Archie C. 72
  Edmund H. 72
  Edmund W. 73
  Elizabeth F. 73
  Elizabeth J. 73
  Faithful M. 73
  George W. 73
  Hannah 73
  Infant 72
  James G. 73
  Mary E. 73
  Sarah F. 73
  Willie 73
SLOAN
  Ann R. 139
  John 139
SLOTKIN
  Nat 165
SMALLING
  Walter R. 73
SMITH
  () 107
  Alexander 107, 112
  Amanda A. 139
  Ann 73
  Augusta L. 73
  Augustine J. 73, 82
  Charles G. 73
  Charles M. 73
  Charlie E. 75
  Charlotte E. 73, 74
  Charlotte V. 52
  Clifton H. 73
  Courtland H. 73, 74
  Daniel 139

Edwin H. 74
Eleanor E. 74
Eliza 75
Eliza W. 74
Elizabeth B. 73
Elizabeth J. 45
Elizabeth P. 74
Elizabeth W. 45, 74
Florence C. 74
Francis L. 74, 75
George 73
George A. 74, 75
Helen 73
Henry 48
Hesselius 139
Hugh 5, 45, 74, 107
Hugh G. 74
Isabella K. 74
J. Berta 139
J. Roberta 139
James H. 74
James S. 74
Jane E. 75
John L. 139
John P. 8
John W. 74
Joseph 133, 140
Julia T. 139
Kathryn F. 75
Larouche J. 29, 75
Maranda 140
Margaret V. 75
Martha J. 140
Mary 107, 133, 140
Mary A. 107
Mary B. 8
Mary C. 29
Mary E. 75
Mary J. 75, 82
Mr. 5
Nancy K. 48
Norma C. 75
Ophelia 74
Ophelia A. 75
Rebecca 112
Robert 73, 75
Robert L. 74, 75
Sally B. 8
Sarah 133
Sarah G. 74, 75
Sarah K. 75

195

Sarah P. 29
Sarah V. 23
Sary 75
Sidney W. 140
Thomas 75, 107, 108, 140
Thomas W. 108
William A. 75
William H. 108
SMITHERS
  Susanna E. 75
  William B. 75
SMOOT
  Julia F. 75
  Sue E. 26
SNOWDEN
  Anna 140
  Edgar 140
  Edith A. 140
  Harold 140
  Hubert 140
  Louisa 140
  Louisa J. 140
  Osmund 140
  William P. 140
SNYDER
  Elizabeth 140
  Mathias 140
SOLBACH
  Bertie S. 76
SOLOMON
  Ann 140
  Samuel 140
SOLOMONSOHN
  Max D. 156
SONDHEIMER
  Leser 157
SOUTHWORTH
  Dora L. 46
SPEAR
  () 108
SPENCER
  James L. 76
SPITTLE
  Lloyd 76
SPOONER
  () 108
SPOTSWOOD
  Alexander 11
STANARD
  Mary E. 19
STANWOOD
  Mary 58
STEELE
  Horatio N. 140
  J.A. 76
  J.H. 76

Margaret 108
Mary C. 76
Sarah J. 76
STEIN
  Caroline 157
  Jacob 157
  Simon 157
STERN
  Samuel 157
STEUART
  Amelia R. 76
  Elias J. 76
  Eliza C. 76
  Elizabeth 76
  James M. 76
  Lizzie 76
  Mary 76
  Sarah A. 76
  William 76
STEVENS
  Mary B. 127
STEVENSON
  Edgar 140
STEWART
  Anna R. 45
  Bettie W. 45
  Eliza D. 77
  Elizabeth 76
  Elizabeth A. 76
  Elizabeth E. 77
  James 9
  James M. 77
  John 108
  John A. 77
  John W. 77
  Margaret S. 77
  Mary 108
  Mary J. 77
  Robert 76
  Sarah A. 76
  Thomas T. 77
  William 77
  William D. 77
STILLARD
  Jennie F. 140
STOKES
  Horace C. 77
  Nettie H. 77
STONE
  Ida 165
  Jane F. 77
  Joseph L. 77
  Julius 165
  Stone 165
STOREY
  George D. 140
  Sarah E. 140

STOUTENBURGH
  Abram 77
  Cornelia H. 77
STOVER
  Lyda A. 77
STRATTON
  Alexander K. 77
  Mary A. 77
STRAUB
  Anna D. 25, 77
  Archie L. 25, 77
  Sandra J. 25
STRAUSS
  Emma 157
  Henrietta 155
  Henry 157
STRAWTHER
  Cassius L. 77
STROMER
  Bernard A. 77
STUART
  Charles E. 77
  Dorothy S. 77
  Elizabeth M. 77
  Harriot E. 78
  Jane B. 60
  Mary F. 77
  Ruth Y. 77
SULLIVAN
  Josephine E. 43
  Mildred C. 78
  William L. 78
SWAIN
  () 78
  Atha K. 78
  B.H. 78
  F.B. 78
  George 78
  George W. 78
  Lizzie 78
  Mary 78
  Mary V. 78
  Rose 78
  Stephen 78
SWAINE
  Jane 140
  Jane A. 140
  Julius G. 140
SWAN
  Mr. 56
SWAURTZ
  Elizabeth 141
SWIFT
  Ann S. 108
  Isaac R. 108
  Mary D. 78
  William R. 78

William T. 108
TO
   Henry W. 141
TALBERT
   Precious 61
TALBOT
   Thomas 78
TALBOTT
   McKenzie 111
TALIAFERRO
   Edmonia B. 78
   John C. 78
   Lucy E. 78
   Marian M. 78
   William H. 78
TATSAPAUGH
   Charles 78
   P. 78
   R.V. 78
   Susanna V. 78
   William 78
TAYLOR
   () 78
   Ann E. 79
   Anna B. 141
   Annas J. 141
   Annie M. 79
   Arabella H. 78
   Arina 141
   Belle H. 28
   Elijah 141
   Eliza J. 110
   Elizabeth A. 141
   Elizabeth B. 125, 141
   George B. 141
   H. Allen 79
   Harriet C. 79
   Henry I. 78
   Jane A. 65
   Jesse 108, 110, 112
   John R. 108
   John T. 141
   Julian 78
   Kathryn 78
   L.I. 79
   Maria 108
   Mary V. 141
   Robert 108
   Robert I. 23, 112
   Robert J. 79
   Rosalie 23
   Rosalie A. 79
   Susan C. 79
   Valentine M. 141
   Vincent 79
   William P. 79
   William R. 79

TEITELBAUM
   Bertha 165
   Bertha G. 165
   Louis M. 165
TEPPER
   Shirley 79
THOM
   David 108
   Mary 108
   William 108
THOMAS
   Amadeo L. 79
   Anna P. 79
   E. 141
   Edgar A. 79
   George 79
   George I. 79
   Hanson 141
   J.W. 79
   John J. 41, 79
   Lucy 62
   M. Armantine 79
   Margret 141
   Maria 79
   Maria A. 79
   Marian M. 79
   Mary A. 79
   Mary J. 79
   Richard A. 79
   Thomas J. 141
   Wiliam H. 79
   William E. 79
   William H. 141
   William P. 79
   Winefred R. 141
THOMPSON
   Archibald 108
   Elizabeth 141
   Henry T. 140, 141
   James 79
   John 80
   Peleg O. 141
   Sabina 80
   Samuel 80
   Sarah E. 140
   Virginia S. 142
THOMSON
   A.H. 26
   Alfred 26
   Alfred H. 26
   Anna D. 26, 80
   James D. 26, 80
   Mary 26
   S.D. 26
   Sarah M. 26

Sue E. 26
THORN
   William 98
THORNTON
   Beverly 142
   Mary E. 142
TOBY
   Nancy 80
   William J. 80
TOMLIN
   Agnes 80
TOOMEY
   Elizabeth 113
TOPPING
   Judith M. 80
   Thomas H. 80
   William R. 80
TORNER
   Arie 157
TORRES
   Esther N. 142
TOWNSEND
   George H. 80
   Ida F. 80
TRAUB
   Morton M. 157
TRAVERS
   Alonza H. 80
   Ann 142
   Henrietta A. 142
   James A. 80
   Lucretia 80
   Lucy A. 142
   Mary A. 80
   Mary J. 61
   Sallie 80
   Thomas 142
TRETCHER
   Eleanor 80
   Thomas 80
TRIPLETT
   Alberta W. 80
   Elizabeth 142
   Elizabeth D. 81
   Ellen M. 81
   George W. 81
   Jane R. 81
   Mary A. 145
   Richard C. 81
   William W. 81
TROTTER
   Bertram T. 81
TRUCKENMILLER
   Kenneth R. 81
   Margaret E. 81
TRUMBLE
   Edward 81

TRUNNEL
  Caroline 142
  Isaac 142
TRUNNELL
  Mary D. 142
  Miriam A. 142
  Samuel 142
  Susan C. 142
TRYTLE
  Frederick 115
  Mary 115
TUBMAN
  Julia F. 81
  Wilhelmina 61
TUCKER
  J.E. 142
  Jane R. 142
TURNER
  () 109
  Cecelia L. 142
  Charles W. 81
  Dewitt C. 142
  Francina W. 109
  George R. 142
  Jane W. 81
TYLER
  Esther M. 81
  Thompson 142
UHLER
  Alfred G. 81
  Edward K. 81
  Eliza G. 81
  John A. 81
  Katharine 81
  Lucile A. 81
  Lucy B. 81
  Lucy L. 81
  Margaret S. 81
  Martha A. 142
  Peter G. 142
  S.H. 81
  Theron R. 81
  William M. 81
UNDERWOOD
  Claudia 38
  Oliver 81
Unknown 150
UPTON
  Julian E. 81
URIE
  Arthur T. 81
  James 81
VAZQUEZ
  Antonio 81
VEITCH
  Alexander 81
  Charles W. 143

Daniel A. 143
Eldrige R. 121, 143
Elizabeth 40
Elizabeth M. 143
Harrison R. 81
Isaac McK. 143
James H. 143
John 143
John A. 143
Martha A. 142, 143
Mary 143
Mary M. 143
Mr. 5
Phebe 137, 143
Rachel 137, 142, 143
Rachel P. 143
Richard 5
Silas 143
William 137, 142, 143
William P. 143
VERNON
  Ernest D. 81
  Robert L. 81
VIA
  Louisa V. 82
VINCENT
  Ellalee F. 82
  Frances S. 82
  John T. 82
VIOLETT
  Ann 82
  Robert G. 143
VIOLETTE
  Elsie A. 82
  T. Hager 82
  Thomas 82
  William J. 82
VIPPERMAN
  Infant 82
VOWELL
  Charles 109
  Charlotte O. 82
  Eliza 82
  Eliza C. 27
  Eliza K. 82
  Elizabeth 82, 83
  James A. 109
  James C. 109
  John C. 23, 27, 75, 82
  John D. 82
  John G. 109

Margaret B. 23
Margaret H. 109
Margaretta 82
Mary 23
Mary A. 109
Mary H. 109
Mary J. 75, 82
Mr. 5
Robert H. 109
Sarah 110
Sarah G. 75
Sarah W. 110
Thomas 5, 82, 83, 109, 110
WADSWORTH
  Laura 40
WALES
  Andrew 110
  Margaret 110
WALKER
  Addie L. 83
  Champe 83
  James W. 83
  Mary 83
  Octavia 83
  Robert 83
WALLACE
  James B. 83
  Kevin G. 83
  Robert B. 83
WALLER
  Constance G. 83
  Robert E. 83
WARD
  Alice 76, 83
  Charles E. 83
  Elizabeth 76
  Jane E. 83
  John W. 83
  Samuel 83
  William 76, 83
WARDEN
  Philip L. 83
  Thomas E. 83
WARFIELD
  Allen A. 83
  Andrew A. 83
  Jane E. 83
  Marshall G. 83
WARING
  Francis 83
  Mary E. 144
  Mary I. 144
WARREN
  Clyde K. 157
WASHINGTON

Edith G. 83
Georgia L. 83
Juliette B. 83
Lelia D. 83
Mason 83
Mason D. 83
Roberta B. 83
WASSERMAN
  Jeanne R. 157
  Stanley B. 157
WATERMAN
  Caroline 157
  Inman H. 157
  Simon 157
WATERS
  Benjamin 144
  Doritha 144
  Georgia A. 144
  Thomas A. 144
  William 144
WATKINS
  Aurelia H. 144
  David G. 144
  Elizabeth 144
  James M. 144
  John T. 144
  Mary E. 144
  Sarah J. 144
  W.T. 144
  William T. 144
WATSON
  Andrew 110
  Elizabeth 45
  Hadlai F. 83
  Nellie 83
WATTLES
  A.J. 17
  Alvin M. 17, 83
  M.E. 17
  Nannie G. 17, 84
  William H. 17
WATTS
  Sara C. 46
WEBESTER
  James 144
  Susannah 144
WEDDERBURN
  Alexander J. 144, 145
  Ann 144
  Augustus 145
  George 145
  Jane S. 144, 145
  Mary Bernard 145
  Sarah A. 145
WEIL
  Albert 157
  Babette 158

Benedict 158
Julia 158
Mollie N. 158
Naomi 157
Sidney 158
WEINBERG
  Joseph 158
WEINER
  Louis J. 165
  Molly L. 164, 165
  Pearl A. 165
WEINTRAUB
  David D. 165
WEIR
  Ella F. 84
  Lillian H. 84
  Paul 84
WEISBAND
  William W. 84
WELBORNE
  David 84
WELCH
  John P. 84
WENDT-WRIEDT
  Adolph J. 84
  Lillie A. 84
WENZEL
  Infant 84
WERTH
  Samuel 149, 161
WEST
  Dorothy V. 84
  Francina 109
  George C. 84
  Linwood M. 84
  Mabel B. 84
  Martha M. 84
WESTCOTT
  Annie 84
  James D. 84
  John 84
  Sarah 84
WESTHEIMER
  Henry 158
WESTON
  Edwin 84
  Rebecca 145
  William 145
WHALEY
  Carl O. 84
  Cecile M. 84
WHEAT
  Benoni 145
  Harriet H. 145
  James S. 145
  Martha J. 145

Mary A. 145
Mary N. 145
WHEELER
  Samuel 145
  Sarah 145
WHITE
  Cornelia H. 77
  E.H. 84
  Edgar D. 34
  Edna H. 16
  Edna V. 84
  Elizabeth A. 110
  Elizabeth D. 84
  J.H. 84
  James H. 16
  John 110
  Mary A. 84
  Mary H. 34
  Neida 84
  R.C. 84
  Robert L. 34
  Thomas M. 77
  Walter C. 84
WHITESTONE
  Melvin 158
  Robert P. 158
  Rosa S. 158
WHITING
  Edith D. 84
  Fairfax E. 84
  Margaret D. 84
WHITMORE
  Anna M. 145
WHITTINGTON
  Harriet F. 27
  Margaret C. 27
  Thomas 27
WHITTLESEY
  Elizabeth G. 145
  Luman 145
WHITTON
  Alice H. 84
  Edith M. 84
  Elizabeth A. 84
  Florence S. 85
  George 84
  Margaret E. 84
  Robert G. 85
WILBAR
  George H. 85
  John T. 85
  Sarah 85
WILBURN
  Sarah 110
WILCOX
  Sophia 146
WILDT

Charles 85
E.C. 85
Edmond C. 85
H.M. 85
Henrietta M. 85
WILKINS
  Helen W. 85
  Leetta E. 17
  Nannie G. 17
WILKINSON
  Bland A. 85
WILLIAMS
  () 110
  Bertha 85
  C.E. 146
  Caroline C. 85
  Dallas C. 85
  Fannie 85
  Harvey 85
  John W. 85
  Laura V. 146
  Margaret D. 85
  Robert 85
  Robert A. 85
  W.A. 146
WILLIAMSON
  Ida M. 85
  Whitfield H. 85
WILLOUGHBY
  Margaret 50
WILSON
  Bruce 110
  Caroline A. 85
  David R. 86
  Deborah A. 85
  Eleanor B. 45
  Eliza J. 110
  Frances A. 86
  Harley P. 85
  Isaac 85
  James 110
  Laura 43
  Margaret 85, 110
  Mary 85
  Mary E. 85
  Mary R. 86
  Robert I. 85, 86
WILTBERGER
  Anna R. 146
  Louveteau E. 146
WILTON
  Ann C. 110
WINDSOR
  Amanda F. 86
  Behetheldon 86
  Edward 49
  Emeline 86

Florence C. 74
Ida B. 37
James H. 86
Julia 49, 86
Kate 86
Mary A. 86
Mary L. 86
Richard W. 86
Susannah 86
Thomas R. 86
WINTERS
  Frances 146
WISE
  Caroline M. 86
  Charles J. 86
  Elizabeth 110
  George 86, 110
  George K. 86
  George P. 86
  Ida V. 86
  John 110
  Margaret 86
WISEMILLER
  Jacob 146
WITBECK
  Adelaide S. 86
  James H. 86
WITHERSPOON
  Marvin E. 86
  Miriam R. 86
WITKIN
  Isadore B. 165
  Mary 165
  Max 165
  Norman S. 165
  Reichel 165
WITMER
  Edmund F. 86
  Elizabeth A. 86
  Elizabeth F. 86
  G.K. 86
  George K. 86
  Isabella F. 86
WOLF
  Ida 158
  Ida B. 158
  James G. 87
  Julius 158
WOLFFORD
  David J. 87
  Edgar B. 87
  Frank P. 87
  Jean 87
  Jennie P. 87
  Vivian R. 87
WOLFORD
  Anna 87

Claude H. 87
David J. 87
Evelyn W. 87
WOLLBERG
  Arthur 158
  Carrie 158
  Carrye 158
  Nathan 158
  Rosalia 158
  Sidney 158
WOOD
  Alice 146
  Arabella F. 87
  C.W. 87
  Clayton E. 87
  Edna D. 87
  Estelle 87
  Evelyn S. 87
  James P. 146
  M. Raymond 87
  Margaret M. 146
  Mary E. 87
  Mollie E. 146
  Ruth L. 87
  S.W. 146
  Selina T. 87
  William D. 87
  William S. 146
  Willie A. 87
WOODEN
  Lucy 87
WOODHOUSE
  Anna M. 87
  William M. 87
WOODY
  Lawrence W. 87
  Ruth 87
WOOLF
  Albert 161
WOOLLS
  William 87
WORSHAM
  Ollie V. 87
WORTHAN
  Mary A. 146
  William A. 146
  William R. 146
WRIGHT
  Daniel 87
  Harriet L. 87
  Helen M. 146
  James B. 87
  Mae R. 87
  Richard M. 146
  Robert L. 87
YEATON
  Sally 110

    William 110
YOAST
    John 110
YOCHUM
    John C. 88
YOUNG
    Elizabeth C. 88
    Francis 110
    James 110
    Jenny 110
    John 88
    Mary 110
    Robert 88
ZEPERNICK
    Mariana 113
ZIMMERMAN
    Adam 135
    Mary C. 135
    Sinah E. 135